Bangladesh

a Lonely Planet travel survival kit

Alex New
Betsy Wager
Jon Mur

Bangladesh

3rd edition

Published by
  Lonely Planet Publications
  Head Office: PO Box 617, Hawthorn, Vic 3122, Australia
  Branches: 155 Filbert St, Suite 251, Oakland, CA 94607, USA
                10 Barley Mow Passage, Chiswick, London W4 4PH, UK
                71 bis rue du Cardinal Lemoine, 75005 Paris, France

Printed by
  Colorcraft Ltd, Hong Kong

Photographs by
  Ian Lockwood   Betsy Wagenhauser
  Jon Murray   Gregory Wait

  Front cover: A Bangladeshi boy, Dhaka (Betsy Wagenhauser)

First Published
  November 1985

This Edition
  June 1996

Although the authors and publisher have tried to make the information as accurate as possible, they accept no responsibility for any loss, injury or inconvenience sustained by any person using this book.

National Library of Australia Cataloguing in Publication Data

Newton, Alex
  Bangladesh

  3rd ed.
  Includes index.
  ISBN 0 86442 296 2.

  1. Bangladesh – Guidebooks. I. Murray, Jon. Bangladesh.
  II. Title. (Series: Lonely Planet travel survival kit).

915.492045

Alex Newton

Raised in Madison, Georgia, Alex Newton joined the Peace Corps in the 1960s. Following almost three years' service in Guatemala as an agricultural adviser, he worked for four years on Wall St as a lawyer. He then studied development economics and French, and ended up in West Africa working on development assistance programmes. Alex is also the author of LP's *West Africa* and *Central Africa*.

He moved on to similar work in Ecuador, where he met Betsy. Alex and Betsy have lived and worked in Bangladesh for five years. Their next move is to Kazakstan.

Betsy Wagenhauser

After eight years of teaching in Dallas, Texas, Betsy headed to Peru in 1986 and eventually ended up at the helm of the South American Explorers Club. For the next seven years, she worked extensively with independent travellers in Peru and Ecuador. She has written and photographed Insight Guides' *South America*, *Peru* and *Ecuador*, and co-authored two editions of *Hiking and Climbing in Ecuador* for Bradt Publications. For several years, she led trips for Wilderness Travel.

These days, writing, photography and the delights of 18 month old Nicola take up most of her time.

Jon Murray

Jon Murray spent time alternating between travelling and working with various publishing companies in Australia before joining Lonely Planet as an editor. He has co-authored LP's *South Africa, Lesotho & Swaziland*, written *New South Wales & the ACT* and updated several other LP books, including *Papua New Guinea* and sections of *Australia*. He lives in Melbourne but spends a lot of time battling blackberries on his bush block near Daylesford.

From Betsy & Alex

We'd like to thank the following friends who made major contributions to this edition: Ian Lockwood, Mike Woodcock, Dave Johnson, Carole & Hallam Murray and their son Quin, Pauline Feltham, Todd Kirschner, Rick Hamburger, Lyn & Lee Morris, Bob Karam, Rob Cunnane, Gretchen Antelman, Tim Lenderking, Kathy Lincoln, the Minnonite Central Committee in Maijdi, Amjad Hossain, the CARE director in Jessore, Valorie Taylor, Lyn Paquette, Drew Sayles, Sue Nesbitt, Kaaren Mirk, Steffie Meyer and the staff at Lonely Planet in Melbourne.

We'd also like to thank the people of Bangladesh; everywhere we have travelled through your country, you have enriched our experiences by your friendliness and hospitality, and inspired us by your perseverance, often under extremely difficult circumstances.

Dedication

This edition is dedicated to Betsy's parents, John and Barbara Wagenhauser of Dallas, Texas who, from the beginning, tolerated the wanderlust with only a mild admonition to 'call us when you find a phone. Until then, we'll assume you're OK'.

This Book

Betsy Wagenhauser and Alex Newton researched and wrote this third edition of *Bangladesh*. Jon Murray researched the second edition in 1990 and Jose Santiago did the first edition in 1985.

From the Publisher

This third edition was produced at LP's Melbourne office. Helen Castle edited the book and took it through production. Rachel Scully and Michelle Glynn assisted with the editing. Kristin Odijk, Joanne Horsburgh and Cathy Lanigan proofed the book. Sharan Kaur provided invaluable editorial guidance.

Adam McCrow coordinated the design and mapping for this book, with Paul Piaia assisting with maps. Thanks to Valerie Tellini for her overall assistance with all aspects of design.

The illustrations were drawn by Mike Woodcock, Verity Campbell and Michael Signal. The cover was designed by Simon Bracken and Adam.

Many thanks also to Md Mohim Ullah Patwary at the Bangladesh High Commission in Canberra, Lou Callan, Marion Gamble, Isabelle Muller, Leonie Mugavin, Julie Young, Shelley Preston and Jon Murray.

Thanks

We greatly appreciate the contributions of the following travellers who put so much effort into writing to us from around the world and telling us of their weird and wonderful experiences:

Florent, C Blok, Ted Booth, Miss A J Brady, Beeye Bubacg, Prior Butler, Louise Cooper, Sally Cowdon, Nicholas J Cupaiuolo, Brett Dawson, Catherine Douxchamps, Mary Frances Dunham, Hanne Finholt, L Fordyce, Nicholas Fry, Oliver Gabersek, Bernhard Hammer, Paul Harris, Stephanie Hill, Adam Hoque, Martin Horn, David & Greeba Hughes, Martin Horn, Derek Ivens, Lynne Kirtley, Frank Kruger, Stefan Liljegren, Claudia Lowe, Paul Madden, Anne-Gmmanvelle Maitre, Paul McKeon, Bryan Meador, Matthew Murphy, Bill Page, Shailesh Panth, T Payne, Brett Pickard, Irwin Rapoport, Janet Raynor, Niels Ronnest, Stefan Samuelsson, Magnus Seger, Salim Sparker Shuvo, Angela Strehl, Marlies Tach, Jael Tan, Adam ul Hoque, Christian van Rossun and Stephen White.

Warning & Request

Things change – prices go up, schedules change, good places go bad and bad places go bankrupt – nothing stays the same. So if you find things better or worse, recently opened or long since closed, please write and tell us and help make the next edition better.

Your letters will be used to help update future editions and, where possible, important changes will also be included in an Update section in reprints.

We greatly appreciate all information that is sent to us by travellers. Back at Lonely Planet we employ a hard-working readers' letters team to sort through the many letters we receive. The best ones will be rewarded with a free copy of the next edition or another Lonely Planet guide if you prefer. We give away lots of books, but, unfortunately, not every letter/postcard receives one.

Contents

Map Legend

BOUNDARIES

.... International Boundary
.... Regional Boundary

ROUTES

.... Freeway
.... Highway
.... Major Road
.... Unsealed Road or Track
.... City Road
.... City Street
.... Railway
.... Underground Railway
.... Tram
.... Walking Track
.... Walking Tour
.... Ferry Route
.... Cable Car or Chairlift

AREA FEATURES

.... Parks
.... Built-Up Area
.... Pedestrian Mall
.... Market
.... Cemetery
.... Forest
.... Beach or Desert
.... Rocks

HYDROGRAPHIC FEATURES

.... Coastline
.... River, Creek
.... Intermittent River or Creek
.... Rapids, Waterfalls
.... Lake, Intermittent Lake
.... Canal
.... Swamp

SYMBOLS

✪ CAPITAL		National Capital
◉ Capital		Regional Capital
⬤ CITY		Major City
● City		City
● Town		Town
● Village		Village
■ ▼		Place to Stay, Place to Eat
⚓ 🍴		Cafe, Pub or Bar
✉ ☎		Post Office, Telephone
❶ ❾		Tourist Information, Bank
● ℗		Transport, Parking
⛪ ⛺		Museum, Youth Hostel
⛽ ⛺		Caravan Park, Camping Ground
✚ ✚		Church, Cathedral
☪ ⛩		Mosque, Burmese Buddhist
⛩ ⛩		Temple, Hindu Temple
✚ ★		Hospital, Police Station

♀ ⛽		Embassy, Petrol Station
✈ ✈		Airport, Airfield
🏊 ❀		Swimming Pool, Gardens
✦ 🐘		Shopping Centre, Zoo
⛳ 🌲		Golf Course, Picnic Site
← A25		One Way Street, Route Number
🏛 ⚑		Stately Home, Monument
⛩ ⬛		Castle, Tomb
⌒ ⛺		Cave, Hut or Chalet
▲ ☀		Mountain or Hill, Lookout
🗼 ⚓		Lighthouse, Shipwreck
)(◎		Pass, Spring
⚑ ⚡		Beach, Surf Beach
∴		Archaeological Site or Ruins
		Ancient or City Wall
⟹ ⟸		Cliff or Escarpment, Tunnel
		Railway Station

Note: not all symbols displayed above appear in this book

Introduction

Bangladesh? Cyclones, floods, famine, unstable governments and people everywhere – at least that's the impression the world's press gives. Combine this with the overpowering proximity of India and Nepal and it is hardly surprising that Bangladesh doesn't rate highly on travellers' itineraries.

What this image doesn't reveal is that Bangladesh offers travel off the beaten path and a variety of attractions quite unusual for a country its size.

Nestled in the crook of the Bay of Bengal and braided by the fingers of the Ganges delta, Bangladesh offers interesting trips through the rural countryside on boats plying the country's innumerable rivers, reputedly the longest beach in the world (and shark-free), and the largest littoral mangrove forest in the world (accessible only by boat unless

you happen to be a royal Bengal tiger), archaeological sites of cultures dating back over 2000 years. As well, it has a fascinating architectural heritage, which includes the remains of ornately carved Hindu temples, beautiful centuries-old mosques and decaying 'Gone with the Wind' mansions of 19th century maharajas.

While the country is mostly riverine plains and flat, making it fantastic for cycling, there are two major hilly areas, both of which are, relatively speaking, sparsely populated. One is in the north-east, where tea estates dot the countryside. The other is in the south-east, east of Chittagong and Cox's Bazar. Known as the Hill Tracts, it's a suprisingly large area of rolling hills covered with verdant tropical forests and populated with colourfully dressed tribal people. Only a fraction of this

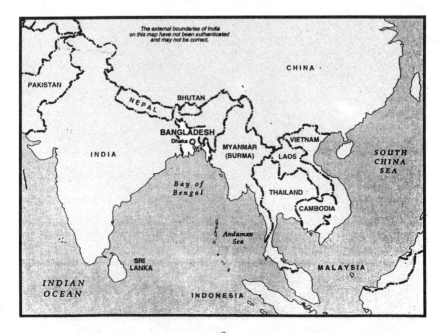

area is open to foreign visitors, but the unrestricted portion is well worth a visit.

In the centre of the country, just below the junction of the two major rivers of the subcontinent, the Ganges (Padma in Bangladesh) and the Brahmaputra (Jamuna), is Dhaka, the capital of the nation and, seemingly, the rickshaw capital of the world. The history of the Old City, established by Mughal sultans, the grand edifices built during British rule, and many peaceful parks and gardens make this a highlight in any visit. Taking one of the city's 350,000-odd rickshaws, which are unquestionably the most colourful in the world, is a 'must'.

Travel by bus, train or aeroplane is quick, easy and amazingly cheap, with only short distances to be covered to reach markedly different environments. But for those who prefer a different kind of adventure or moving at a more leisurely pace, enjoying rural life along the way, travel by boat is the only way to go.

Travellers looking for adventure in unexplored areas are 'missing the boat' by joining the crowds headed for India and Nepal, overlooking Bangladesh en route. While it can't offer quite the variety of cultures and ancient monuments, life along the rivers is fascinating, the countryside of Bangladesh is lush and beautiful, and the air is by far cleaner (except on the crowded streets of Dhaka behind a polluting bus or baby taxi).

Despite being the world's most crowded major country, Bangladesh is predominantly rural, with only two large cities. The rural countryside feels relaxed, and it gives a sense of spaciousness with incredible vistas. It is also friendly – travellers crossing from India have been agreeably surprised to find border officials offering them cups of tea rather than reams of forms to fill in. The National Tourist Corporation's former slogan acknowledges the country's dearth of visitors, but like them you could do worse than use it to your advantage – 'Come to Bangladesh before the tourists'.

Facts about the Country

HISTORY

The history of Bangladesh has been one of extremes: of turmoil and peace, prosperity and destitution. It has thrived in the glow of cultural splendour and suffered under the ravages of war. Throughout its tumultuous history it has known internal warfare, suffered invasion upon invasion, witnessed the rise and fall of mighty empires and several religions, and benefited from the trade and culture brought from foreign lands.

Some medieval European geographers located paradise at the mouth of the Ganges, and although paradise was not found here, amazingly enough, Bengal was probably the wealthiest part of the subcontinent until the 16th century.

Stretching from the lower reaches of the Ganges River on the Bay of Bengal and north almost to the foothills of the Himalaya, the Bengal region of the subcontinent is the gateway to Myanmar (Burma) and South-East Asia, making control over it vital to successive Indian empires. Its strategic position has ensured a place in the political, cultural and religious conflicts and developments of the subcontinent through the millennia.

Early History

Perhaps the earliest mention of the region is in the Hindu epic the *Mahabharata* (the 'Great Battle' – 9th century BC), which tells of Prince Bhima's conquest of eastern India, including Varendra, an ancient kingdom in what is now Bangladesh. References are made to several ethnic groups inhabiting the area (eg the Pundras, Vangas and Suhmas). By the 5th and 6th centuries BC, Aryan culture had spread eastward from the Indus River in Pakistan to dominate most of northern India. Although culturally homogeneous, the Bengal region comprised small, squabbling states until the formation of the powerful kingdom of Magadha, with its capital at Patna on the Ganges.

The region's history becomes less obscure from 325 BC, when Alexander the Great set upon India after his conquest of Persia. Alerted to this formidable threat, troops from the lower Ganges, known to the Greeks as Gangaridae, united under a non-Aryan native king of the Nanda dynasty. This huge army of infantry supported by 4000 trained war elephants and horses was too much for Alexander's troops who were already struggling with the oppressive heat and lack of supplies. Without giving battle Alexander retreated from India, never to return.

Chandragupta Maurya, fired by tales of the exploits of Alexander the Great, ascended the Magadhan throne and set about creating an empire, then known as Pundravardhana Bhukti. He succeeded, and it eventually spread right across northern India under his grandson, the Emperor Ashoka, one of the classic figures of Indian history. Ashoka's conversion to Buddhism in 262 BC had a long-lasting effect on the religious life of the area. Even as late as the 7th century AD, Chinese pilgrims still found Buddhism prevalent in Bengal, though in fierce conflict with Hinduism.

The Mauryan Empire, under Ashoka, controlled more of India than any subsequent ruler prior to the British. Following his death the empire went into a rapid decline and finally collapsed in 184 BC. It was not until the 4th century AD that northern India, including Bengal, was once again united under imperial rule, this time by the Guptas, during whose reign the arts flourished and Buddhism reached its zenith. Except for the kingdom of Sumatata, the various independent principalities in Bengal came to an end with the rise of the Gupta dynasty.

The Guptas succumbed to a wave of White Hun invasions, and in the 6th century AD Sasanaka founded the Gauda Empire in Bengal. It was eventually overthrown by the warrior-king Sri Harsa, whose empire ruled the Bengal area until it was toppled, into

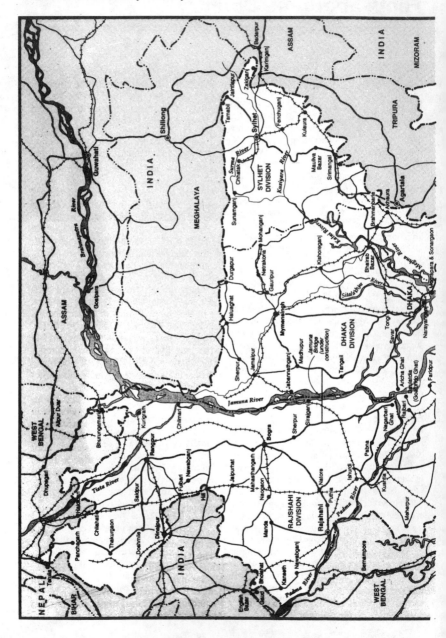

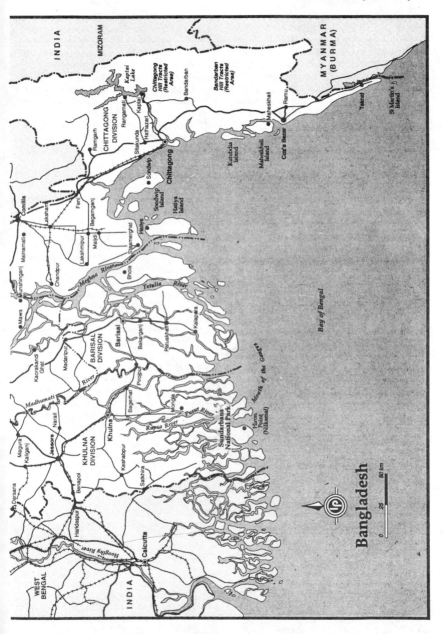

anarchy and chaos, in the 8th century AD. Buddhism was in decline and Hinduism was experiencing a resurgence; over the next couple of centuries, while northern India broke into a number of separate kingdoms, the Bengal area established a separate political identity, but was without any central authority to control the disrupting elements within the realm.

Out of the intolerably chaotic political and social conditions, a Kshatriya tribal chief, Gopala, from Varendra ultimately emerged as an elected leader. He introduced a settled government and became the founding figure of the Pala dynasty (8th to 12th centuries

Found at the Mainimati ruins in Chittagong Division, this bronze Avalokitesvara dates from the 10th-11th centuries, when Buddhism was already in decline.

AD). The Palas were Buddhists who claimed to have descended from the sea and the sun. They continued their royal patronage of Buddhism while politically tolerating the Hindus. Dharmapala succeeded his father Gopala and established the gigantic Somapura Vihara in Varendra, known today as the ruins of Paharpur Monastery.

During the 9th century the Pala dynasty was considerably weakened by a line of imbecile kings, and in the 11th century the Hindu Senas from south India replaced the Palas as rulers in Bengal. But in less than a century both Palas and Senas, Buddhists and Hindus, were swamped by the tide of Islam.

The Muslim Period

Muslim power had been creeping towards India from the Middle East for centuries before Mohammed Bakhtiar, a Khiljis from the Turkistan region of Central Asia, appeared on the scene. With only 20 men, and by means of a bold and clever stratagem, Bakhtiar captured Bengal in 1199, and brought the area under the rule of the Sultanate of Delhi, the centre of Muslim power which already held sway over most of northern India.

For a short period the Mameluk Sultanate was established in Bengal, but in the 14th century this was overrun by the hordes of Timur (better known in the west as Tamerlane), and the Tughluk Sultanate was formed. The influx of Muslims from Samarkand, Balkh and Abyssinia, and of Persians from Shiraz continued, and under the Muslims Bengal entered a new era. Cities developed, palaces sprang up along with forts, mosques, mausoleums and gardens, roads and bridges were constructed, and prosperity brought a new cultural life.

The Afghans arrived in 1520 and contributed further to the urbanisation of the land. In particular, the city of Gaud on the Indian border emerged as a cosmopolitan metropolis.

In 1526 the Sultanate of Delhi was overthrown by Babur, a descendant of both Timur and Genghis Khan, and the Mughal Empire under this Central Asian leader reached out to encompass most of northern India. It was not until 1576, however, that Babur's grandson Akbar finally defeated the Bengali Sultan Daud Karrani at the Battle of Tukaroi and Bengal became a province of the Mughal Empire.

Gaud remained the centre of power in Bengal until the capital was moved to Dhaka in 1608. Under the Mughal viceroys, urbanisation continued, art and literature flourished, overland trade expanded and Bengal was opened to world maritime trade. Intellectual and cultural life at this time was influenced mainly by the Persians, particularly by the Sufis, Muslim mystics who seek direct experience of divine love and wisdom, and who recite, or write, mystical love poetry.

Glorious at its peak, the Mughal Empire ushered in another golden age in India, only to be outdone by the country's final great colonial power – the British.

The European Period

With the growth of international maritime trade and commerce, Europeans began to establish themselves in the region. The Portuguese had founded settlements as early as the 15th century, and were soon joined by the East India Company: a London-based trading firm that had been granted a royal charter by Queen Elizabeth I in 1600, giving them a monopoly over British trade with India.

After a few initial setbacks – the Portuguese were ousted from their foothold in 1633 by Bengali opposition, and the British failed in an attempt to capture Chittagong in 1686 – the European juggernaut was unstoppable. The British managed to negotiate trade terms with the authorities in Bengal, and established a fortified trading post at Calcutta, dealing mainly in cotton, raw silk, yarn, sugar and saltpetre.

Following the death of Aurangzeb in 1707 came the decline of Mughal power, and the provincial governors of the once great empire began to assume autonomy. In 1740 Sarfaraz Khan, the viceroy of the three provinces of Bengal, Orissa and Bihar, was overthrown by Ali Vardi Khan, a subordinate

official in charge of the administration of Bihar. This heralded the rise of the independent dynasty of the nawab of Bengal, with whom the Englishman Robert Clive came in contact.

The East India Company's trading post at Calcutta was a thriving concern by now and Calcutta was fast becoming a great centre of trade and commerce. The role of Robert Clive in establishing British control over Bengal is well known. Originally a mere clerk with the East India Company, he rose to become the local head of the Company, and the effective ruler of the province, after a series of wars against local potentates. In 1756 Suraj-ud-Daula, the 21 year old Nawab of Bengal, attacked the British settlement of Calcutta. The British inhabitants unlucky enough not to escape were packed into an underground cellar, where most of them suffocated during the night in the infamous 'Black Hole of Calcutta'.

A year later Clive retook Calcutta and in the Battle of Plassey defeated Suraj-ud-Daula. As a result the British became the de facto rulers of Bengal, and the East India Company governed the province through puppet nawabs, effectively exercising its *raj* (sovereignty) over the province. This was the start of British government intervention in Indian affairs. The company's control over Bengal aroused concern in London, leading to the passage of an act regulating its power. Following the Indian Mutiny, or First War of Independence, of 1857, during which Bengal had been used as a secure base for British operations, the British government took control of India from the East India Company.

British Raj

Even the Raj machine found that it didn't escape the influence of the area. The British engineers found that the rivers here were sometimes beyond their taming, and the earlier British settlers in this backwater came to be considered not quite *pukka* (genuine) by their more proper counterparts elsewhere in India. Quite a number of the chaps 'went native', and they even spent their time playing a silly game they called polo.

It has been said that the British Raj ushered Bengal into another period of growth and development, but Bangladeshi historians hotly dispute this. They consider the dictatorial agricultural policies of the British in east Bengal, and the establishment of the *zamindar* (landowner) system, as being responsible for draining the country of its wealth, damaging the social fabric and directly contributing to today's desperate conditions.

Zamindars were independent rent collectors who administered areas under their jurisdiction, for the Raj. Although many of them were given or adopted the title of *raja* (ruler or landlord), they were really entrepreneurs. In addition, they were nearly always Hindus, which grated on the predominantly Muslim peasantry of east Bengal.

The introduction of the English language and the British educational, administrative and judicial systems established an organisational and social structure unparalleled in Bengal in its breadth and dominance. There were new buildings, roads, bridges, a railway system and continued urbanisation. Calcutta became one of the most important centres of commerce, education, culture and the arts on the subcontinent.

The establishment of the British Raj was a relief to the Hindus but a catastrophe for the Muslims. The Hindus immediately began to cooperate with the British, entering British educational institutions and studying the English language. The Muslims on the other hand refused to cooperate, preferring to remain landlords and farmers.

Bengal's religious dichotomy formed a significant basis for future conflict. Unlike the rest of India, the people of Bengal were predominantly Muslim and from early on, Islamic fervour against the British was strong, flaring up whenever any crop or other local product was made uneconomic by government policy.

At the end of the 19th century Bengal was an overgrown province of 78 million people, comprising Bengal, Bihar and Orissa. A massive earthquake struck the country in 1897, causing havoc over large areas of present-day Bangladesh. Many buildings and stately *rajbaris* (zamindari palaces) that caved in were never repaired; today they are decaying historical monuments. In 1905 Lord Curzon, the Viceroy of India, decided to partition Bengal for administrative purposes into East Bengal and Assam, and West Bengal, Bihar and Orissa. The new province of East Bengal and Assam, with a population of 31 million people, had its capital at Dhaka.

The Indian National Congress, which had been formed in 1885, was originally supported by both Hindus and Muslims. But the division of Bengal was seen as a religious partition, prompting the formation of the All India Muslim League in the following year. Its purpose was the protection of Muslim interests, as the Congress was increasingly being perceived as a Hindu power group.

This first partition of Bengal was physically defined by the Brahmaputra and the Padma rivers. East Bengal prospered, Dhaka assumed its old status as capital and Chittagong became an important sea port.

Although the partition of Bengal was opposed by Hindus and Muslims alike, when the split province was reunited in 1912, the Muslims began to have doubts. They feared Hindu social, economic and even political dominance and continued to press for Muslim autonomy.

At the same time the imperial capital of the British Raj was moved to Delhi, and although Calcutta remained an important commercial, cultural and political centre, the rest of Bengal was neglected. Political agitation increased over the next few decades as did the violent enmity between Muslims and Hindus. Although there was a movement in favour of a united Bengal, the Muslims supported repartition and the formation of a Muslim state separate from India.

Independence

As the Indian National Congress continued to press for self-rule for India, the British began to map out a path to independence. At the close of WWII it was clear that European colonialism had run its course and Indian independence was inevitable. Moreover, the UK no longer had the desire or power to maintain its vast empire, and a major problem had developed within India itself.

The large Muslim minority realised that an independent India would be a nation dominated by Hindus and that despite Mahatma Gandhi's fair-minded and even-handed approach, others in the Indian National Congress would not be so accommodating or tolerant. The country was divided on purely religious grounds with the Muslim League headed by Muhammad Ali Jinnah, representing the majority of Muslims, and the Indian Congress Party, led by Jawaharlal Nehru, commanding the Hindu population.

India achieved independence in 1947 but the struggle after the war had been bitter, especially in Bengal where the fight for self-government was complicated by the conflict between Hindus and Muslims. The British realised any agreement between the Muslim League and the Indian National Congress was impossible, so the viceroy, Lord Mountbatten, seeing no other option, decided to partition the subcontinent.

East Pakistan

The two overwhelmingly Muslim regions of pre-partition India were on the exact opposite sides of the subcontinent, in Bengal and the Punjab. In Bengal the situation was complicated by Calcutta, with its Hindu majority. There, jute mills and a developed port contrasted with Muslim-dominated East Bengal, also a major jute producer, but with virtually no manufacturing or port facilities.

The Muslim League's demand for an independent Muslim home state was realised in 1947 with the creation of Pakistan. This was achieved by establishing two separate states, East and West, on opposite sides of Indian territory. For months, a huge exodus took place as Hindus moved to India and Muslims moved to East or West Pakistan.

But despite the fact that support for the creation of Pakistan was based on Islamic solidarity, the two halves of the new state had little else in common. The instability of the arrangement was obvious, not only in the geographical sense, but for economic, political and social reasons as well.

The people of East Pakistan spoke only Bangla (known as Bengali in West Bengal), while the West Pakistanis spoke Urdu, Pushtu, Punjabi and Sindhi; the diet of the East Pakistanis consisted mainly of fish and rice while that of the West Pakistanis was meat and wheat.

The country was administered from West Pakistan, which tended to direct foreign aid and other revenues to itself, even though East Pakistan had more people and produced most of the cash crops. From early on these differences and inequalities stirred up a sense of Bengali nationalism that had not been reckoned with in the struggle for Muslim independence.

The Bengalis of East Pakistan had no desire to play a subordinate role to the West Pakistanis. The resentment was exacerbated by the fact that when the British left, most of the Hindus in the administrative service fled en masse to India, leaving a vacuum that could only be filled by the trained West Pakistanis and not by the local Muslims. Nor did West Pakistanis show a great deal of respect for Bengalis – the president of Pakistan, a West Pakistani, reportedly said that Bengalis 'have all the inhibitions of downtrodden races and have not yet found it possible to adjust...to freedom'. There was dissatisfaction in all spheres of Bengali life.

When the Pakistan government declared that 'Urdu and only Urdu' would be the national language, a language that virtually no one in East Bengal knew, the Bengalis decided this was the last straw. The primacy given to Urdu resulted in the Bangla Language Movement which rapidly became a Bengali national movement and the real beginning of the move towards independence. There were riots in Dhaka in 1952 during which 12 students were killed by the Pakistan army. Democracy gave way to military government and martial law.

The Awami Party, led by Sheikh (pronounced shake) Mujib Rahman, emerged as the national political party in East Pakistan, and the Language Movement became its ideological underpinning.

The catastrophic cyclone of 1970 devastated East Pakistan, killing some half a million people, and while foreign aid poured in, the Pakistan government appeared to do little. Support for the Awami League peaked and in the 1971 national elections it won 167 of the 313 seats, a clear majority. Constitutionally the Awami League should have formed the government of all Pakistan, but the president, faced with this unacceptable result, postponed the opening of the National Assembly.

Riots and strikes *(hartaals)* broke out in East Pakistan. At Chittagong, a clash between civilians and soldiers left 55 Bengalis dead. When President Khan secretly returned to West Pakistan after talks with Sheikh Mujib in March 1971, Pakistani troops went on the rampage throughout East Pakistan: burning down villages, looting shops and homes, and indiscriminately slaughtering civilians.

The War of Liberation
At the Race Course rally of 25 March 1971 in Dhaka (at what is now Ramna Park), Sheikh Mujib stopped just short of declaring East Pakistan independent. In reality, however, Bangladesh (land of the Bangla speakers) was born on this day. Sheikh Mujib was arrested, taken to West Pakistan and thrown into jail. This ignited the smouldering rebellion in East Pakistan.

When the Mukti Bahini (Bangladesh Freedom Fighters) captured the Chittagong radio station, Ziaur Rahman announced the birth of the new country and called upon its people to resist the Pakistani army. President Khan responded by sending more troops to quell the rebellion. In a classic piece of misjudgment, he had earlier claimed that 'the autonomy issue has been created by a few intellectuals. A few thousand dead in Dhaka and East Pakistan will be quiet soon'.

The ensuing war was a short but bloody one. General Tikka Khan, 'the Butcher of Baluchistan', was instructed to rid the country of Sheikh Mujib's supporters and his troops began the systematic slaughter of the Mukti Bahini and other 'subversive' elements such as intellectuals and Hindus.

A few army units made up of East Pakistanis rebelled in time to avoid capture, but they were heavily outnumbered and without supplies. By June the struggle became a guerrilla war, with more and more civilians joining the Mukti Bahini. With the whole countryside against them, the Pakistan army's tactics became more brutal. Napalm was used against villages.

West Pakistan had taken Dhaka and secured other major cities, and by November 1971 the whole country suffered the burden of the occupying army. The searches, looting, rape and slaughter of civilians continued and during the nine months from the end of March 1971, 10 million people fled to refugee camps in India. Rape was so widespread and systematic that it appeared to be an attempt to change the racial make-up of the country. Clouds of vultures cast ghastly shadows all over the country.

Border clashes between Pakistan and India became more frequent as the Mukti Bahini, who were being trained and equipped by India, were using the border as a pressure valve against Pakistan's onslaught. Finally, the Pakistan air force made a pre-emptive attack on Indian forces on 3 December 1971 and it was open warfare. The end came quickly. Indian troops crossed the border, liberated Jessore on 7 December and prepared to take Dhaka. The West Pakistan army was being attacked from the west by the Indian army, from the north and east by the Mukti Bahini and from all quarters by the civilian population.

It's a chilling insight into the military mentality that, during a particularly savage war, the Indian commander's surrender demand to his old school chum commanding the Pakistan army should be: 'My dear Abdullah, I am here. The game is up. I suggest that you give yourself up to me'.

By 14 December the Indian victory was complete, and Pakistan's General Niazi signed the surrender agreement on 16 December. Some Bangladeshi historians think that this was in the nick of time, as the

The Slaughter of the Intellectuals

Immediately following Sheikh Mujib's arrest on March 26, all hell broke out. Blaming the Hindu intellectuals for fomenting the rebellion, the generals immediately sent their tanks to Dhaka University and began firing into the halls killing students. This was followed by the shelling of Hindu neighbourhoods and a selective search for intellectuals, business people and other alleged subversive elements. One by one they were captured, hauled outside the city and shot in cold blood. Over the ensuing months, the Pakistani soldiers took their vicious search for subversives to every village. By then, if there had ever been a distinction made between intellectuals and Hindus, it was gone. When captured, men were were forced to lift their lungis to reveal if they were circumcised; if not, they were slaughtered.

While estimates vary widely, probably close to a million people died in the conflict. Years later, General Tikka Khan, who was initially in command during the Savar slaughter, admitted to murdering 'only' 35,000 intellectuals. And the murderers were never punished; indeed today they are heroes. Tikka, for example, retired in comfort and years later, in 1989, the 'grand old man' of the Pakistani army, as he was affectionately called, became the Governor-General of Punjab Province. ■

US navy's 7th Fleet was steaming up the Bay of Bengal. They were coming ostensibly to evacuate Americans from Dhaka but it was feared that the real purpose was to aid their Pakistani allies.

On his release from jail, Sheikh Mujib took over the reins of government, announcing the establishment of the world's 139th country.

Bangladesh

The People's Republic of Bangladesh was a country born into chaos; shattered by war, with a ruined economy and a totally disrupted communications system, the country seemed fated to continuing disaster. Pakistan's infamous pogrom against intellectuals had almost destroyed the new country's educated class and it appeared that Sheikh Mujib, though a skilful leader in wartime, did not have the peacetime ability to heal the wounds.

The famine of 1973-74 set the war-ravaged land and its people back even more. A state of emergency was declared in 1974 and Sheikh Mujib proclaimed himself president. The abuses and corrupt practices of politicians and their relatives, however, prompted a military coup in 1975. Sheikh Mujib and his entire household, except a daughter in London, were slaughtered.

Khandakar Mushtaq Ahmed became president, declared martial law and banned all political activities. A counter-coup four months later brought Brigadier Khalid

Musharaf into power – for four days. He was overthrown and killed, and power was assumed by a military triumvirate led by Abusadet Mohammed Sayem, the Chief Justice of the Supreme Court. As president and chief martial law administrator, he governed for nearly two years, with the heads of the armed services as his deputies.

In late 1976 the head of the army General Ziaur Rahman, who had led the Mukti Bahini during the War of Independence, took over as martial law administrator and, following the resignation of President Sayem in April 1977, assumed the presidency.

The overwhelming victory of President Zia (as Ziaur Rahman was popularly known) in the 1978 presidential poll was further consolidated when his newly formed Bangladesh Nationalist Party (BNP) won two-thirds of the seats in the parliamentary elections of 1979. Martial law was lifted and democracy and stability returned to Bangladesh. Zia, who proved to be a competent politician and statesman, turned more and more to the west and the oil-rich Islamic countries, assistance began pouring in and over the next five years the economy went from strength to strength.

During a military coup attempt in May 1981, President Zia was assassinated. There was no obvious successor, so Justice Abdul Sattar was appointed as acting president. Faced with a population in a political frenzy, a general election was held in which Sattar, as candidate for the BNP, won 66% of the vote. He formed a cabinet and the country appeared ready to settle down. The population's peaceful return to the rule of the law was a reflection of the stability that Zia had created.

However, there was increasing concern over government methods and on 24 March 1982 General Hossain Mohammed Ershad seized power in a bloodless coup, becoming the country's 7th head of state since independence just 11 years earlier. Once again Bangladesh was placed under martial law. Ershad announced a mixed cabinet of politicians and army officers, and pledged a return to parliamentary rule within two years. As Zia had done, he formed his own political party, the Jatiya Party, and then solidified his power by handing out highly valuable plots of land in Baridhara to various generals.

The pledge to hold elections was never honoured. The general election scheduled for 1985 was cancelled and in its place Ershad held a referendum in an attempt to pacify his critics. The opposition parties dismissed this as a farce, and many refused to take further part in the political process.

Thereafter, the government periodically made vague announcements that elections would be held soon, and while these were rapturously greeted by the local press as proof that Bangladesh was indeed a democracy, nothing ever came of them. Despite Ershad's disregard for both the pledge and the spirit of democracy, the country progressed economically during the late 1980s. In early 1990, however, the economy began to unravel and by the summer massive rallies and hartaals were being held in the streets.

Zia's wife, Begum Khaleda Zia, with no political experience, was put forward as the head of the BNP. Her steadfast call for Ershad's resignation created a favourable image. As military support waned, Ershad had no choice but to resign. Shortly thereafter he was thrown in jail to await trial on charges of corruption. A neutral caretaker government was appointed to oversee parliamentary elections in early 1991.

The ensuing campaign was reasonably free and open. Sure of victory, the Awami League, headed by Sheikh Hasina and supported by the older generation involved in the struggle for independence, waged an uninspired campaign. When the votes were counted, they had about 33% of the vote compared to the BNP's 31% but the BNP won about 35 more seats in parliament. Democracy once again took roots.

Several months later, the country was hit by the worst cyclone since 1970, killing an estimated 150,000 people. This, however, was only a temporary setback. The economy was soon back on track and the Dhaka stock market began to draw the attention of some speculative foreign investors.

While the economy ticked along reasonably well at the macroeconomic level, on a microeconomic level things were not so good. The number of destitute people was increasing. Dhaka city elections in 1994, which were won by the Awami League, sent a strong signal to the BNP that all was not well. In 1995, with parliamentary elections scheduled for early 1996, the Awami League began calling hartaals every few weeks and demanding that the BNP step down a month before the elections and hand the government over to a caretaker government. Since there was no constitutional provision for this action, the BNP rejected the proposal and as a result, all major opposition parties boycotted the February 15 elections. Voter turnout was around 5% and widespread reports of ballot-box stuffing by polling officials verified the opposition's claim that a free and fair election could not be held, and further undermines the legitimacy of the BNP government.

GEOGRAPHY

Although geographers have divided Bangladesh into as many as 54 distinct geographical regions, the most obvious features are that it's very, very flat and the rivers are correspondingly vast. The two hilly areas are the hills of sedimentary rock around Sylhet, which mark the beginnings of the hills of Assam, and the short, steep ridges of the Chittagong Hill Tracts, which run along the Myanmar border.

Bangladesh has a total area of 143,998 sq km, roughly the same size as Wisconsin or England and Wales combined. It is surrounded to the west, north-west and east by India, and shares a south-eastern border with Myanmar for 283 km. To the south is the Bay of Bengal.

The topography is characterised by alluvial plains, bound to the north by the submontane regions of the Himalaya; the piedmontane areas in the north-east and the eastern fringes adjacent to Assam, Tripura and Myanmar are broken by the forested hills of Mymensingh, Sylhet, and Chittagong. The great Himalayan rivers, the Ganges and the Brahmaputra, divide the land into six major regions, which correspond to the six governmental divisions: north-west (Rajshahi), south-west (Khulna), south central (Barisal), central (Dhaka), north-east (Sylhet) and south-east (Chittagong). Because most of these areas lie on a major fault, seismologists warn that another massive earthquake like the one in 1897 could occur.

The alluvial river plains, which dominate 90% of the country, are very flat and never rise more than 10m above sea level. The only relief from these plains occurs in the north-east and south-east corners of the country where the hills rise to an average of 240m and 600m, respectively. These hills follow a north-south direction. The highest peak in Bangladesh is Mt Keokradong (1230m),

which is about 80 km south-west of Chittagong in the Hill Tracts.

Overall, Bangladesh has no great mountains or deserts, and is characterised more by wooded marshlands and jungles, with forest regions in Sylhet, Mymensingh, the Sundarbans, the Chittagong Hill Tracts, and Tangail in Dhaka Division. These forest regions constitute 15% of the total land area.

Almost all of Bangladesh's coastline forms the Mouths of the Ganges, the final destination of the Ganges River, and the largest estuarine delta in the world. The coastal strip from the western border to Chittagong is one great patchwork of shifting river courses and little islands. The Sundarbans, a vast area of coastal forest, rises only a metre above sea level and is a delta in the making. Over the whole delta area, which extends into India, the rivers make up 6.5% of the total area.

The south-eastern coast, south from the city of Chittagong, is backed by the wooded Arakan Hills which overlook a sandy coast for about 120 km through to the settlement of Teknaf at the southernmost point.

In all of Bangladesh the only place which has any stone is a quarry in the far north-western corner of the country bordering India. That's one reason you'll see bricks being hammered into pieces all over the country: the brick fragments are substituted for stones when making concrete.

The Great Indian Earthquake of 1897

Bangladesh hasn't had an earthquake for so long that no one seems to take seriously it is one of the world's major earthquake zones and that a 'big one' is just waiting to happen.

Bangladesh has experienced seven earthquakes measuring more than seven on the Richter scale this century. The 'whopper' was the 1897 earthquake which had an epicentre 230 km from Dhaka and reached 8.7 on the Richter scale. It was felt all over Bangladesh.

In the far north-western corner near India, the Kantanagar Temple was the country's premier nava-ratna (nine-towered) shrine. Sadly, all nine towers collapsed during the earthquake. In Comilla, the only saptadasha (17-towered) structure, the octagonal Jagannath Temple, suffered a similar fate. If it seems a little odd looking, now you know why.

Between these two points the damage was equally bad. The Hussaini Dalan in Dhaka has the same 'not-quite-right' look about it. The original elevated roof fell in during the earthquake and was replaced by a flat one. In Rangpur, the beautiful Tajhat Palace remains in good condition but its then-new owner, Govinda Lal, was buried alive under the debris of his own house nearby. All of the Dighapatia Palace in Natore, except its mosque-like dome, dates from 1897; the original palace underneath was destroyed by the tremors.

The wide swath of destruction leaves no doubt that Bangladesh is indeed in a major seismic zone and that earthquakes are high on the list of potential disasters facing this country. ∎

Rivers

Rivers are the most important geographical feature in Bangladesh, and it is rivers which created the vast alluvial delta. The outflow of water from Bangladesh is the third highest in the world, after the Amazon and the Congo systems.

Bangladesh's rivers have been described as 'young and migratory', and even in the last 100 years there have been massive changes of course. This is not new. The history of the country is full of important cities becoming ghost towns because the rivers they were built on silted up or changed course; the earliest inscription found in the country exhorts people to store grain in expectation of future floods. Many of the little lakes and ponds scattered around the country are the equivalent of the Australian billabongs – lagoons created when branches of meandering rivers are cut off.

Annual flooding during the monsoon season is part of life in Bangladesh. But after the 1988 floods, some experts began speculating whether the flooding is getting worse and whether deforestation in India and especially Nepal, which causes increased runoff, may be the reason. Other experts are not so sure there has been a change. Regardless, there has been increased pressure to 'do something' and find a 'permanent solution'. Part of the problem of doing anything, however, is that the country depends for its fertility on regular flooding, and simply building massive dykes along riverbanks could be disastrous for agricultural output.

The Brahmaputra-Jamuna and the lower Meghna are the widest rivers, with the latter expanding to around eight km across in the wet season, and much more when it is in flood.

The Ganges, which begins in the Indian state of Uttar Pradesh, enters Bangladesh from the north-west through Rajshahi Division. It joins the Brahmaputra in the centre of the country, north-west of the capital, Dhaka. The Ganges and the Brahmaputra rivers both receive new names once they pass into Bangladesh: the Ganges becomes the Padma, while the Brahmaputra is known as the Jamuna. It is these great rivers and the countless tributaries that flow from them that have the most apparent effect on the landform – constant erosion and flooding over the alluvial plains change the course of rivers, landscapes and agriculture. The Jamuna alone is estimated to carry down 900 million tonnes of silt each year.

Seasonal Floods

If you arrive here by air during the monsoon season, you'll be astounded by how much of the country appears to be under water – around 70%. And this will probably be just the normal flooding that occurs. Imagine what it must be like when there's a real flood! Many first-time visitors to Bangladesh assume that the flooding is due to heavy rainfall in the country during that time of year. In fact, it has little to do with local rainfall – it's mostly water coming from the Ganges, Meghna and the Brahmaputra rivers.

For Bangladeshis, annual flooding is a fact of life. Wading through waist-high water to the nearest tube well for potable water is just part of living in difficult circumstances. Much of the flooding, which affects about a third of the country, is regarded by farmers as beneficial, replenishing worn soils with nutrients. It's when the rivers rise above their normal limits that problems arise.

The last great flood was in 1988 when all three of the country's major rivers reached flood levels at the same time. The devastation was enormous; some 2000 people drowned. The worst-hit area was the small islands near the edge of the Jamuna River; hundreds were totally submerged. In Dhaka, even houses on fairly high ground were inundated and Zia airport was covered with water and had to be shut down.

After the 1988 flood, the World Bank helped to develop a Flood Action Plan (FAP) designed to reduce the potential for flooding. The original FAP ran into a barrage of criticisms. Environmentalists claimed that massive construction works were not the answer: levees would interfere with the migration paths of fish and concrete embankments would cut off the regular beneficial floods that over millennia Bangladeshis had learned to adapt to. The answer was not flood control but controlled flooding. Environmentalists seem to have won the day because the revised FAP now calls for improved flood forecasting and disaster management. ■

CLIMATE

The climate of Bangladesh is subtropical and tropical with temperatures ranging from an average daytime low of 21°C in the cold season to a top of 35°C in the hot season. Annual rainfall varies from 1000 mm in the west to 2500 mm in the south-east and up to 5000 mm in the north near the hills of Assam.

Three-quarters of the annual rainfall occurs between June and September. The 90% to 95% humidity in this season is almost unbearable for some travellers. The humidity remains high all year round, producing the thick fogs of winter, and making chilly nights in the north feel much colder than they are.

Bangladesh has three main seasons: the monsoon or wet season from late May to early October; the cold season from mid-October to the end of February; and the hot season from mid-March to mid-May. There are two cyclone seasons – May to June and October to November.

Rajshahi Division shares some of neighbouring north India's extremes of climate. It is the hottest region in the country in summer, and between the end of March and the end of April the *pashi*, a blistering wind, blows through the day. In winter it can get quite cold at night, down to 3°C some years, when freezing fogs bring normal life to a standstill and many poor people die.

In the cold season the weather is drier and fresh, and the days are usually sunny with clear blue skies. Temperatures range from 5°C overnight in the far north to 22°C during the day and rainfall is negligible, although even in winter a brief thunder shower may come along.

Early March is still reasonably pleasant with tolerable humidity, warm days and nights and clear skies. But by April, as the monsoon approaches, the temperature rises to around 40°C during the day and 29°C overnight. With increasing humidity, this time of the year can be almost intolerable. Lethal hail storms are also quite common, with reports of some hail stones weighing half a kg. The winds that provide this unusual weather whirl up from the Bay of Bengal, then U-turn at the Himalaya and carry their

The Cyclones of 1970 & 1991

Every few years it seems Bangladesh is hit by another disaster. While there are periodic floods and droughts, the most catastrophic by far in terms of human life are cyclones.

Bangladesh is in the worst area in the world for cyclones because of a unique combination of factors: a large tide (five metres near Sandwip Island), a funnelling coast configuration which increases the height of waves, low flat terrain, and frequent severe tropical storms which produce an average of one major cyclone every three years. The worst seasons are May to June and October to November, and the area where damage tends to occur most frequently is in the east around Chittagong and Cox's Bazar.

People still talk about the 1970 cyclone when between 300,000 and 500,000 people lost their lives. The 1991 cyclone which occurred at midnight during the month's peak high tide was stronger, affected over twice as many people and destroyed four times as many houses. However, the death toll of between 140,000 and 200,000 was less than half that of 1970.

A major reason for the reduction of fatalities was the presence of storm shelters; a number of which had been constructed since 1970. As you travel around the Cox's Bazar area you'll definitely see a few; some are multi-functional, serving as schools too. More shelters and stronger embankments have been built since 1991. ■

icy cargo back to Bangladesh. They are known as *guarni jour*.

The usual starting date for the monsoon is somewhere between late May and mid-June. It doesn't rain solidly all day every day – there tends to be an initial downpour, followed by clear skies. The air feels cleaner and sweeter-smelling and the rain appears to relieve the oppressive heat of the hot season.

Although there are only three observable seasons in Bangladesh, the locals have six:

Basanto (spring)
    February to April
Grishma (summer)
    April to June
Barsha (rainy)
    June to August
Sharat (autumn)
    August to October
Hemanto (misty)
    October to December
Sheet (winter)
    December to February

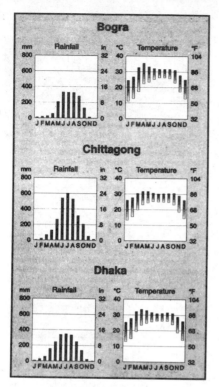

ECOLOGY & ENVIRONMENT

With the occurrence of global warming, believed by many scientists to be caused by the greenhouse effect, Bangladesh, as one of the 10 countries in the world most vulnerable to a rise in sea level, will be drastically affected. Present predictions indicate the sea will rise by eight to 30 cm by 2030, and 30 to 110 cm by 2100. A 100 cm rise in the Bay of Bengal would result in a loss of 12% to 18% of the country's land area.

Loss of land is just one consequence – severe flooding and reduced agricultural potential are almost inevitable. Seasonal flooding will become wider, deeper and more prolonged because a higher sea level will retard drainage. This will increase the salinity of ground water. Tidal waves during cyclones are likely to be more severe.

This is a cruel twist of fate, since Bangladesh, as a poor, agricultural society, has contributed very little to global warming. Even with assistance from the Dutch, who are helping to devise a strategy to cope with rising water levels, the question remains whether Bangladesh will have the capacity to develop and apply the appropriate technology.

FLORA & FAUNA

Like most of the northern flatlands of the subcontinent, Bangladesh is both subtropical and tropical. This has given rise to a great variety of flora and fauna.

Flora

About 10% of Bangladesh is still forested. Half of the remaining forest is in the Chittagong Hill Tracts and a further quarter in the Sundarbans, with the rest scattered in small pockets throughout the country.

The forests fall distinctly into three regional varieties: the forests of the tidal zones along the coast, often mangrove but sometimes hardwood, in much of the Sundarbans; the forests of *sal* (hardwood) trees around Dhaka, Tangail and Mymensingh; and the upland forests of tropical and subtropical evergreens in the Chittagong Hill Tracts and parts of Sylhet.

Even away from the forests, Bangladesh is a land of trees. Lining the old Trunk Road in the west are huge rain trees, and every village is an arboreal oasis, often with spectacular banyan or *oshot* trees. The red silk-cotton or kapok tree is easily spotted throughout the countryside in February and March, when it loses its leaves and sprouts a myriad of red blossoms. Teak was introduced into the Hill Tracts last century, and the quality approaches that of Myanmar; it's much better than Indian teak.

Given that half the country is located in the tropics, flowering plants make up an integral part of the beauty of Bangladesh. Each season produces its special variety of flowers. Among them, the prolific water hyacinth flourishes. Its carpet of thick green leaves and blue flowers gives the impression that solid ground lies underneath. Other decorative plants which grow easily are jasmine, water lily, rose, hibiscus, bougainvillea, magnolia, and an incredible diversity of wild orchids in the forested areas.

Fauna

Bangladesh is home to the royal Bengal tiger and others of the cat family such as leopards and the smaller jungle cat. Tigers are almost exclusively confined to the Sundarbans, but their smaller relations prey on domestic animals all over the country. There are three varieties of civet, including the large Indian civet which is now listed as an endangered species. Other large animals include Asiatic elephants (mostly migratory herds from Bihar), a few black bears in Chittagong Division, wild pigs and deer. Monkeys, langurs, gibbons (the only ape on the subcontinent), otters and mongooses are some of the smaller animals. There were once wild buffalo and rhinoceros, but all became extinct this century.

Reptiles include the sea tortoise, mud turtle, river tortoise, pythons, crocodiles and a variety of poisonous snakes. The voluble gecko lizard is, appropriately, known as *tiktiki*. Marine life includes a wide variety of both river and sea fish.

The royal Bengal tiger is a powerful animal, often growing to more than two metres in length and 290 kg in weight. In Bangladesh, the tiger is now only found in the Sunderbans, where its population is thought to be around 400.

Bird-Watching

Between the natural and human problems of Bangladesh, it's difficult to imagine that the country can boast of being the habitat to more than 650 species of birds, almost half of those found on the entire subcontinent.

Tucked in between the Indian subcontinent and the Malayan peninsulas, Bangladesh attracts both the Indian species in the west and north of the country, and the Malayan species in the east and south-east. It is also conveniently located for the migrants heading south towards Malaysia and Indonesia, and those which are moving south-west to India and Sri Lanka. In addition, there are a number of Himalayan and Burmese hill species which move into the lowlands during the winter. Despite the fact that many of these species are rare or localised and that the overall number of birds has declined in the past two decades, bird-watching in Bangladesh can be rewarding.

Within the Dhaka Division, the Madhupur Forest, south-west of Mymensingh, is an extremely important habitat worthy of national protection. This area is great for a variety of owls, including the popular and rare brown wood owl, wintering thrushes and a number of raptors, to mention a few. The Jamuna River floods regularly, and from December to February provides winter habitats for waterfowl, waders and the occasional black stork.

Lying close to the Himalaya, the Sylhet area has extensive natural *haors* (pronounced 'howers', wetlands) in this low-lying basin and during the winter season is home to huge flocks of wildfowl. Outstanding species include the rare Baer's pochard and Pallas' fishing eagle, along with a great number of ducks and skulkers. Also important habitats are the remaining fragments of evergreen and teak forests, especially along the Indian border near the Srimangal area. The blue-bearded bee-eater, red-breasted trogan and a wide variety of forest birds, including rare visitors, are regularly seen in these forests. Preservation of these forests and haors is critical for sustaining the variety and rarity of this wildlife.

One of two important coastal zones is the Noakhali region, with emphasis on the islands near Hatiya, where migratory species and a variety of wintering waders find suitable refuges. These include large numbers of the rare spoonbilled sandpiper, Nordman's greenshank and flocks of Indian skimmers.

The Sundarbans, the second important coastal zone, is the richest for all kinds of wildlife, and the most difficult to penetrate. With its miles of marshy shorelines and brackish creeks, it supports a great number of wetland and forest species, along with large populations of gulls and terns along the south coast. Eight varieties of kingfishers have been recorded here including the brown-winged, white-collared, black-capped and the rare ruddy kingfisher.

Overall the most exciting time of year for bird-watching is during the winter from November to March. See the Books section in the Facts for the Visitor chapter for a list of field guides.

Endangered Species

It is well known that the royal Bengal tiger is an endangered species. The government recently set aside three specific areas within the Sundarbans as tiger reserves, but numbers are low. See the Sundarbans National Park section of the Khulna Division for more information.

Other species which are rare or under threat include Indian elephants, hoolock gibbons, black bears and the Ganges River dolphin. Reptilian species under threat include the Indian python, the crocodile and various turtles.

Many of the diverse bird species are prolific, however, some are vulnerable, including Pallas' fishing eagle and the rare Baer's pochard.

National Parks & Reserve Areas

There is a dismal lack of designated national parks, reserves and conservation areas in Bangladesh. With millions of people to feed, perhaps it's asking too much to make good agricultural land off-limits. However, the situation is as complicated as a Gordian knot, since in many ways survival depends on intact natural areas. Unfortunately, due to intense human pressure, these are disappearing fast. Added to that, designated parks and reserves are not strictly controlled and blatant misuse, even by those who are paid to protect them, is an everyday occurrence.

Bhawal National Park More commonly known as Rajendrapur National Park, it is located in the Dhaka Division, about 38 km north of Dhaka city. The area mostly comprises regrowth sal forest and open picnic spots. There are a few walking trails.

Sundarbans Reserve This is the finest natural area in the entire country, mostly due to its impenetrable jungle forests and maze of rivers. Located in the southern half of the Khulna Division, it's part of the world's largest mangrove forest and home to the Bengal tiger.

Madhupur Forest Reserve This is a degraded sal and mixed forest with some remaining old growth; it's roughly 130 km north-west of Dhaka (three hours by car) on the road between Mymensingh and Tangail. Over the past 20 years its size has been cut in half, but it continues to be a very interesting forest rich with wildlife.

Lowacherra Forest Reserve Some eight km east of Srimangal in the greater Sylhet area, this hilly sal forest is similar in size to Madhupur Forest, though the species of wildlife varies slightly.

Telepara/Satcheri Forest Reserve This mixed evergreen/teak forest is about 60 km south-west of Srimangal. Within its boundaries is a sandy basin which is excellent for bird-watching.

Singra Forest Reserve In the Rajshahi Division, well north of Dinajpur, this reserve is a fairly uniform sal forest with mixed woodland on the boundary.

GOVERNMENT & POLITICS

Bangladesh is a constitutional republic with a multiparty parliamentary democracy in which elections by secret ballot are held on the basis of universal suffrage. The theoretical head of state is the president, who is elected by the members of parliament for a five year term and can hold office for no more than two terms, whether or not they are consecutive. Under the present government, the president is Abdur Rahman Biswas. Although the president appoints the prime minister, the real executive power rests with the prime minister, presently Begum Khaleda Zia.

As in the UK, the prime minister must call elections at least every five years. In the 1991 elections, the BNP won a majority of the 300 seats up for election, and in the February 1996 elections, which were boycotted by the major opposition parties, the BNP won an overwhelming majority.

An additional 30 seats are reserved for women and since they are allocated by parliament, this effectively rewards the majority party with 30 more seats. Women can contest any elected seat in parliament, and have won seats in the past two elections. While the presence of women in parliament and of Zia as the head of government is said to demonstrate the country's commitment to women's participation in the government, opponents claim it's only show because at the cabinet and sub-cabinet levels, women are conspicuously absent.

The indigenous tribal people who, like in the Indian constitution, are referred to in the Bangladesh constitution as the 'backward section of citizens', have no seats specifically reserved for them, but some members from minority groups are in the BNP government.

The opposition is led by Sheikh Hasina Wajed (daughter of Sheikh Mujib Rahman) and her Awami League. While there are many other parties, the most significant ones are the Jatiya Party (former President Ershad's party) and the Jamaat-i-Islami, the major Islamic political party.

Although 87% of the population is Muslim, Bangladesh is constitutionally defined as a secular democracy. Unlike in many Islamic countries, the Muslim clergy, the mullahs, do not hold sway in national politics.

Administratively, the country is divided into six divisions: Dhaka, Chittagong, Sylhet, Rajshahi, Khulna and Barisal. Each division is in turn divided into lesser units. It is at these lower levels that the government has the most impact on people's daily lives. But while elections are held for lower-level positions, local governments have only a democratic veneer because elections are held infrequently and elected officials, once in office, are not very responsive to the public.

Politics & Students

Probably nowhere in the world do students play such a pivotal role in politics as in Bangladesh. There's always news about another gun-toting student riot at Dhaka University. Dormitory bombings and assassinations of student leaders are common everyday occurrences. Since independence, some 55 people have been killed due to student riots on campus, many killings occurring as a result of inter-faction disagreements.

Students today are empowered by recent tradition, in large part from the key role they played in the War of Liberation. When the war started it was no mistake that the Pakistanis aimed their tanks first at Dhaka University. Many students were among the intellectuals targeted for massacre.

Today the main political parties view students' support as crucial and court their allegiance by supporting student activists. Most of these 'permanent students', who live on campus for years, are popularly thought to be paid political activists.

As a result, many of the state universities have become the scene for ongoing clashes between the major parties. After every bloody clash the universities close down, sometimes for weeks. This pattern constantly repeats itself, followed by the invariable public outcry for the government to 'do something' – which it rarely does. ∎

Farakka Dam: The Politics of Water

You can't stay very long in Bangladesh without hearing or reading something about the Farakka Dam. The dam was built on the Ganges in 1974, just 15 km from the Bangladesh border, for the ostensible purpose of diverting water during the dry season to the Hooghly River in West Bengal, to improve the navigability of the port of Calcutta. This did not occur and the port, which is 190 km up-river from the Bay of Bengal, is doomed. Undaunted, India has dropped that argument and now says it needs the water for irrigation instead.

Today, India siphons off increasingly large quantities of water for this purpose and as a result, the flow of the Ganges downriver during the dry season has dropped to about 15% of its former level. Bangladesh predicts that in another 10 years the flow during the dry season will completely stop.

The environmental consequences for Bangladesh are severe. Some rivers draining from the Ganges are now completely silted up in the dry season, losing all navigability. Reduced flow also increases saline intrusion from the Bay of Bengal into the south-west, threatening the fragile ecology of the Sundarbans and reducing ground water levels. And the most immediate effect is that thousands of hectares of land which could formerly be irrigated for a third crop now lay dry during the winter. Bangladesh estimates that the cumulative agricultural loss is around US$500 million annually.

The dam was constructed without any signed agreement between the governments for water-sharing and the Indian government has since refused to convert a 1985 Memorandum of Understanding on usage into a permanent arrangement. With virtually no leverage for bringing India to the bargaining table, Bangladesh is truly 'up the creek'. ■

Relations with India

On the international front, Bangladesh is very friendly with the West and has sent troops around the world to help out in hot spots including the Gulf War, the invasion of Haiti and the war in Bosnia. But with neighbouring India, Bangladesh won't lift a finger.

Basically, the two countries are at political odds with one another. Religious conflicts over the centuries between Hindus and Muslims are an underlying reason. During the Raj era, Hindus were favoured by the British, adding fuel to Muslim resentment against the wealthier Hindus. While Bangladeshis have a close affinity with West Bengalis because of their common language, relations with the national government are on a different footing. When Nehru agreed to bind the area of Bangladesh with Pakistan at the time of Indian independence, the Bengalis felt like pawns. And the Indian army's assistance years later in bringing the Pakistani army to its knees during the War of Liberation was viewed, quite rightly, more as a matter of self-interest.

Today, their most contentious issue is Farakka Dam, which during the dry season enables India to siphon off water from the Ganges, to the great detriment of Bangla-desh. As long as this issue remains unresolved, regional cooperation between the two countries seems doomed.

National Flag

First flown 'officially' from the rebel Bangladesh embassy in Calcutta when the War of Liberation began, the Bangladesh flag is green for the lush country (not for Islam, as some fundamentalists would prefer) with a red circle for the bloodshed at the country's creation.

ECONOMY

Bangladesh is quite poor, with the average per capita income hovering around US$225. On the United Nations Human Development Index, a development scale based on a combination of gross national product, literacy and life expectancy, Bangladesh is ranked 146th of 173 – ahead of 27 other countries and neck and neck with Nepal. Approximately US$2 billion per annum has been pumped into the country over the past decade or more, but aid levels are now falling significantly. Food aid is one-third of what it was 15 years ago because the country now produces most of what it consumes.

Still unable to shed its 'basket case' image,

the country continues to attract foreign aid from a large number of organisations from around the globe including aid agencies such as UNICEF, UNDP, UNESCO, WHO, ODA, USAID, GTZ and Danida. Much of it has gone into the family planning sector; the country's rapidly declining birth rates are the result. For years foreign aid has provided over 50% of the government's development budget, but the figure is now less than 30% and declining rapidly. The Bangladesh government maintains that as long as foreign

Jute in Decline

In the 19th century, Bengal was known for its production of jute, the 'golden fibre'. The humid climate was perfect for growing jute and jute sacks were in demand worldwide. Today, polythene has nearly destroyed the industry – even grain donated from abroad arrives in plastic bags. Although Bangladesh still produces 80% of the world's jute, the industry is in rapid decline. It now accounts for only 13% of total exports, down from 62% in 1982. Cheap jute carpets and jute handicrafts for export are helping the industry to survive, but whether this biodegradable natural fibre will make a comeback remains to be seen. ■

donors increase access to their markets (especially the garment market) to offset the decreased aid levels, it won't complain. To some extent, this has been happening.

On the macroeconomic level, Bangladesh has a liberalised market-oriented economy and no major political party seems to question this overall policy, only its implementation. The structural adjustment programme of the BNP government is an attempt to create a positive investment climate which involves conservative fiscal and monetary policies which have resulted in low inflation rates (around 2%), low bank interest rates, a doubling in domestic savings rates, low fiscal deficit (around 5%) and minimal fluctuation in exchange rates. Exports have been growing annually at an impressive 20% and foreign reserves have grown to US$3 billion.

Despite these results, the annual growth in the economy remains arrested at around 4.5%, which is actually lower than in the early 1980s when economic reforms began. Due to strong pressure from trade unionists, the government has been moving at a snail's pace in privatising state enterprises, particularly the large jute factories; these losing enterprises continue draining huge sums from the state coffers. Also, while the country is now close to self-sufficiency in rice, agricultural production has been stagnant since 1991. Excluding garments, the manufacturing sector's annual growth, too, is only fair at just 4.5%. The only growth sectors are fisheries and livestock which are of relatively minor importance.

The main reason, however, for the mediocre growth rate is that the country is failing to attract investment. Foreign investment shot up briefly in 1994 but then went dramatically down in 1995 as the country's political situation heated up. So despite recent articles calling Bangladesh 'The Emerging Tiger' *(Euromoney)* and 'the best investment choice on the Indian sub-continent' *(The Emerging Stock Market Report)* and despite being allowed 100% ownership, foreign investors are staying away because of the volatile political situation.

The one really bright spot is the ready-made

Foreign Remittances

In terms of foreign currency reserves, Bangladesh, with about US$2.5 billion in the coffers, is doing quite well. This is largely due to the country's overpopulation – one of its few benefits. Every year thousands of Bangladeshis leave to look for work in the Middle East and Asia, especially Malaysia where as many as 160,000 work legally and undoubtedly many more illegally. Many send money back to their families in Bangladesh.

The amount of remittances is increasing at a phenomenal rate and now totals US$1.3 billion plus another half billion or so thought to come in through unofficial channels. Foreign remittances represent about half the country's total export earnings – more than from garment exports. However, for the workers abroad, it's a trade-off; for substantially higher pay they endure a fairly pathetic life, alone in a strange country and often receiving little respect. While many return after just a few years, others remain and prosper. ∎

garment industry with an annual growth of a phenomenal 22%. Incredibly low wages (between US$20 and US$30 a month) and a relatively disciplined workforce are Bangladesh's drawing cards. Most of the 2200 garment factories are in and around Dhaka and Chittagong, and women, mostly from poor families, hold nearly 90% of the more than one million jobs. Bangladesh is now the largest supplier of T-shirts to Europe and it's the seventh largest apparel supplier to the US. Entrance into the brand-name market seems to be the next step.

Child Labour

Use of child labour (children under 14 years of age) in the garment factories became a major issue in 1994 when the US Congress threatened to prohibit Bangladesh-made textiles from entering the US, which is the largest market for Bangladesh-made garments. The issue is complex because in Bangladesh these children (estimated at between 50,000 and 100,000) barred from working in export industries will not go to school; they'll probably end up with worse jobs, such as brick-breaking in the hot sun, begging or, worse, prostitution. Many of the children come from families with no fathers and many young siblings; they have no choice but to work.

Nevertheless, because of pressure from the US, use of child labour has been greatly reduced. As part of the agreement with the Bangladesh Garment Manufacturers for firing these children, some US assistance is being given to establish primary education programmes. Unfortunately these programmes will only help a few thousand. ∎

POPULATION

The population of Bangladesh is close to 120 million, making it the most densely populated country in the world, with the exception of several city-states (Singapore, Malta and Hong Kong). On a per sq km basis, it is three times more populated than India and seven times more populated than China. Nevertheless, what is not well known is that there are several other sizable areas in the world which are just as crowded – Java (Indonesia's principal island), for example, has a population density equal to Bangladesh's.

Despite the density of population, rural Bangladesh (which is where most of the people are) is only beginning to feel crowded. There aren't endless sprawls of depressing slums and industrial wastelands, mainly because land is too precious to sprawl over and industrial development is still fairly low. The countryside is green and lovely and the air is clean. Anyone flying from Kathmandu or Delhi will see a marked visual difference in the air quality.

The country's family planning programme has been remarkably successful. Fertility rates have declined dramatically, from 6.3 births per woman in 1975 to 3.4% by 1993. The average desired family size is now under three children. The average population growth rate was down to 2.3% in 1995 and was well below the economic growth rate. The use of contraceptives grew from 19% in 1981 to 45% in 1995, significantly higher than in India. Despite this successful decline in population growth, the country's population is expected to double in another 35 to 40 years, eventually levelling off between 230 and 280 million people.

PEOPLE

Perhaps because of their country's bloody birth, the proud nationalism of Bangladeshis extends to their concept of themselves as a people. It seems a bit forced, but some academics here argue that Bangladeshis have always been a separate cultural and even racial unit on the subcontinent. This is somewhat fancifully stretched to include the tribes of the Chittagong Hill Tracts, and is used as a justification for their forced integration into the mainstream culture.

It took the Aryan invaders 1000 years to tame the jungles of the Gangetic plain and reach Bengal, and on the way the meat-eating warriors evolved into contemplative Hindus. It is claimed that the region's original Dravidian tribe, the Bangs, were pushed by the Aryan invaders into the jungles of the delta but were not initially conquered. Here, their culture developed and, as one author put it, 'unlike many other Dravidian tribes the Bangs...were intelligent, imaginative and nomadic'. The late arrival of the by now less aggressive Brahmin culture resulted in integration with the locals, rather than conquest and outcast status as happened to other aboriginal tribes on the subcontinent.

The Bangladeshi pride in ancestry is balanced by the Islamic slant of intellectual life which tends to deny the achievements of the preceding Buddhist and Hindu cultures. The antipathy to Hinduism isn't just religious – it was the Hindu zamindars who grew rich on the toil of the Muslim peasantry under the Raj. The zamindars' lifestyle of 'wine and women' isn't approved of (nor is song in some fundamentalist circles), and the Tantric overtones of Buddhism are regarded as depraved.

Bangladesh has been a melting pot of peoples and cultures for a very long time. Peoples from Myanmar and the Himalaya, Dravidians (the original inhabitants of the subcontinent), and the invading Aryans made up the first blend of people here. With the arrival of the Mughals, people from all over the Islamic world settled here.

The Dravidians, with their racial origins in the Deccan Plateau, are mainly Hindus and constitute about 12% of the population. The Muslims, who make up 87%, are of Dravido-Aryan origin. The original tribal people still exist, mainly in the Chittagong Hill Tracts, though they now number less than 1% of the total population. Many of the tribes have been converted to Christianity, although animism still strongly influences their beliefs and practices. The Tibeto-Burmese inhabitants are mainly Buddhists and less than 1% of the population is Christian.

The Muslims and Hindus have a cultural affinity with West Bengal and speak Bangla, while the Buddhists have their own distinct culture and dialects related mainly to that of Burma and the tribal culture of eastern India. Apart from the tribal people, the Christian people here mostly have Portuguese names and are usually English-speakers.

The family sticks together, even in the more westernised middle classes, and most people have a 'home village' to which they return on weekends or holidays. This is so

Poverty

Despite an economic growth rate which exceeds the population growth rate, the situation of the country's poor – about half the population – is dire, despite signs of marginal improvements. The benefits of growth need to 'trickle down' more. Statistics show, for instance, that while the population with virtually no land (one-fifth of a hectare or less) remains constant at 47%, the proportion of absolute landless (19%) is increasing.

Other statistics show that the literacy rate is barely improving and, most startlingly, that the people may be shrinking. A recent study showed that children aged 11 years have lost height and weight between 1937 and 1982. The study may be flawed but no one would dispute that the huge percentage of children who are malnourished is not declining. Because of these dire statistics, the World Bank has altered course slightly and now has a $60 million nutrition project targeting children under age five. ■

Child Nutrition

Child malnutrition is perhaps Bangladesh's gravest problem. Many children are doomed even before birth. Women are more likely to be malnourished than men, and many are iodine deficient. Because of the mother's deficiency, each year some 20,000 children are born with mental or physical handicaps. Simply adding iodine to salt would help tremendously but this has not yet been done.

Almost half of the babies born in Bangladesh have low birth weights (under 2.5 kg). The mother's malnutrition is just one cause. Others include hard physical work during pregnancy, repeated infections, the very young age of mothers, and close birth spacing. Maternal mortality (400 per 10,000 births) is also an element. In rural areas with few doctors, women know they will die if an oversized baby is unable to pass through the pelvis. Consequently, many women restrict their diets during pregnancy. Ironically, recent research shows that head size rather than overall weight causes the problems and this is not affected by diet.

Malnourishment continues as the children grow. Of those under five years of age, 69% are malnourished and 12% are decidedly 'stunted and wasted'. As many as 500,000 children die each year due to complications arising from malnutrition.

Deficiency in vitamin A is another major problem. The occurrence of night-blindness among Bangladeshi children is one of the highest in the world. Thousands of children become blind annually and almost half of these children die within a year. Low intake of vegetables and frequent attacks of diarrhoea are two of the principal causes of this deficiency. ■

pervasive that an unquestionable excuse for, say, your laundry not being returned on time is 'the room boy has gone to his home village'.

Tribal People

The tribal population of Bangladesh numbers almost one million. They live generally in the hilly regions north of Mymensingh, the Sylhet area, and more than half a million are concentrated in the wooded Chittagong Hill Tracts. Others live in urban areas such as Chittagong and Cox's Bazar.

The tribes living in the Hill Tracts of Chittagong include the Chakmas, Moghs, Mrus, Murungs, Lushais, Kukis, Bams, Tripuras, Saks, Tangchangyas, Shandus, Banjugis and the Pankhars. The Chakmas constitute the major tribe here, and next to them are the Moghs, who are also found in Cox's Bazar and the Khepupara region near Patuakhali. These tribes are sometimes collectively known as Jhumias, from *jhum*, their method of slash-and-burn agriculture. Because vast areas of their territory now lie under the waters of Kaptai Lake, and because of land appropriation by plains settlers, their sustainable 10 year rotation of cultivation has been cut to three, which doesn't give the forest time to regenerate properly.

The tribes in the Sylhet Hills – the Khasis, Pangous and the Manipuris – usually have their settlements on the hilly frontier area at the foot of the Khasi-Jaintia Hills. Some of them have become businesspeople and jewellers in Sylhet.

The Garos (or Mandi, as they call themselves), Hanjongis, Hadis, Dahuis, Palais and the Bunas live in the hilly regions north of Mymensingh in Haluaghat, Sreebardi, Kalmakanda and the Garo Hills, and some live west of Mymensingh around the Madhupur forests.

Other tribal groups, such as the Santals, Oraons, Hus, Mundus and Rajbansis, are scattered in urban settlements in Rangpur, Dinajpur, Bogra, Rajshahi, Noakhali, Comilla and Bakerganj.

The tribes in the Mymensingh Hills were originally nomads from the eastern states of India and those in the Chittagong Hill Tracts originate from Myanmar. The tribal groups have their own distinct cultures, art, religious beliefs, superstitions, farming methods and attire. Many of the tribes are Buddhist, though some still retain their animist religion which, to some extent, has been influenced by Hinduism. Centuries ago, the offering of human sacrifices was part of the ritual of some tribes who believed that slaying another man endowed the slayer with the victim's attributes.

Rice and wine are the staple food of these

hill people, but included in the tribal menu are snakes, beetles, crabs, fish, snails, pigs, dogs, buffaloes, deer, ants and chickens. Many of the tribes influenced by Hinduism, along with the Chakmas, Moghs and Marmas who are Buddhist, cremate their dead. Others, such as the Khasis, bury their dead and place headstones on their graves.

The dwellings of the hill people are usually bamboo huts, either on stilts or flat on the ground, and their farming methods are ancient. Some still retain curious traditional customs such as the stone-lifting ceremony of the Khasis, which may have originated from Tibet or even the northern mountain areas of Pakistan.

Many of the tribes still have very little contact with the outside world, but as modern civilisation begins to encroach on their territories, more and more of the younger villagers are moving to the urban areas for employment. The Chakmas, for instance, now make saris and tribal jewellery and have established or joined weaving industries. They have begun to accept western education and clothing, and even use western medicine in lieu of herbs and mantras.

Within the broad racial group of the plains people who make up the vast majority of Bangladeshis are subgroups who, although apparently integrated into the culture, continue to live strikingly different lives. The Baurs, for example, are wandering beggars whose sexual freedom is abhorred by the mainstream, but they are good musicians and are welcomed at weddings and parties.

River Gypsies

Bangladesh's river gypsies, the Badhi or Badhja, make up about 50% of the river-boat people of the country and are mainly low-caste Hindus. They move as a clan from one river to another, selling herbal medicine and jewellery which includes the pink pearls they gather from river oysters. During the monsoon, when the rivers swell and streams extend to outlying villages, the Badhi scatter far and wide to trade; but in winter they move back to their usual havens such as Mirpur, Savar and the Dhakeswari River.

Their houseboats are very tidy, neat and clean with shelves for garments, bedding, pots and pans. Each houseboat holds a family, generally with just two or three children. There seem to be few elderly river gypsies. The gypsies live their whole lives afloat but development, even in Bangladesh, is starting to number their days. Motorised vessels, manufactured jewellery and modern medicine have made inroads and some gypsies now send their children to school. Still, modernisation is a slow process in Bangladesh, and it's likely to be a long, long time before the houseboats disappear.

EDUCATION

Primary education was declared compulsory in 1991, but due to inadequate government support there is an abysmal lack of classrooms and teachers. The facilities that do exist are overcrowded and suffer from a shortage of textbooks and other resources. Extreme poverty compounds the situation, and many school-age children have to work or care for younger siblings out of necessity. Most parents, facing tons of work and seeing little relevance in what their children are learning at school, take them out after a year or two. As a result, 65% of the population is illiterate and the situation is not improving significantly. For women, the figure is 78%.

Secondary education covers classes six to 10, culminating with the first national examination at the end of 10 years of study – the Secondary School Certificate. Secondary education is not free; tuition, textbooks and supplies must be paid for by the student. In some areas, there are separate schools for girls and boys, though the quality of the buildings and facilities vary. Private schools, ranging in tuition from US$10 to US$200 a month, offer the best alternative for those who can afford it.

ARTS

The people of the Bengal region share a similarity of language, dress, music and literature across the national boundaries. Certainly the Bengali passion for politics and poetry seems to spill across the border

Bangladesh Rural Advancement Committee (BRAC)

Started in the early 1970s as a relief organisation during the War of Independence, BRAC later expanded its activities into development work, including rural credit, skill development and health care. BRAC is best known, however, for its non-formal primary education programme. This programme supplements the government primary education system by catching those in the rural areas, particularly girls, who never enter grade one or who drop out within a year.

BRAC targets children of illiterate destitute people, particularly the landless. Today, it's renowned as an innovator in the field of education. Class hours are flexible and scheduled around work demands on children's time, and at least 70% of the students (ages eight to 16) are girls.

The curriculum focuses on just a few subjects which are relevant and useful for the pupils and their families – Bangla, English, arithmetic, and social studies which includes training in health, hygiene, nutrition, horticulture, safety and the community. Teachers, 80% of whom are women, are usually married with at least nine years of schooling and receive 13 days training and a nominal monthly allowance from BRAC. The teaching method is participatory, with students divided into groups of six. Students in each group learn from each other, with the teacher acting as a facilitator, and while there are periodic informal tests, there are no formal annual exams.

Today, there are over 30,000 schools in operation covering over 70% of the country's district-level *thanas*. Student enrolment is now close to one million and drop-outs, the government system's biggest problem, are few. A good number, following the standard three years of schooling, enter public schools at an advanced level.

However, not everyone is happy with BRAC. *Mullahs* (traditional Muslim religious leaders) have accused the programme of being Christian, even tearing down schools; their real gripe seems to be that BRAC is educating women. Despite this, the programme's success has drawn such international attention that BRAC is now branching out to help organisations in other developing countries, especially Africa, to do the same. ■

between West Bengal and Bangladesh. The region also has a multifaceted folk heritage, provided by its ancient animist, Buddhist, Hindu, and Muslim roots. Weaving, pottery and terracotta sculpture are some of the earliest forms of artistic expression. During the Hindu and Buddhist periods, the historic legends and religious deities were depicted in terracotta. The necessities of clothing and utensils for cooking provided another medium for aesthetic creation.

Literature, too, had a place early on. Oral traditions of verse, in the forms of Hindu and Buddhist translations and local mythology, were preceded by itinerant theatre performing groups, whose rural wanderings date back 2000 years. Even today poetry is taken seriously by the Bangladeshis, who consider themselves, at heart, to have the depth of passion and sensitivity of a poet.

Folk Art

Most of the traditional culture is folk culture although, except for the revival in weaving and dyeing, about the only places you'll see concrete examples of it are museums.

Weaving had always held a special place in the artistic expression of the country. In the 7th century, the textiles of Dhaka weavers were finding their way to Europe, where they were regarded as *textiles ventalis*, fabrics woven of air. These fine cotton muslins, woven centuries ago in the old capital of Sonargaon, are still plied by traditional weavers in Tangail, though the exquisite fineness of the thread is no longer available. The most artistic and expensive ornamental fabric is the *jamdani*, or loom-embroidered muslin or silk, exclusively woven for the imperial household centuries ago. Evolving as an art form under the influence of Persian design, the jamdani gained a unique position in the world of weaving. Floral, geometric and animal designs are used in these fabrics.

Needlework, with its roots in antiquity, has become a cottage industry. Most well known are the *naksui kantha*, embroidered, quilted patchwork cloths produced by village women, and holding an important place in village life. They are used as trousseaux, and the embroidery depicts and keeps alive local history and myth. There are women's cooperatives that now produce the kantha commercially, and examples can be found in handicraft stores in Dhaka and Chittagong.

The most pervasive form of popular culture, the paintings on rickshaws and trucks, also upholds local history and myth. Many paintings are just rehashes of film posters, but some, especially on trucks, are very fine naive art. Make an effort to look at some before you get overwhelmed by the sheer quantity. One recurrent motif is a winged creature with a woman's head. This is the *buraq*, which carried Mohammed on his ride from Jerusalem to heaven and back.

Folk Theatre

The *jatra*, or folk theatre, is common at the village level, and usually takes place during harvest time or at *melas*, village fairs. The performances, conducted with much music and dance, were traditionally based on religious, folk, or historic themes which served to preserve the lore of the village. Today's dramas mainly centre on social or political themes, and have become an effective means of communication. *Kabigan* is a form of folk debate conducted in verse. This is most common during festivals.

Literature

Best known in the literature of Bangladesh are the works of the great Bengali poets Rabindranath Tagore and Nasrul Islam, whose photos are – somewhat curiously – displayed in restaurants and barber shops. Tagore received international acclaim after being awarded the Nobel Peace Prize for Literature in 1913, though he always remained close to the Bangladeshi heart. Despite his Hindu upbringing, Tagore wrote from a strong cultural perspective which transcended any particular religion. He celebrated 'humble lives and their miseries' and supported the concept of Hindu-Muslim unity. His love for the land of Bengal is reflected in many of his works, and a portion of the lyrics in one of his poems was adopted as the national anthem.

The 'rebel poet' and composer Nasrul Islam is considered the national poet of Bangladesh. During the time the country was suffering under colonial rule, Islam employed poetry to challenge intellectual complacency and spark feelings of nationalism.

Music & Dance

Traditional Bengali music is gradually being subsumed by the cultural dominance of Indian music. Classical music, *uchamgo*, is similar to Indian classical music, but tends to be more simple and wistful than vigorous. Village songs, *pelligiti*, are more lively, but the themes of love and loss continue. Popular music is likewise sentimental and is usually played on acoustic instruments, a great relief after Indian film music. A popular singer of modern songs is Shumana Huq; her cassettes are available everywhere. The bamboo flute is a folk instrument with a haunting tone, and even on Dhaka's noisy streets you'll occasionally hear one.

There are many folk dances, but classical dance is largely borrowed from Indian models and is frowned upon by the more severe religious leaders.

Architecture

There are far more temples and palaces in Bangladesh than most people realise, and hunting for these old structures can be half the fun. In a country with very little stone and with an extreme tropical climate, buildings don't last long especially when they aren't maintained or are damaged by iconoclasts of opposing religions. Nevertheless, the government has done a reasonably good job at preserving the major Muslim and Buddhist historical monuments and many of them are quite beautiful.

As a general rule, the Hindu monuments haven't been given the same amount of attention, particularly the old Hindu rajbaris. Even those being used as government buildings, such as the once magnificent Tajhat Palace in Rangpur, are being allowed to decay.

Pre-Mauryan & Mauryan – 4th to 2nd Century BC

The term *bangla* is associated with the indigenous architecture of this period. The bamboo-thatched hut with a distinctively curved roof, still seen in villages today, known as a bangla, is the most ancient architectural form known in the country. This word is most likely a derivation of *bangala*, which means the people who live on mounds. *Bang* was the name of the tribe and *ail* means divider. Even then the annual rains and floods of the delta made it essential to live on elevated mounds.

Chinese annals mention that as early as the 5th century AD the region was a prosperous Buddhist country, boasting many stupas, temples and monasteries, all made of brick.

Gupta Buddhist – 4th to 8th Century AD

The traditional design of a stupa for this period consisted of a square plinth surmounted by a circular one and topped by a solid dome which tapered off sharply near the top. The traditional design of the cell which the monks lived in, a three metre square cube, was established during this period. The only variation was the addition of an ornamental pedestal placed in a few cells, like those found in Paharpur.

The great brick temples and monasteries at Mahasthangarh and Comilla were already in existence during this time, however, it is not known if the great Paharpur temple dates from this period.

Architecture seems to have fallen from favour during the Pala period (8th to 12th century) because no important structures, either Buddhist or Hindu, have been discovered from this era.

Sena Dynasty – 12th to 13th Century

During this period Hindu temples were constructed which had a pronounced Indian influence. Perfect specimens are to be found in Puthia, near Rajshahi. Much later, the Indian design of Hindu temples was replaced by purely local architecture. The temple in Kantanagar near Dinajpur is a good example.

The Muslim Period – 12th to 17th Century

From the 12th to 16th century a variety of Muslim styles penetrated the region's architecture.

The Turkistan Khiljis period from the 13th to 15th centuries is noted mainly for its mosques, such as the numerous ones around Bagerhat (near Khulna), including the famous Shait Gumbad Mosque, the Goaldi Mosque at Sonargaon, and the Kusumbha Mosque north of Rajshahi.

From 1576 to 1757 the Mughals ruled Bengal and made some improvements on the simple design of preceding Muslim architecture although they did not follow the traditional designs employed in India. The best examples are the Lalbagh Fort, Khan Mohammad Mridha's Mosque and the Sat Gumbad Mosque, all in Dhaka.

The Portuguese Influence

European Renaissance architecture was introduced by the Portuguese via their colony in Goa. Palaces during this period took on a baroque style.

British Raj Period

The most notable buildings constructed during the British Raj were the Hindu rajbaris, mostly built around one century ago, and some public buildings, constructed during the first two decades of the 20th century.

Rajbaris With Hindus dominating economic life under the Raj, it was natural that the most substantial houses were built by them. Rajbaris is the generic name for the palaces built by the big zamindar landowners who often adopted the title of raja (ruler or landlord). The European Renaissance style had become popular in Europe and was emulated by rich Hindu zamindars in Bangladesh. There is a striking resemblance of many of the Hindu zamindar palaces, especially the Puthia and Murapara palaces, to the famous Senate House in Cambridge.

Although they are essentially very large Georgian or Victorian country houses, the cosmopolitan ideas of their owners were usually expressed in a barrage of neo-Renaissance features, such as Corinthian, Ionic and Doric columns. The architects also adopted domes, which were often decorated with a series of windows and columns. The halls and staircases usually occupied the central areas.

Hindu outlook on life can be seen in the decoration, which is often a mixture of various styles – it's odd to see a Hindu goddess peering out from a classical Greek frieze. Many of the rajbaris had separate Hindu temples, which are sometimes just as interesting as the rajbaris.

Today, most of these stately rajbaris are in ruins, having been vacated at partition, and the more intact examples are now usually neglected government buildings or schools. A few in the rural areas are deserted and you can roam through them at will. The Natore rajbari stands out in this respect. Two of the rajbaris are in excellent condition: Ahsan Manzil in Dhaka, which is now a museum, and Dighapatia Palace in Natore, which is now a government building. The Folk Art Museum in 'Old

Sonargaon' is a rajbari which is being slowly repaired. Many of the others are still very much intact, with most of their exterior features still present.

Some Sonali Bank branches, such as the one in Dinajpur, are in elaborate buildings which once housed rich zamindars' private banks, abandoned hurriedly at partition. The buildings are often worth checking out.

Dating from the mid-1700s, the rajbari in Natore is one of the country's oldest, featuring Corinthian columns and a large reception hall lit by clerestory windows, which were originally fitted with coloured glass.

Public Buildings Most of the public structures built during the British era reflect an interesting combination of the Renaissance and Mughal styles. The beautiful Old High Court Building in Dhaka is predominantly Renaissance in style but many other buildings combine both styles including Curzon Hall and Salimullah Muslim Hall at Dhaka University, North Brooke Hall near Sadarghat in Dhaka and Carmichael College in Rangpur. Their layout is typically Renaissance but the ornamentation is mostly Mughal: horseshoe arches, octagonal minarets, towering pinnacles and ornamented parapets. If you're in Rajshahi, you'll see a number of old public buildings of the Raj era; most are now used as schools.

Many of the old government Circuit Houses resemble the British bungalow style, with high-pitched corrugated iron roofs and low verandahs. The most notable example is the one in Chittagong (now a museum).

Curzon Hall is a fine example of architecture from the European-Mughal era. Built in 1905, it is located at Dhaka University.

Modern Buildings
The most notable modern building in Bangladesh is unquestionably the striking National Assembly building, which was designed by the American architect Louis Kahn – it's one of his masterpieces. Very typical of Kahn's style, it incorporates huge bold geometrical patterns.

The Baitul Mukarram Mosque's orthodox Islamic architecture is interpreted with very sharp and spare lines. It's best at night when its moodily lit wall looming out of the darkness at the top of Nawabpur Rd looks a little like a drive-in movie screen. ■

SOCIETY & CONDUCT

Apart from the obvious religious differences, Bangladesh does not differ markedly from the culture found in the Indian state of West Bengal. Centuries of isolation, even when foreign powers ruled, have produced people, customs and values that are typically Bengali in nature. On the surface, Bangladeshis may appear to be abrupt, unsophisticated and at times aggressive. At the heart of things, they are warm, hospitable and exceedingly helpful. If you find yourself in a jam, don't be surprised by the Bangladeshis who will go out of their way to help you. For many it is a duty to assist a guest in their country.

Traditional Culture

More than 80% of the population live in rural villages. Even for the city dwellers, there is a strong connection to the 'home village'. Most earn their living from the land, either by farming their own, which is becoming less common as the population increases, or by working for someone else. Rural lives are bounded by dependency: on the elders of the family, on the employer or village patron, or on some other authority figure. Loyalty to the group is an essential cultural value, and one that carries over to urban life.

At the core of this group is the extended family which forms the basis of social and economic life in Bangladesh and remains a cornerstone despite the shift towards nuclear families, a product of growing urbanisation. The head of the household assumes much of the responsibility and provides for parents, children and other relatives. They all may occupy one house or compound area, and establish separate kitchens as the family grows and more independence is sought. When a son marries, his wife is brought to the family home and assumes the duties outlined by her mother-in-law. The family is a tightly knit group, not only for economic and protective reasons, but as a major centre of recreational and social activity.

The concept of privacy is not a part of the culture in Bangladesh and you will probably see this exemplified most in the Bangladeshi habit of staring at the unusual – be it an activity, event or person. Foreigners especially can draw the crowd by merely stepping out onto the street. Depending on the circumstances and locale, a group of 30 tightly knit spectators crowding in to get a look is not unusual. Even better are the 'saviours' who come to the rescue, knock back the closest of the crowd, only to stand there and stare for themselves. For most westerners, this is an extremely uncomfortable custom, if not downright annoying. And it only gets worse because it's never-ending.

The only solution is to understand plainly that the prohibition against staring is essentially a western one, has no place in Bangladeshi tradition, and that absolutely no harm is meant. To be fair, the person being stared at is probably the most interesting thing that has happened to the starer all week. Given this, it is still sometimes difficult to keep the right perspective. When a little respite is needed to save the sanity, try ducking into a nearby shop. In most cases, the proprietor will courteously offer you a seat, chase away the lingerers, and send the shop assistant off to fetch you a cup of tea.

The most common form of dress for men is a lungi and an ordinary shirt. Trousers and other western clothing are popular among the younger generation and businesspeople, though once at home almost everyone reverts to traditional dress. The lungi is a cylindrical, skirt-like garment which is wrapped and tied at the waist. A T-shirt or button-down shirt is worn over it. The Indian-style Punjabi suit, an open-collared tunic worn over loose-fitting pants, is also a popular style of dress.

The majority of women wear a sari, a six foot length of material wrapped in a rather complicated fashion around their bodies. Worn under this is a short blouse and a plain cotton skirt. A *salwar kameez*, a long dress-like tunic worn over baggy trousers, is the modern woman's alternative to the sari. A long scarf called a *dupatta* or *orna*, is draped backwards over the shoulders to cover the chest. One end of the scarf can be used to cover the head for an even more modest appearance.

The subcontinent head-waggle is an ubiquitous form of non-verbal communication. Wagging the head from side to side in response to a question may mean 'no', or 'not sure', while a single tilt to one side is a sign of assent or agreement.

Women

Bangladeshi women bear the brunt of many of the country's problems. Numerous pregnancies from puberty to menopause, hard work and a poor diet mean that many women suffer ill health. With the stresses of a patriarchal society and, in rural areas, taboos from much older cultures, it isn't surprising that the rates of mental illness and suicide among women are high.

One thing that the visitor may notice quite quickly is the absence of women on the streets and in the marketplace. All the shopkeepers, produce sellers and hawkers are men; the outright majority of those doing the buying, the tea-sipping, and the standing around are men. Strict purdah, the practice of keeping women in seclusion according to the Koranic injunction to guard women's modesty and purity, is not widely observed in Bangladesh. It is sometimes found in the middle to lower-class families who tend to be the most conservative element of society, but most of the poorer segment cannot afford the luxury of idle females. The generally progressive upper-class, with the benefit of an urban education, consider themselves too sophisticated to put up with it.

Even in the absence of purdah, however, cultural tradition and religious custom serve to keep women 'under wraps', and relationships between men and women outside of the family are very formal.

The birth of a daughter is met with less fanfare than that of a son. The sum of a girl's training is usually directed towards the family, home, and eventually motherhood. Formal education is not a given, especially if there are sons who require the family's financial resources in order to be schooled. In rural areas, only 25% of primary school

Grameen Bank

Founded in 1976, the Grameen Bank now operates in half the country's 68,000 villages and has US$500 million in assets. It is as much a cult as a business, and founder Mohammed Yunus is its 'guru'.

Yunus opposes the traditional concept that a borrower must be educated to be risk-worthy and that micro-loans can't be profitable. He feels that if financial resources are available to poor landless people at existing commercial terms, millions of small families with millions of small pursuits can create a development wonder.

Grameen Bank targets destitute women and under its lending formula, prospective borrowers form groups of five neighbours who vet each others' loan requests and ensure weekly paybacks. If one member fails to pay, the group receives no further loans; peer pressure tends to keep things straight. Interest rates are 20%. Loans can vary from US$65 to around US$1000 but the average is US$120, typically enough to purchase a cow, a sewing machine or a silkworm shed. Most loans (91%) go to women because Yunus believes they are more reliable; women tend to plough money into the needs of the family while men more often spend it on themselves. By the bank's statistics, the default rate is around 2% and it claims that about a third of the borrowers have crossed the poverty line.

The programme is not without its sceptics. The bank's claims are difficult to verify because of slow reporting. Its default rate calculation may be suspect; some say that by normal banking standards the rate would be much higher. With so much foreign money pouring into the bank, it's not clear whether the bank is a sustainable institution and thus a viable model for other countries and institutions lacking such resources.

Repayments of loans begin after the first week; many borrowers complain that this is too limiting. Some don't know how they'll use the loan, but because the money is there and they're eligible, they accept it. Reportedly, some borrowers lie about the purpose of the loan and use it for personal reasons such as dowry demands.

Regardless of the unresolved issues, Grameen Bank is politically popular, highly visible, and has made an impact. Similar programmes have emerged; BRAC has one that is almost identical, with similar default rates and slightly more flexible repayment schedules. The benefits to women borrowers are immeasurable. Through working collectively and with the growth of self-esteem, they can improve their deplorably low status in Bangladesh. ■

students are female; a big percentage of girls are not enrolled at all. The overall illiteracy rate for women rises above 80%. Most marriages are arranged by the parents, and in rural villages the general marriageable age for girls is well below the legal minimum of 18 years.

There are a number of development projects which have sprung up over the past few years directed at women's concerns. These focus on training programmes, health care and legal representation that are intended to foster independence and self-sufficiency. Grameen Bank has become an international success story by lending small amounts of money to individual rural women.

An alternative development model proposed by UBINIG, a private organisation concerned with social research and policy critique, involves improving Bangladesh's economic position and raising the economic and social status of women through village-based industries. See the Work section in the Facts for the Visitor chapter for more information about this organisation.

Dos & Don'ts

Within the Bangladeshi culture, there are a number of social conventions which stem from Islamic and other much older customs. Being sensitive to local custom will make travelling easier and provide a broader perspective of the people and their lifestyle.

Koranic injunctions make it clear that men and women cannot safely form friendships or interact beyond the most formal level. If they do, the worst will happen – the woman will be deprived of her purity and be ruined for life. Among the educated upper-class, there is less regard for strict adherence to the social norms, but among the general population the roles are clearly defined. Public physical contact between men and women – between travelling companions, even married ones, or with Bangladeshis – is unacceptable. A man offering a handshake to a member of the opposite sex may be acceptable, but it's better to wait and let them make the first move.

On the other hand, physical contact between men is quite common. There's nothing out of the ordinary for two men to walk down the street holding hands and in no way indicates homosexuality; it's just the custom. Village boys always seem to want to get in on the act by shaking hands with foreigners, teenage boys sometimes aim especially for women, but if this gets out of hand you can gracefully refuse.

> **Hand Greeting**
> The common hand greeting is a salute. The right palm faces out with thumb down and, for men, the backs of the fingers nearly touch the right side of the forehead over the eyebrow. For women, it's a little different. The right hand is slightly cupped and brought up to the area between the eyes, but not quite making contact. ∎

Modesty in dress, more so for women, is extremely important. Sleeveless shirts and shorts or short skirts are definitely out. For details, see What to Wear in the Women Travellers section of the Facts for the Visitor chapter. Bangladeshi men don't normally wear shorts or sleeveless shirts; a man dressed this way would not necessarily offend, but would certainly attract even more attention.

The left hand is considered unclean, as Asians use their left hand for toilet purposes. It is courteous to receive or give anything using only the right hand, but it is especially important when offering or receiving food. You may see bread being torn using both hands, but the food that goes into the mouth will be in the right hand. Likewise, water may be drunk from a glass with the left hand because it is not being directly touched. Bangladeshis eat with their hands, and in the smaller towns and villages, you may be hard pressed to find an eating utensil.

Feet are also considered unclean and shoes are generally removed before entering a home. Sitting with a foot pointing toward another person is discourteous, as is stepping over part of someone's body. The thumb's up signal is considered rude.

RELIGION

Only Indonesia, India and Pakistan have a larger Muslim population than Bangladesh. A century ago, Hinduism represented a third of the country, but now only 12% of the people are Hindus. Some Buddhism and Christianity also exists.

Islam

Bangladesh's Muslim majority is almost entirely Sunni. Although there is a vocal fundamentalist minority whose leaders have influence in the government, the War of Liberation affected the attitude to fundamentalist Islam. This is because some fanatics collaborated with the Pakistanis because of their belief that rebelling against Pakistan, the 'land of the pure', was a crime against Islam.

Pirs are religious leaders whose status is something like a cross between that of a bishop and a sage. They are associated with Sufism, the mystical interpretation of Islam. In much the same way that people maintain their clan roots in a home village or district, many people have a pir to whom their family or village looks for spiritual (and sometimes political) leadership. The largest Sufi centre in Bangladesh is Dewanbag Pak Darbar Sharif, two km east of Kanchur Bridge on the Dhaka-Chittagong highway.

The annual Biswa Ijtema, an international Muslim gathering and second in size only to the *hajj* (pilgrimmage) to Mecca, is held on the outskirts of Dhaka, usually in January.

During the month-long observance of Ramadan, Muslims are prohibited from eating between sunrise and sunset, and this might affect your eating habits too.

Prayer times occur five times during the day: just before dawn, 12.30 pm, 5.45 pm, 5.45 pm (just after sunset) and around 7.15 pm. These times can vary according to season, especially the pre-dawn and sunset times.

Hinduism

Hinduism in Bangladesh lacks the pomp and awe of the religion in India, but because of that it's possible to understand it here more easily – people are very willing for you to watch and even participate in Hindu ceremonies. It's always worth checking out any Hindu temple you come across in case something is happening, or just to meet people whose colourful cosmos can be a relief from the austere Muslim majority's. In many larger towns there is a Rama Krishna Mission which might have information on festivals.

Buddhism

Buddhists are today a tiny minority of the population and are mostly tribal people. The Buddhist culture which once flourished here and made Bangladesh a major pilgrimage centre had faded under pressure from Hinduism before the arrival of Islam, but its influence lingered in the styles of sculpture and the generally relaxed way of life. Some scholars claim that Tantric Buddhism, now largely confined to Himalayan countries, began here.

The temples and monasteries in Chittagong Division, especially around Cox's Bazar, reflect the influence of neighbouring Myanmar (Burma) rather than a continuation of Bangladesh's Buddhist past.

Christianity

Although there is a very small Christian population here, mostly comprising descendants of Portuguese settlers, there is quite a strong Christian presence courtesy of the foreign aid organisations. There are also a number of missionary groups that have found their footing in rural areas through the operation of development projects and health care programmes. Since overt proselytising is strictly forbidden by the Muslim government, these groups tend to focus on providing aid to the needy and serving the few Christians within the community rather than making converts. For this reason, the missionaries in Bangladesh tend to be a bit more relaxed about religious matters and are quite open to receiving the rare western visitor who may turn up.

LANGUAGE

Bangla, or Bengali, as it is known in West Bengal, is the national language of Bangladesh.

and the official language of the state of West Bengal in India. Bengali, or Bangla, is the easternmost of the Indo-European languages and finds its roots in the local speech of Bengal, Pali, which is a *'prokrit'* or vernacular language. In addition to Arabic, Urdu and Persian words, the Sanskrit of Brahmin Hindus was assimilated into the local speech, giving Bengali a strong resemblance to Hindi, with some variation in pronunciation. The ·vocabulary was further expanded through contact with European traders and merchants. Today, Bangla has a number of regional variations but remains essentially the same throughout Bangladesh.

History

The modern development of Bangla as a symbol of the cultural separateness of Bangladesh began under the British. In keeping with the Raj's policy of working within local cultures, Bangla was taught to officers who used it in their dealings with locals. This resulted in the fusion of the vernacular of the peasants with high-caste literary Bangla, which had fallen into disuse under Muslim rulers who favoured Urdu. The Hindus took enthusiastically to Bangla as a way of reasserting their cultural heritage, and the 19th century saw a renaissance in Bangla literature. Rabindranath Thakur (known as Tagore to the western world) gave Bangla (Bengali) literature kudos when he won the Nobel Prize for literature in 1913.

It wasn't until partition, and the departure of most of the Hindu ruling class, that Bangladeshi intellectuals felt the need for Bangla as a means of defining their culture and nationalism.

There are much fewer English speakers in Bangladesh than in India. It's surprising how many conversations you can have in which you *think* that you're being understood. English has lapsed for three main reasons – there aren't distinct regional languages which make a lingua franca necessary; the nationalism which sprang up after independence; and the havoc wreaked on the education system during the Pakistani pogroms against intellectuals.

English is again a compulsory subject in schools, but it will be a long time before the answer to any query isn't 'Sit down. You will take tea?'. A little effort in speaking Bangla will be appreciated. You will find that most billboards and street signs are written in Bangla script only.

There are a few Bangla phrasebooks available in Dhaka in the New Market bookshops. The Heed Language Centre in Dhaka produces a useful Bangla-English/English-Bangla dictionary and a basic course instruction booklet. There is also the Lonely Planet *Bengali phrasebook*.

Pronunciation

Pronunciation of Bangla is made difficult by the fact that the language includes a variety of subtle sounds with no equivalents in English.

If you find you're not being understood, try emphasising the first and last syllables of words, even if that isn't the correct pronunciation.

a	as in '**fa**ther'; sometimes as in '**bo**ne'
b	as in the English 'b' but often as 'v'
c	as in '**ch**ant'
y	as in '**bee**t'
e	as in '**be**t'
ch	as in '**sh**ow'
i	as in '**bee**t'
j	as in '**g**enre'
o	as in '**bo**ne'
s	usually as in '**sh**ow'; sometimes as in '**s**ummer'
u	as in '**pu**t'
v	as a cross between 'v' and 'w'
w	as a cross between 'v' and 'w'
z	as in '**g**enre'

An *a* is sometimes added to the end of a word ending in *r*; for example, the Star Mosque in Dhaka is pronounced (and is becoming officially known as) the *Ishtara* Mosque.

Useful Verbs

Two useful verbs are *ace*, meaning 'There is' or 'has', and *lagbe*, meaning 'need'. You can ask *khana ace?* 'Is there food?' or *bangti ace?* 'Do you have change?' The negative form of *ace* is simply *nai.* Saying *baksheesh nai* means you don't have any *baksheesh* to give. You can say *pani lagbe* (lit: water is needed), or say *lagbe na* (lit: don't need) to turn down any unwanted offer.

Greetings

Accha, the subcontinent's ambiguous 'OK/Yes/I see' is used widely, but the local slang equivalent is *tik assay* or just *tik. Ji* or *ha* is more positive – if the rickshaw wallah answers *accha* to your offered price, expect problems at the other end; if it's *tik* or *ji* he won't demand more money. Well, not much more, anyway.

Men might hear people greet them with *bahadur*, an honorific implying that you're wise and wealthy and should pay top price. Married or otherwise 'respectable' women might be addressed as *begum*, roughly the equivalent of 'Madam'. However, most often you will be referred to as *bondhu* ('friend').

'Please' and 'Thank you' are rarely used in Bangla, instead these sentiments are expressed indirectly in polite conversation.

Hello.	*Nomaskar* or *Asalaam walaikhum.* (lit: peace be unto you)
(common response)	*Walaikhum asalaam.* (lit: unto you, also peace)
Goodbye.	*Khuda hafiz.*
See you later.	*Pore dekha hobe.*
See you again.	*Abar dekha hobe.*

Basics

Excuse me/Forgive me.	*Mahp korun.*
Yes.	*Ji.*
No.	*Na.*
Not any/None.	*Nai.*
It's all right/No problem.	*Tik ace.*
What is this?	*Eta ki?*

Where?	*khotai?*
When?	*kokhon?*
How far?	*khoto dur?*
How much?	*khoto?*

Small Talk

How are you?	*Kamon acen/ apni kamon acen?*
I'm well.	*Bhalo aci.*
What is your name?	*Apnar nam ki?*
My name is ...	*Amar nam ...*
What country are you from?	*Apnar des ki?*
My country is ...	*Amar des ...*
How old are you?	*Khoto boyos?*
Do you like ...?	*Apnar ... bhalo lagge?*
I like it very much.	*Amar khub bhalo lagge.*
I don't like ...	*Amar ... bhalo lagge na.*
What do you want?	*Ki lagben?*
Do you smoke?	*Cigarette khaben?*
It's available.	*Pawa jai.*
It's not available.	*Pawa jai na.*

Language Difficulties

I (don't) understand.	*Ami bujhi (na).*
Do you speak English?	*Apni English/ Ingreji bolte paren?*
I speak a little Bangla.	*Ami ektu Bangla bolte pari.*
Please write it down.	*Likhte paren.*
How do you say ... in Bangla?	*Banglai ... ki bole?*

Getting Around

I want to go to ...	*Ami ... jabo.*
Where is this bus going?	*Ey bas khotai jabe?*
What time does the ... leave/arrive?	*Khoto somoy ... charbe/poicharbe?*
boat	*nowkha/launch*
bus	*bas*
train	*tren*
car	*gari*
rickshaw	*riksha*

Directions

Where is ...?	... khotai?
How far is ...?	... koto dur?
I want to go to Dhaka.	Ami Dhaka jabo.
I'm going to Chittagong.	Chittagong jabo.
Go straight ahead.	Soja jan.

left	bame
right	dane
before/after	age/pore
above/below	upore/nice
east/west	purbodik/poscim
north/south	uttor/dokkhin
here/there	ekane/okane

Around Town

For many words, such as 'station', 'hotel' and 'post office', the English word will be understood.

Where is the toilet?	Paykhana kothai ace?
Where is the ...?	... khotai?
What time does it open/close?	Khoto shomoy khole/bondo-hoy?

bank	bank
change (money)	bangti
embassy	embassy
hospital	hashpatal
market	bajar
mosque	masjid
palace	rajbari
post office	post offish
temple (Hindu)	mandir
town	gram

Accommodation

Is there a hotel/guesthouse to stay nearby?	Kache kono hotel/guesthouse jaiga ache ki?
Do you have a room?	Rum ace?
How much is it per night/per person?	Ek dine/ek jon thakte khoto taka lagbe?
I'd like to book a room.	Ami ekta rum book korbo.
for one person	ekjon thakbe
for two people	duijon thakbe

Is there a toilet?	Paykhana ace?
Can I see the room?	Rum dekhte pari?

Shopping

How much does it cost?	Dam khoto?
It's too expensive.	Eta onek besi dam.

bookshop	boyer dokan
chemist/pharmacy	oshuder dokan
clothing store	kaporer dokan
laundry	kapor dhobar dokan

Food

I'm a vegetarian.	Ami shudhu shobji khay.
breakfast	nasta
lunch	dupurer khabar
dinner	rater khabar
restaurant	restaurant

beef	gorur mangso
bread	roti/nan
chicken	murgi
chilli	moric
egg	dim
fish	mach
food	kabhar
fruit	phol
meat	mangso
milk	dudh
mutton	khasir
rice	bhat
salt	lobon
sugar	cini
tea	ca
vegetable	sobji
water	pani
yoghurt	doy
(sweetened) yoghurt	(misti) doy

Health

I need/My friend needs a doctor.	Amar/amar bondhu daktor lagbe.
I'm a (diabetic/epileptic).	Amar (diabetes/mirki rog) ache.

I'm allergic to antibiotics/penicillin.	*Amar antibioticse/ penicilline allergy ache.*
I'm pregnant.	*Ami pregnant.*
antiseptic	*savlon*
aspirin	*aspirin*
condoms	*condoms*
nausea	*vomi-bhab*
tampons	*tampons*

Time & Dates

What is the time?	*Khoto bajha?*
hour	*ghonta*
day	*din*
week	*sopta*
month	*mas*
year	*bochor*
date (calendar)	*tarikh*
today	*áj*
tonight	*aj rate*
tomorrow	*agamikal*
yesterday	*gotokal*
in the morning	*sokale*
in the afternoon	*bikale*
night	*rat*
all day/everyday	*sob din*
always	*sob somoy*
now	*ekhon*
later	*pore*
Monday	*sombar*
Tuesday	*mongolbar*
Wednesday	*budhbar*
Thursday	*brihospotibar*
Friday	*sukrobar*
Saturday	*sonibar*
Sunday	*robibar*

Numbers

Counting up to 20 is easy, but after this it becomes complicated as the terms are not sequential. In Bangla 21 is not *bis-ek* or *ek-bis* but *ekus*; 45 is actually *poy-collish* but the simpler *pa'c-collish* is understood.

1	১	*ek*
2	২	*dui*
3	৩	*tin*
4	৪	*car*
5	৫	*pa'c*
6	৬	*choy*
7	৭	*sat*
8	৮	*at*
9	৯	*noy*
10	১০	*dos*
11	১১	*egaro*
12	১২	*baro*
13	১৩	*tero*
14	১৪	*codo*
15	১৫	*ponero*
16	১৬	*solo*
17	১৭	*sutaro*
18	১৮	*atharo*
19	১৯	*unis*
20	২০	*bis*
30	৩০	*tiris*
40	৪০	*collis*
50	৫০	*poncas*
60	৬০	*sat*
70	৭০	*sottor*
80	৮০	*asi*
90	৯০	*nobboy*
100	১০০	*ekso*
1000		*ek hajar*
100,000		*ek lakh*
10,000,000		*ek crore*
½		*chare*
¼		*choa*
¾		*pone*
1½		*derta*
2½		*arai*

Emergencies

Please help me!	*Amake sahajo koren!*
Go away!	*Jao!*
Call a doctor/the police.	*Daktor/polis lagbe.*
I've been robbed (of things).	*Amar jinnish churi hoyechi.*
I've been robbed (of money).	*Amar taka churi hoyechi.*
I'm lost.	*Ami hariye ghecchi.*

Facts for the Visitor

Although few travellers in the Indian subcontinent include Bangladesh on their itinerary, there are many foreigners working here on various development projects. So Bangladesh is by no means entirely unequipped to deal with foreigners. Indeed, the country has a national tourist organisation, the Parjatan Corporation, and seems bent on attracting tourists. Dhaka's Zia international airport has been upgraded to cope with the ever-increasing flow of visitors, mostly on business or in transit.

PLANNING
When to Go

Tropical Bangladesh can be visited year round; each seasonal phase offers a different quality to the warm climate. It's hottest during the pre-monsoon spring from April to mid-June when both temperature and humidity climb steadily to an uncomfortable level. By mid-June when the monsoon begins things cool off slightly, though the days remain quite muggy. The whole country begins to fill up with water, the bulk of it coming down the rivers from the Himalaya. This is a fascinating time of year for travelling albeit not without some difficulty.

As the rivers swell and overtake their tributaries, most low-lying land around the major river systems becomes inundated. In some rural areas only the elevated highway is above the flood line, along with clusters of raised settlements that become islands in the vast expanse of water. It begins to cool off and dry up by October, and between November and February the weather is at its best, especially December/January when it gets rather chilly in the evenings.

Maps

Lonely Planet has published a *India & Bangladesh* travel atlas. For a more detailed map of the country, purchase the new *Bangladesh Guide Map* by The Mappa; it costs Tk 50. The Mappa also publishes the best Dhaka map – *Dhaka City Guide Map*. You'll find the latter two in Dhaka at IDEAS on Gulshan Ave, at the Sonargaon and Sheraton bookshops, at The Mappa offices (☎ 817-260) in the city centre at 146/5 Green Rd, and possibly at the New Market (the south-eastern corner). The Bangladesh Guide Map definitely has errors, but it's far better than the many older, locally produced maps on the market, which are terrible. The older Dhaka city maps are just as bad except for the Parjatan *Dhaka Tourist Map*, which is a vast improvement over past editions.

When to Go

One reason potential visitors to Bangladesh sometimes end up skipping over the country is the perception that the climate must be unbearable year round. While some foreigners do complain about the weather, many more find it delightful between mid-October and early March when temperatures drop. For about one month during this period you may even have to wear a light sweater in the evening and, in the far north, something even heavier. During the rest of that five-month period, the air-con is off, the fans are on and the nights are truly fantastic.

No one likes the hot season but some people actually look forward to the monsoon when the skies are often cloudy, noticeably reducing temperatures. And it doesn't rain every day by a long shot. High temperatures (typically around 32°C at noon) are not the problem during the summer; it's the incredible humidity which makes the climate feel hotter than it is. You won't go for very long without sweating or being rained on. The Bangladeshis don't mind the rains; sometimes the men, with only their lungis on, just get soaked and enjoy it.

So don't cross out a trip to Bangladesh just because it's the monsoon season. The chances are that you'll find the climate tolerable. But if you hate humidity and heat, then go in the winter. ■

What to Bring

The weather is warm year round, so you don't need to bring much clothing with you: light, cotton clothing in summer; rainproof jacket for the monsoon (or buy a sturdy cloth umbrella here); woollen pullover or light jacket for chilly winter nights, especially in the north. Shorts are unacceptable in public for women except when they're jogging and even then they may get hassled by men. Men can wear shorts in public but it is not advisable when you're in traditional areas as it will only make you stand out more, thus increasing the staring.

Steep gangplanks and slippery decks are a major part of travel here, so bring shoes with a good grip. Rubber thongs (flip-flops) can be bought here and are good for lounging around the hotel and protecting your feet from fungal infections in the shower.

Bearing in mind the strength of the tropical sun, it would be a good idea to bring a hat, sun cream and sunglasses. To keep mosquitoes away, bring some roll-on repellent. Coils for your room at night are available everywhere.

In rural areas where electricity is unreliable and many streets are unlighted, a torch is handy. Batteries can be bought locally and inexpensively, but they don't last as long as those brought from home. A sturdy water bottle or canteen holds up better than the local bottled water containers which tend to leak. A lock for the occasional dodgy hotel door would be handy, and a universal sink plug may be useful.

Tampons are not normally available in Bangladesh, although you might sometimes find them in shops at the Sonargaon and Sheraton hotels in Dhaka. Sanitary napkins, however, are sold all over the country and their quality is quite acceptable.

SUGGESTED ITINERARY

The following represents just one of the many possibilities for a tour of up to four weeks:

- Dhaka – Dhaka is very crowded but can be fascinating if you're willing to explore (two or three days)
- Old Sonargaon (half day)
- Savar and Dhamrai (half day)
- Mymensingh (one day)
- Madhupur Forest (one day, two if you camp)
- Srimangal (two days)
- Sylhet (two days)
- Chittagong (one day)
- Rangamati, Chittagong Hill Tracts (one day transit, two to three days visiting)
- Cox's Bazar (two or three days)
- Sundarbans (two to four days transit, two days visiting)
- Bagerhat (one day)
- Bogra (one day)
- Paharpur (one day)
- Dinajpur (two days)
- Rajshahi, Puthia & Natore (two days)

TOURIST OFFICES

The Bangladesh Parjatan Corporation is the national Bangladesh tourist office. It provides tourist information, runs tours from Dhaka and has tourist offices at four locations in Dhaka. The best place for information, especially on tours and trips to Rangamati, is the main Parjatan office on Old Airport Rd, Tejgaon (☎ 317-836, 817-855/9; fax 817-235). It also has offices at the Dhaka Sheraton Hotel (☎ 509-479), Sonargaon Hotel (☎ 811-641, 814-937) and Zia international airport (☎ 894-416). Usually, all these offices are not very helpful.

Parjatan also advertises that you can get tourist information at its seven hotels outside Dhaka, in fact they can do little more than help you find a rental car. These hotels are in Bogra, Chittagong, Cox's Bazar, Rajshahi, Rangamati, Rangpur and Sylhet. See the individual city sections in the relevant chapters for details.

VISAS & DOCUMENTS
Passport

You must have a passport. Police are usually very helpful and rarely hassle foreigners. In Dhaka, unlike in India, having your passport on you isn't necessary. If it's back at the hotel, you should have no worry (if it's in a security box) but to be on the safe side it's a

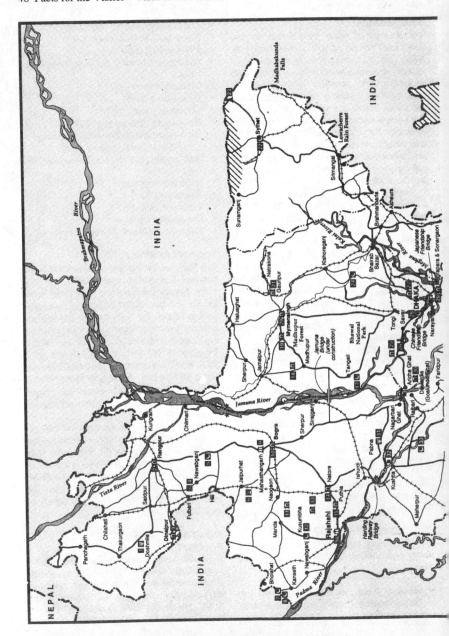

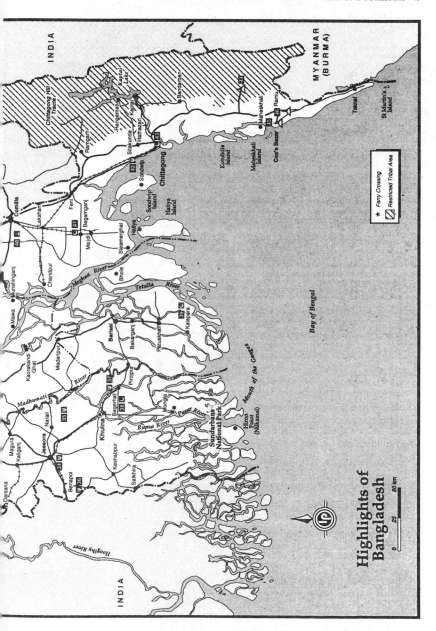

Highlights of
Bangladesh

Highlights

A - Muslim
B - Hindu
C - Rajbari
D - British-era Public Building
E - Tribal Monument
F - Museum
G - Buddhist
H - Burmese Buddhist
I - Other

1   Kantanagar Temple (B)
2   Tajhat Palace (C) & Carmichael College (D)
3   Dinajpur Rajbari (C) & Krishna Temple (B)
4   Sitakot Vihara Monastery (G)
5   Sura Mosque (A)
6   Paharpur Temple & Monastery (G)
7   Khania Dighi Mosque (A) & Chhota Sona Mosque (A)
8   Darasbari Mosque (A), Shah Niamatullah Mosque & Mausoleum (A) & Tahkhana Moghal Palace (A)
9   Mahasthangarh Citadel (G, B & F)
10 Nawab Chowdhury's Palace (C)
11 Dubalhati Palace (C)
12 Kusumbha Mosque (A)
13 Tahirpur Palace (C)
14 Natore Rajbari (C) & Dighapatia Palace (C)
15 Puthia Palace (C), Shiva Temple (B), Govinda Temple (B) & Jagannath Temple (B)
16 Baro Kuthi (I) & Varendra Research Museum (F)
17 Atia Mosque (A)
18 Dhonbari Nawab Palace (C) & Mosque (A)
19 Muktagacha Palace (C)
20 Mymensingh Rajbari (C)
21 Gauripur Palace (C)
22 Shah Jalal Mosque (A)
23 Jaintiapur Megaliths (E)
24 Shah Mohammed Mosque (A)
25 Baliati Palace (C)
26 National Martyrs' Memorial (I)
27 Murapara Palace (C)
28 Lalbagh Fort (I), Khan Mohammad Mirdha's Mosque (A), Dhakeswari Temple (B), Bara Katra (I), Armenian Church (I), Star Mosque (A), Ahsan Manzil (C & F), Northbrooke Hall (D), Curzon Hall (D), Old High Court (D), Supreme Court (D), Sat Gumbad Mosque (A), Rose Garden (C), Ruplal House (C), National Museum (F) & National Assembly (I)
29 Sardarbari (C & F), Goaldi Mosque (A) & Painam Village (C)
30 Teota Palace (C)
31 Jor Bangla Temple (B), Sitlai Palace (C) & Taras Rajbari (C)
32 Tagore Lodge (I)
33 Sailkupa Mosque (A)
34 Chanchra Siva Temple (B)
35 Raja Ram Temple (B)
36 Sonabaria Temple (B)
37 Kodla Math Temple (B)
38 Shait Gumbad Mosque (A), Bibi Begni's Mosque (A), Nine-Domed Mosque (A), Ronvijoypur Mosque (A), Chunakhola Mosque (A), Singar Mosque (A) & Khan Jahan's Tomb (A)
39 Masjidbara Mosque (A)
40 Mainimati Ruins (F & G) & WWII Memorial Cemetery (I)
41 Bajra Shahi Mosque (A)
42 Chandranath Temple (B)
43 Qadam Mubarak Mosque (A), Zia Memorial Museum (D & F), Ethnological Museum (F), Railway Station (D) & WWII Memorial Cemetery (I)
44 Lama Bazar Khyang (H)
45 Aggameda Khyang (H)
46 Ramu Khyang (H)

good idea to carry a photocopy with you. Travelling without your passport to another part of the country, however, would not be wise.

Visas

All visitors to Bangladesh must have a visa. You can get them from all neighbouring countries and generally the process is simple and straightforward. However, if your stay will not exceed 15 days, there's no real reason to get one before arriving because visas are issued at the airport. The fee varies according to nationality: US$21 for Ameri-cans and Australians, US$13 for Germans, US$37 for Canadians, US$41 for the French and UK£40 for Britons. If you later decide to extend your stay, extensions are easily obtained.

If you'll be staying for more than 15 days, you'll probably be better off getting one at home. The fees are the same as those issued at the airport. In Washington, the Bangladesh embassy requires two photos and payment by money order (include a self-addressed envelope with applications made by mail). Applications in person are received from 9 am to noon and passports can be collected the following day from noon. The process at the embassy in London is similar except that the applicant is asked to provide the name of two contacts in Bangladesh.

On rare occasions, the London office has been known to refuse visas or limit their duration to one month (UK£40) when the traveller was a member of Amnesty International or other similar organisation.

Bangladesh has embassies in many countries in the region. However, the consulate in Calcutta is unpredictable and the embassy in Nepal has on rare occasions refused to issue a visa if you're flying from Kathmandu to Dhaka on an airline other than Biman.

The Bangladesh embassy in Delhi (take bus No 450 from Connaught Place to Moolchand Hospital) accepts applications on weekdays between 10 am and noon; you can pick up your passport in the afternoon. Fees in Delhi and Kathmandu are in line with what they cost at Dhaka airport. See Bangladesh High Commissions & Embassies Abroad in the Embassies section of this chapter for contact details.

If you have no choice but to wait until you arrive in the region, the chances are excellent that you'll face no problems whatsoever. If an embassy tells you that you don't need a visa, be sceptical. Some Australians and Canadians, for example, have been told by Bangladesh consular offices in Bangkok and Calcutta that they don't need visas.

Visas valid for six months from the date of issue and good for stays of three months are the norm. However, if you don't request a three month visa, you may end up with a visa valid for only one month. There's no difference in price.

Requests for visas for stays longer than three months are usually denied. However, if you're persistent, requests based on the demands of a job are more likely to be successful and you might be one of the lucky few who get a visa valid for a six month stay. The cost is often slightly more (eg UK£52 for Britons in London).

Visa Extensions Apply for visa extensions in Dhaka at the Passport & Immigration Office, 2nd floor, 17/1 Segunbagicha Rd, 400m east of the Supreme Court (behind No 13/1). Bring one photo. Extensions up to a total stay of three months are generally easy to obtain. If you received a 15 day visa at the airport, you should have the extension the same day if you apply before 11 am. If you've been there three months and wish to extend beyond that, the process will often take up to a week or more, and there is no assurance that you'll receive it. The better reason you have for needing the extension and the more convincing you are, the better your chances are.

Try not to overstay your visa – there is a charge of Tk 500 per day for each day extra! In some cases, they have charged travellers even more, given no receipt and refused to explain the extra charge – corruption is rampant in cases of requests to extend stays longer than three months. So start the process early – at least a week before the expiration date if you've already been there three months.

The office is open Saturday to Thursday from 8 to 11 am for receiving applications (in triplicate) and routine extensions can usually be collected after 2.30 pm, although a wait of a day is not unusual. Fees for one month visa extensions vary according to nationality, eg Tk 850 for Americans and Australians, Tk 900 for the Dutch and Tk 1500 for Britons. Some Britons, however, have been charged as much as Tk 2600. If you can't get an extension, it's fairly easy to leave and get another three month visa in Nepal or India, however, the consulate in Calcutta may refuse if they see you've just completed a three month stay.

Travel Permits

Permits are required if you wish to visit the Chittagong Hill Tracts or the Sundarbans during your stay. You will also need a permit if you wish to go to India by road having arrived by air.

The Ministry of Home Affairs, which issues permits to visit the Chittagong Hill Tracts, is at the Secretariat Building on Abdul Gani Rd. They need five passport photos and 10 to 14 days to process applications, which are free and now routinely approved.

The District Forestry Office (☎ 20665, 21173) in Khulna issues permits to the Sundarbans. Permits are issued on the spot and cost Tk 2.5 per person per day. See Travel Permits to the Sundarbans in the Khulna section of the Khulna Division chapter for more information.

If, having entered by air, you leave Bangladesh via a land border crossing, a road permit is required. This can be obtained in Dhaka from the Passport & Immigration office, 2nd floor, 17/1 Segunbagicha Rd. It's open from 8 am to 1 pm every day except Friday. Two passport photos are required but there is no fee. The process usually takes 24 hours, sometimes 48 hours, and you don't have to leave your passport.

To enter India from Sylhet you no longer need a permit unless you are driving. These are obtained from the Indian high commission in Dhaka. See Foreign Embassies in Bangladesh in the Embassies section later in this chapter for contact details.

Travel Insurance

A travel insurance policy to cover theft, loss and medical problems is a good idea. There is a wide variety of policies available and your travel agent will be able to make recommendations. The policies handled by STA Travel and other student travel organisations are usually good value. Some policies offer lower and higher medical-expense options but the higher ones are chiefly for countries such as the US which have extremely high medical costs. Check the small print:

- Some policies specifically exclude 'dangerous activities' which can include scuba diving, motorcycling, even trekking. If these activities are on your agenda you don't want that sort of policy.
- You may prefer a policy which pays doctors or hospitals direct rather than you having to pay now and claim later. If you have to claim later make sure you keep all documentation. Some policies ask you to call back (reverse charges) to a centre in your home country where an immediate assessment of your problem is made.

- Check if the policy covers ambulances or an emergency flight home. If you have to stretch out you will need two seats and somebody has to pay for it!

Driving Licence

A driver's licence might conceivably be useful as a second identification document in some instances but unless you'll be driving to Bangladesh, a licence is of no use because there are no self-drive car rentals.

If you are driving to Bangladesh you will need an International Driver's Licence, a *carnet de passage en douane* (a document obtained from the motoring organisation in the country of registration of the vehicle, which guarantees that you will not sell the vehicle abroad without paying the appropriate import duties), and preferably an entry permit from either the Bangladesh consulate in Calcutta or their high commission in Delhi. See Bangladesh High Commissions and Embassies Abroad in the Embassies section later in this chapter for contact details.

International Health Card

An International Health Certificate is theoretically required to enter the country but foreigners are not asked to show it.

Business Cards

You will find having business cards extremely useful. In the business world you are nobody without one and in social settings one of the first things people often do is to exchange them. Obviously the masses don't carry cards.

EMBASSIES
Bangladesh High Commissions & Embassies Abroad

Australia
    35 Endeavour Street, Red Hill, Canberra, ACT 2603 (☎ (06) 295-3328)
Belgium
    29-31 Rue Jacques Jordaens, 1050, Brussels (☎ (02) 640-5500)
Bhutan
    Plot No 111G-3, Upper Chubachu, PO Box 178, Thimpu (☎ 2539)

Brazil
SHIS, QL-10, Conj. 01 Casa 17, Brasilia-DF (☎ (61) 248-4830, 248-4905)

Canada
85 Range Rd, Suite No 402, Ottawa, Ontario KIN 8J6 (☎ (613) 236-0138/9)

China
42, Guang Hua Lu, Beijing (☎ (1) 532-521, 532-3706)

France
5 Square Petrarque, 75016 Paris (☎ (1) 47-04-94-35, 45-53-41-20)

Germany
Bonner Strasse 48, 53173 Bonn (☎ (0228) 352-525, 362-940)

Hong Kong
Room 3807, China Resources Building, 26 Harbour Rd, Wanchai (☎ (5) 827-4278/9)

India
56 Ring Rd, Lajpat Nagar 111, New Delhi (☎ (11) 683-4065, 683-4668)
9 Circus Ave, Calcutta 700 017 (☎ (33) 247-5208, 247-0341)
Kunjahan Rd, Agartala 799 006, West Tripura (☎ 4807, 5260)

Indonesia
Jalan Situbondo No 12, Menteng, Jakarta (☎ (21) 314-1690, 310-2705)

Italy
Via Antonio Bertoloni 14, Rome 00197 (☎ (6) 803-3595, 807-8541)

Japan
7-45 Shirogane, 2 Chome, Minato-ku, Tokyo 108 (☎ (03) 3442-1501/2)

Kenya
Ole Odume Rd, PO Box 41645, Nairobi (☎ 562-875/6)

Malaysia
204-1, Jalan Ampang 50450, Kuala Lumpur (☎ (3) 242-3271, 242-2505)

Myanmar (Burma)
56 Kaba Aye Pagoda Rd, Yangon (☎ (01) 51174, 51378)

Nepal
Naxal, Bhagabati Bahal, GPO 789, Kathmandu (☎ 414-943, 414-265)

Pakistan
House 24, St No 28, F-6/1 Islamabad (☎ (51) 826-885, 213-885)
9 Choudhury Khaliquzzaman Rd, Karachi C'01 (☎ (21) 516-597, 568-3984)

Philippines
2nd floor, Universal Re Bldg, 106, Paseo De Roxas, Makati, Metro Manila (☎ (2) 817-5001, 817-5010)

Russian Federation
6 Zemledel Cheski Perculok, Moscow (☎ (95) 246-7900)

Singapore
06-07 United Sq, 101 Thompson Rd, Singapore 1130 (☎ 225-0075)

Sri Lanka
286 Bauddhaloka Mawatha, Colombo 7 (☎ 502-198, 502-397)

Sweden
Sturegatan 6 (4th floor), 11435 Stockholm (☎ (08) 605-501, 605-511, 625-591)

Switzerland
65, rue de Lausanne, 1202 Geneva (☎ (22) 449-340/9)

Thailand
House No 727, Thonglor, Soi-55, Sukhumvit Rd, Bangkok, 10110 (☎ (2) 235-3639)

UK
28 Queen's Gate, London SW7 5JA (☎ (0171) 584-0081)
31-33 Guildhall Building, 12 Navigation St, Birmingham, 42 4NT (☎ (021) 643-2386)
28-32 Princess St, 3rd floor, Manchester, MI 4LB (☎ (061) 236-4853, 236-1064)

US
2201 Wisconsin Ave NW, Suite 300, Washington DC 20007 (☎ (202) 342-8373; fax 333-4971)
211 East 43rd St, Suite 502, New York NY 10017 (☎ (212) 599-6767, 599-6850)

Foreign Embassies in Bangladesh

The main embassies travellers are likely to have to deal with are those from neighbouring countries for which visas may be required – that is, Myanmar (Burma), India, Nepal and Thailand. Details are as follows:

India
The high commission is at House 120, Road 2, Dhanmondi, Dhaka (☎ 504-897). Visas are generally valid for up to one month but multiple-entry visas are now easy to obtain and cost the same. You need two passport photos and must pay a fee which varies with nationality. For Australians, Americans and Britons, the fee is Tk 805. The office is open Saturday to Thursday from 8.30 am to 4.30 pm and if you apply before 10.30 am visas can be collected the next day after 2.30 pm.
Travel permits to Assam, Shillong, etc are no longer required unless you'll be driving but permits to other eastern regions are still required and never granted.

Myanmar
The embassy is at House No 89/B, Road 4, Banani (☎ 601-915) and receives visa applications between 9.30 am and 12.30 pm, Sunday to Thursday. The application form is very simple and visas are issued routinely in 24 hours. The

cost, which is the same for all nationalities, is Tk 400 for a visa valid for one month and good for a stay of 14 days. Visas valid for stays of 28 days and one year are also available. Bring five photographs.

Nepal
The embassy is at Lake Rd 2, UN Rd, Baridhara, Dhaka (☎ 602-1790), facing the US embassy. The office is open Sunday to Thursday from 8.30 am to 1 pm and visas are issued within 24 hours. Bring one passport photo. The fee, which is the same for everyone, is Tk 600 for visas valid for stays of 15 days and Tk 1000 for stays up to one month. Since obtaining a visa at the airport in Kathmandu requires no photo and costs the same (US\$15/25 respectively), most people get them there.

Thailand
The embassy is at House 12, Road 59, Gulshan, Dhaka (☎ 601-475), and will move to 18 Sohrawarde Ave soon. If you'll be staying in Thailand for not more than 15 days, there's no need to get a visa as you can get a 15 day nonextendable transit visa at the airport in Bangkok. Visas issued by the Thailand embassy in Dhaka are generally valid for two months. Take two passport photos and Tk 500 (free for some Scandinavian countries) between 9 am and noon, Sunday to Thursday. Applications made early in the morning can be processed in 24 hours.

Other diplomatic offices in Dhaka include:

Australia
184 Gulshan Ave, Gulshan (☎ 600-091/5)
Belgium
22 Gulshan Ave, Gulshan (☎ 600-138)
Bhutan
House 5/E, Gulshan Ave, Gulshan (☎ 605-840)
Canada
House 16/A, Road 48, Gulshan (☎ 883-639)
Denmark
House 1, Road 51, Gulshan (☎ 881-799)
France
13 Park Rd, Baridhara (☎ 601-049)
Germany
178 Gulshan Ave, Gulshan (☎ 884-735/6/7)
Italy
Corner of Road 74 & Road 79, Gulshan (☎ 882-781/2/3)
Japan
Dutabash Rd, Baridhara (☎ 608-191/2/3)
Malaysia
House 4, Road 118, Gulshan (☎ 887-759/60)
Netherlands
House 49, Road 90, Gulshan (☎ 882-715/6)
Norway
House 9, Road 111, Gulshan (☎ 883-880)

Pakistan
House 2, Road 71, Gulshan (☎ 885-388/9)
Russian Federation
House 9, Road 79, Gulshan (☎ 888-147)
Sweden
73 Gulshan Ave, Gulshan (☎ 884-761/2/3)
Switzerland
House 31/B, Road 18, Banani (☎ 885-529)
UK
13 UN Rd at Dutabash Rd, Baridhara (☎ 882-705/6/7)
US
9 Park Rd at Madani Ave, Baridhara (☎ 884-700/1/2)

CUSTOMS

The usual 200 cigarettes, one litre of alcohol rule applies. Foreigners are allowed to bring in US\$5000 and Tk 300 without declaration. For Bangladeshis the amounts are US\$2500 and Tk 300. Don't be surprised if border officials don't know the exact amounts.

On departure tourists are allowed to reconvert 25% of the total foreign currency encashed in the country. This is only possible at the airport in Dhaka, and you will need your encashment slips as proof. These rules, like many others in Bangladesh, are a little vague. Don't arrive at the airport with a huge wad of taka for conversion, especially if your plane is leaving in the middle of the night. Despite assurances you might have been given, the bank might be 'closed' or claim that it has insufficient dollars, and the bank staff who happen to be hanging around will change your money at rip-off rates.

MONEY
Costs

Bangladesh is a very cheap country to travel in if you're prepared to travel on a budget, perhaps even slightly cheaper than India – but the quality of budget food, accommodation and travel is low. One woman travelling alone reported having averaged only US\$4 a day during her recent stay of several weeks. This required going 2nd class on trains, travelling on local buses, staying at hotels in the Tk 50 range (typically tiny rooms with overhead fans plus a tolerably clean bath which may or may not be attached), and eating at the very cheapest restaurants (Tk 15 a meal).

Travelling at this level does not mean you'll have a buggy room every night; a good percentage of cheap hotels are quite decent. However, to escape nerve-shattering buses and avoid stomach bugs, you'll have to move up a notch, although it's still quite inexpensive (US$10-15 a day).

Carrying Money
Petty theft in Bangladesh is fairly rare. Nonetheless, it's a good idea to use a money belt when you're going about town, especially in Dhaka, and to make use of safe deposit boxes if you're staying at a top-end hotel.

Cash & Travellers Cheques
Cash and travellers cheques in US dollars are preferred by banks to British pounds. Outside Dhaka and Chittagong you'll have problems changing pounds. Even in touristy Cox's Bazar, only Uttara Bank appears to accept British currency and travellers cheques.

In Dhaka, many foreigners use American Express. As a general rule it refuses to cash travellers cheques other than its own, but if you have dollar-denominated travellers cheques issued by other American banks, there's a good chance they'll make an exception.

Under Central Bank policy, banks are not allowed to give you any foreign currency when cashing travellers cheques. However, if you're leaving the country soon and you bring your airline ticket to the bank to prove it, you can obtain up to US$300 in US dollars with your travellers cheques. ANZ/Grindlays and American Express are the best for this.

Many banks, including Standard Chartered Bank, will not cash travellers cheques if you don't have the receipt showing proof of purchase. So be sure to bring it along.

Credit Cards
Credit cards, especially Visa, American Express and Diners, are widely accepted at major hotels, guesthouses and restaurants in Dhaka and Chittagong but virtually nowhere else. American Express cardholders can obtain cash or travellers cheques with their cards; the fee for travellers cheques is 1% even for Gold Card holders.

International Transfers
If you need to have money transferred to you in Bangladesh, it can be done in 24 hours or less with American Express: phone someone at home and tell them to go by the nearest American Express office, give them the money in cash and direct them to credit it to you (full name and passport number) in Dhaka. One traveller reported having cash in hand within 12 hours of the phone call. Using the ANZ/Grindlays branch in Dhaka, another traveller reported waiting only three days for the money to arrive, including the time it took for his telegram to get to the UK.

It's possible to spend some time in Bangladesh without seeing a coin – prices for foreigners tend to be rounded up to the nearest taka. Torn-note phobia isn't as bad here as in India but you do sometimes find that a tear means that a note will be refused. Banks will usually exchange them.

Currency
The principal unit of money is the taka (Tk, pronounced 'tahka') which is divided into 100 paisas. There are 10, 20 and 50 paisa, and Tk 1 and Tk 5 coins. There are notes in denominations of Tk 1, Tk 5, Tk 10, Tk 20, Tk 50, Tk 100 and Tk 500.

Currency Exchange
Exchange rates have been very stable, with only a very slight devaluation of the taka each year, and there is essentially no black market. However, bringing cash or travellers cheques in currencies other than the US dollar and British pound is not advisable.

Current exchange rates include:

A$1	=	Tk 31
US$1	=	Tk 41
UK£1	=	Tk 63.5
1 DM	=	Tk 28
FF1	=	Tk 8
Can$1	=	Tk 30
NZ$1	=	Tk 28
IRs 100	=	Tk 114.5

Changing Money

Standard Chartered Bank and ANZ/Grindlays are best if you have British pound cash or travellers cheques, including those of Thomas Cook. However, ANZ/Grindlays' commissions at Tk 300 per cheque are ridiculously high compared with Standard Chartered's at Tk 65/90 for each US$50/100 travellers cheque.

American Express, ANZ/Grindlays and Standard Chartered Bank also have branches in Chittagong; ANZ/Grindlays has branches in other major cities such as Khulna. The government-owned Sonali and Janata banks usually change money, although some of their rural branches won't. Uttara and Pubali will often change money; other private commercial banks include Eastern Bank, National Bank, United Commercial Bank and The City Bank.

Tipping

Baksheesh (BAK-sheesh), in the sense of a tip or gift rather than a bribe (an admittedly fine line), is seemingly demanded in almost every situation with foreigners and Bangladeshis alike. So much so that if it isn't demanded you can suspect that some 'pre-emptive' baksheesh has been built into the price. However, travelling around the more remote rural areas where foreigners are rarely seen, you may go for days without having baksheesh demanded of you.

In cities and large towns it will often be demanded constantly even after repeating *nai* (none) several times and this can be extremely annoying. Your status as a foreigner invariably raises the hope of receiving a tip.

In restaurants, Bangladeshis almost never tip, but at expensive restaurants in Dhaka frequented by foreigners, waiters often expect them to leave a small tip, typically in the 5% range.

See Coping with Beggars in the Dangers & Annoyances section later in this chapter for more information.

Bargaining

Most transactions require bargaining. This can be fun and is a normal part of life, not an attempt to rip you off. The perfect deal is one in which both parties are satisfied, so always leave room to manoeuvre. It often takes only a very small increase in your offer for the vendor to feel that honour has been satisfied. A rule of thumb is to offer about half of the original price and work up from there.

For those who absolutely detest the bargaining ritual, decide ahead of time what the item is worth to you. If the vendor's price is lower, you've come out ahead. If it's higher, state your price and be willing to leave it if it's not accepted. In most cases, vendors know when you mean business, and if your offer is a fair one, they won't let you get too far away before agreeing.

Bear in mind that most vendors live hand-to-mouth and a few extra taka are going to help them more than it's going to hurt you.

POST & COMMUNICATIONS
Sending Mail

The postal system in Bangladesh works surprisingly well, despite the impression you get upon entering most post offices. Inside, it's dark and gloomy and you have to wait around for an attendant to show up, and then they won't know how much postage to put on your letter back home. Well, you start wondering, if you leave it there, will it make it past the first rubbish bin? The answer is yes, and it will take 10 to 15 days to get there.

Receiving Mail

Receiving packages is also possible, but probably not worth it. When a small Christmas present came for some foreigners at the Dhaka GPO, it was stamped with the date of arrival, a mere six days after it was posted from Australia. Three months later it finally found its way into their post office box, just in time for Easter! If you're going to be in the country long enough to receive a package, or if you think luck is on your side, you'll eventually find the one person at the GPO who admits he knows the procedure. Make sure you don't lose the scrap of paper which appeared at poste restante to notify you of the package arrival. Postal hours are 9 am to 3 pm Saturday to Thursday.

The poste restante service in Dhaka is at the main GPO on Abdul Gani Rd; upon entering the main hall, it's the first door on your right. Service is not the best and the person responsible for keeping the box sometimes leaves early. When looking for letters, be sure to ask to see the 'second' box after going through the main stack. For mysterious reasons, they store some letters in a completely different place.

Telephone & Fax

International calls are very easy to make as many phones have direct dial service via satellite. Rates are 25% lower all day Friday and on other days from 11 pm to 8 am. Local calls present no problems, but between cities it is often difficult to hear the other end. The only way to make a 'public' phone call is to use the telephone and fax services available at numerous small business centres in Dhaka, Chittagong and even some smaller towns; they're usually well marked. Charges are about double the actual telephone rate, eg Tk 120/130/140 a minute to Australia/Europe/America. If you use one of the major hotels instead of the small business centres, you'll pay two or three times as much.

The numbers for long-distance information are 103 (domestic) and 162 (foreign). International operators speak English; many other operators do not. See the table following for a list of local area codes.

BOOKS

There's remarkably little published in the west about Bangladesh, and while there's a lot of publishing going on in the country, it's mostly by very small companies operating out of individual bookshops, as was the case in Europe 200 years ago.

University Press Ltd (UPL) is a Dhaka publishing company with an impressive list of current titles covering a wide range of topics of interest to the traveller. See the Bookshops section in the Dhaka chapter for more information.

Most books are published in different editions by different publishers in different countries. As a result, a book might be a

Area Codes			
Town	Telephone code	Town	Telephone code
Bagerhat	0401	Moulvibazar	0861
Barisal	0431	Mymensingh	091
Bogra	051	Natore	0771
Chandpur	0841	Narayanganj	0671
Chittagong	031	Pabna	
Comilla	081	Panchagarh	0562
Cox's Bazar	0341	Rajshahi	0721
Dhaka	02	Rangamati	0351
Dinajpur	0531	Rangpur	0521
Faridpur	0631	Savar	
Feni	0331	Saidpur	0552
Jessore	0421	Srimangal	0862
Kushtia	071	Sylhet	
Maijdi	0321	Tangail	0921
Mongla	0402	Thakurgaon	0561

hardcover rarity in one country while it's readily available in paperback in another. Fortunately, bookshops and libraries search by title or author, so your local bookshop or library is best placed to advise you on the availability of the following recommendations.

Lonely Planet

Also published by Lonely Planet are the *India & Bangladesh* travel atlas and *Bengali phrasebook*.

Guidebooks & Travel

There are no other guidebooks to the country currently available. *A Handbook for Travellers in India, Nepal, Pakistan, Bangladesh & Sri Lanka* (John Murray, London, 1978) with a short and fairly useless section on Bangladesh is sadly out of print. This solemn guidebook was first published last century; if you spot a second-hand copy, grab it. *On the Brink in Bengal* by Francis Rolt (John Murray, London, 1991) is the only travelogue written about the country, with a strong focus on encounters with the minority tribal populations. This, too, is out of print, but worth reading if you can get a copy.

Bangladesh by B L Johnson (Heinemann Educational Books, London) is one of the few general books on the country published in the west. *The Tropical Traveller* by John Hatt (Pan, London) is a good general introduction to tropical travel.

History & Politics

Most histories of Bangladesh or the Bengal region are published either in Dhaka or Calcutta. Titles include:

Travellers' Impressions

Whether their visit was weeks, years or centuries ago, travellers' interests seem to be the same – the prices, the climate, the people, the curiosities and so on. Some impressions of Bangladesh:

Fa Xien
A 5th century Chinese Buddhist pilgrim, Fa Xien came here via the Karakorams where the Gupta imperial power held sway. He visited Buddhist pilgrimage centres in northern India and was impressed all the way through by the great structures and the prosperity of the land.

Xuan Zhang
Another Chinese Buddhist traveller, who also came here via the Karakorams, but two centuries later. Xuan Zhang was similarly amazed by the numerous towering temples, stupas and large monasteries where thousands of *bhikkus* (monks) lived and which he described as 'ornaments of the earth, as high as mountain peaks, obstructing the very course of the sun with their lofty and imposing towers'. He probably exaggerated a little.

Marco Polo
Travelling as an emissary of Kublai Khan in the 14th century, the famed Venetian traveller came close to the southern borders of China but may never have actually visited Bangala. Hence his information certainly does not sound first-hand. He described Bangala as a province close to India and of southern China, populated by wretched idolaters with a peculiar language.

Ibn Battuta
A Moroccan from Tangier, this 14th century visitor noted how inexpensive Bangala was. He stocked up on female slaves who seem to have been available at bargain basement prices that century. Of Bangala he wrote that: 'There are innumerable vessels on the rivers and each vessel carries a drum and when vessels meet each of them beats a drum and they salute one another'.
He visited Sylhet to see a famous Persian saint who lived in a cave and fasted for 10 days and drank cow's milk on the 11th. 'He would then remain standing all night in prayer.' The saint apparently said his prayers in Mecca each morning but was present in his cave the rest of the day. He also paid a special visit to Mecca each year on the occasion of the Id festival.
'We travelled down the river for 15 days (from Sylhet to Sonargaon),' wrote Ibn Battuta, 'between villages and orchards just as if we were going through a bazar. On the banks are waterwheels, orchards, villages to the right and left like those on the Nile River'. He discovered that there were numerous religious mendicants, Sufis and fakirs and described the land as having an abundance of the essentials of life and as being scenic and luxuriant. In summer, he reported, the creeks and inlets steamed up and as they went through them they had a 'vapour bath'. The people in the west generally, he continued, were oppressed and called the land Dazaki-i-pur Niamat – 'a hell crammed with blessings'.

Mu Huang
This Chinese traveller visited Sonargaon in the 15th century, probably as a seaman. He described foreign vessels arriving and lying at anchor in estuaries while small boats ferried them to the inland river port. He was similarly impressed by the general prosperity of the land, and its wealthy cities with their palaces, temples and gardens. Like Ibn Battuta he noted that there were many Sufis and fakirs.

Zaheed Beg
In the 17th century this Mu ghal visitor observed that no one liked the country. Mughal officials and military officers stationed here demanded increased salaries, higher ranks and payment in cash. It was an unhealthy land and Zaheed Beg, on being nominated as viceroy of Bangala, exclaimed: 'Ah .... your majesty could find no better place to kill me than Bangala'. ■

Bangladesh: Emergence of a Nation by AMA Muhith, (UPL, 1992).

Bangladesh: From Mujib to Ershad by Lawrence Ziring (UPL, 1994).

The Separation of East Pakistan by Hasan Zaheer (UPL, 1994).

Pakistan – Failure in National Integration by Rounaq Jahan (UPL, 1994).

Francis Buchanan in Southeast Bengal edited by Willem van Schendel (UPL, 1994) is an 18th century chronicle providing some of the earliest detailed information about rural Bangladesh.

Historical Geography of Ancient & Early Medieval Bengal by Amitabha Bhattarcharya (Calcutta).

Tribal Culture in Bangladesh by Abdus Sattar (Dhaka).

An Economic Geography of Bangladesh by Haroun El Rashid.

The History of Bengal 1200-1757 by J N Sakkar.

Glimpses of Old Dhaka by S M Tarfu (Calcutta).

Other titles include:

A Tale of Millions by Rafiqul Islam (Chittaranjan Sahu, Dhaka, 2nd edition, 1981) is the story of the War of Liberation told by a senior army officer who was one of the first to rebel. It goes into great detail about his engagements and is a bit sketchy on everything else, but it's a reasonable read.

Of Blood & Fire by Jahanara Imam (Academic Publishers, 1990) tells the story of the war from the perspective of a Dhaka housewife.

Arguing with the Crocodile; Gender and Class in Bangladesh by Sarah C. White (UPL, 1992) raises key issues concerning class relationships and women's impact on social policy within the community.

No Better Opinion? by Hameeda Hossain, Roushan Jahan and Salma Sobhan (UPL, 1993) looks at the role of women as cheap labour in industry.

In Quest of Empowerment by Ainon Nahar Mizan (UPL, 1994) documents the Grameen Bank impact on women's power and status.

The Fifty Percent by Salma Khan (UPL, 1992) reveals the persistent pattern of excluding women from development activities and focuses on the need for investment in women to help generate surplus economy.

The following books are available internationally:

Heroes by John Pilger includes an incisive analysis of the 1970 floods and the ensuing war.

In fictional terms, the graphic, almost surreal account of the 1971 war in Salman Rushdie's *Midnight's Children* is hard to beat.

Lajja (Shame) by Taslima Nasrin. The Bangladeshi counterpart to Rushdie, Nasrin made international waves and became a 'persona non grata' in Bangladesh where her novel was banned. Set during the 1992 Muslim-Hindu clash over the destruction of the Babri Masjid in India, her fictional Hindu family, loyal Bangladeshis, become targets for the violence provoked by Muslim fundamentalists. It's a painful story to read, but one that should be told.

Architectural history is well covered in three locally produced, illustrated volumes by Dr Nazimuddin Ahmed:

Discover the Monuments of Bangladesh (UPL, 1984).

Buildings of the British Raj in Bangladesh (UPL, 1986).

Epic Stories in Terracotta (UPL, 1990).

Several titles which focus on history in legend and myth are:

Folk Tales of Bengal by Lal Behari Dey (Uccharan Press, Calcutta, 1993). The 1st edition was printed in 1883.

The Myths of Bangladesh, Anwarul Karim (Kustia, 1988).

Princess Kalaboti and Other Tales by Niaz Zaman (UPL, 1988).

General

A few titles have emerged which examine Bangladesh from a variety of perspectives:

Bangladesh: Reflections on the water by James J. Novak (UPL, 1994) is the best all-round introduction to the country and gives a personal and penetrating overview of the land and its people.

Bangladesh: the Guide by Elaine Bigalow (AB Pub, 1995) provides useful insights for a greater understanding of the culture.

A Quiet Violence by Betsy Hartmann and James Boyce (UPL, 1990) is the account of two Americans who lived for nine months in a small rural village.

The Rickshaws of Bangladesh by Robert Gallagher (UPL, 1992) is a study of the ubiquitous rickshaw and its impact on the economy and society.

The Art of Kantha Embroidery by Naiz Zaman (UPL, 1994), illustrated by line drawings and photographs, examines the technique of *kantha* embroidery and the rural women involved in its production.

Sailing Against the Wind by Trygve Bolstad and Eirik Jansen (UPL, 1992) illustrates with over 100 colour photographs of the traditional sailing boats which are sadly being replaced by motorised vessels.

Tanti by John Warren (IDEAS, 1989) looks at handloom weaving and traditional weavers in a series of superb colour and B&W photos.

There are a number of field guides to birdwatching in the Bangladesh region:

Pictorial Guide to the Birds of the Indian Subcontinent is, though unwieldy, the best field guide specific to the area. The 1994 edition is now available in the UK and US.

Where to Watch Birds in Asia by Nigel Wheatly is a good, hands-on guide to particular areas on the continent.

Dave Johnson, a long-term resident in Bangladesh, and Paul Thompson are authoring a field guide, complete with details of numerous field trips, to species in Bangladesh. It ought to be available in Dhaka's main bookshops by the end of 1996.

FILMS

The great majority of films shown in cinemas are imports from India, with the usual themes of romance or personal triumph accompanied by lots of singing and dancing. Around 50 films are produced locally each year, however, most of these are little more than copies of the more popular Indian films.

The country's most acclaimed film is *Surjo Dighal Bari* (The House Along the Sun).

NEWSPAPERS & MAGAZINES

The press in Bangladesh is relatively free. Newspaper ownership and articles, for example, are not subject to government restriction, and there are hundreds of daily and weekly publications, mostly in Banglas. However, the government does seek to influence newspapers through the placement of advertising, one admitted criterion being the objectivity of the reporting. The government also owns the only newsprint mill in the country, with the power to deny newsprint. Local press owners are sometimes harassed. Three editors of one newspaper were arrested and put in jail for printing a satirical fable mocking Islamic clerics who misinterpret the Koran. Foreign publications are subject to censorship only on rare occasions. A *Time* magazine edition in 1994 with an objectionable photo of a model wearing a dress with verses from the Koran embroidered on it was censored.

There are eight English-language daily newspapers. The one with the most international news and, reputedly, the most unbiased reporting is *The Independent*, which is reasonably good, with quite a few interesting articles, often from foreign newspapers. *The Bangladesh Observer* is also fairly good. Others include *The New Nation*, *The Financial Express*, *The Daily Star* and *The Bangladesh Times*. Most are about 16 pages long and cost Tk 5. English usage in many papers is often bizarre – one editorial warned that the situation was deteriorating and that 'the ostriches have come home to roost'!

The best weekly is the *Dhaka Courier*; it's independently minded and critical of both leading political parties. The *Holiday* often has some interesting articles as well. Other weekly magazines, some of which are in English, are a hotch-potch of thoughtful articles and illiterate drivel.

French-language weekly newspapers can be found at the Sonargaon and Sheraton hotels, however, for copies of the most recent weeklies and monthlies visit the library at Alliance Française (see Libraries in the Information section of the Dhaka chapter for more information). *Le Fleuve* (The River) is a monthly newspaper on Bangladeshi culture published jointly by Alliance Francaise and the French embassy.

RADIO & TV

There is a TV station in Dhaka which has coverage throughout the country. Most programmes are in Bangla. However, there are increasing numbers of English-language programmes and movies, including world news at 10 pm, often preceded by American serials. BBC news is transmitted daily between 7 and 8 am followed, except on Fridays, by CNN from 8 to 11.20 am. Top hotels often have cable TV, which is also available to private residences in Dhaka.

Radio Bangladesh broadcasts English-language news nightly at 11.05 pm.

PHOTOGRAPHY
Film & Equipment
Colour print film is available everywhere and processing is quite good. Slide film, mainly Fujichrome, is available at a few places in Dhaka – see the Photography section in the Dhaka chapter.

Photography
Rural Bangladesh is extremely photogenic, and it's at its best in the morning and evening when a golden glow descends on the land and colours are vivid. A polarising filter will help reduce glare and intensify colours, especially river photographs. Avoid taking landscape photos in the middle of the day when the tropical sun washes out colours.

Restrictions
It is said that film processing places reserve the right to destroy negatives depicting 'obscene subjects', though what generally happens is that they just make their own copies along with yours.

Photographing People
One aspect of photography unique to Bangladesh is the people. Rather than being turned down by individuals who don't want you to take their picture, here you'll have to be quick if you don't want the whole village in your photograph of a peaceful sunset over the river.

Candid photos will have to be fast for the same reason, so you'll find an autofocus lens invaluable. If there are two of you, each can take turns being the 'decoy' who attracts most of the attention while the other gets the shots. Children flock to cameras like moths to a flame and it often works to point your camera in the opposite direction of the scene you want to photograph. They'll all congregate in front of your lens, allowing you to turn quickly and take your picture.

You'll undoubtedly end your trip with some great people shots.

TIME
Bangladesh has one time zone: one hour behind Thailand, 15 minutes ahead of Nepal, half an hour ahead of India, six hours ahead of GMT, 10 hours ahead of New York (11 hours during daylight-saving time), four hours behind EST in Australia and five hours ahead of France.

ELECTRICITY
The electricity is 220 V, 50 cycle AC. The two-prong connection is round rather than flat; various adaptors are available at most hardware shops but they may not fit all plugs.

WEIGHTS & MEASURES
Officially Bangladesh is metric, but some local measures are still in use. The *tola*, used by goldsmiths and silversmiths, equals 11.66g, and 16 *ana* equals one *tola*. For weights in general, a *seer* equals 850g and a *maund* is 37 kg. Land may be measured using *katha*, 80 sq yd, and *bigha*, 1600 sq yd. Large amounts of taka are invariably quoted in *lakh*, 100,000 and *crore*, 10 million. Yards are used interchangeably with metres, and miles are often confused with kilometres.

LAUNDRY
There are no do-it-yourself laundrettes in Bangladesh and no individuals in the business of washing clothes either. Dry cleaners, which are not always easy to find, exist in Dhaka, Chittagong and some other major cities. They are likely to starch everything unless you tell them otherwise. It may be possible to have your washing done at your hotel, however, this is often fairly expensive. It is probably easier to do it yourself. Most cheap hotel rooms have small washbasins in attached bathrooms (but no plugs).

HEALTH
Travel health depends on your predeparture preparations, your day-to-day health care while travelling and how you handle any medical problem or emergency that does

develop. While the list of potential dangers can seem quite frightening, with a little luck, some basic precautions and adequate information few travellers experience more than upset stomachs.

Travel Health Guides

There are a number of books on travel health:

Staying Healthy in Asia, Africa & Latin America by Dirk Schroeder (Moon Publications). Probably the best all-round guide to carry, as it's compact but very detailed and well organised.

Travellers' Health by Dr Richard Dawood (Oxford University Press). Comprehensive, easy to read, authoritative and also highly recommended, although it's rather large to lug around.

Where There is No Doctor by David Werner (Macmillan). A very detailed guide intended for someone, like a Peace Corps worker, going to work in an underdeveloped country, rather than for the average traveller.

Travel with Children by Maureen Wheeler (Lonely Planet Publications). Includes basic advice on travel health for younger children.

Predeparture Preparations

Health Insurance See Travel Insurance in the Visas & Documents section of this chapter for details.

Medical Kit A small, straightforward medical kit is a wise thing to carry; it should include:

- Aspirin or paracetamol (acetaminophen in the US) – for pain or fever.
- Antihistamine (such as Benadryl) – useful as a decongestant for colds and allergies, to ease the itch from insect bites or stings, and to help prevent motion sickness. There are several antihistamines on the market, all with different pros and cons (eg a tendency to cause drowsiness), so it's worth discussing your requirements with a pharmacist or doctor. Antihistamines may cause sedation and interact with alcohol so care should be taken when using them.
- Antibiotics – useful if you're travelling well off the beaten track, but they must be prescribed and you should carry the prescription with you. Some individuals are allergic to commonly prescribed antibiotics such as penicillin or sulpha drugs. It would be sensible to always carry this information when travelling.

- Loperamide (eg Imodium) or Lomotil for diarrhoea; prochlorperazine (eg Stemetil) or metaclopramide (eg Maxalon) for nausea and vomiting. Antidiarrhoea medication should not be given to children under the age of 12.
- Rehydration mixture – for treatment of severe diarrhoea. This is particularly important if travelling with children, but is recommended for everyone.
- Antiseptic such as povidone-iodine (eg Betadine), which comes as a solution, ointment, powder and impregnated swabs – for cuts and grazes.
- Calamine lotion – to ease irritation from bites or stings.
- Bandages and Band-aids – for minor injuries.
- Scissors, tweezers and a thermometer (note that mercury thermometers are prohibited by airlines).
- Cold and flu tablets and throat lozenges
- Insect repellent, sunscreen, chapstick and water purification tablets.
- A couple of syringes, in case you need injections. Ask your doctor for a note explaining why they have been prescribed.

Ideally antibiotics should be administered only under medical supervision and should never be taken indiscriminately. Take only the recommended dose at the prescribed intervals and continue using the antibiotic for the prescribed period, even if the illness seems to be cured earlier. Antibiotics are quite specific to the infections they can treat. Stop immediately if there are any serious reactions and don't use the antibiotic at all if you are unsure that you have the correct one.

In many countries, if a medicine is available at all it will generally be available over the counter and the price will be much cheaper than in the west. However, be careful if buying drugs in developing countries, particularly where the expiry date may have passed or correct storage conditions may not have been followed. Bogus drugs are common and it's possible that drugs which are no longer recommended, or have even been banned, in the west are still being dispensed in many Third World countries.

Some people like to leave unwanted medicines, syringes etc with a local clinic or missionaries, rather than carry them home; try to leave these items with a reputable group.

Health Preparations Make sure you're healthy before you start travelling. If you are embarking on a long trip make sure your teeth are OK; you don't want to have dental problems along the way. However, Dhaka has an outstanding dentist, David Johnson (☎ 882-849), and if you have a lot of work to do (eg root canals) you can probably pay for your trip by using him instead of a more expensive dentist in the west.

If you wear glasses bring a spare pair and your prescription. Losing your glasses can be a real problem, although at DIT II Circle in Gulshan, Dhaka you can get new spectacles competently made up in approximately four days for about Tk 1000, possibly faster if you pay extra.

If you require a particular medication take an adequate supply, as it may not be available locally. Take the prescription or, better still, part of the packaging showing the generic rather than the brand name (which may not be locally available), as it will make getting replacements easier. It's a wise idea to have a legible prescription or a letter from your doctor with you to show you legally use the medication – it's surprising how often over-the-counter drugs from one place are illegal without a prescription or even banned in another.

Immunisations Vaccinations provide protection against diseases you might meet along the way.

It is important to understand the distinction between vaccines recommended' for travel in certain areas and those required by law. Essentially the number of vaccines subject to international health regulations has been dramatically reduced over the last 10 years. Currently yellow fever is the only vaccine subject to international health regulations. Vaccination as an entry requirement is usually only enforced when coming from an infected area.

Occasionally travellers face bureaucratic problems regarding cholera vaccine even though all countries have dropped it as a health requirement for travel.

On the other hand a number of vaccines are recommended for travel in certain areas. Although no immunisations are required to enter Bangladesh some vaccinations are recommended for your own personal protection. All vaccinations should be recorded on an International Health Certificate, which is available from your physician or government health department.

Plan ahead for getting your vaccinations since some of them require an initial shot followed by a booster while some vaccinations should not be given together. Most travellers from western countries will have been immunised against various diseases during childhood but your doctor may still recommend booster shots against measles or polio, diseases still prevalent in Bangladesh. The period of protection offered by vaccinations differs widely and some are contraindicated if you are pregnant.

Vaccinations include:

Cholera A cholera vaccination is not required to enter the country. Protection is poor and it lasts only six months. It is contraindicated for pregnancy. Although cholera is endemic to Bangladesh, the risk is extremely low because outbreaks are attacked immediately and effectively by the International Centre for Diarrhoeal Disease Research, Bangladesh (ICDDR/B), in Dhaka.

Hepatitis A The most common travel-acquired illness which can be prevented by vaccination. Protection can be provided in two ways – either with the antibody gamma globulin or with a new vaccine called Havrix.

Havrix provides long term immunity (possibly more than 10 years) after an initial course of two injections and a booster at one year. It may be more expensive than gamma globulin but certainly has many advantages, including length of protection and ease of administration. It is important to know that being a vaccine it will take about three weeks to provide satisfactory protection – hence the need for careful planning prior to travel.

Gamma globulin is not a vaccination but a ready-made antibody which has proven very successful in reducing the chances of hepatitis infection. It should be given as close as possible to departure because it is at its most effective in the first few weeks after administration and the effectiveness tapers off gradually between three and six months.

Typhoid Available either as an injection or oral capsules. Protection lasts from one to five years depending on the vaccine and is useful if you are travelling for long periods of time in rural, tropical areas. You may get some side effects such as pain at the injection site, fever, headache and a general unwell feeling. A new single-dose injectable vaccine, which appears to have few side effects, is now available but is more expensive. Side effects are unusual with the oral form but occasionally an individual will have stomach cramps.

Polio A booster of either the oral or injected vaccine is required every 10 years to maintain our immunity from childhood vaccination. Polio is a very serious, easily transmitted disease which is still prevalent in many developing countries including Bangladesh.

In the US, the Center for Disease Control (CDC) has established a number (☎ (404) 332-4559) for international travellers providing recommendations for vaccinations, by region. It is easier and cheaper to reach this 24-hour number at a low-toll time, including weekends.

In London, travellers can get all recommended vaccinations except rabies at the Hospital for Tropical Diseases at 4 Pancras Way, NW1 OPE and at Trailfinders Immunisation Centre (☎ (0171) 938-3999), 194 Kensington High St. Trailfinders also sells first-aid kits (UK£13).

In Australia, travellers can get vaccinations, at the Traveller's Medical and Vaccination Centre in Sydney (☎ (02) 9221-7133) at 2nd floor, Dymocks Building, 428 George St, and in Melbourne (☎ (03) 9602-5788) at 2nd floor, 393 Little Bourke St.

In France, the main vaccination centre in Paris is the Institut Pasteur, 209 boulevard de Vaugirard, 75015 Paris (☎ (1) 45 68 81 98). Vaccinations are also available at Air France, aerogare des Invalides, 2 rue Esnault-Pelterie, 75007 Paris (☎ (1) 43 20 13 50).

Basic Rules

Care in what you eat and drink is the most important health rule; stomach upsets are the most likely travel health problem but the majority of these upsets will be relatively minor. Don't become paranoid, trying the local food is part of the experience of travel.

Water The number one rule is usually *don't drink the water* and that includes ice. However, well over 90% of Bangladeshis have access to potable water. There are tube wells all over the country. The source of the water is pure and there is little potential for contamination because of the sealed metal pumps. So if you take the water directly from the tube well, you should have no problem other than the ever-present possibility that your stomach can get upset merely from not being accustomed to the water – which can happen anywhere you travel. You should be more worried about the glass than the water.

Try to keep a canteen with you so that you can fill it up with water from the well yourself. While tap water in Dhaka is pumped from wells, the chances are reasonable that the water will be contaminated by transmission through old pipes.

If you don't know for certain that water is safe always assume the worst. Locally bottled water in Bangladesh and soft drinks are fine and they are both quite inexpensive. Take care with fruit juice, particularly if water may have been added. Milk should be treated with suspicion as it may be unpasteurised. Boiled milk is fine if it is kept hygienically and yoghurt, which is available in a sweetened form *(misti doi)*, is always good. Tea or coffee should also be OK since the water should be boiled.

Water Purification The simplest way of purifying water is to boil it thoroughly. Vigorous boiling for five minutes at sea level should be sufficient to kill all major water-borne bacterial diseases and viruses.

Simple filtering will not remove all dangerous organisms, so if you cannot boil water it should be treated chemically. Chlorine tablets (Puritabs, Steritabs or other brand names) will kill many but not all pathogens. They will not kill giardia and amoebic cysts. Iodine is very effective in purifying water and is available in tablet form (such as Potable Aqua) but follow the directions care-

A: On board the Rocket. (Jon Murray)
B: A girl in Muslim headdress. (Gregory Wait)
C: Chittagong nappy. (Jon Murray)
D: A river-boat rower. (Gregory Wait)

E: A Bangladeshi boy. (Gregory Wait)
F: A dignified Muslim ascetic. (Jon Murray)
G: Girls in a field near Paharpur. (Jon Murray)

Top: Morning mist over brickwork foundations at Mahasthangarh.
Bottom Left: Scissor-action rowing is common on Chittagong harbour.
Bottom Right: Devotees threshing rice at the Ghandi ashram, Joyag.

fully and remember that too much iodine can be harmful. Iodine is contraindicated in pregnancy.

If you can't find tablets, tincture of iodine (2%) or iodine crystals can be used. Four drops of tincture of iodine per litre or quart of clear water is the recommended dosage; the treated water should then be left to stand for 20 to 30 minutes before drinking.

Iodine crystals can also be used to purify water but this is a more complicated process, as you have to first prepare a saturated iodine solution. Iodine loses its effectiveness if exposed to air or damp so keep it in a tightly sealed container. Flavoured powder will disguise the taste of treated water and is a good idea if you are travelling with children. Iodine is contraindicated for pregnancy.

Food Salads and fruit should be washed with purified water or peeled where possible.

Ice cream is usually OK if it is a reputable brand, but beware of street vendors and of ice cream that has melted and been refrozen. Thoroughly cooked food is safest but not if it has been left to cool or if it has been reheated. Take great care with shellfish or fish and avoid undercooked meat. If a place looks clean and well run and the vendor also looks clean and healthy then the food is more likely to be safe. In general, places that are packed with locals will be fine while empty restaurants are questionable.

Street food which is fried on the spot is usually quite safe. However rice dishes and curries sold on the street, typically for rickshaw wallahs, is questionable because the dishes are cooked at home and reheated on the streets. Restaurants which depend largely on repeat business are generally OK.

Nutrition If you don't like Bengali food, if you're travelling hard and fast and therefore missing meals, or if you simply lose your appetite, you can soon start to lose weight and place your health at risk.

Make sure your diet is well balanced. Boiled eggs, soupy yellow lentils (dhal) and peanuts, which are all widely available on the streets are all safe ways to get protein.

Fruit you can peel (bananas, mangoes and papaya for example) is usually safe and a good source of vitamins. Try to eat plenty of rice and bread. If you're not eating enough, it's a good idea to take vitamin and mineral supplements.

Especially during the dry season make sure you drink enough, don't rely on feeling thirsty to indicate when you should drink. Not needing to urinate or very dark yellow urine is a danger sign. Always carry a water bottle with you on long trips. Excessive sweating can lead to loss of salt and therefore muscle cramping. Salt tablets are not a good idea as a preventative but adding salt to food can help.

General Health A normal body temperature is 37°C or 98.6°F; more than 2°C (4°F) higher indicates a high fever. A normal adult pulse rate is 60 to 100 per minute (children 80 to 100, babies 100 to 140). You should know how to take a temperature and a pulse rate. As a general rule the pulse increases about 20 beats per minute for each °C (2°F) rise in fever.

Respiration rate (breathing) is also an indicator of illness. Count the number of breaths per minute: between 12 and 20 is normal for adults and older children (up to 30 for younger children, 40 for babies). People with a high fever or serious respiratory illness (like pneumonia) breathe more quickly than normal. More than 40 shallow breaths a minute may indicate pneumonia.

In western countries with safe water and excellent human waste disposal systems we often take good health for granted. It is important for people travelling in areas of poor sanitation to be aware of this and adjust their own personal hygiene habits, eg washing your hands before a meal, it's quite easy to contaminate your own food.

Clean your teeth with purified water rather than straight from the tap. Avoid climatic extremes, keep out of the sun when it's hot, dress warmly when it's cold. Avoid potential diseases by dressing sensibly. You can get worm infections through bare feet or dangerous coral cuts by walking over coral without shoes. You can avoid insect bites by covering bare skin when insects are around, by screening windows or beds or by using insect repellents. Seek local advice, if you're told the water is unsafe due to jellyfish or crocodiles, don't go in. In situations where there is no information, discretion is the better part of valour.

Environmental Hazards

Sunburn In the tropics you can get sunburnt surprisingly quickly, even through cloud. Use a sunscreen and take extra care to cover areas which don't normally see sun, eg your feet. A hat provides added protection and use zinc cream or some other barrier cream for your nose and lips. Calamine lotion is good for mild sunburn.

Heat Exhaustion Dehydration or salt deficiency can cause heat exhaustion. Salt deficiency is characterised by fatigue, lethargy, headaches, giddiness and muscle cramps and in this case salt tablets may help. Vomiting or diarrhoea can deplete your liquid and salt levels. Anhydrotic heat exhaustion, caused by an inability to sweat, is quite rare. Unlike the other forms of heat exhaustion it is likely to strike people who have been in a hot climate for some time, rather than newcomers.

Heat Stroke This serious, sometimes fatal, condition can occur if the body's heat regulating mechanism breaks down and the body temperature rises to dangerous levels. Long, continuous periods of exposure to high temperatures can leave you vulnerable to heat stroke. Avoid excessive alcohol or strenuous activity when you first arrive in a hot climate.

The symptoms are feeling unwell, not sweating very much or at all and a high body temperature (39°C to 41°C). Where sweating has ceased the skin becomes flushed and red. Severe, throbbing headaches and lack of coordination will also occur, and the sufferer may be confused or aggressive. Eventually the victim will become delirious or convulse. Hospitalisation is essential, but meanwhile get victims out of the sun, remove their clothing, cover them with a wet sheet or towel and then fan continually.

Fungal Infections Fungal infections are most likely to occur on the scalp, between the toes or fingers (athlete's foot), in the groin (jock itch or crotch rot) and ringworm on the body. You get ringworm (which is a fungal infection, not a worm) from infected animals or by walking on damp areas, like shower floors.

To prevent fungal infections wear loose, comfortable clothes, avoid artificial fibres, wash frequently and dry carefully. If you do get an infection, wash the infected area daily with a disinfectant or medicated soap and water, and rinse and dry well. Apply an antifungal powder like the widely available Tinaderm. Try to expose the infected area to air or sunlight as much as possible and wash all towels and underwear in hot water and change them often.

Jet Lag Jet lag is experienced when a person travels by air across more than three time zones (each time zone usually represents a one-hour time difference). It occurs because many of the functions of the human body (such as temperature, pulse rate and emptying of the bladder and bowels) are regulated by internal 24-hour cycles called circadian rhythms. When we travel long distances rapidly, our bodies take time to adjust to the 'new time' of our destination, and we may experience fatigue, disorientation, insomnia, anxiety, impaired concentration and loss of appetite. These effects will usually be gone within three days of arrival, but there are ways of minimising the impact of jet lag:

- Rest for a couple of days prior to departure; try to avoid late nights and last-minute dashes for travellers cheques, passport etc.
- Try to select flight schedules that minimise sleep deprivation; arriving late in the day means you can go to sleep soon after you arrive. For very long flights, try to organise a stopover.
- Avoid excessive eating (which bloats the stomach) and alcohol (which causes dehydration) during the flight. Instead, drink plenty of non-car-

bonated, non-alcoholic drinks such as fruit juice or water.

- Avoid smoking, as this reduces the amount of oxygen in the aeroplane cabin even further and causes greater fatigue.
- Make yourself comfortable by wearing loose-fitting clothes and perhaps bringing an eye mask and ear plugs to help you sleep.

Infectious Diseases

Diarrhoea A change of water, food or climate can all cause the runs; but more serious is diarrhoea due to contaminated food or water. Despite all your precautions you may still have a mild bout of travellers' diarrhoea but a few rushed toilet trips with no other symptoms is not indicative of a serious problem. Moderate diarrhoea, involving half a dozen loose movements in a day, is more of a nuisance. Dehydration is the main danger with any diarrhoea, particularly for children where dehydration can occur quite quickly. Fluid replacement is the mainstay of management.

Drink large quantities of unsweetened liquids such as tea (weak and without milk), bouillon soup and bottled water. A good preparation is: the juice of one orange and a quarter of a teaspoon of salt together with 250 ml of water. With severe diarrhoea a rehydrating solution is necessary to replace minerals and salts and they are sold in all pharmacies throughout Bangladesh. Stick to a bland diet as you recover.

Lomotil or Imodium can be used to bring relief from the symptoms, although they do not actually cure the problem. Only use these drugs if absolutely necessary, eg if you *must* travel. For children under 12 years Lomotil and Imodium are not recommended. Under all circumstances fluid replacement is the most important thing to remember. Do not use these drugs if the person has a high fever or is severely dehydrated.

In certain situations antibiotics may be indicated:

- Watery diarrhoea with blood and mucous. (Gut-paralysing drugs like Imodium or Lomotil should be avoided in this situation.)
- Watery diarrhoea with fever and lethargy.

- Persistent diarrhoea not improving after 48 hours.
- Severe diarrhoea, if it is logistically difficult to stay in one place.

The recommended drugs (adults only) would be either norfloxacin 400 mg twice daily for three days or ciprofloxacin 500 mg twice daily for three days. 'Cipro' is available in some of the better pharmacies in Bangladesh.

The drug bismuth subsalicylate has also been used successfully. It is not available in Australia. The dosage for adults is two tablets or 30 ml and for children it is one tablet or 10 ml. This dose can be repeated every 30 minutes to one hour, with no more than eight doses in a 24 hour period.

The drug of choice in children would be co-trimoxazole (Bactrim, Septrin, Resprim) with dosage dependent on weight. A five day course is given.

Ampicillin has been recommended in the past and may still be an alternative.

Giardiasis The parasite causing this intestinal disorder is present in contaminated water. The symptoms are stomach cramps, nausea, a bloated stomach, watery, foul-smelling diarrhoea and frequent gas. Giardiasis can appear several weeks after you have been exposed to the parasite. The symptoms may disappear for a few days and then return; this can go on for several weeks. Tinidazole, known as Fasigyn, or metronidazole (Flagyl) are the recommended drugs for treatment. Either can be used in a single treatment dose. Antibiotics are of no use.

Dysentery This serious illness is caused by contaminated food or water and is characterised by severe diarrhoea, often with blood or mucus in the stool. There are two kinds of dysentery. Bacillary dysentery is characterised by a high fever and rapid onset; headache, vomiting and stomach pains are also symptoms. It generally does not last longer than a week, but it is highly contagious.

Amoebic dysentery is often more gradual in the onset of symptoms, with cramping abdominal pain and vomiting less likely;

fever may not be present. It is not a self-limiting disease: it will persist until treated and can recur and cause long-term health problems.

A stool test is necessary to diagnose which kind of dysentery you have, so you should seek medical help urgently. In case of an emergency the drugs norfloxacin or ciprofloxacin can be used as presumptive treatment for bacillary dysentery, and metronidazole (Flagyl) for amoebic dysentery.

For bacillary dysentery, norfloxacin 400 mg twice daily for seven days or ciprofloxacin 500 mg twice daily for seven days are the recommended dosages.

If you're unable to find either of these drugs then a useful alternative is co-trimoxazole 160/800 mg (Bactrim, Septrin, Resprim) twice daily for seven days. This is a sulpha drug and must not be used by people with a known sulpha allergy.

In the case of children the drug co-trimoxazole is a reasonable first-line treatment. For amoebic dysentery, the recommended adult dosage of metronidazole (Flagyl) is one 750 mg to 800 mg capsule three times daily for five days. Children aged between eight and 12 years should have half the adult dose; the dosage for younger children is one-third the adult dose.

An alternative to Flagyl is Fasigyn, taken as a two gram daily dose for three days. Alcohol must be avoided during treatment and for 48 hours afterwards.

Cholera Vaccination against cholera is not very effective. The bacteria responsible for this disease are waterborne, so attention to the rules of eating and drinking should protect the traveller.

Outbreaks of cholera are generally widely reported, so you can avoid such problem areas. The disease is characterised by a sudden onset of acute diarrhoea with 'rice water' stools, vomiting, muscular cramps, and extreme weakness. You need medical help – but treat for dehydration, which can be extreme. If there is an appreciable delay in getting to the ICDDR/B hospital in Dhaka, begin taking tetracycline. The adult dose is

250 mg four times daily. It is not recommended for children aged eight years or under nor for pregnant women. An alternative drug is Ampicillin. People who are allergic to penicillin should not be given Ampicillin. The adult dosage is two 250 mg capsules, four times a day.

Remember that while antibiotics might kill the bacteria, it is a toxin produced by the bacteria which causes the massive fluid loss. Fluid replacement is by far the most important aspect of treatment.

Viral Gastroenteritis This is caused not by bacteria but, as the name suggests, by a virus. It is characterised by stomach cramps, diarrhoea, and sometimes by vomiting and/or a slight fever. All you can do is rest and drink lots of fluids.

Hepatitis Hepatitis is a general term for inflammation of the liver. There are many causes of this condition: drugs, alcohol and infections are but a few.

The discovery of new strains has led to a virtual alphabet soup, with hepatitis A, B, C, D, E, G and others. These letters identify specific agents that cause viral hepatitis. Viral hepatitis is an infection of the liver, which can lead to jaundice (yellow skin), fever, lethargy and digestive problems. It can have no symptoms at all, with the infected person not knowing that they have the disease. Travellers shouldn't be too paranoid about this apparent proliferation of hepatitis strains; hep C, D, E and G are fairly rare (so far) and following the same precautions as for A and B should be all that's necessary to avoid them.

Viral hepatitis can be divided into two groups on the basis of how it is spread. The first route of transmission is via contaminated food and water (leading to hepatitis A and E) and the second route is via blood and bodily fluids (resulting in hepatitis B, C and D).

The following strains are spread by contaminated food and water:

Hepatitis A This is a very common disease in most countries, especially those with poor standards of sanitation. Most people in developing countries are infected as children; they often don't develop symptoms, but do develop life-long immunity. The disease poses a real threat to the traveller, as people are unlikely to have been exposed to hepatitis A in developed countries.

The symptoms are fever, chills, headache, fatigue, feelings of weakness and aches and pains, followed by loss of appetite, nausea, vomiting, abdominal pain, dark urine, light-coloured faeces, jaundiced skin and the whites of the eyes may turn yellow. In some cases you may feel unwell, tired, have no appetite, experience aches and pains and be jaundiced. You should seek medical advice, but in general there is not much you can do apart from resting, drinking lots of fluids, eating lightly and avoiding fatty foods. People who have had hepatitis must forego alcohol for six months after the illness, as hepatitis attacks the liver and it needs that amount of time to recover.

The routes of transmission are via contaminated water, shellfish contaminated by sewerage, or foodstuffs sold by food handlers with poor standards of hygiene.

Taking care with what you eat and drink can go a long way towards preventing this disease. But this is a very infectious virus, so if there is any risk of exposure, additional cover is highly recommended. This cover comes in two forms: Gamma globulin and Havrix. Gamma globulin is an injection where you are given the antibodies for hepatitis A, which provide immunity for a limited time. Havrix is a vaccine, where you develop your own antibodies, which gives lasting immunity.

Hepatitis E This is a very recently discovered virus, of which little is yet known. It appears to be rather common in developing countries, generally causing mild hepatitis, although it can be very serious in pregnant women.

Care with water supplies is the only current prevention, as there are no specific vaccines for this type of hepatitis. At present it doesn't appear to be too great a risk for travellers.

The following strains are spread by contact with blood and bodily fluids:

Hepatitis B This is also a very common disease, with almost 300 million chronic carriers in the world. Hepatitis B, which used to be called serum hepatitis, is spread through contact with infected blood, blood products or bodily fluids, for example through sexual contact, unsterilised needles and blood transfusions or via small breaks in the skin.

Other risk situations include having a shave or tattoo in a local shop, or having your body pierced. The symptoms of type B are much the same as type A except that they are more severe and may lead to irreparable liver damage or even liver cancer.

Although there is no treatment for hepatitis B, a cheap and effective vaccine is available; the only problem is that for long-lasting cover you need a six month course.

Persons who should receive a hepatitis B vaccination include anyone who anticipates contact with blood or other bodily secretions, either as a health-care worker or through sexual contact with the local population, particularly those who intend to stay in the country for a long period of time.

Hepatitis C This is another recently defined virus. It is a concern because it seems to lead to liver disease more rapidly than hepatitis B.

The virus is spread by contact with blood – usually via contaminated transfusions or shared needles. Avoiding these is the only means of prevention, as there is no available vaccine.

Hepatitis D Often referred to as the 'Delta' virus, this infection only occurs in chronic carriers of hepatitis B. It is transmitted by blood and bodily fluids. Again there is no vaccine for this virus, so avoidance is the best prevention. The risk to travellers is certainly limited.

Typhoid Typhoid fever is another gut infection that travels the faecal-oral route – ie contaminated water and food are responsible. Vaccination against typhoid is not totally effective and it is one of the most dangerous infections, so medical help must be sought.

In its early stages typhoid resembles many other illnesses: sufferers may feel like they have a bad cold or flu on the way, as early symptoms are a headache, a sore throat, and a fever which rises a little each day until it is around 40°C or more. The victim's pulse is often slow relative to the degree of fever present and gets slower as the fever rises – unlike a normal fever where the pulse increases. There may also be vomiting, diarrhoea or constipation.

In the second week the high fever and slow pulse continue and a few pink spots may appear on the body; trembling, delirium, weakness, weight loss and dehydration are other symptoms. If there are no further complications, the fever and other symptoms will slowly diminish during the third week. However you must get medical help before this because pneumonia (acute infection of the lungs) or peritonitis (perforated bowel) are common complications, and because typhoid is very infectious.

The fever should be treated by keeping the victim cool and dehydration should also be watched for.

The drug of choice is ciprofloxacin at a dose of one gram daily for 14 days. It is quite expensive and may not be available. The alternative, chloramphenicol, has been the mainstay of treatment for many years. In many countries it is still the recommended antibiotic but there are fewer side affects with Ampicillin. The adult dosage is two 250 mg capsules, four times a day. Children aged between eight and 12 years should have half the adult dose; younger children should have one-third the adult dose.

People who are allergic to penicillin should not be given Ampicillin.

Worms These parasites are most common in rural, tropical areas and a stool test when you return home is not a bad idea. They can be present on unwashed vegetables or in under-cooked meat and you can pick them up through your skin by walking in bare feet. Infestations may not show up for some time, and although they are generally not serious, if left untreated they can cause severe health problems. A stool test is necessary to pin-point the problem and medication is often available over the counter.

Tetanus This potentially fatal disease is found worldwide, occurring more commonly in undeveloped tropical areas. It is difficult to treat but is preventable with immunisation. Tetanus occurs when a wound becomes infected by a germ which lives in soil and in the faeces of horses and other animals, so clean all cuts, punctures or animal bites. Tetanus is also known as lockjaw, and the first symptom may be discomfort in swallowing, or stiffening of the jaw and neck; this is followed by painful convulsions of the jaw and whole body.

Rabies Rabies is a fatal viral infection found in many countries and is caused by a bite or scratch by an infected animal. Dogs are noted carriers as are monkeys and cats. Any bite, scratch or even lick from a warm-blooded, furry animal should be cleaned immediately and thoroughly. Scrub with soap and running water, and then clean with an alcohol or iodine solution. If there is any possibility that the animal is infected medical help should be sought immediately to prevent the onset of symptoms and death. In a person who has not been immunised against rabies this involves having five injections of vaccine and one of immunoglobulin over 28 days starting as soon as possible after the exposure. Even if the animal is not rabid, all bites should be treated seriously as they can become infected or can result in tetanus.

A rabies vaccination is now available and should be considered if you are in a high-risk category – eg if you intend to explore caves (bat bites can be dangerous), work with animals, or travel so far off the beaten track that medical help is more than two days away.

Meningococcal Meningitis Neighbouring Nepal is one of the countries noted for recurring epidemics of meningitis. If you'll be trekking there following your visit to Bangladesh, you should be particularly careful as the disease is spread by close contact with people who carry it in their throats and noses, spread it through coughs and sneezes and may not be aware that they are carriers. Lodges in the hills where travellers spend the night, are prime spots for the spread of infection.

This very serious disease attacks the brain and can be fatal. A scattered blotchy rash, fever, severe headache, sensitivity to light and neck stiffness which prevents forward bending of the head are the first symptoms. Death can occur within a few hours so immediate treatment is important.

Treatment is large doses of penicillin

given intravenously, or, if that is not possible, intramuscularly (ie in the buttocks). Vaccination offers good protection for over one year but you should also check for reports of current epidemics. If you're going to Bangladesh from Nepal, you can get the vaccination in Kathmandu from the International Clinic (☎ 410-893) in Balawatar across from the north end of the Soviet embassy.

Tuberculosis (TB) Tuberculosis is a bacterial infection which is widespread in many developing countries. It is usually transmitted from person to person by coughing, but may be transmitted through consumption of unpasteurised milk. Milk that has been boiled is safe to drink and the souring of milk to make misti doi or cheese (Comilla cheese) kills the bacilli.

Typically, many months of contact with the infected person are required before the disease is passed on so it is not considered a serious risk to travellers. The usual site of the disease is the lungs, although other organs may be involved. Most infected people never develop symptoms. In those who do, especially infants, symptoms may arise within weeks of the infection occurring and may be severe. In most, however, the disease lies dormant for many years until, for some reason, the infected person becomes physically run down.

Symptoms include fever, weight loss, night sweats and coughing. Vaccination against tuberculosis may prevent serious disease so is recommended especially for young children if they are likely to be heavily exposed to infected people.

Diptheria Diphtheria can be a skin infection or a more dangerous throat infection. It is spread by contaminated dust contacting the skin or by the inhalation of infected cough or sneeze droplets. Frequent washing and keeping the skin dry will help prevent skin infection. The mainstay of treatment of the diphtheria throat infection is an intravenous infusion of diphtheria antitoxin. The antitoxin is produced in horses so may be associated with allergic reactions in some

people. Because of this it must be administered under close medical supervision. Antibiotics such as erythromycin or penicillin are then given to eradicate the diphtheria bacteria from the patient so that it is not transmitted to others. A vaccination is available to prevent the throat infection.

Sexually Transmitted Diseases Sexual contact with an infected sexual partner spreads these diseases. While abstinence is the only 100% preventative, using condoms is also effective. Gonorrhoea, herpes and syphilis are the most common of these diseases; sores, blisters or rashes around, the genitals, discharges or pain when urinating are common symptoms. Symptoms may be less marked or not observed at all in women. Syphilis symptoms eventually disappear completely but the disease continues and can cause severe problems in later years. The treatment of gonorrhoea and syphilis is with antibiotics.

There are numerous other sexually transmitted diseases, for most of which effective treatment is available. However, there is no cure for herpes and there is also currently no cure for AIDS.

HIV/AIDS HIV, the Human Immunodeficiency Virus, may develop into AIDS, Acquired Immune Deficiency Syndrome. HIV is a major problem in many countries. Any exposure to blood, blood products or bodily fluids may put the individual at risk.

In many developing countries transmission is predominantly through heterosexual sexual activity. This is quite different from industrialised countries where transmission is mostly through contact between homosexual or bisexual males, or via contaminated needles shared by IV drug users. Apart from abstinence, the most effective preventative is always to practise safe sex using condoms. It is impossible to detect the HIV-positive status of an otherwise healthy-looking person without a blood test.

HIV/AIDS can also be spread through infected blood transfusions – screening of blood used in transfusions is virtually nonexistent in Bangladesh. It can also be spread by dirty needles – vaccinations, acupuncture, tattooing and ear or nose piercing can be potentially as dangerous as intravenous drug use if the equipment is not clean. If you do need an injection, ask to see the syringe unwrapped in front of you, or better still, take a needle and syringe pack with you overseas – it is a cheap insurance package against infection with HIV.

Fear of HIV infection should never preclude treatment for serious medical conditions. Although there may be a risk of infection, it is very small indeed.

HIV is not yet a major problem in Bangladesh. In early 1996, there were eight officially 'reported' cases of HIV/AIDS, but without HIV screening (there are no tests available to the general public), there is no way of knowing the actual figure. Most foreign health professionals working in Bangladesh, however, theorise the number to be much higher. Because of the country's close proximity to India (which has a very high incidence), high STD (sexually transmitted disease) rates, high rates of migration and a large number of prostitutes, these rates are expected to shoot up sharply.

Insect Borne Diseases

Malaria This serious disease is spread by mosquito bites. It is not a problem in Dhaka but in other areas of the country, particularly the Sylhet and Chittagong areas, it is becoming increasingly endemic.

If you are travelling in endemic areas it is extremely important to take malarial prophylactics. Symptoms include headaches, fever, chills and sweating which may subside and recur. Without treatment malaria can develop more serious, potentially fatal effects.

Antimalarial drugs do not prevent you from being infected but kill the parasites during a stage in their development.

There are a number of different types of malaria. The one of most concern is falciparum malaria. This is responsible for the very serious cerebral malaria. Falciparum is the predominant form in many malaria-prone areas of the world. Contrary to popular belief cerebral malaria is not a new strain.

The problem in recent years has been the emergence of increasing resistance to commonly used antimalarials like chloroquine, maloprim and proguanil. Newer drugs such as mefloquine (Lariam) and doxycycline (Vibramycin, Doryx) are often recommended for chloroquine and multidrug-resistant areas.

Expert advice should be sought, as there are many factors to consider when deciding on the type of antimalarial medication, including the area to be visited, the risk of exposure to malaria-carrying mosquitoes, your medical history, and your age and pregnancy status. It is also important to discuss the side-effect profile of the medication, so you can work out some level of risk versus benefit ratio. It is also very important to be sure of the correct dosage of the medication prescribed to you. Some people have inadvertently taken weekly medication (chloroquine) on a daily basis, with disastrous effects.

While discussing dosages for prevention of malaria, it is often advisable to include the dosages required for treatment, especially if your trip is through a high-risk area that would isolate you from medical care. In the US, physicians who are not able to find a supply of mefloquine can call ☎ (800) 526-6367 for information.

The main messages are:

1. Primary prevention must always be in the form of mosquito-avoidance measures. The mosquitoes that transmit malaria bite from dusk to dawn and during this period travellers are advised to:
* wear light coloured clothing
* wear long pants and long sleeved shirts
* use mosquito repellents containing the compound DEET on exposed areas (overuse of DEET may be harmful, especially to children, but its use is considered preferable to being bitten by disease-transmitting mosquitoes)
* avoid highly scented perfumes or aftershave
* use a mosquito net – it may be worth taking your own

2. While no antimalarial is 100% effective, taking the most appropriate drug significantly reduces the risk of contracting the disease.

3. No one should ever die from malaria. It can be

diagnosed by a simple blood test. Symptoms range from fever, chills and sweating, headache and abdominal pains to a vague feeling of ill-health, so seek examination immediately if there is any suggestion of malaria.

Contrary to popular belief, once a traveller contracts malaria he/she does not have it for life. Two species of the parasite may lie dormant in the liver but they can also be eradicated using a specific medication. Malaria is curable, as long as the traveller seeks medical help when symptoms occur.

Dengue Fever There is no prophylactic available for this mosquito-spread disease; the main preventative measure is to avoid mosquito bites. A sudden onset of fever, headaches and severe joint and muscle pains are the first signs before a rash starts on the trunk of the body and spreads to the limbs and face. After a further few days, the fever will subside and recovery will begin. Serious complications are not common but full recovery can take up to a month or more. Fortunately, unlike in Sri Lanka, in Bangladesh cases of dengue fever are extremely rare and travellers have little to worry about.

Filariasis This is a mosquito-transmitted parasitic infection which is found in many parts of Africa, Asia, Central and South America and the Pacific. There is a range of possible manifestations of the infection, depending on which filarial parasite species has caused the infection. These include fever, pain and swelling of the lymph glands; inflammation of lymph drainage areas; swelling of a limb or the scrotum; skin rashes and blindness. Treatment is available to eliminate the parasites from the body, but some of the damage they cause may not be reversible. Medical advice should be obtained promptly if the infection is suspected.

Typhus Typhus is spread by ticks, mites or lice. It begins with fever, chills, headache and muscle pains followed a few days later by a body rash. There is often a large painful

sore at the site of the bite and nearby lymph nodes are swollen and painful. Treatment is with tetracycline, or chloramphenicol under medical supervision.

Tick typhus is spread by ticks. Scrub typhus is spread by mites that feed on infected rodents and exists mainly in Asia and the Pacific Islands. You should take precautions if walking in rural areas in Bangladesh. Seek local advice on areas where ticks pose a danger and always check your skin carefully for ticks after walking in a danger area such as a tropical forest. A strong insect repellent can help, and serious walkers in tick areas should consider having their boots and trousers impregnated with benzyl benzoate and dibutylphthalate.

Cuts, Bites & Stings

Snakes Bangladesh has a variety of poisonous snakes. To minimise your chances of being bitten always wear boots, socks and long trousers when walking through undergrowth where snakes may be present. Don't put your hands into holes and crevices, and be careful when collecting firewood.

Snake bites do not cause instantaneous death and antivenenes are usually available. Keep the victim calm and still, wrap the bitten limb tightly, as you would for a sprained ankle, and then attach a splint to immobilise it. Then seek medical help, if possible with the dead snake for identification. Don't attempt to catch the snake if there is even a remote possibility of being bitten again. Tourniquets and sucking out the poison are now comprehensively discredited.

Bedbugs & Lice Bedbugs live in various places, but particularly in dirty mattresses and bedding. Spots of blood on bedclothes or on the wall around the bed can be read as a suggestion to find another hotel. Bedbugs leave itchy bites in neat rows. Calamine lotion or Stingose Spray may help.

All lice cause itching and discomfort. They make themselves at home in your hair (head lice), your clothing (body lice) or in your pubic hair (crabs). You catch lice through direct contact with infected people or by sharing combs, clothing and the like. Powder or shampoo treatment will kill the lice and infected clothing should then be washed in very hot water.

Women's Health

Gynaecological Problems Poor diet, lowered resistance due to the use of antibiotics for stomach upsets and even contraceptive pills can lead to vaginal infections when travelling in hot climates. Maintaining good personal hygiene, and wearing skirts or loose-fitting trousers and cotton underwear will help to prevent infections.

Yeast infections, characterised by a rash, itch and discharge, can be treated with a vinegar or lemon-juice douche, or with yoghurt. Nystatin, miconazole or clotrimazole suppositories are the usual medical prescription. Trichomoniasis and gardnerella are more serious infections; symptoms are a smelly discharge and sometimes a burning sensation when urinating. Male sexual partners must also be treated, and if a vinegar-water douche is not effective medical attention should be sought. Metronidazole (Flagyl) is the prescribed drug.

Pregnancy Most miscarriages occur during the first three months of pregnancy, so this is the most risky time to travel as far as your own health is concerned. Miscarriage is not uncommon, and can occasionally lead to severe bleeding. The last three months should also be spent within reasonable distance of good medical care. A baby born as early as 24 weeks stands a chance of survival, but only in a good modern hospital. Pregnant women should avoid all unnecessary medication, but vaccinations and malarial prophylactics should still be taken where possible. Additional care should be taken to prevent illness and particular attention should be paid to diet and nutrition. Alcohol and nicotine, for example, should be avoided.

Women travellers often find that their periods become irregular or even cease while they're on the road. Remember that a missed period in these circumstances doesn't necessarily indicate pregnancy. There are health posts or Family Planning clinics in urban centres throughout Bangladesh, where you can seek advice and have a urine test to determine whether or not you are pregnant.

TOILETS

Bangladesh has Asian-style toilets, which are level with the ground and have foot pads either side, requiring the user to squat. Public facilities are few and far between, however, many small restaurants have them. As water is plentiful, most toilets are reasonably clean. Finding a toilet is not always possible in the rural backcountry, nor is complete privacy. For women, in a desperate situation a skirt will make this awkward position a little less so.

WOMEN TRAVELLERS

Attitudes to Women

Sexual harassment of foreign women in Bangladesh isn't as blatant as in some other patriarchal countries, but it's wise to be a little careful. Keep in mind that women are not touched by men in this society. Even a casual tap on the shoulder is not appropriate, but because you're a foreigner, it might happen. The best thing to do is to show clearly, yet tactfully, that you object to being touched. That should end the matter. Most people are genuinely friendly and interested in what you're doing; it's a matter of not letting things get out of hand.

In the cities, it's not easy to meet Bangladeshi women, whose domain is the home. However, it is easier here than in some other Muslim countries, and gender discrimination is an issue among educated people. This is partly due to Bangladesh's relatively relaxed attitudes and partly because of the large part women played, by taking up arms, during the War of Liberation. You might find that women consider themselves to be Bangladeshis and Muslims first; feminism is a means to improving their society, not creating a new one.

A way *not* to meet women, unfortunately, is to meet men – they're unlikely to introduce to their families a woman they've met outside the home. However, it's very easy to interact with rural women in the villages. For them, a foreign woman travelling around is almost beyond belief and due to their sheltered existence, a woman visitor causes great excitement.

It's rare for Bangladeshi women to go out at night without men, so much so that popular belief has it that lone women at night, especially in rickshaws for some reason, must be prostitutes.

In a Bangladeshi middle-class home you would most likely be expected to eat first with the men while the women of the household tuck themselves away in another part of the house, or dutifully serve the meal. In rural areas, you might not eat with either, but be served first, and separately, as a gesture of respect. Accept either graciously. Protest would cause great embarrassment on the part of your host.

Most mosques don't allow women inside, although a few do have a special women's gallery. If in doubt, ask.

Women, with or without men, are sometimes unwelcome in bottom-end hotels. This knee-jerk reaction can sometimes be overcome if you hang around long enough to show that you aren't a foreign degenerate. On the other hand, staying in one of these cheaper establishments, especially if you are solo, is generally more trouble than it's worth. It's hard to change attitudes that are so deeply ingrained in the culture. Mid-range hotels who are accustomed to foreigners are the best bet. Unmarried couples are better off simply saying they're married although this leads to questions about children and the number of years married and so on.

On BIWTC (Bangladesh Inland Waterway Transport Corporation) boats there's sometimes a special section for women, although it's usually very crowded. There are often women's waiting rooms at railway stations. On buses, unaccompanied women are expected to sit at the front, and if you want to find a seat, glaring at a man in a seat near the front will usually procure one.

Safety Precautions

Practically anything out of the ordinary attracts a crowd in Bangladesh, and foreigners, both men and women, are the biggest drawing cards. Sometimes it's difficult to tell whether the attention is of a sexual nature or just plain curiosity. When in doubt, ignore it. A loud protest will usually dissuade the persistent, although you may then have the problem of disengaging your chivalrous rescuers.

Conforming to the local notion of a respectable woman is your best protection, although just being a solo traveller raises doubts. The other side of the harassment coin, and almost as much of a nuisance, is that people are constantly making elaborate arrangements to protect you from harassment.

How you carry yourself also subtly determines how you are treated. Women who are tentative, appear unsure or seem to be helpless are potential targets for harassment. A woman who is assertive can ask for space and usually get it.

Dhaka's Old City at night is supposedly a no-go area for solo women. In any crowd beware of bag-snatchers.

A Woman Traveller in Bangladesh
I'm surprised how easy it is to be a female traveller in Bangladesh. You always get a seat on the buses (in the front), and people will always move away and let you through when it's crowded. I could walk into any crowded, cheap restaurant for a coke or snacks and the locals would squeeze together and clear a table for me. I would be served immediately even though quite a few others were waiting. I lined up in a terrible, long queue at the post office but was immediately directed to the front of the line. You've got to get used to people staring at you though. After all they don't see many tourists.
Hanne Finholt, Norway

Many of the staff at Parjatan offices in Dhaka are women, but their wealthy background could make their advice suspect. 'That would not be suitable for you' might mean that it's dangerous for a woman, but is more likely to mean that a person of your class wouldn't do that sort of thing – a foreign passport confers upper-class status.

What to Wear

Modest clothing is a must, although opinions differ as to whether it's bare arms or ankles which are most likely to mark you as disreputable. While Bangladeshi men often wear western clothes almost no women do, so investing in a *salwar kameez* (a long dress-like tunic worn over baggy trousers) is a good idea if things become intolerable. A *dupatta* (long scarf) to cover your head increases the appearance of modesty and is a handy accessory.

That being said, foreign women tend to be exempt from many social customs. You can get away with wearing baggy trousers and a long loose-fitting shirt in most parts of the country. Long, loose skirts are also acceptable and provide the added advantage of privacy in the absence of a public toilet.

Organisations

A good place to find out about the situation concerning women in Bangladesh is at the feminist bookshop run by UBINIG in Dhaka (see Bookshops in the Dhaka chapter).

GAY & LESBIAN TRAVELLERS

In a country with such strong taboos against any mingling between sexes, it's little wonder that there is a high degree of sexual repression in Bangladesh, and not surprising that authorities deny the existence of homosexuality. Unofficially, many believe homosexuality is quite prevalent, especially among men. There is little known about the prevalence of lesbianism.

The penal code (leftover from the Raj) punishes homosexual acts with deportation, fines and/or prison, however, these laws are hardly ever used.

The dark ages are still here; under pressure from outside agencies to inform the general public of the risk of AIDS, the government health department distributed posters to rural villages that depict a skull and crossbones and claim simply that 'AIDS kills'. HIV positive travellers to Bangladesh would be wise to be discreet.

DISABLED TRAVELLERS

While Bangladesh struggles under the weight of its own disabled and impoverished people, it's little surprise that nothing has been done to accommodate the disabled traveller. In fact, with the terminally cracked (or absent) footpaths, Asian-style squat toilets, overcrowded buses, and absence of elevators in all but the finest buildings in Dhaka, it would seem that the country has contrived to keep out all but the most fit and able. While this is not the case, the fact of the matter is that disabled travellers to Bangladesh would have a number of obstacles (literally!) to surmount.

SENIOR TRAVELLERS

Stifling heat for much of the year, basic facilities (if that!), simple accommodation, uninspired cuisine, rough public transport would all seem to deter senior travellers to Bangladesh. In our travels around the country, however, we have come across a fair number of older people working as volunteers, many on a short term basis, while others have come to visit family members. Many have enjoyed their experiences and discovered in the process that from the inside Bangladesh is not the 'basket case' the world press would have everyone believe. A number of clean, comfortable hotels and guesthouses in the more popularly visited regions provide a pleasant haven for travellers who don't want to 'rough it', and private vehicles with drivers are available almost anywhere for getting around.

TRAVEL WITH CHILDREN

In a society with an abundant child population, travelling with children in Bangladesh can be quite pleasant. Children are an integral part of a Bangladeshi's life, and foreign children are especially fascinating and draw a lot of attention. You may find yourself fending off would-be nannies who want to take your child on a tour of the village, or perhaps you'll happily take advantage of the impromptu childcare service! Older children will find instant playmates wherever they go.

From a health standpoint, deep tube well water is safe without treating, and dishes of boiled rice and unspiced *dhal* (watery lentils), scrambled or boiled eggs, oatmeal and a variety of fruits and vegetables should be enough to keep the little ones satisfied. Keeping hands clean and dirty fingers out of the mouth is a common concern to parents of toddlers, though we have to admit that our own toddler has never developed any maladies as a result of the 'free reign' we've given her.

If long journeys on cramped public transport is asking too much of little travellers, private transport is a reasonable option that allows for periodic rest stops and space for catnaps. Most hotels and guesthouses happily accommodate travellers with children, and you'll find that throughout Bangladesh special effort is made for those with children in tow. Lonely Planet's *Travel with Children*, by Maureen Wheeler, is a collection of experiences from travelling families, and includes practical advice on how to avoid the hassles and have a rewarding experience when travelling with your kids.

DANGERS & ANNOYANCES

Bangladesh is a very friendly country, and to travellers arriving from India this is immediately obvious and a great relief. There are few serious dangers and the worst annoyance is an accumulation of minor irritations. After a while the crowds get on your nerves, the baksheesh demands become infuriating, and you don't even want to discuss the possibility of sponsoring an immigrant to your country.

Bangladeshis are quite a volatile people – loud arguments in public places are a constant background noise – so be careful about venting your frustrations too openly.

Despite the poverty the crime rate is surprisingly low. Even pickpocketing on the crowded buses is not as endemic as in some other Asian countries. *Dacoity* (armed robbery) on buses is on the increase and on some routes night buses are more prone to attack. Don't be tempted to use your size advantage in the unlikely event that you're confronted with bandits – messy weapons like knives, acid bulbs and home-made shotguns are popular. You're in much more danger from more mundane robbery like bag-snatching, although even this isn't particularly common.

Crowds are one thing any foreign traveller in Bangladesh will have to accustom themselves to. They appear wherever you may go, but are especially inquisitive in the rural areas where they are less likely to have seen foreigners before.

Almost every conversation you have with an English speaker ends with, 'You will help me go to your country?' This becomes a real nuisance, no matter how much you sympathise. It might be a good idea to arm yourself with your country's immigration selection criteria (most embassies have a pamphlet) and the address of your embassy in Dhaka.

One of the standard questions you'll be asked is 'What is your religion?' If your answer is 'atheist', be prepared for some startled reactions, and things might even get a little heavy. Saying you are 'humanist' might be better.

Drugs

Cheap grass is becoming increasingly available in Bangladesh and especially in Dhaka. Rickshaw wallahs are a common supplier and foreign high school students are a principal target. However, travellers are unlikely to be offered drugs except, possibly, those staying at top-end hotels. Expensive hashish and cheap grass are sold around the international hotels in Dhaka, for instance, but you'd be unwise to accept the offer. Bangladesh has the death penalty for trafficking in drugs and Dhaka's Central Jail already has a foreigner or two languishing through long sentences. Commuted sentences are not an option. Don't trust the dealers either – turning you in for some baksheesh isn't likely to bother gentlemen whose stock of merchandise includes their sisters.

If a man asks furtively 'Smoking?', it's usually not a prelude to offering you drugs but an invitation to give him a cigarette.

Getting Things Done

Government paper work is about average for a developing country. However, Islamic good manners mean that in almost any official dealing your status is that of an honoured guest with privileges, rather than a customer with rights. Being rude or losing your temper definitely doesn't work here – Bangladeshis are proud people and their clerks aren't a ground-down *babu* class. Just accept that things will take time and be prepared to drink a lot of tea.

Coping with Beggars

A few of the more disturbing aspects of travelling in Bangladesh are encounters with extreme poverty and the preponderance of beggars. Many travellers find themselves taken aback by the impoverishment that confronts them at seemingly every turn. After a little time travelling around the country, one becomes better able to distinguish true poverty from the simple, hardworking lifestyle and things begin to look a little more optimistic.

Despite this, there are very needy people everywhere and begging is a way of life for many of them. Begging is an accepted practice and giving alms is an important requirement of Islam.

There are all levels of beggars. The 'professionals' are the most insistent and will not necessarily be content with a single taka note from a wealthy foreigner. Many of these beggars, mostly found in the larger cities, are controlled by an illegal syndicate, or mafia. Sadly, much of what they receive is turned over to the *mustans* (bosses). Women with babies, and small children are the major recruits, probably because of their vulnerability. Independent beggars will gratefully accept what is offered and move on to the next potential source. The word most commonly used by beggars is baksheesh, which in this case means alms or donation. In other contexts, it may refer to a tip or a bribe.

Begging tends to stir up conflicting emotions and many travellers agonise over this issue. Dealing with it is a personal decision. Some opt to give nothing, realising that there will always be someone else who needs help and a single taka will not cure what ails this country. Others, recognising their privileged position, choose to have small change readily available. Perhaps you could buy a bagful of *chapatis* (flat bread) and give those out rather than takas. Some resolve to give money to reputable development organisations, either in Bangladesh or back home, which have a philosophy of self-sufficiency as opposed to hand-outs.

The advantage in giving is that the beggar will move on as soon as he/she has received something, but otherwise often lingers in case you change your mind.

The disadvantage is although it generally takes only a taka or two to satisfy beggars, you'll be making the situation more difficult for future travellers, especially in Dhaka, Chittagong and Cox's Bazar where their presence is most felt.

LEGAL MATTERS

Drug offences are very stiff in Bangladesh and can result in the death penalty if the quantities seized are considerable. Any person, including foreigners, caught smuggling virtually any amount of drugs or gold often end up with prison sentences for life. As a matter of practice, the courts permit those charged with crimes to have access to a lawyer. Foreigners should not expect their embassies to come to their rescue. Apart from contacting relatives back home and recommending local lawyers, they can do little else.

BUSINESS HOURS

Banking hours on Saturday to Wednesday

are 9 am to 3 pm, and on Thursday, 9 am to noon. The official day off is Friday. Government offices are open Saturday to Thursday from 8 am to 2 pm. Private businesses generally operate between 9 am to 6 pm except Fridays, while consumer shopping, including bazars, varies from 9 or 10 am to 8 or 10 pm. Many individual shops close on Fridays, but each bazar has its own particular closing day.

PUBLIC HOLIDAYS

The following holidays are observed nationally, and government offices, banks and most businesses are closed.

February
> *Amar Ekushe* (21 February) – Also known as Shaheed Day or the National Day of Mourning, this holiday is a tribute to the Bengali students who successfully opposed the government's attempts to deny the Bangla language the status of state language. On 21 February 1952 several students from the Language Movement were killed, and subsequently awarded martyr status. This is a potentially chaotic day as it celebrates a crucial event on the path to independence, but it also legitimises student protest and all the rival factions attempt to claim the mantle of saviours of the country.

March
> *Independence Day* (26 March)

April
> *Pohela Boisakh* (14 April) – Bengali New Year

May
> *May Day* (1 May)

June
> *Bank Holiday* (30 June)

November
> *National Revolution Day* (7 November)

December
> *Biganj Dibash* (16 December) – Victory Day
> *Christmas Day* (25 December)
> Bank Holiday (31 December)

SPECIAL EVENTS

A festival in Bangladesh – as in Pakistan, India and Nepal – is usually called a *mela*. It is often a time when all religions – Muslims, Hindus, Buddhists and Christians – join in the celebrations. Melas could be likened to a spectator sport, but one where everybody joins in despite their allegiances. Festivals may be related to harvests and other religious rites and ceremonies of the Hindus and Buddhists. Minor melas are mainly related to weddings, exhibition fairs or even election victories.

Islamic Festivals

Muslim holidays, known as *Eids*, follow a lunar calendar. The dates depend on the physical sighting of the moon, and almost invariably occur 11 days earlier each year. Along with public holidays, these special events are observed nationally, and government offices, banks and most businesses are closed. Projected dates for major Muslim events in the next few years are in the table below.

December-January
> *Shab-e-Barat* – This holiday marks the sighting of the full moon 14 days before the start of Ramadan. The night of *barat* (record), according to Mohammed, is the time that God registers all the actions men are to perform in the ensuing year. It is a sacred night when alms and sweets are distributed to the poor.
> *Jamat-ul-Wida* – Start of the month of Ramadan and the fasting period.
> *Ramadan* – Referred to as *Ramzan* in Bangladesh, this month-long period of fasting is not technically a festival (nor is it a month-long period of public holidays), but warrants mention here as an important Muslim ritual. Fasting, the third pillar of Islam, incurs merit whenever

Islamic Festival Dates				
Event	*1996*	*1997*	*1998*	*1999*
Shab-e-Barat	7 Jan	27 Dec	16 Dec	5 Dec
Jamat-ul-Wida	21 Jan	10 Jan	31 Dec ('97)	20 Dec ('98)
Eid-ul-Fitr	22 Feb	10 Feb	31 Jan	20 Jan
Eid-ul-Azha	29 April	18 April	8 April	28 March
Eid-e-Miladunnabi	29 July	18 July	7 July	26 June

observed, but is an absolute duty during Ramzan. For the entire month, between sunrise and sunset, abstinence from food, liquids, including swallowing one's own spit, smoking, impure thoughts, and physical pleasures is obligatory. The fast begins at dawn as soon as a white thread is distinguished from a dark one, though in most villages and cities the broadcasted morning call to prayer is signal enough. When the evening call to prayer is heard, the fast is broken with the *Iftar* (meal).

Iftari (food eaten at Iftar) can be wonderful. Traditional offerings include samosa, shingara, piaju, beguin, alu chop, various kabobs, and moori and cheera preparations.

The meal taken about 30 minutes before dawn is called *Sehri*. For many reasons, extreme poverty being only one of them, many Bangladeshis do not fast during Ramzan. Snack shops in the larger cities will stay open during the day, but put up curtains across the door so that diners will receive a little anonymity. In smaller villages, it may be more difficult to come up with a meal during the day. Plan accordingly.

January-February
  Eid-ul-Fitr – One of the two major Muslim holidays, it celebrates the end of Ramzan with the sighting of the new moon. It's a holiday as important to Muslims as Christmas is to many westerners. Shops and offices are closed for two days during this period of celebration, and transportation becomes a nightmare as many Bangladeshis travel to their home villages. The festival is characterised by alms-giving and prayer, along with feasting, merriment, new clothes and gifts. *Eid Mubarrak* (or Happy Eid) is the common greeting.

March-April
  Eid-ul-Azha – Known as the Eid of Sacrifice or informally as Bloody Eid, this two day festival, is the other major Muslim holiday which is 69 days after Eid-ul-Fitr. It remembers Abraham's sacrifice of his son Ishmael, celebrated with the slaughter of a cow, sheep or goat. After the morning prayers, the head of the family takes the animal to the entrance of the house, faces it toward Mecca and kills the animal painlessly with one quick slash of the throat. The meat is divided equally among the poor, friends and family. During the week preceding the festival, open-air fairs do a brisk trade in cattle and goats; the animals brightly adorned with ribbons, garlands and tassels. This festival also marks the beginning of the *hajj* (pilgrimage) to Mecca.

May
  Moharram (Azhura) – Martyrdom of the Prophet's grandson, Imman Hussain in Karbala.

June-July
  Eid-e-Miladunnabi – Birth of the Prophet Mohammed.

Hindu Festivals

Hindu and Buddhist holidays also follow a different calendar but they generally fall at much the same date each year.

January
  Saraswati Puja – Towards the end of January, clay statues of Brahma's consort Saraswati are made in preparation for this ceremony held around the beginning of February. The goddess of knowledge is always depicted playing a *veena* (an Indian stringed instrument) and accompanied by a swan, but outside these limitations there's a lot of variety.

February-March
  Holi Festival – The Festival of Colours is celebrated in late February/early March in Bangladesh. Commonly known as the spring festival, it is celebrated, less so here than in other countries, with the throwing of coloured water and powders.

June-July
  Rath Jatra – This festival celebrates Jagannath, the lord of the world and a form of Krishna, along with his brother and sister. These three images are set upon a Jagannath (chariot) and pulled through the streets by devotees. The seven metre chariot in Dhamrai, 32 km north-west of Dhaka, is typical. It's used in the big mela held there every year during the full moon in late June/early July. Smaller festivals take place in other towns.

October
  Durga Puja – The most important Hindu festival celebrated in this country. Statues of the goddess Durga astride a lion, with her 10 hands holding 10 different weapons, are placed in every Hindu temple. Celebrations last for four days culminating on the day of the full moon when the statue is moved to the banks of a river or pond amidst much dancing and drum-beating. Sometime after sunset the goddess is carried into the water to dissolve. A huge festival takes place along the Buriganga in Dhaka. Country boats can be hired to watch the celebrations from the middle of the river.

LANGUAGE COURSES

The best place for learning Bangla is at HEED (Health Education Economic Development) Language Training Centre (☎ 603-632) at House 38 on Green Rd at the intersection with Pantha Path, 500m south-west of Farm

Gate. The normal course lasts three months (8 am to noon) and costs about Tk 4000 a month. If you don't have three months to spare, you could pay for just one month and then drop out.

WORK

Work opportunities in Bangladesh are fairly limited. People with special teaching skills are sometimes able to land jobs at the American School or the French School. There are also numerous donor agencies that are, on occasion, looking for people with certain skills on a temporary basis and the pay is good. Working on a pro bono basis is quite feasible as there are a large number of PVOs (private voluntary organisations) and some are receptive to outside help. Places in or near Dhaka where you might inquire include the Centre for the Rehabilitation of the Paralysed (CRP) at Savar (see the boxed story about CRP in the Savar section of the Dhaka Division chapter for details), Badda Self Help Centre (☎ 607-879), 332 Uttar Badda, off Rampura Rd, and Centre for the Rehabilitation and Training of Destitute Women (CRTDW) (☎ 812-213), House 2, Road 11, Mohammadpur.

UBINIG (☎ 318-428), 5/3 Barabo Mahanpur Ring Rd, Shamoli, Dhaka, runs a feminist bookshop in Dhaka, and while its office isn't really set up to handle visitors, they do have some literature and can arrange for female researchers and journalists to spend time in villages.

ACCOMMODATION

There are international standard hotels in Dhaka but most accommodation in Bangladesh is well down the price scale.

Unmarried couples won't find things as difficult as in some Muslim countries, but there will be the odd cheap hotel unwilling to condone such behaviour. Lodgings in remote villages tend to be less forward-thinking.

Hotels

The word 'hotel' can mean a hotel or restaurant; the correct term for a hotel is 'residential hotel'.

Lower-end establishments often make this distinction on their signs, and you'll avoid confusion by using this term when looking for a cheap hotel.

Many hotels don't have English signs and there are lots of buildings that look like they might be hotels but aren't, so it's useful to learn to recognise the word 'hotel' in Bangla script. A few examples are given here:

হোটেল

হোটেল

হোটেল

Although you can find very cheap accommodation you get what you pay for. Very tiny rooms with fans and shared bathrooms, maybe mosquito nets as well, typically cost around Tk 30/50 for singles/doubles. Apart from their deficiencies in space and hygiene, bottom-end places sometimes refuse to accept foreigners; you'll get a queer look and be told that there's no room. This is particularly true of the central area in Dhaka. Outside of Dhaka, this happens only rarely. If it's late and you're desperate, you might try hanging around the foyer for a while. An English speaker may strike up a conversation with you and help you get a room.

The biggest hassles in hotels are the friendly room boys, some of whom simply won't leave you alone. If you stay at the very cheapest hotel in town you may find that your door is made with two or three slabs of wood; cracks between them offer scope for Peeping Toms.

Middle-level hotels are better value, and there are lots of them. Expect to pay around Tk 70/110 for singles/doubles with attached bathroom, more in Dhaka. For this you'll usually get a small room with a slightly softer bed (beds in Bangladesh are usually larger and more comfortable than those in India) and a bathroom with a cold shower and an Asian-style squat toilet, usually quite clean. Almost all rooms have fans and mosquito netting – in this guide, unless stated otherwise, you can assume that mid-range hotels have them.

Parjatan's eight hotels are expensive by Bangladeshi standards (eg Tk 500 to Tk 800 for a room) but they're modern and decent.

Rest Houses & Circuit Houses

There are various government rest houses and circuit houses (guesthouses) but they aren't officially accessible to travellers. However, if there are rooms available and you mumble something about being embassy-connected (having a passport is a vague connection), the district commissioner will often let you stay, especially if there is no top-end hotel in town. These circuit houses are often the nicest places in town. Rooms are usually spacious and you can usually eat there as well.

The Archaeology Department has rest houses at Paharpur, Mainimati and Mahasthan. They generally accept travellers if there's room but you book a room by contacting the chief of the regional office in Bogra (for Paharpur and Mahasthan) or, better, the head office in Dhaka (see the Information section in the Dhaka chapter for the address). If you just show up, there's still a fair chance of getting a room. The rooms are basic but very cheap, typically Tk 50, and there will usually be a caretaker there to prepare food. It's quite unusual for travellers to stay in them; a little knowledge of local archaeology will smooth your way.

Guesthouses

The Forestry Office has guesthouses in five forest areas: Sundarbans, Cox's Bazar, Lowacherra Forest near Srimangal, Madhupur Forest Reserve near Mymensingh and Bhiwal National Park north of Dhaka. Foreigners are allowed to stay at them but you must, without exception, book a room in advance with the Forestry Officer of the region where the park is located. These guesthouses vary widely in price, from nothing to Tk 500 for a room. Reservations by phone are sometimes possible.

Many companies, such as the gas company or the Rural Electrification Board (REB), have guesthouses all over the country; occasionally it's possible to stay at them, sometimes without prior booking in Dhaka. They're also very cheap at around Tk 60 a person.

If you're cycling around Bangladesh, finding a place to sleep in small villages is not nearly as difficult as you might think. Many villages too small to support a hotel, have guesthouses with one or two rooms so they can offer government officials a place to stay should they come to town. Foreigners are always welcomed to stay provided there's space. The price is typically Tk 30 a room and they're usually quite decent and spacious.

FOOD

Bangladeshi food is influenced, like in the rest of the Indian subcontinent, by the regional variations of its history. Bangladesh, once an outpost of the Mughal Empire, now retains part of this heritage through its cuisine. Spicy *kebabs* and *koftes* (meatballs) of all kinds are available. This has combined to form a mix with the more southern, vegetarian cuisine.

In low-end restaurants, it's rare to see women eating, but they are welcomed. Some mid-range restaurants have family rooms, often just a curtained booth, where women and families are supposed to eat. These offer a welcome opportunity to go 'off stage' for both men and women.

In Dhaka you can also find excellent Indian, Thai, Chinese and Korean restaurants, but outside Dhaka the only cuisine that you'll find besides Bangladeshi food is Chinese and it's only served at top-end restaurants. There are Chinese restaurants everywhere, even in small towns such as

Savar and Benapol. Prices typically range from Tk 50 a dish, double that in Dhaka.

Snacks

Breads and biscuits are available everywhere, and in some small towns they might be all that you feel like eating. 'Salt' biscuits are usually not salty, just not the usual extremely sweet variety.

Local 'fast foods' are plentiful and rarely cost more than Tk 3 or Tk 4, but try to find them freshly cooked and hot. Some of the more common snacks include:

aloe – a fried vegetable cutlet.
chokputi – hot chickpeas with potato, egg, spices and tamarind sauce.
luchi – a tasty and crusty fried preparation, usually with dhal.
moghlai paratha – a paratha stuffed with vegetables and spices, delicious for breakfast.
chapati – round and thin bread made from grilled unfermented dough.
paratha – thin flat bread (like a chapati) lightly fried in oil or butter.
puri – deep-fried bread stuffed with dhal.
samosa – an Indian-style, wheat-flour pastry triangle stuffed with vegetable or minced meat with spices.
shingara – very similar to a samosa but round with a slightly heavier filling, typically of potatoes or liver, and spices.

Main Dishes

Overall, Bangladeshi food is not nearly as varied as in nearby India, and many dishes begin to look and taste the same after a while. A typical meal would include a curry (or massala) made with meat (beef, mutton, chicken or fish) or egg and vegetables cooked in a hot spicy sauce with mustard oil; yellow watery lentils *(dhal* or *jhal)* and plain rice. Rice is considered a higher status food than bread, therefore at people's homes you will generally not be served bread.

Bhuna (or bhoona), which you'll find on lots of menus, is a cheaper cut of meat in a rich, spicy gravy. Another common dish is *dopiaza*, which is served with the same kinds of meat or fish. Finding purely vegetarian dishes can be quite difficult because in Bangladesh meat is highly prized. Ask for *bhaji*, which can be any kind of fried vegetable, such as squash or green beans. A mixed vegetable dish would be *shabji bhaji*. At fancy dinners, an all-vegetarian meal would not be well received.

The three main forms of rice dishes which you're likely to encounter are *biryani*, rice with chicken, beef or mutton; *pulao* (or pilao), fried and spiced like the biryani but without the meat; and *baht* which is just plain rice. Rice and dhal mixed together and cooked is called *khichuri*. In restaurants, chicken tikka is also common and usually served with Indian-style *naan*, a slightly puffed whole-wheat bread cooked in a tandoori oven.

Fish is part of the staple diet; however, river fish are becoming scarce and more sea fish are appearing on menus. During the summer, when storms keep fishers from the Bay of Bengal, sea fish in restaurants are likely to be frozen and a little suspect. Make sure river fish are properly cooked, and beware of heads and entrails as they contain some nasty parasites.

The fish – broiled, smoked or fried – you are most likely to eat is probably *hilsa* or *bekti*. Smoked hilsa is very good, but is mainly available at five-star prices in big hotels. Bekti is a variety of sea bass with lots of flesh and few bones. It's one of the best fish you'll eat and is served in middle-range restaurants along with prawn and crab dishes.

Beef is widely available, although the quality is low, and cows are rumoured to be smuggled across from India, leaving their 'sacred' status at the border.

Kebabs come in a wide variety including *sheesh kebab*, which is prepared with less spice and usually with mutton or beef, and *shami kebab*, made with fried minced meat. Koftes are minced meatballs cooked in gravy.

Desserts

The Bangladeshis have a sweet tooth and many sugar-loaded desserts are made. Even their yoghurt, known as *misti doi*, is sweetened. It's virtually impossible to get normal fresh yoghurt except with difficulty in the bigger cities. Other sweet things include:

firni – rice pudding cooked with milk, sugar, flavouring and nuts, popular at Eid celebrations.
pais – similar to firni.
kheer – rice pudding with thick milk.
halva – a common light-brown dessert made with carrot or pumpkin, butter, milk and sugar.
keora – a milk and sugar combination flavoured with a floral extract, usually rose.
molidhana – another milk-based dessert similar to halva.
pitha – a blanket term for all kinds of cakes or pastries including specific varieties such as *chitol, dhupi, takti, andosha, puli, barfi* and *pua*.
rasgula & kalojam – two popular Indian-style desserts, milk-based and made with sugar, flour and ghee.
ras malai – round sweets floating in a thick milk.
sooji – wheat cream, almond and pistachio nuts.
sundesh – a milk-based dessert, one of the best available.
shirni – rice flour with molasses or sugar.
shemai – vermicelli cooked in milk and sugar.
zorda – sweetened rice with nuts.
jarda – yellow sweet rice with saffron, almonds and cinnamon.

DRINKS

Taking water from the tap is not as safe as taking it direct from one of the many tube wells throughout the country. Tap water doesn't always come from tube wells and the water can be contaminated in the pipes. In addition, the glass you drink from may be contaminated. For these reasons, people in Dhaka, for example, are advised to boil and filter their water. In a restaurant, even if the water comes from a tube well, it can easily be contaminated by the glass. Bring a canteen or water bottle and fill it up yourself from the tube wells. It's also possible to buy bottled water in much of Bangladesh, including in the larger towns but usually not in the smaller ones. Because it's locally bottled, the price is not high (Tk 15 to Tk 20, Tk 25 in restaurants). When buying bottled water from outdoor stalls, ensure that the plastic cap has not been tampered with. Recycling takes many forms, including 'rebottling' water.

Nonalcoholic Drinks

The milky sweet tea known as *cha* costs Tk 1 to Tk 2 a cup and is available everywhere. It's slightly better than the Indian version as each cup is made individually, rather than stewing all day. This also means that it's no problem getting tea without sugar (say *chini na* or *chini sera*), but as sweetened condensed milk will be used it doesn't make all that much difference.

The magic words to get a pot of tea, usually with just one weak tea bag, are 'milk separate'. Miming a tea bag produces hilarity but not much else. Coffee is difficult to find and those who can't do without should consider buying a jar of instant in Dhaka.

International soft drinks, such as Pepsi, Coke and Sprite, are readily available throughout the country and cost between Tk 7 and Tk 8. Getting them cold or 'cool-ish' is fairly easy. Fresh lime sodas are generally available at the better restaurants in Dhaka and at some of the top-end hotels outside of Dhaka.

Coconut milk is a fine, safe and refreshing drink. A whole young coconut costs about Tk 3. On the other hand, *lassi*, the refreshing yoghurt drink found throughout India, is not so common in Bangladesh.

Alcoholic Drinks

The only places where commercial alcohol is sold in Bangladesh is at the Sonargaon, Sheraton, Purbani and Zakaria hotels in Dhaka, the Agrabad in Chittagong and the Saymen and Shaibal in Cox's Bazar. There's also a restaurant at the wharf in Chittagong (see the Chittagong chapter) which sells it. On rare occasions, you can find a few cans of beer being sold illegally in shops; the price is at least Tk 100 a can.

Hindu and tribal people are generally not adverse to drinking alcohol, typically their own brews made of rice. On the tea estates, which are worked predominantly by Hindus, the drinking of local brew, especially during festival time, is quite common. On New Year's Eve in Dhaka, Muslim rickshaw wallahs desperate to celebrate will sometimes offer Tk 20 for a can of beer from foreigners who appear to be carrying some.

In the countryside you may encounter a drink called *tari*, made from coconut palms. When it is fresh, it is cool and sweet; but when it is fermented it becomes the local beer. Many palm trees have a decidedly notched appearance due to repeated tapping. It is universally known as 'coconut toddy', but only found in non-Muslim areas like the Chittagong Hill Tracts. *Kesare rose* is the rural liqueur, made from date molasses. It is mixed with hot water and tastes like brandy or cognac. A bottle costs about Tk 10.

ENTERTAINMENT

There are plenty of cinemas in Bangladesh but 99% of the films are from India. You could check the English-language press for foreign films, but don't expect to find anything interesting. Nevertheless, even if you don't understand a word, Indian films and the few local ones can be entertaining, not least for their noisy audience participation! If you have access to a video, there are plenty of video shops in larger towns.

The large American and British communities have social clubs in the Gulshan area of Dhaka (the American Recreation Association and the Bagha Club), as do the Australians, Germans, Canadians, Dutch and Scandinavians. On certain days, members from other clubs are welcomed and club members are likely to invite you in as their 'guest' even though they've just met you at the gate.

Another way to meet foreigners is to join the Hash House Harriers on their twice weekly runs in Dhaka. Call the Marines at the US embassy, the British high commission (before 3 pm) or the Bagha Club for the location, which is different for each run.

SPECTATOR SPORT

Women don't play much sport, except for badminton, which is one of the country's most popular sports. Floodlit village courts are everywhere, and if you can play you'll have no problem in meeting people – if you're male. A knowledge of events in the world of test cricket is a good conversational

standby. Bangladeshis barrack for Pakistan, so Imran Khan, now retired, is not a name to take in vain. European football is now very popular, and games can get as unruly as those in the west when minor skirmishes escalate into major brawls.

THINGS TO BUY

You don't get hassled to buy things here, mainly because there isn't very much produced with a tourist market in mind. Even quality post cards are hard to come by.

Things *not* to buy are products made from wild animals and reptiles, all of which are under pressure to survive in this crowded country. Even if a leopard skin for sale really is 20 years old, how do you think the stock will be replenished if you buy it?

Souvenirs include jewellery, garments, brasswork, leatherwork, ceramics, jute products, artwork, woodcarvings and clay or metal sculptural work. Unique items include pink pearls, fine muslin, *jamdani* or silk saris, jute doormats, wall pieces, glass bangles, seashells and conch shell bangles and reed mats. Quality is generally quite high and the prices are very low.

Jute carpets, if you have the room, are a real deal. The better ones look exactly like and feel similar to oriental wool carpets. There is a good selection of colours, designs and sizes. They don't last as long as the real thing, but for US$50 a two metre by three metre (six feet by nine feet) jute carpet will cover your floor for five or more years. Hotel Sonargaon in Dhaka has a jute carpet shop where the prices are affordably fixed by the government.

Maybe the best thing to buy in all of Bangladesh is a piece of authentic rickshaw art. It's lightweight and easy to pack in the flat of your bag or backpack. Rickshaw art is not a tourist industry, so you'll have to shop where the rickshaw wallahs shop. The few centrally located shops are on Bicycle Street, a local name for the area where most bicycle parts, and a few whole bicycles, are sold. (See the Bangsal Rd heading in the Old Dhaka section of the Dhaka chapter for details.) You'll see painted rectangular tin and vinyl pieces and see how these are attached to the rickshaw. The tin pieces are cheaper and last longer than the vinyl which tends to crack when folded. Quality varies among shops, but expect to pay Tk 40/80 for a tin/vinyl piece. If you don't see what you like, ask for others which are usually kept in bundles behind the counter. Bargain hard, the shopkeepers are beginning to realise they've got a lucrative market.

The chain of Aarong shops has a good range of high quality goods, although fixed prices are higher than could be bargained for on street stalls. Aarong has shops in Dhaka, Chittagong and Sylhet; see the city sections in the relevant chapters for locations.

You may decide to replace everything in your backpack, or improve your stock of T-shirts. The garment industry is one of the biggest exporters of western clothing, and you can buy seconds and overruns at the enormous Banga Bazar, sometimes referred to as Gulistan market. Clothing ranges from Calvin Klein jeans to baby rompers. See the Dhaka chapter for more details.

Bangladesh hasn't much to offer in the way of leather clothing – if India is on your itinerary wait until you get to Delhi.

Getting There & Away

AIR

Many travellers use Dhaka as the gateway to the subcontinent because of the availability of cheap fares from Europe. Some of the lowest fares offered by London bucket shops and other discount agencies to, for example, Kathmandu, are often with Bangladesh's Biman Airlines via Dhaka, so many travellers passing through are headed in that direction. From Bangkok you may be able to get some extra-low fares with Biman at some of the special discount agencies in that city; otherwise Biman's fares are no cheaper than those of other airlines in the region.

Note, however, that while fares from Europe and Bangkok (also Singapore and Malaysia) are often bargains, fares out of Bangladesh are expensive. And compared to fares of flights originating in India, those from Dhaka seem even more expensive. In general, fares out of India are half those in Dhaka. Flying from Dhaka to Calcutta, for example, costs US$43 while flying from Calcutta to Dhaka is US$22. So if you're headed from Dhaka to, say, Karachi, you'll save big money going to Calcutta and purchasing your ticket there.

Biman tickets between South-East Asia and the subcontinent or Europe often include a free night's stopover in a luxury hotel in Dhaka. Travellers who want to see Bangladesh could try postponing their onward trip until the next morning. If you decide to do this make sure that you hang onto your passport as transit passengers are sometimes asked to surrender them. Whether you do stay on in Bangladesh or not, make sure that your ticket clearly says that Biman is paying for the accommodation or you might get hit with the bill.

There are many good travel agents in Dhaka. If the agency doesn't have a computer facility, find one that does. The best agencies are listed in the Dhaka chapter, and all of them accept payment by credit card or by travellers cheques. Biman also accepts travellers cheques, but if you cancel, you won't get a refund until the cheques have been cleared. If you pay in cash, make sure that they endorse your encashment certificate.

Europe

If price is your only concern, go with Aeroflot. It flies from various cities in Europe to Moscow where you connect with an onward flight to Dhaka. From London the flight takes as little as 18 hours if connections are good. Aeroflot's fares from Europe are truly unbeatable if you deal through a discount agency – as low as £396 return from London! (Returning from Dhaka with Aeroflot will cost you about US$450 one way to London and US$550 to Paris.)

The next-best deals are with Biman, which offers direct service to Dhaka from London, Paris, Amsterdam, Brussels, Frankfurt, Rome and Athens, usually with stops in the Middle East (Bahrain, Abu Dhabi, Dubai etc) and India. If you're travelling from Amsterdam or Brussels, for example, you can connect with the twice-weekly flight from New York which usually stops at one or the other. The return fare to Kathmandu via Dhaka is the equivalent of only US$700. From London, the same deal with Biman will cost you only £480 compared to over £600 on any other airline. Alternatively you can fly to other Asian cities such as Calcutta or Bangkok and connect to Dhaka from there. Most of these extra-low fares are obtainable only through discount agencies.

The best airlines serving Dhaka from Europe are British Airways (four times weekly), KLM (twice weekly), Emirates Air (three times weekly, with a change in Dubai) and Gulf Air (four times weekly, with a change in Bahrain or Abu Dabi). Emirates Air offers unbeatable service but taking it requires a change of planes. If you purchase your ticket through a discount agency, the fare won't be so much higher.

Air Travel Glossary

Apex Tickets Apex stands for Advance Purchase Excursion fare. These tickets are usually between 30 and 40% cheaper than the full economy fare, but there are restrictions. You must purchase the ticket at least 21 days in advance (sometimes more) and must be away for a minimum period (normally 14 days) and return within a maximum period (90 or 180 days). Stopovers are not allowed, and if you have to change your dates of travel or destination, there will be extra charges to pay. These tickets are not fully refundable – if you have to cancel your trip, the refund is often considerably less than what you paid for the ticket. Take out travel insurance to cover yourself in case you have to cancel your trip unexpectedly – for example, due to illness.

Baggage Allowance This will be written on your ticket; you are usually allowed one 20 kg item to go in the hold, plus one item of hand luggage. Some airlines which fly transpacific and transatlantic routes allow for two pieces of luggage (there are limits on their dimensions and weight).

Bucket Shops At certain times of the year and/or on certain routes, many airlines fly with empty seats. This isn't profitable and it's more cost-effective for them to fly full, even if that means having to sell a certain number of drastically discounted tickets. They do this by off-loading them onto bucket shops (UK) or consolidators (USA), travel agents who specialise in discounted fares. The agents, in turn, sell them to the public at reduced prices. These tickets are often the cheapest you'll find, but you can't purchase them directly from the airlines. Availability varies widely, so you'll not only have to be flexible in your travel plans, you'll also have to be quick off the mark as soon as an advertisement appears in the press.

Bucket-shop agents advertise in newspapers and magazines and there's a lot of competition – especially in places like Amsterdam and London which are crawling with them – so it's a good idea to telephone first to ascertain availability before rushing from shop to shop. Naturally, they'll advertise the cheapest available tickets, but by the time you get there, these may be sold out and you may be looking at something slightly more expensive.

Bumped Just because you have a confirmed seat doesn't mean you're going to get on the plane – see Overbooking.

Cancellation Penalties If you have to cancel or change an Apex or other discount ticket, there may be heavy penalties involved; insurance can sometimes be taken out against these penalties. Some airlines impose penalties on regular tickets as well, particularly against 'no show' passengers.

Check In Airlines ask you to check in a certain time ahead of the flight departure (usually two hours on international flights). If you fail to check in on time and the flight is overbooked, the airline can cancel your booking and give your seat to somebody else.

Confirmation Having a ticket written out with the flight and date on it doesn't mean you have a seat until the agent has confirmed with the airline that your status is 'OK'. Prior to this confirmation, your status is 'on request'.

Courier Fares Businesses often need to send their urgent documents or freight securely and quickly. They do it through courier companies. These companies hire people to accompany the package through customs and, in return, offer a discount ticket which is sometimes a phenomenal bargain. In effect, what the courier companies do is ship their freight as your luggage on the regular commercial flights. This is a legitimate operation – all freight is completely legal. There are two shortcomings, however: the short turnaround time of the ticket, usually not longer than a month; and the limitation on your luggage allowance. You may be required to surrender all your baggage allowance for the use of the courier company, and be only allowed to take carry-on luggage.

Discounted Tickets There are two types of discounted fares – officially discounted (such as Apex – see Promotional Fares) and unofficially discounted (see Bucket Shops). The latter can save you more than money – you may be able to pay Apex prices without the associated Apex advance booking and other requirements. The lowest prices often impose drawbacks, such as flying with unpopular airlines, inconvenient schedules, or unpleasant routes and connections.

Economy Class Tickets Economy-class tickets are usually not the cheapest way to go, though they do give you maximum flexibility and they are valid for 12 months. If you don't use them, most are fully refundable, as are unused sectors of a multiple ticket.

Full Fares Airlines traditionally offer first class (coded F), business class (coded J) and economy class (coded Y) tickets. These days there are so many promotional and discounted fares available that few passengers pay full fare.

Lost Tickets If you lose your airline ticket, an airline will usually treat it like a travellers' cheque and, after enquiries, issue you with a replacement. Legally, however, an airline is entitled to treat it like cash, so if you lose a ticket, it could be forever. Take good care of your tickets.

MCO An MCO (Miscellaneous Charges Order) is a voucher for a value of a given amount, which resembles an airline ticket and can be used to pay for a specific flight with any IATA (International Air Transport Association) airline. MCOs, which are more flexible than a regular ticket, may satisfy the irritating onward ticket requirement, but some countries are now reluctant to accept them. MCOs are fully refundable if unused.

No Shows No shows are passengers who fail to show up for their flight for whatever reason. Full-fare no shows are sometimes entitled to travel on a later flight. The rest of us are penalised (see Cancellation Penalties).

Open Jaw Tickets These are return tickets which allow you to fly to one place but return from another, and travel between the two 'jaws' by any means of transport at your own expense. If available, this can save you backtracking to your arrival point.

Overbooking Airlines hate to fly with empty seats, and since every flight has some passengers who fail to show up (see No Shows), they often book more passengers than they have seats available. Usually the excess passengers balance those who fail to show up, but occasionally somebody gets bumped. If this happens, guess who it is most likely to be? The passengers who check in late.

Promotional Fares These are officially discounted fares, such as Apex fares, which are available from travel agents or direct from the airline.

Reconfirmation You must contact the airline at least 72 hours prior to departure to 'reconfirm' that you intend to be on the flight. If you don't do this, the airline can delete your name from the passenger list and you could lose your seat.

Restrictions Discounted tickets often have various restrictions on them, such as necessity of advance purchase, limitations on the minimum and maximum period you must be away, restrictions on breaking the journey or changing the booking or route etc.

Round-the-World Tickets These tickets have become very popular in the last few years; basically, there are two types – airline tickets and agent tickets. An airline RTW ticket is issued by two or more airlines that have joined together to market a ticket which takes you around the world on their combined routes. It permits you to fly pretty well anywhere you choose using their combined routes as long as you don't backtrack, ie keep moving in approximately the same direction east or west. Other restrictions are that you (usually) must book the first sector in advance and cancellation penalties then apply. There may be restrictions on how many stopovers you are permitted. The RTW tickets are usually valid for 90 days up to a year.

The other type of RTW ticket, the agent ticket, is a combination of cheap fares strung together by an enterprising travel agent. These may be cheaper than airline RTW tickets, but the choice of routes will be limited.

Standby This is a discounted ticket where you only fly if there is a seat free at the last moment. Standby fares are usually only available directly at the airport, but sometimes may also be handled by an airline's city office. To give yourself the best possible chance of getting on the flight you want, get there early and have your name placed on the waiting list. It's first come, first served.

Student Discounts Some airlines offer student-card holders 15% to 25% discounts on their tickets. The same often applies to anyone under the age of 26. These discounts are generally only available on ordinary economy-class fares. You wouldn't get one, for instance, on an Apex or an RTW ticket, since these are already discounted.

Tickets Out An entry requirement for many countries is that you have an onward or return ticket, in other words, a ticket out of the country. If you're not sure what you intend to do next, the easiest solution is to buy the cheapest onward ticket to a neighbouring country or a ticket from a reliable airline which can later be refunded if you do not use it.

Transferred Tickets Airline tickets cannot be transferred from one person to another. Travellers sometimes try to sell the return half of their ticket, but officials can ask you to prove that you are the person named on the ticket. This may not be checked on domestic flights, but on international flights, tickets are usually compared with passports.

Travel Periods Some officially discounted fares, Apex fares in particular, vary with the time of year. There is often a low (off-peak) season and a high (peak) season. Sometimes there's an intermediate or shoulder season as well. At peak times, when everyone wants to fly, both officially and unofficially discounted fares will be higher, or there may simply be no discounted tickets available. Usually the fare depends on your outward flight – if you depart in the high season and return in the low season, you pay the high-season fare. ■

The US

There are basically two ways to Bangladesh from the US. From the west coast, virtually everyone flies to Dhaka via Bangkok or Singapore. You could also fly direct to India and connect from there, but this costs more.

From the US east coast, most people fly via Europe. Biman (☎ (212) 808-4477), which has the only direct flights from North America to Dhaka, and Gulf Air offer the best deals. Biman's DC 10s depart New York on Monday and Friday evenings, stopping en route at Brussels or Amsterdam and Delhi but without changing planes. The fare with a four month return restriction is US$1246. If you purchase this through a consolidator, the price will be less.

Gulf Air offers lower fares from New York and its service is reputedly better. You must switch planes en route but connections are good. It's represented by Tradewinds Travel (☎ (800) 438-4853). The return fare from New York with a minimum seven day/maximum one year stay, no advance purchase required, is US$904 (including tax).

If you live near a city serviced by British Airways or KLM, you can often get special return excursion fares flying all the way with those airlines for around US$1400. You could fly, for instance, on KLM to Amsterdam and connect there with its twice-weekly flight to Dhaka, or on British Airways to London and connect with one of its four weekly flights from London to Dhaka.

To shop around for the best discount agency fares, check the Sunday travel sections of papers like the *New York Times* or the *Los Angeles Times*. Typical return fares from the west coast to Dhaka via Bangkok start at around US$1125. Silver Wings Travel (15456 Ventura Blvd, Suite 102, Sherman House, Los Angeles), for example, offers that price on Thai Airlines with a six month return restriction. It also offers the identical fare to Delhi on Singapore Airlines, with the same return restriction. Fares to Hong Kong are also a good bargain from around US$600 one-way; cheap fares are easy to obtain onwards from Hong Kong.

Australia

From Australia, the easiest way to get to Bangladesh is to fly to Bangkok or Singapore and fly from there to Dhaka, or to fly to Calcutta in India and fly or travel by land into Bangladesh. See the following Asia section for more details of transport from Bangkok or Calcutta. Advance purchase air fares from the Australian east coast to Bangkok are from A$915 one-way or A$1317 return. You should be able to find similar fares without the advance purchase restrictions through travel agents. The advance purchase fares to Calcutta are A$932 one-way, A$1283 return; again you can hunt around travel agents for a better deal.

Asia

There are flights between all the neighbouring Asian countries – Thailand (daily), India (daily), Nepal (five times a week), Pakistan (five times a week), Myanmar (Burma; on Wednesdays) – and Bangladesh. All connections are direct to Dhaka International Airport, apart from daily flights between Calcutta and Chittagong and Biman's Thursday flight between Yangon (Rangoon) and Dhaka via Chittagong.

India Biman has at least two flights every day between Dhaka and Calcutta, and Indian Airlines has four weekly flights as well. Both airlines charge the same for the 35-minute flight. However, the fare is US$22 (US$43 return) if you purchase the ticket in Calcutta and US$43 ($86 return) if you purchase it in Dhaka. You can also fly between Delhi and Dhaka four times a week on British Airways and twice weekly on Biman; the one-way fare for the 2½ hour flight is US$175.

If you want to fly clockwise from Dhaka-Delhi-Kathmandu-Dhaka (or counter clockwise), you can get a 25% discount if you use Biman for the Dhaka-Delhi and Dhaka-Kathmandu segments and Indian Airlines or Royal Air Nepal for the Kathmandu-Delhi segment. This is known as the special 'SARC' fare (a special regional fare on national airlines) and comes to US$324, or

US$26 less than the Dhaka-Delhi return fare on Biman or British Airways.

Nepal There are flights five days a week between Dhaka and Kathmandu; Biman and Singapore Airlines are the only airlines serving this route. The flight takes 65 minutes and the one-way fare is US$107 on either airline.

Thailand Thai Airlines, Biman and Druk Air fly Bangkok to Dhaka. Thai Airlines has flights every day and Biman has almost as many; the normal one-way fare is US$251. Druk Air offers the best deal; it charges only US$176 but has flights only twice a week. However, if you purchase your ticket from one of the many discount agencies in Bangkok, you'll get a much better deal.

Myanmar The only flight between Yangon and Dhaka is Biman's Wednesday flight via Chittagong. The one-way fare for the 1½-hour flight is US$184. Flying via Bangkok, which you can do almost daily, costs 65% more, ie US$304 one-way.

Bhutan Druk Air offers the only service between Dhaka and Paro and the fare is high (US$175 one-way). There are only two flights a week. If the schedule isn't convenient, you could also fly to Paro via Calcutta, using Druk Air and Biman; connections are good and the cost is only marginally more.

Hong Kong Dragon Air has direct flights twice a week to Hong Kong from Dhaka while Thai Airways and Cathay Pacific Airlines offer service to Hong Kong via Bangkok. The one-way fare is US$307 (US$304 on Thai) and there are flights every day.

LAND

India is still the only official land border crossing for foreigners to/from Bangladesh. While the idea of crossing into Myanmar may hold appeal it is unlikely to become possible in the immediate future.

India

Road Permit If, having entered by air, you leave via a land border crossing, a road permit is required. This can be obtained from the Passport & Immigration office (2nd floor, 17/1 Segunbagicha Rd) in Dhaka. It's open from 8 am to 1 pm every day except Friday. Two passport photos are required but there is no fee. The process usually takes 24 hours, sometimes 48 hours, and you don't have to leave your passport.

If you drive from Bangladesh in your own vehicle, two permits are required. One from the Indian High Commission (☎ 504-897), House 120, Road 2, Dhanmondi, Dhaka, and one from the Bangladesh Ministry of Foreign Affairs (☎ 883-260/1/2), Pioneer Rd, facing the Supreme Court in Segun Bagicha (in the city centre).

Border Crossings The situation with crossings to/from India is vague. The main crossings are at Benapol/Haridispur (near Jessore, on the Calcutta route), Chilahati/Haldibari (in the far north, on the Siliguri-Darjeeling route) and, most recently, along the entire eastern border with India (eg, at Tamabil/Dawki, in the north-east corner on the Shillong route, and east of Brahmanbaria on the route to Agartala in the Tripura region). If officials tell you that you cannot cross elsewhere, be sceptical because we have letters to the contrary from travellers. In recent years travellers have crossed at Bhurungamari/Chengrabandha (in the north, well east of Chilahati, an alternate route to Siliguri and Darjeeling), Hili/Balurghat (north-west of Bogra) and Godagari/Lalgola (west of Rajshahi on the Padma River, an alternate route to Calcutta). It may also be possible to pass at Satkhira (south-west of Khulna).

The problem is that these lesser crossings witness so few westerners passing through (maybe only once or twice a year) that everyone assumes it's impossible. Getting the correct story from Indian and Bangladeshi officials is virtually impossible. The truth is probably that crossing at these lesser routes is simply more variable and never certain. If you do use one of the minor crossings, be sure you don't leave the border without a stamp in your passport, otherwise you're sure to run into problems when leaving the country.

Via Benapol This is the main overland route into Bangladesh, made generally by train from Calcutta. It's a half-hour rickshaw ride to the immigration checkpost, then walking distance to the actual border. Inside Bangladesh it is a Tk 6 rickshaw ride to the bus station in Benapol, where you can catch buses to Jessore (one to 1½ hours). Because this is such a crowded crossing point, you can easily spend two hours going through immigration on both sides. See the Benapol section in the Khulna Division chapter for more details.

Via Chilahati This is the main overland route into Bangladesh from the north and is generally made by bus or train from Darjeeling or Siliguri to Haldibari. It's a two-hour rickshaw ride from Haldibari to Hemkumari at the Indian border; slow buses also cover this stretch. From Hemkumari to Chilahati (five km), the Bangladesh border town, is about a four km hike. From there you can take the twice-daily local train or a bus south to Saidpur; either way the trip takes several hours. See the Chilahati section in the Rajshahi Division chapter for more details.

Via Tamabil The bus from Sylhet to Tamabil takes about 2½ hours. The border at Tamabil/Dawki opened up to foreigners in 1995, providing direct passage to/from Shillong. If border officials mention anything about a permit, remain steadfast. No permit is required unless you're taking a vehicle.

Via Godagari One recent traveller reports that this infrequently used crossing is 'open for Bangladeshis' but 'variable for foreigners'. Another notes that leaving through Godagari poses no problem but that if coming from Lalgola on the Indian side, it would be difficult to find this crossing as there is quite a lot of walking through fields

involved. You need both rupees and taka for ferry crossings on the way and there are no exchange facilities either at the border or in Lalgola.

Via Hili Regarding this equally minor crossing, one recent traveller reports:

At Balurghat/Hili, crossing for foreigners is a very painful experience. After a long rickshaw ride (1½ hours along a deteriorating brick road) to Hili, the customs formalities took forever; everything in my rucksack was examined in minute detail and my camera opened. The strange demand that I take off my boots (on three separate occasions) later became clear as it was explained that the last foreigner to go through (four months before) had been a German caught smuggling gold hidden in his boots. So maybe I was just lucky. It is possible to cross this way however, and on the Indian side there is a regular bus from the border to Balurghat from where there is a direct overnight luxury bus service to Calcutta.

Via Bhurungamari The border crossing in the north at Bhurungamari, north-east of Rangpur, is rarely used by travellers. If you're entering Bangladesh, you'll find getting to the Indian border town of Chengrabandha from Siliguri is easy. There are buses every 45 minutes between 6 am and 1 pm (the last bus); the fare is Rs 20 and the 70 km trip takes 2½ hours. The Indian immigrations office opens at 9 am. Outside, you can change your rupees into taka. Exporting rupees from India is illegal and they will be confiscated if found on you. However, officials are usually very friendly and don't perform searches.

Upon entering Bangladesh, you'll be questioned by officials and then told to proceed to Bhurungamari, one km away. It's a tiny village, and if you're caught here for the night your only option may be to sleep on the floor of one of the bus offices. There are also a few very basic food stalls. You can take buses direct to Rangpur (5½ hours), Bogra (eight hours) or Dhaka (15 hours). The fare is Tk 50 to Rangpur, Tk 80 to Bogra and around Tk 170 to Dhaka.

Myanmar

Overland routes between the subcontinent

and Myanmar have been closed since the early 1950s. Even if the border were to be opened to foreigners in the future (it is periodically opened for Bangladeshis), roads across the frontier are in bad condition.

Given the understandable fascination that Myanmar's off-limits border areas have for many travellers, some have been tempted to make a discreet trek across the Bangladesh border into Rakhine (Arakan). However, while this may have been fun in the past, and

the eventual punishment meted out by the government was formerly not too severe, times have changed. This is not recommended.

LEAVING BANGLADESH

The airport departure tax for international flights is Tk 300. See the section on Money in the Facts for the Visitor chapter for details of currency restrictions; and the Land section in this chapter for information on road permits, if you're leaving by land.

Warning
The information in this chapter is particularly vulnerable to change: prices for international travel are volatile, routes are introduced and cancelled, schedules change, special deals come and go, and rules and visa requirements are amended. Airlines and governments seem to take a perverse pleasure in making price structures and regulations as complicated as possible. You should check directly with the airline or a travel agent to make sure you understand how a fare (and ticket you may buy) works. In addition, the travel industry is highly competitive and there are many lurks and perks.

The upshot of this is that you should get opinions, quotes and advice from as many airlines and travel agents as possible before you part with your hard-earned cash. The details given in this chapter should be regarded as pointers and are not a substitute for your own careful, up-to-date research. ■

Getting Around

Internal transport in Bangladesh is so cheap that everyone uses it all the time, whether it be air, land or water transport. The rule is: if you want a seat get there early and learn to shove, kick and gouge like the rest of your travelling companions. District-wide strikes by launches, buses and even rickshaw wallahs are not uncommon, but rarely all at the same time, so with a little ingenuity you shouldn't ever be totally stuck.

The distinguishing feature of internal travel in Bangladesh is the presence of a well developed and well used system of water transport. You will find that in a country where rivers and streams outstretch roads in total distance, water transport is very interesting, especially on the smaller rivers where you can see life along the banks.

Nevertheless, travelling by boat is slow compared to travelling by bus and it's usually avoidable, so many travellers never go out of their way to take a long trip, settling instead for a short ferry ride across a river or two. This is a big mistake – going to Bangladesh and not taking a trip down a river is like going to the Alps and not skiing or hiking. Travelling on river-boats is a high point of a visit to Bangladesh for many travellers.

AIR

Bangladesh Biman, the national carrier, links all divisions with Dhaka, but flying between divisions is not possible. Domestic flights are cheap but are still more than three times 1st-class train fares. There is a Tk 50 depar-

ture tax on internal flights. See the map following for destination and fare details of flights with Biman.

As in India, private airlines are now beginning to appear on the scene. The first is Aero Bengal Airlines which has two daily flights to Barisal from Dhaka's old airport in the city, and may soon be flying to other cities not covered by Biman. It has two 17-seater Chinese planes and fares are about 50% higher than those of Biman. Unlike Biman, Aero frequently cancels flights during the monsoon season due to inclement weather.

The Rocket Experience
On the riverbanks the panorama changed continuously – from lush, tropical jungle with mangroves, to vast expanses of paddy fields dotted with brightly coloured figures at work. Sometimes we saw people leading their cattle or goats across narrow bridges made of no more than a couple of palm-tree trunks; at other times there were fisher people's huts on stilts with nets hanging out to dry. But most memorable was a potters' village of hump-backed, thatched roofs opposite the ferry terminal at Kawkhali, where newly fired terracotta pots were stacked in herring-bone patterns along the bank. What a contrast to the enormous brick factories with tall industrial chimneys that lined the approach to Dhaka the following morning.

Hallam & Carole Murray

BUS

Bus drivers in Bangladesh are among the world's most reckless, as evidenced by the incredible number of bus accidents occurring every day. It's almost impossible to take even a one hour trip without seeing at least one major bus accident. Each time (as the newspapers invariably report) the driver – knowing full well that if he stays around, the angry survivors will beat him to death – absconds from the scene and is nowhere to be found.

The number of buses on the highways is hard to believe. Travelling between Dhaka and Comilla (a two hour trip) you'll pass about 500 buses – an average of four buses every minute!

The country has an extensive system of, passable roads. The main problem with them is that they aren't really wide enough for two buses to pass without pulling onto the verge, which is inevitably crowded with rickshaws and pedestrians. All this involves a lot of swerving, yelling and horn blowing, and can be extremely hard on the nerves. A couple of cigarette filters make good emergency ear plugs.

When your bus encounters a river crossing it generally comes on the ferry with you, and the smoky queues of buses waiting to be loaded is one of the more frustrating aspects of travel here. If you don't mind paying another fare you can always leave your bus and get on one at the head of the queue.

For the lengthy (around two hour) ferry crossings of the mighty Padma and Jamuna, you have to leave your bus and pick up another one from the same company waiting on the other side. These major inland *ghats* (landings) are a mass of boats, people and vehicles, so expect to be confused – pick out someone on your bus and follow them off the ferry. In any case, the bus assistant continues with the passengers, so you're unlikely to get left behind if you take a while finding your bus after the crossing.

You probably won't be allowed to do as the locals do and ride on top of the bus. It's illegal but the police don't bother to stop it. If you do ride on top, remember that low trees kill quite a few people each year.

Most bus stations are located on the outskirts of towns, often with different stations for different destinations. This helps reduce traffic jams in town (if you've come from India you'll appreciate the difference) but it often means quite a trek to find your bus. Chair coach companies, however, usually have their own individual offices, often in the centre of town, and it's at these offices, not at the major terminals, that you must reserve your seat.

Chair Coach Buses Chair coaches are distinguished by their adjustable seats (and more leg room). Where possible, take one of these large modern buses. They are not faster on the road – nothing could possibly go faster than the usually out-of-control ordinary buses! However, departure hours are fixed and seats must be reserved in advance, so unlike regular buses, there's no time wasted filling up the seats and aisles. In addition, they are less crowded, often with no people in the aisles. And most importantly for taller people, there's plenty of leg room.

Most chair coach services between Dhaka and cities on the western side of the country operate at night, typically departing sometime between 5 pm and 9 pm and arriving in Dhaka at or before dawn. Chair coaches plying the Dhaka-Chittagong route, however, travel mostly during the day.

There are two classes of chair coach – those with air-con and those without. Air-con chair coaches operate primarily on the Dhaka-Chittagong and Chittagong-Cox's Bazar routes, and cost about twice those without air-con. All chair coaches are express buses but not vice versa.

The most famous service in the country are the Green Line buses connecting Dhaka with Chittagong and Cox's Bazar. Not only do their waiting rooms have air-con but snacks and drinks are served on board, and the buses screen videos. Service is punctual, non-stop and slightly faster than the train.

Ordinary Buses Among the ordinary buses, there are express buses and local ones which stop en route. The latter charge about 25% less but are slow. In more remote areas, local buses may be your only option. Most buses are large, but there are a few minivans (coasters).

The government's Bangladesh Road Transport Corporation (BRTC), whose buses generally leave from a separate BRTC station, is being driven out of business by the private companies. It may be just as well as BRTC buses tend to be in much worse condition. On the other hand, they are sometimes slightly cheaper and tend to be slower, which in Bangladesh can not only be a blessing but also a life saver.

Ordinary buses are seemingly made for midgets; the leg room does not allow anyone to sit with their knees forward. On long trips, this can be very uncomfortable so try and get an aisle seat.

Women travelling alone sit together up the front, separate from the men. Women travelling with their husbands normally travel together, in the men's section. Bus attendants often treat women with a bit of disdain, but with foreigners, both women and men, they are usually very helpful and try to give them the best seats.

On long-distance bus trips cha stops can be agonisingly infrequent and a real hassle for women travellers – toilet facilities are indeed rare and sometimes hard to find when they do exist.

TRAIN

Trains are a lot easier on the nerves, knees and backside than buses, and those plying the major routes are actually quite good, at least in 1st class. However, travelling between Dhaka and western Bangladesh is complicated by unbridged rivers requiring ferry crossings, circuitous routing to the north via Mymensingh and different gauges.

The longest river crossing is on the Jamuna between Dhaka and Rajshahi divisions, where there's a three hour ferry crossing and a change of trains to contend with. Travelling from, say, Bogra to Dhaka takes twice as long by train than by bus, while between Dhaka and Chittagong the travel time by either is virtually the same.

In the eastern zone of the country, the railway system may be improving slightly with the recent purchase of 20 trains from Germany. In contrast, the railway system in the western zone, which has had only one station renovated since independence and relies on engines purchased from Hungary 30 years ago, continues to deteriorate.

Inter City (IC) trains are frequent, relatively fast, clean and reasonably punctual, especially in the eastern zone. Fares in 1st class are fairly high, about a third more than an air-con chair coach, but in *sulob* (2nd class with reserved seating and better carriages than ordinary 2nd class) the fare is comparable to that in a chair coach without air-con

---

Bus Adventures

Travelling from Sylhet to Dhaka, we expected just another teeth-cracking hair-pulling bus ride typical of Bangladesh bus travel. What we got was so much more. The first hour and a half was smooth enough. Then trouble struck. A dump truck full of stones simply would not let us pass. Our driver's hands were calloused from honking the horn and the male passengers on our bus were visibly (and audibly) impatient. Finally, on a slow section of road, a man jumped from our moving bus and ran up to the truck driver's window. A few sharp words (and blows!) were exchanged and our man returned. We were then allowed to pass.

But the adventure wasn't over; the incident demanded further road justice. Our driver forced the truck to stop on the shoulder and 10 or 12 passengers on our bus ran to the truck, pulled the driver and passengers from the truck, and beat them for a few minutes. Our passengers returned, vindicated, and we were off again. As our bus blared into the next small town, we hit a traffic jam and it all flared up again. This time about 20 were involved with the melee. Luckily, the local law arrived to cart the whole kicking-yelling-pushing bunch down to the police station. After two hours, the groups (apparently reconciled) returned and we were back on the road for the remaining ride into Dhaka.

Todd Kirschner & Rick Hamburger, US

JON MURRAY

BETSY WAGENHAUSER

Top: Truck painting is a widespread expression of popular culture.
Bottom: Rickshaws and baby taxis dominate this street near New Market, Dhaka.

Top Flooded land south of Bagerhat, Khulna Division.
Middle: Paddling cargo through a carpet of water hyacinth.
Bottom: Traditional river-boat on the Tongi River near Dhaka.

and the trip is a lot more pleasant. You may find that train fares for some routes are cheaper, however, than quoted here, as the government is experimenting with lower fares on the routes where there are popular bus services, such as Dhaka-Chittagong.

There really isn't much difference between 1st class and sulob except space – 1st class has three seats across, facing each other and separated by a table, while sulob has four seats across without tables. Air-con 1st class is popular but limited; you'll have to reserve at least several days in advance to get a seat.

There are generally no buffet cars but sandwiches (eg hamburgers), Indian snacks and drink are available from attendants. Second-class cars, with unreserved seating, are always an over-crowded mess and on mail trains your trip will be even slower. However, you may come out of the experience with a few good stories.

The only sleepers are on the night train between Dhaka and Sylhet, Chittagong and Sylhet and Chittagong and Dhaka. The fare is about 40% more than 1st class. However, on many other trains the 1st-class compartments are sleeping compartments, and who's to stop you climbing into an upper bunk for a nap? If the carriage is full of other people with the same idea there's a fair chance that few of them have 1st-class tickets – the conductor will evict them if you ask. While locals often use baksheesh to upgrade their tickets, it's unlikely that you'll get away with it.

There is no longer a 3rd class, but the distinction is semantic, as 2nd class on the poorly maintained local trains is very crowded and uncomfortable, though is remarkably cheap – less than a third that of 1st class. Unreserved 2nd class has at least two levels above it (1st class and sulob, and sometimes 1st air-con and 1st sleeping), so it's really 3rd class and feels like it. On some trains, such as between Dhaka and Mymensingh, there are only 2nd-class compartments.

For IC and mail trains, ticket clerks will naturally assume that you, as a seemingly rich foreigner, want the most expensive seats unless you make it clear otherwise. Buying tickets on local trains is a drag because they

don't go on sale until the train is about to arrive, which means that while you're battling the ticket queue all the seats are being filled by hordes of locals. It's almost always better to take a bus than a local train.

Printed timetables are not available, so understanding the convoluted rules of train travel is not easy, even for railway staff. Finding someone who speaks English and is knowledgeable about the exact schedules can be quite difficult.

Dhaka's modern Kamalpur station is the exception; schedules are clearly marked on large signs in Bangla and English. However, you'll have to double check to make sure they are correct. Some schedules, particularly on the Dhaka-Sylhet route, change by half an hour or so between the summer and winter seasons, and the signs may not have been updated. You can phone the station, but enquiries in person are more likely to yield a reliable result. When making enquiries, it's best to keep things as simple as possible – specify when and where you want to go, and which type of train you want to catch.

If your queries are too much for counter staff, try the District Information Officer (DIO) at Kamalpur station (in the Administration annexe just south of the main station building) – where you'll at least get a cup of cha.

If the crowds who silently follow you around the platform get you down (and they will), ask for the waiting room to be unlocked, or establish yourself in the office of an official who speaks English. Rural railway stations are prone to power failures – hang onto your luggage if the lights go out.

BOAT
Ferry
The river is the traditional means of transport in a country that has 8000 km of navigable rivers, though schedules, even for the ferries crossing the innumerable rivers, are prone to disruption. During the monsoon, rivers become very turbulent and flooding might mean relocation of ghats; during the dry season, silting might make routes inaccessible. Winter fogs can cause long delays, and

mechanical problems on the often poorly maintained boats are not unknown.

The main routes are covered by the Bangladesh Inland Waterway Transport Corporation (BIWTC), but there are ,many private companies operating on shorter routes and some competing with the BIWTC on the main ones. Private boats tend to be slower and less comfortable but cheaper than BIWTC boats. It always seems to be private boats which are involved in the occasional disaster. Bangladesh averages about five major ferry sinkings a year, frequently at night and with an average of 100 people drowning at each one.

Classes On all craft with 1st-class tickets, you must book in advance to be assured of a cabin. On popular routes, especially the Rocket (paddle wheel) route between Dhaka and Khulna, you may have to book a couple of weeks ahead during the dry season. If you're catching a boat at one of the smaller stops, your reservation for a 1st-class cabin will have to be telegraphed to another office and may take some time. Inter-class and deck-class tickets can be bought on board, so there's always a scramble for room. In deck class you may find your ability to sleep in cramped, noisy spaces stretched to the limit. Bedding is provided only in 1st class.

If you haven't managed to book a 1st-class cabin, it's worth boarding anyway and buying a deck-class ticket, as you may be offered a crew member's cabin. Renting a crew cabin is a common and accepted practice, but it's technically against the rules, so there's scope for rip-offs. Don't necessarily believe the crew member when they tell you that the fee you pay them is all that you will have to pay – you need to buy at least a deck-class ticket to get out of the ghat at the other end of the trip, and other hastily thought-of hidden charges may crop up. Some travellers have even had these sorts of problems when renting the captain's cabin.

It's a hassle finding the ship assistant, but if you want to avoid the possibility of minor rip-offs, involve him in negotiations for a crew cabin. He is the person responsible for matters relating to passengers and accommodation.

If you travel deck or inter class (and having a crew berth counts as deck class), you can't use the pleasant 1st-class deck, from where the best views are to be had. You might of course be able to sneak in, but don't complain too loudly if you're thrown out. You aren't *really* special, just rich. Anyway, you can insinuate yourself onto the walkway near the wheelhouse, where the views are better – but it's rare to find yourself more than five metres above water level in Bangladesh.

Travellers on a really tight budget who can't even afford the crew berth might try going up to the 1st-class dining room to sleep there. Once again, it's a bit arrogant to complain if you're thrown out.

Tips In winter, thick fog can turn a 12 hour trip into a 24 hour one, although the captain sometimes doesn't decide that it's unsafe to proceed until he has a very close encounter with a riverbank. If you're travelling deck class, make sure that you're sleeping somewhere where you won't roll off the boat if it comes to a sudden stop!

Porters waiting to leap on docking ferries jostle and fidget like swimmers on the starting blocks – if you don't fancy a swim, don't stand in front of them. The BIWTC routes are shown in the Ferry Routes table. Also, see the relevant sections in the Division chapters for schedules and fares.

The country's major ferry crossing is at Aricha, which is at the confluence of the country's two largest rivers, the Jamuna and the Padma. Ferries operate between Aricha (east bank), Nagarbari (west bank) and Daulatdia (Goalundo Ghat). So if you're heading from Dhaka north-west to, say, Bogra, you'll take the Aricha-Nagarbari ferry (usually about three hours, including bus changes), and if you're heading west to Khulna Division, including Jessore, you'll take the Aricha-Daulatdia ferry (about two hours).

Ferries from Aricha to Daulatdia or Nagarbari depart approximately hourly between 6 am and 10 pm and take about 40 vehicles;

Ferry Routes		
From	*To*	*Frequency (in each direction)*
Barisa	Chandpur & Dhaka	daily
Bahadurabad	Chilmari	daily
Barisal	Chittagong	1 weekly
Barisal	Hularhat (Sea truck)	6 weekly
Chittagong	Hatiya Island	2 weekly
Chittagong	Kutubdia Island	daily
Dhaka	Barisal/Mongla/ Khulna(Rocket)	4 weekly
Kumira	Guptachara (Sondwip Is)	daily
Manpura	Mirzakalu	1 weekly
Steamerghat	Hatiya Island	daily

the last ferries from Daulatdia and Nagarbari depart at midnight and 1.30 am respectively. If you're driving, for two people and a car you'll pay Tk 161 for the Nagarbari ferry and Tk 123 for the Daulatdia ferry.

If you're heading for the Khulna Division you can also take the Mawa-Kaorakandi Ghat ferry. This ferry crossing is slightly shorter than at Aricha but the wait may be longer as there are less frequent crossings. The Sirajganj to Bhuapur ferry crossing north-west of Tangail, which is not used very much, will end with the completion of the Jamuna bridge.

It's amazingly relaxing just watching the countryside drift by. If you're lucky you may spot a sluggish river dolphin. Sometimes you're gliding over thick growths of water chestnut, close to the jungle-covered bank; at other times you're churning along a river so wide that neither of the banks are visible.

The Rocket This is a generic name given to special BIWTC paddle wheel steamers that run four times weekly between Dhaka and Khulna, stopping at Chandpur, Barisal, Mongla and five other lesser ports en route. If you're heading to the Sundarbans, Calcutta or the Muslim ruins at Bagerhat, travelling by the Rocket is a great way to go for a major part of the journey. The journey

all the way to Khulna takes about 30 hours, departing from Dhaka at 6 pm and arriving at Khulna at 3 am the following night.

There are four Rockets, the best two being the *Ghazi* and the *MV Masood*, which are the most recently refurbished. These two Rockets are not particularly glamorous by Mississippi paddle wheel standards, but they do have paddle wheels, two levels and in 1st class a protected deck with comfortable cane seats. On rare occasions, the BIWTC has to substitute a non-paddle wheeler for the real thing. The Rocket operating on your trip is pretty much hit or miss. Regardless of which boat you take, 2nd class (Tk 220) and deck class (Tk 135) are crowded, but possible if you are on a budget.

The front half of the upper deck of the old paddle wheel steamer is reserved for 1st-class passengers. This is no tourist boat as most of them are, typically, Bengalis. There are eight cabins in this section – four doubles and four singles. The cost is Tk 915 if you go the entire distance. Inside, floors are carpeted, and each cabin has a washbasin and a narrow bunk bed or two with reasonably comfortable mattresses, freshly painted white walls, wood panelling and good lighting. Bathrooms with clean toilets and showers are shared.

The central room has overhead fans to cool things off, a long sofa plus four tables for dining. Guests have a choice between Bengali and Continental meals and they're both quite adequate. The cost is only Tk 45 (Tk 22 for breakfast). You can also buy bottled water (Tk 25). Outside, you can sit on the deck in cushioned wicker chairs and have the stewards serve tea and biscuits as you cruise the Ganges delta.

In Dhaka, tickets are available from the well marked BIWTC office in the modern commercial district, Motijheel, a block down from the landmark Purbani Hotel. Book in advance. The boat leaves from Badam Tole, a pier one km north of Sadarghat terminal on the Buriganga River. Leaving from Khulna, you should be allowed to sleep the night before in your cabin; departure is at 3 am. They move the boat to a different anchorage for the night so get aboard early, then sometime after midnight the boat steams back to the loading dock.

Traditional River-Boats

There are about 60 types of boats plying the rivers of Bangladesh. Steamers are only one type; the remaining 59-odd are traditional wooden boats of all shapes and sizes, some with sails but most without. It's a big mistake to think that steamers are the only way to travel in Bangladesh. Some travellers prefer the smaller boats plying the smaller rivers; this is the only way to see the life along the riverbanks. Out on the wide Padma, you'll see lots of big launches, traditional boats and maybe some river dolphins, but you won't see people fishing with their nets, children waving from the shore, farmers working in the paddy fields, or women walking along the banks in their colourful saris.

The problem with taking boats on the minor rivers – and the reason why travellers almost never do this – is finding out where to take them and where they're heading. There is no 'system'; you simply have to ask around. If you see two towns on a map with a river connecting them, you can be sure that boats travel between them, and if there's no obvious road connecting them there will be lots of passenger boats plying the route.

A great river for taking a cruise is right in the Dhaka area – the Tongi (TONG-gee) River. See the Around Dhaka section in the Dhaka chapter for details.

CAR

Travelling by car has two possibilities: either you'll be driving your own vehicle, or you'll be the passenger in a rental car, which comes complete with its own driver.

Owner-Drivers

The import of a vehicle requires a *carnet de passage en douane*, from the country in which the vehicle is registered. Later, the vehicle must be exported. The Automobile Association of Bangladesh (☎ 402-241) is at 3/B Lower Circular Rd, Mogh Bazar, Dhaka.

Driving in Bangladesh takes a bit of guts.

On the major highways, you'll be pushed onto the curb every 10 minutes or so by large buses hurling down the road. Dhaka presents its own unique driving perils because of the vast number of rickshaws and baby taxis (three-wheeled auto-rickshaws). The incredibly dexterous rickshaw wallahs and mad baby taxi drivers dart in an out of lanes, causing near misses nearly every few seconds. And just because you're in a one-way lane doesn't mean you can't expect to face a vehicle or two coming straight at you, seemingly oblivious to the road laws (if there are any!).

Traffic is heavy and when jams occur, you'll be surrounded by so many rickshaws you may think you'll never get out. But unlike in Bangkok, Manila and other Asian cities with notorious traffic jams, those in Dhaka generally don't last very long.

Rental

Self-drive rental cars are not available in Bangladesh, and that's probably a good thing – even the biggest and the shiniest cars here are covered in scratches and dents, and the road law is vague at best. Fortunately, renting cars with drivers has become very easy and the price is lower than in Europe and North America. Considering the ease and low cost of renting cars in Bangladesh, it's surprising how rarely travellers do it.

In Dhaka, there are innumerable companies in the business; the best ones are listed under Car in the Getting Around section of the Dhaka chapter. Expect to pay about Tk 1500 a day for a car without air-con and about Tk 2000 for a vehicle with air-con, plus petrol which costs only Tk 14 a litre. There are no other extras except one: when you stay out of town overnight, you must pay for the driver's lodging (about Tk 60 a night) and food (Tk 50 a meal is reasonable). They don't try to hide this, but make sure you determine beforehand what those rates will be so as to avoid any misunderstandings. Insurance isn't required because you aren't the driver.

Outside of Dhaka, the cost of renting vehicles is typically about a third less if you don't go through Parjatan, around Tk 1000 a day plus petrol for a van without air-con. In cases where no information is available your best bet is go to the top hotel in town and ask the manager who to contact. You negotiate with the driver but if you go through Parjatan they rake off 50% from the driver's price. If this approach fails, try a development organisation in the area, such as Care or Danida; the chances are that they or their drivers will know of someone in the business. Outside of Dhaka, any taxi is also a rental car, however, there are so few taxis available that finding one can be difficult – try the airport when a plane arrives. You will not find taxis outside of Dhaka, Sylhet, Khulna, Saidpur and Rajshahi.

BICYCLE

Bangladesh is ideal for cycling and is an interesting way to see the country. With the exception of the tea-estate regions in the Sylhet Division and the Chittagong Hill Tracts, it is perfectly flat; you can peddle around very easily with a single-gear bike.

Just because you may be travelling around the Indian subcontinent without a bike doesn't preclude your doing this. When you get to Bangladesh, you can buy a new Chinese bike for around Tk 4000 (US$100). In Dhaka, Bicycle Street in the old section is the best of several places to look. When you leave the country, there's a good chance that you will be able to sell it for half the price. You might even set up a purchase-back scheme with the bike seller. Tools for repair are hardly needed because everywhere you go you'll find people who can repair bikes. Rickshaws, remember, are everywhere!

The cities, particularly Dhaka and Chittagong, are places to cycle. Be warned though, heading out of Dhaka in any direction is a major hassle. However, if you're on your way by 5.30 am, you'll zip out of there (or any city) in a breeze, quickly and without the slightest problem. Alternatively, hop on a train with your bike, get off when you arrive at a major town and start your trip from there. And when you're arriving at Dhaka or Chittagong and you don't want to deal with the traffic you can simply hail any bus or baby taxi and ride in from there, with your bike on top.

The trick to cycling in Bangladesh is to avoid the major highways as much as possible; two buses trying to pass another bus at the same time is a frequent sight. All you can do is try to get off the road and out of their way.

While keeping off the major highways is not always possible, look for back roads that will get you to the same destination. Unfortunately, maps of Bangladesh lack sufficient detail or are notoriously bad to be of help here. Nevertheless, we've travelled in areas where maps show no trails and our experience is that if you're travelling between two major towns trails virtually always exist between them. So long as you're not in complete marshland there is bound to be a path. Most paths are bricked and in good condition, and even if it's just a dirt path, bikes will be able to pass during the dry season. And a river won't hinder your travel as there's invariably a boat of some sort to take you across. See the Around Dhaka section of the Dhaka chapter and the Sylhet Division chapter for some suggested cycling routes.

The ideal time to go cycling is in the dry season from mid-October to late March; during the monsoon many tracks become impassable.

LOCAL TRANSPORT

In Dhaka and Chittagong, motorised transportation has increased tremendously in the last few years; traffic jams in certain areas of central Dhaka are a nightmare. The problem continues to be due more to rickshaws than cars but vehicles too are now causing traffic jams.

What is most disturbing to people is the total chaos that seems to pervade in the streets, with drivers doing anything they please – certainly the police can't control them. The foolish traveller, unable to control anything in this mad environment, will fret to no end. Others will sit back in their baby taxi or rickshaw and enjoy the crazy scene. Accidents do happen and sometimes people are killed, but the odds of your being involved are still fairly slim.

Taxi

There are precious few taxis in Bangladesh. In Dhaka, the only place you'll find them are at the airport and at the Sonargaon and Sheraton hotels – you cannot hail a taxi in the street. In Chittagong, the same applies – you'll find a few taxis at the airport and at the city's leading hotel, the Agrabad. In Sylhet, Khulna, Saidpur and possibly Rajshahi, you'll see no taxis except for a few at the airport. They are not marked, so you'll have to ask someone to point them out to you. At Zia international airport in Dhaka,

taxi drivers now demand Tk 400 to virtually anywhere in the city.

Rickshaw

In Bangladesh, all rickshaws are bicycle driven. Unlike in Calcutta, there are none of the human-puller variety. Rickshaw wallahs (drivers) usually do not speak English and often don't know much of the layout of their town beyond their own area. So if you'll be going a good distance and you're not sure where you're going, don't expect them to be able to help much in locating your destination; you probably won't be able to explain yourself anyway.

Fares vary a lot and you must bargain if

Bangladesh by Bike

Upon our arrival in Bangladesh, we decided to see a bit of the country that would be our home. A bicycle trip would give us a good preview and Calcutta, less than 50 km from the Bangladesh border, was a suitable destination. A return to Dhaka by air would let us cover maximum distance in minimum time.

Calcutta is about 240 km from Dhaka as the crow flies, so we followed the crows and avoided the heavily used highway.

The route was wonderfully conceived. Except for the first 30 km out of Dhaka and the last 30 km into Calcutta, there was virtually no traffic. (Not to mention that somewhere in the middle 65 km-section there was virtually no road!) Using the best available map (a scrap of paper with certain village checkpoints highlighted), we pedalled along the backroads of Bangladesh.

The village checkpoint system was our key to success. Each preselected village was within a day's walk of the next, ensuring that almost any local we asked would know of its location.

At the main traffic circle south of Dhaka, we took the Khulna road, crossed the Chinese Friendship bridge and headed for Mawa (checkpoint No 1) on the Padma River. There we waited for the big ferry, drank a few cold Cokes and provided the main entertainment for a crowd of about 40.

Once across the river, we headed down the near-deserted road toward Bhanga (checkpoint No 2). Rice paddies and rural settlements flashed by in a series of instant replays. We replenished our water supply from tube wells.

Bhanga is a hub of activity. Buses, rickshaws, food stalls and people competing for space at dusty intersections. We bolted down a dinner of samosas and chapatis while straddling our bikes and fending off the ever-swelling crowd.

At the main intersection of Boritola (checkpoint No 3), an astonished traffic policeman pointed out the right-hand turn to Mukshudpur (checkpoint No 4). The air was thick with mosquitoes at sunset and the bumpy brick road gradually deteriorated into an even bumpier, potholed track.

We left Dhaka too late in the morning to make it to Mukshudpur before nightfall. We were still pedalling when darkness settled around us with black finality.

That day we'd mastered the art of small-boat ferrying. These country rowboats, sitting inches out of the water, routinely transport cycles and other cumbersome objects. The first crossing or two (there would be many before we saw Calcutta) were a little precarious until we got used to the shifty balance. Our last such crossing for the day would have been at Mukshudpur but the boatman had gone home for the night. Our only option was a narrow, bamboo-pole bridge about 15 cm wide, spanning 10 metres of wet, murky darkness.

As we pondered the physics of guiding two fully loaded bikes across the rickety structure, out of nowhere came a local who silently shouldered the first bike and deftly crossed the bridge. A second trip had us both across without a hitch. Our next problem was solved by another 'guardian angel' who led us to a nearby guesthouse.

you care about paying twice as much as locals, but it still isn't very expensive. In any case it is simply unrealistic to expect to pay exactly what Bangladeshis do. If you can get away with paying a 25% premium, you'll be doing exceptionally well. Around Tk 30 per hour or Tk 3 per km with a minimum fare of Tk 5 is normal, and up to double that in Dhaka. To hail a rickshaw, wave your hand downwards – the usual mode of waving your arm upwards used in the west appears to a Bangladeshi as 'Go away! To hell with you!'.

It's important to get a firm agreement of the fare to avoid hassles at the other end, a nod of the head doesn't count. When bargaining, make your first offer only a taka or two below the fair price, as rickshaw wallahs

seem satisfied if they've beaten you up by any amount. If you have no idea of the correct fare it's hard to get the wallah to make an offer, even to the extent of losing the fare to another rickshaw – try offering Tk 4 or Tk 5.

On the other hand if, having agreed on a fare, the wallah yells it out to all the other wallahs who then start laughing, that's your cue to get out and take another rickshaw for half the price. If the driver doesn't understand you, pull out the amount you want to pay and show him; he'll understand that.

Passers-by will often help to get the fare down to the local price, but in rural areas they're just as inclined to begin bargaining for baksheesh for the wallah before he's even thought about it.

The Mukshudpur guesthouse would have been difficult to recognise without help. What looked like a deserted, semi-deteriorated building in the dark, opened to reveal a room with a double bed complete with fresh sheets, mosquito netting and a clean basic toilet. The wizened man who, as the appointed caretaker, went about his caretaking duties with a practised formality, added to a sense of unreality.

After a blissful sleep, we glided silently out of Mukshudpur in the wet, predawn mist toward the village of Kashiani (checkpoint No 5). The entire scene could not have been more rural. The track narrowed to a footpath as we vied for space with men carrying farm tools and women balancing water urns on their hips. Naked children greeted us and field labourers paused as we rolled past. Pungent bursts of onion and coriander punctuated the air, and only occasional bursts from a nearby generator interrupted the serenity.

Footpaths and bumpy tracks slowed our progress, but it was great to be out and we felt no urge to hurry. Past Kashiani we hardly noticed the several short ferry crossings, and all too quickly we were in Kalna (checkpoint No 6) and then Lohagara (checkpoint No 7). By the time we got to Narail (checkpoint No 8), the road improved considerably. In another fifteen km we were in Jessore. It seemed we were going to make it after all.

It was early afternoon when we navigated Jessore's traffic-laden streets, an abrupt change from the peaceful countryside. Overcoming the temptation to stop, we pushed on the last 30 km to the border town of Benapol.

Our experience of Bangladesh was slight, but in no time we knew that Benapol was not one of its highlights. The town is one long, gravelly, dusty street, haphazardly lined with trucks and food stalls. Guesthouse is not a term used here.

After a number of enquiries, we were finally led down a narrow alley to a shed-like structure. The concrete room was a jumble of unmade beds and mosquito netting. Smiles masked our misgivings, and we decided to look at the other options. Within an hour, we were out of options, humbly returning to bargain for the room.

The border formalities the next morning were straightforward despite the lines of people and the officer's request for our nonexistent road permit. As the main attraction, we proceeded to the front of the line for processing, and an hour later were pedalling down the tree-lined Indian highway toward Calcutta.

The first difference we noticed was that even the smallest of settlements had refrigeration. The first cold lime soda went down so sweetly that it was hard to resist stopping at every village.

By mid-afternoon the third day we reached the outskirts of Calcutta. No signs suggested its proximity, but the increase in overloaded buses and smoke-spewing trucks was enough. We rode as far as the airport on the eastern edge of the city and called it quits.

We found a guesthouse, the Tutimeer, a few km west of the airport, with hot water and air-con for a very reasonable price. Alternating between streams of hot water and blasts of cool air, we soaked in the comfort, enjoyed a sense of accomplishment and relished the thought that we would not have to straddle a bike for at least another week. ■

Driving a Rickshaw

Most travellers, even those who frequently travel in these colourful vehicles, never bother to get on a rickshaw and pedal it for a few metres. Try it – and give your rickshaw wallah a big laugh. It takes more effort than you would imagine and once you've tried it you'll definitely empathise with the driver. (You might not even feel so bad when you think you've overpaid him.) After steering one of these tipsy machines, you'll really appreciate the drivers' dexterity in avoiding all manner of potential accidents at the last second. Try turning a corner as you would on a bicycle and you'll end up in a ditch.

We met two travellers who gave the rickshaw driving experience a try for a km or so. The wallahs of course had never seen a foreigner driving a rickshaw. For them it was a real hoot, not only watching their awkward attempts, but being pulled as well. One warning: choose a wide, empty road to practise. Rickshaws are brutes to steer and slow to stop. And, it's amazing how much damage they can cause if you run into something! ∎

Baby Taxi

In Bangladesh, three-wheeled auto-rickshaws are called baby taxis. Like rickshaws, baby taxis are covered with paintings and trimmings, making them unquestionably the most colourful three-wheelers on earth. Also like the rickshaws, the drivers almost never own their vehicles; they're owned by powerful fleet owners called *mohajons* who rent them out on an eight hour basis. And like rickshaws they're designed to take two or three people but entire families can and do fit. Unlike rickshaws, they pollute the air.

In Dhaka and Chittagong, baby taxis are everywhere – most people use these instead of regular taxis. Rickshaws are also used all over these two cities but generally for shorter distances. Faster and more comfortable than rickshaws, on most trips, baby taxis cost about twice as much. You'll also find them at Dhaka and Chittagong airports, and they charge less than half the taxi fare. Outside of these two metropolises, baby taxis are much rarer. In towns such as Rangpur, Dinajpur and Barisal, they virtually do not exist.

You can go from one side of Dhaka to the other for Tk 50; from the airport you'll pay double because of their waiting time. The minimum fare is about Tk 20 compared to about Tk 5 for rickshaws, so for short distances rickshaws are much more economical. For long distances, the price difference can be minuscule.

In addition to colourful baby taxis, every so often you'll see a similar vehicle which is slightly narrower and, if you look closely, is driven by a motorised chain like a bicycle – and it will be devoid of rickshaw art decoration. This is a *mishuk* (mee-SHUK). If you patronise the baby taxis; you'll be helping to keep rickshaw art alive and well!

Tempo

This is a larger version of a baby taxi, with a cabin in the back. Tempos run set routes, like buses, and while they cost far less than baby taxis, they're more uncomfortable because of the small space into which the dozen or so passengers are squeezed. On the other hand, they're a lot faster than rickshaws and as cheap or cheaper. Outside Dhaka and Chittagong, they're a lot more plentiful than baby taxis; you will find them even in relatively small towns.

ORGANISED TOURS

There are several companies offering tours of Dhaka, including short river-boat rides along the Buriganga or Sitalakhya rivers; see the Organised Tours section in the Dhaka chapter. There are also companies, including the government's Parjatan tourist agency, which offer all-inclusive package tours to the Sundarbans, the tea estates in Sylhet Division, the Chittagong Hill Tracts, and to Cox's Bazar. You'll find more information in Organised Tours under the Information sections of the Sylhet and Chittagong division chapters.

Dhaka

In the past few years the capital city of Dhaka has grown enormously, both in population and area size. As is the case elsewhere around the globe, much of the expansion is due to the influx of economic refugees from the countryside. From a population of around one million in 1971, Dhaka has exploded to close to eight million. It's now the world's 20th largest city and is expected to reach the top 10 within 10 to 15 years. The only way to escape the pandemonium of crowded streets is to head out of town!

Dhaka is the rickshaw capital of the world. There are more here (over 300,000) than in any other city, and they are by far the most colourfully painted as well. Riding one is always a highlight of any trip here, and the art work makes great souvenirs.

History

Dhaka, previously merely a small town dating from the 4th century, first received principal status during the reign of the Mughal Emperor Jahangir. In 1608, Emperor Jahangir appointed Islam Khan Chisti as the Subahdar of Bengal. Khan then proceeded to transfer the capital from Rajmahal to Dhaka, which upon his arrival in 1610 he renamed Jahangirnagar. It lost its provincial capital status in 1704 to Murshidabad, but for over half a century afterwards it remained the commercial centre of the region until the British centralised everything in Calcutta, reducing Dhaka to a district headquarters. By the end of the 18th century, Dhaka had lost almost three-quarters of its population and the muslin cloth trade almost completely vanished.

During the Mughal period, Dhaka became the chief commercial emporium, so much so that forts were built along the riverbanks to protect the city from Portuguese and Mogh pirates. In 1626 the Mogh pirates and their Portuguese allies briefly took Dhaka, and from 1639 to 1659 the capital was moved to Rajmahal, leaving Dhaka as the administra-

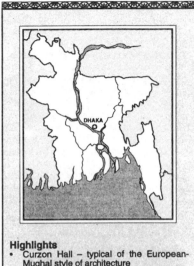

Highlights
- Curzon Hall – typical of the European-Mughal style of architecture
- Rose Garden – an elegant rajbari featuring Corinthian columns
- Sat Gumbad Mosque – a Mughal-style mosque featuring seven bulbous domes
- Ahsan Manzil – popularly known as the Pink Palace
- Dhakeswari Temple – the city's oldest Hindu temple
- National Assembly – designed by Louis Kahn

tive centre. This had the effect of encouraging a greater concentration of commerce; and maritime trade brought with it industry, Islamic education and increasing sophistication in the arts. As many as 100 vessels arrived annually to unload their cargo at Narayanganj and to load up with rice, sugar, fats, oilseeds and wax. Exotic goods were imported from central Asia, Persia, Afghanistan and Turkey, and the influx of foreign money resulted in cowrie shells being replaced by silver as the local currency.

Dhaka remained the capital under the Mughals until 1704 when they moved it to Murshidabad. Under the Mughals, Dhaka's prosperity was considerably enhanced: they built mosques, palaces, caravanserais, bazars and gardens. This development began to attract European traders from southern India.

Five Augustinians, led by Father Bernard de Jesus, arrived in Dhaka in 1599 and established the first Christian mission in the area. In 1616 it became their official missionary centre for the region. They were followed by Portuguese traders who were given the area of Ichamata, about 18 km from the city centre, now called Ferringi Bazar. Some of these traders entered the service of the Mughals.

They were soon followed by the Dutch who established their trading posts in Dholai Khal, a more favoured place, right in the centre of the commercial area. In 1682 the French arrived and, like the Dutch, sided with the Mughals against the Portuguese and Mogh pirates. The area north of Dholai Khal was assigned to the Europeans by the Mughals, and it was in this section of the city that they had their headquarters, residences and churches.

The Church of Our Lady of the Holy Rosary was built there by the Portuguese in 1677 and it's the oldest church in Bangladesh. The Portuguese, the Dutch and the French all vied for influence with the Mughals. The Armenians and Greeks also arrived on the scene.

Like the Greeks, the Armenians concentrated on inland trade and it was they who pioneered the jute trade in the second half of the 19th century until they were overtaken by the British monopolies. In 1666 the East India Company established a trading post in Dhaka, but fell afoul of the Mughal Viceroy, Shaista Khan. Dhaka's decline as a maritime trade centre had already begun, however, as Narayanganj began to lose ground to the new port of Satgaon, later to become Calcutta. The East India Company extended its power to such an extent that by 1757 it controlled all of Bangala except Dhaka,

which it took eight years later. The Mughal Nawab of Bangala, Naim Nizamat, was allowed to govern under the British. It was under the British auspices during the late 18th and early 19th centuries that the dominant forms of current economic development were established: vast plantations of indigo, sugar, tobacco, tea and, of course, jute. At the same time the other European powers were eased out; the Dutch surrendered their property to the British in 1781. In 1824, after almost six decades of indirect rule, the British finally took over direct control and administration of the city.

In 1887 Dhaka became a district, and in 1905 Bengal was divided into east and west, the eastern section incorporated Assam, with Dhaka as its capital. From this point on, Dhaka again began to assume some measure of importance as an administrative centre. Government buildings, churches, residential enclaves and educational institutions transformed it into a city of prosperity. During the existence of East Pakistan, Dhaka was classed as a subsidiary capital and it was not until independence in 1971 that Dhaka once again achieved capital city status.

Orientation

Dhaka is an unplanned city but conceptually it's not so difficult to figure out. When you're in the streets surrounded by hundreds of rickshaws, however, you'll probably feel otherwise. Three facts stand out about the city's plan. Firstly, it's basically oriented south to north, with the bustling Buriganga River forming the southern boundary and Zia international airport being the northern limit.

Secondly, the city can be conveniently divided into three areas. Old Dhaka is a compact maze of crowded bazars and narrow streets lying between the northern bank of the Buriganga and Fulbaria Rd. About two km to the north is where the much larger 'modern' city begins, stretching about seven km northward to the Military Cantonment. Beyond are the suburbs, including the Cantonment (a restricted area) and the relatively upmarket residential quarters of Banani,

Gulshan and Baridhara. Virtually all of the city's top restaurants are located in these three quarters, as are the best guesthouses, almost all of the embassies and their clubs, and most handicraft shops.

Thirdly, most major arteries run north-south, giving the city plan a five-finger appearance. Starting in the east these include: DIT Rd/Shaheed Suhrawardi Ave, which starts in Malibagh and extends north to the east of Baridhara; Airport Rd, which starts as Mogh Bazar Rd in the city centre and heads northward past Banani, eventually connecting with Shaheed Suhrawardi Ave and passing Zia international airport; Kazi Nazrul Islam Ave, which starts in the heart near Dhaka University and passes the National Museum and the Sheraton and Sonargaon hotels en route to the busy Farm Gate intersection where it becomes Airport Rd and later Sadar Rd; the shorter Begum Rokeya Sarani Ave starts in the area around the National Assembly and heads north towards Mirpur; and Mirpur Rd, which starts as Azimpur Rd near the Lalbagh Fort in Old Dhaka, passes New Market and continues through Dhanmondi towards Gabtali (GAB-toh-lee) bus station.

The heart of the modern city is Motijheel (moh-tee-JEEL) which is the commercial district where you will find most of the banks, travel agents and airline offices. Major landmarks here include the National Stadium, the Shapla (Lotus Flower Fountain) Circle on Inner Circular Rd and the Raj-era Supreme Court just north of Dhaka University.

An important road in the central area is North-South Rd, heading south from Kakrail Rd past the GPO and the Gulistan (Fulbaria) bus station into Old Dhaka, leading indirectly all the way towards the Buriganga River. The intersection of North-South and Fulbaria Rds is known as Gulistan Crossing. In the old section, streets become much narrower, and wandering around becomes confusing. Some of the major landmarks include, from east to west, the busy Sadarghat boat terminal where most boats dock on the Buriganga; Islampur Rd; the tall

Shahi Mosque in Chowk Bazar; and Lalbagh Fort.

Even in the modern section, travelling around is complicated by the fact that the main roads are known by the names of the areas through which they pass, rarely by their official name. Adding to the confusion is the fact that side streets and lanes often take the same name as the nearby main road. If the driver of your rickshaw, bus or baby taxi doesn't speak English, you'll be better off giving sections of the city or landmarks, and addresses only after you get there.

Between 5 and 8 pm the streets are especially full of people going home. Traffic jams aren't like those in Bangkok, but they are getting noticeably worse. Friday morning is the best time for wandering around and, although few commercial businesses are open, a number of public markets and tourist sites can be visited. Some shops reopen in the afternoon, when traffic on the streets picks up.

Information
Tourist Offices The main office of the Parjatan (☎ 817-855/6; fax 817-235), the national tourism organisation, is on Airport Rd, just north of the intersection with Bijoy Sarani Ave. It's not set up to give general tourist advice; the only things it offers are its tourist brochures, car rentals and various tour options. Parjatan also has offices at Zia international airport (☎ 894-416) and the Sheraton Hotel (☎ 509-479). The car rental division (☎ 319-561) is adjacent to the main office.

Money Banks available in Dhaka include:

American Express
 Inner Circular Rd just south of Shapla Circle, Motijheel (☎ 956-1751/2, 956-1496/7)
 Sonargaon Hotel (☎ 812-011, 811-005)
 Gulshan Ave, DIT II Circle, Gulshan (☎ 883-635, 881-904)
ANZ/Grindlays Bank
 2 Dilkusha Rd next to the Hotel Purbani, Motijheel (☎ 956-3908/9)
 Corner Mirpur Rd & Road 5, Dhanmondi (☎ 864-240, 863-507)

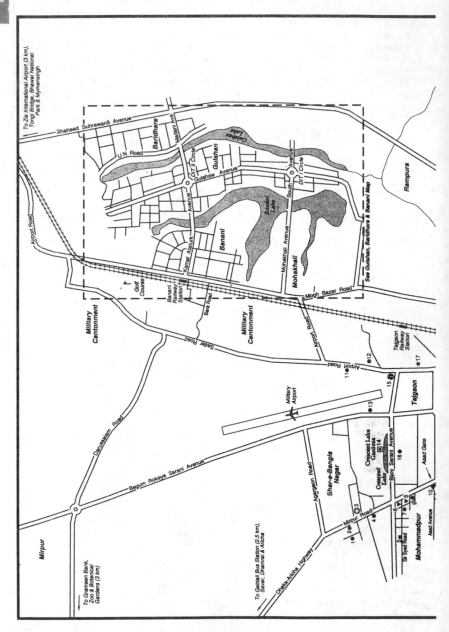

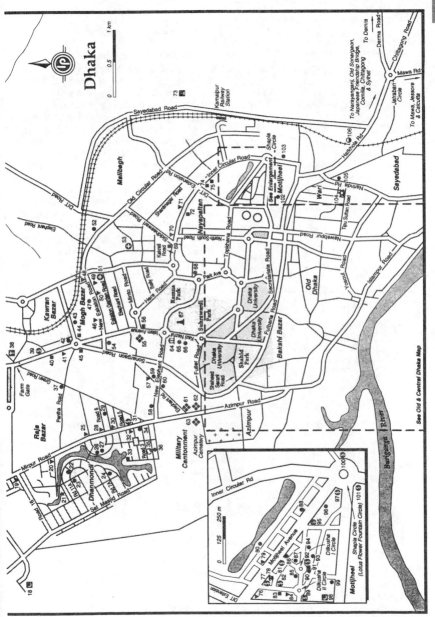

116 Gulshan Ave, Gulshan (☎ 881-014, 884-221)

Kazi Nazrul Islam Ave, between Farm Gate and the Sonargaon Hotel (☎ 812-019, 812-009)

Citibank
122 Motijheel, north of Dilkusha II Circle (☎ 956-2355/9)

Eastern Bank
Dilkusha II Circle, Motijheel (☎ 236-360/1)

Janata
Dilkusha I Circle, Motijheel (☎ 240-000)

National Bank
18 Dilkusha Rd, Motijheel (☎ 230-622, 236-505)

Sonali Bank
Shapla Circle, Motijheel (☎ 955-0426/7)
Zia international airport (☎ 894-437)

Sonargaon Hotel
Kazi Nazrul Islam Ave, Kawran Bazar (☎ 812-011, 811-005). Will change cash at fair rates but changes travellers cheques for guests only.

Standard Chartered Bank
Inner Circular Rd just south of Shapla Circle,

Motijheel (☎ 956-1465/6)
14 Kemal Ataturk Ave, Banani (☎ 881-718/9)

Post & Communications The GPO is near the Baitul Mukarram Mosque on Abdul Gani Rd on the corner of North-South Rd. When mailing parcels, you may be asked to have your boxes sewn in cloth and sealed, especially if the package is quite large. If sewing is required, you might check another branch to see if it's more flexible. At the GPO, there are parcel wallahs who will sew packages up; they can be found in a shelter to the left of the building.

Receiving parcels takes determination as there's only one clerk in the building who's prepared to admit that he knows the procedure. Make sure you don't lose the scrap of paper you received from poste restante notifying you that a parcel had arrived.

If you prefer to use a courier for sending

PLACES TO STAY	PLACES TO EAT	OTHER
5 MCC Guesthouse	19 Xenial Chinese Restaurant	1 Archaeology Department (Permits for Rest Houses)
33 Care Guesthouse	20 Chilis Chinese Restaurant	2 Max-Taxi Car Rental
40 Hotel Super Star	25 Coopers Pastry Shop	3 Suhrawardi Hospital
44 Sonargaon Hotel	28 Magdonalds Chinese Restaurant	4 Limousin Rent-A-Car
45 Sundarban Hotel	30 Ming House Chinese Restaurant	7 OXFAM
56 Sheraton Hotel & Indian Airlines	32 Chung King Chinese Restaurant	9 MCC Office
69 Hotel Razmoni Isha Kha	41 Cooker's-7 Fast Food Restaurant	10 Aarong Handicrafts
72 Hotel Midway International	46 Pizza Garden	11 The Bookworm Bookshop
74 Hotel Parabat, Hotel Arina, Shahagh Paribahan Bus Lines & Saudia Bus Lines	48 Tai King Chinese Restaurant	12 Prime Minister's Office
75 Hotel Al-Belal, Hotel Eastern & Green Line Bus	49 Mikado Restaurant	13 Old Airport (Aero Bengal Flights)
83 Hotel Pacific	50 Chop Sticks Restaurant	14 Zia Uddyan (Zia's Tomb)
91 Hotel Purbani International	57 Xian Restaurant (Chinese & Thai)	15 Parjatan Tourist Office
	70 Nightingale Restaurant & Dragon Air	16 National Assembly
PLACES TO EAT	71 Pizza Land	17 Police Station
6 Sung Palace Chinese Restaurant	76 Cafe Jheel	18 Sat Gumbad Mosque
8 VIP Chinese Restaurant & Intense Business Service	79 Crescent Garden Restaurant	21 Dhanmondi Police Station
	84 Hotel Park	22 UN Development Program (UNDP)
		23 World Food Program
		24 Care Office
		26 Russian Cultural Institute

parcels, try DHL (☎ 956-0108) at 94 Motijheel, and also at House 1, Road 95, Gulshan (☎ 600-191). Also recommended are Federal Express (☎ 956-0108) at 96 Motijheel, and also at Bilquis Tower, Road 46, Gulshan (☎ 602-373).

There are small business centres around the city offering fax, telephone or photocopying, including one several blocks south of the GPO on North-South Rd opposite Hotel Grand Palace; Intense Business Service (☎ 818-315) on Mirpur Rd, about one km east of the National Assembly; and numerous others around DIT II Circle in Gulshan.

One of the better services is Lita Corp (☎ 610-674; fax 888-962) on Kemal Ataturk Ave just west of DIT II Circle; it's open until around 10.30 pm. Lita's telephone and fax rates are good: Tk 100 to India, Nepal and Sri Lanka; Tk 120 to Asia; Tk 130 to Europe; and Tk 140 to Australia, Africa and the Americas.

Film & Photography There are lots of photo studios around the city, the highest concentration being around DIT II Circle in Gulshan. A roll of colour film (36 prints) costs Tk 110 (Fujicolor) to Tk 160 (Kodachrome), and Tk 240 to Tk 300 to develop. Most photo studios give same-day service and some have one hour service. The quality of the processing is quite good. Some do B&W passport photos; the cost is around Tk 100 for four and Tk 250 for 10.

Padma Colour (☎ 508-557), upstairs at 52 New Elephant Rd (ask rickshaws for the Science Laboratory to get to the area), is a good place for film and processing, and it sells Fuji slide film (Tk 175 for a role of 36). Processing can be done the same day. In the same building is a good camera repair shop.

27 Food & Agriculture Organisation (FAO)	62 Chandni Chowk Bazar	90 Singapore Airlines
29 World Health Organisation (WHO)	63 New Market	92 ANZ/Grindlays Bank
	64 National Museum	93 Borak Travels (Aeroflot)
31 ANZ/Grindlays Bank	65 Public Library	94 BIWTC (Reservations for the Rocket)
34 Alliance Française	66 Institute of Arts & Crafts	
35 Indian High Commission	67 Greek Memorial & Shishu Park	95 Pubali Bank
36 Goethe Institute	68 Shilpakala Academy & National Art Gallery	96 Bengal Airlift (Qantas, Royal Air Nepal, Air France & Gulf Air)
37 Heed Language Centre		
38 Holy Rosary Church	73 Dharmarajikha Buddhist Monastery	97 Sonali Bank
39 ANZ/Grindlays Bank		98 Rajuk Mosque
42 Gulf Air & KLM	77 ANZ/Grindlays Bank	99 Cathy Pacific Airlines
43 Bangladesh Tours Car Rental	78 Business Centre	100 Bangladesh Bank, British Airways & Travel Centre
47 The Guide (Tour Agency)	80 DHL & Federal Express Couriers	
51 Holy Family Hospital	81 Janata Bank	101 American Express & Standard Chartered Bank
52 Aarong Handicrafts	82 Citibank	
53 Monowara Hospital	85 University Press Bookshop	102 Banga Bhavan (President's Residence)
54 Dhaka Tours Car Rental	86 Rajbithi Travels (Aero Bengal Airlines)	
55 Paribag Super Market (Karika Handicrafts)	87 Biman Airlines	103 HAC Enterprises (TWA Travel Agency)
58 Jute Carpet Shops	88 Emigrates Air & Korean Air	104 Baldha Gardens
59 Padma Colour Photo Shop	89 JJB Building, Eastern Bank & Citibank	105 Old Christian Cemetery
60 Monno Ceramics		106 Sayedabad Bus Terminal
61 Gausia Market		

Travel Agencies In the central area, one of the best travel agencies for making airline reservations is Bengal Airlift (☎ 241-337/8; fax 863-945) at 54 Motijheel Ave, not far from Shapla Circle. It's a large agency with terminals for Air France, Qantas and several other airlines.

Other agencies in Motijheel, all good, are Travel Centre (☎ 251-760, 233-859) in Nahar Mansion, 150 Motijheel Ave; Hac Enterprise/TWA Airlines (☎ 955-2208, 955-2491), 5 Inner Circular Rd, 150m south of Shapla Circle; Rajbithi Travels (☎ 237-896), 99 Karim Chamba, a block north of Biman; and Vantage Travel (☎ 813-021) at the Sonargaon Hotel.

In Gulshan, you can't beat Travel Channel (☎ 605-513, 604-629). It has its own terminals and is on a short back street off Road 133 near the north-east corner of DIT I Circle. Professionally operated, it accepts credit cards and will deliver tickets to you.

Bookshops In the central area, the best place for books about Bangladesh is unquestionably University Press (☎ 956-5441/4). It's on the 2nd floor of the Red Crescent building at 114 Motijheel, just west of the Biman Airlines office, and is very poorly marked. It's open Saturday to Thursday from 9 am to 5 pm, and has an excellent catalogue.

The Sheraton and Sonargaon hotels both have very small bookshops which carry international newspapers and magazines, maps of Dhaka and Bangladesh, a few interesting books on Bangladesh plus some recent blockbusters. For second-hand books, try New Market on Mirpur Rd. Entering the market from the south, turn left and head towards the end, which is where all the book and map stalls are located.

In the greater Gulshan area, there are three good places for books. The largest is University Press/Samarkand, which is also a cafe. It's located at House 49 on Road 35 in Gulshan, behind Gulshan mosque, and is very poorly marked. It carries many of the same books sold at the main outlet in Motijheel. IDEAS, on Gulshan Ave 300m south of DIT I, has an interesting range of books, including handicrafts, social issues, art and poetry.

UBINIG (☎ 318-428), 5/3 Barabo Mahanpur Ring Rd in Shamoli run a feminist bookshop.

Finally, there's The Bookworm (☎ 881-230), on Airport Rd between the Prime Minister's office and the military cantonment. This is the best place to go if you're looking for popular novels, including recent best sellers. It also carries books on Bangladesh.

Libraries Travellers desperate for books and conversation in English should try the British Council Library (☎ 500-107/8) at 5 Fuller Rd in the Dhaka University area or the USIS library (☎ 862-550/1) on the 4th and 5th floors of the Jiban Bima Bhaban building facing Dilkusha II Circle in Motijheel. The latter is open Sunday to Wednesday from 11 am to 4 pm.

Other libraries include the Alliance Française (☎ 504-732) at 26 Mirpur Rd, just north of Road 3 in Dhanmondi; the Goethe Institute (☎ 507-325), nearby at House 23, Road 2, Dhanmondi; Dhaka University Library (☎ 505-161/2); and Dhaka Public Library (☎ 500-831) on Mymensingh Rd near the National Library.

Laundry Dry cleaners are hard to find; try US Dry Cleaners at DIT II Shopping Centre on Gulshan Ave.

Hairdressers You'll find cheap barbers everywhere, but the best place in town for both women and men is Nelo's Salon (☎ 604-643) at House 7, Road 78, Gulshan.

Medical Services For emergency medical care, contact Dr Wahab (☎ 881-454, 605-947). His office is at House 3 on Road 12 in Baridhara. The best hospital is likely to be the new Gulshan Hospital at the eastern end of Road 71 in Gulshan; it's due for completion in late 1996. Until then, use Monowara Hospital (☎ 839-529) in Mogh Bazar, one km east of the Sheraton Hotel.

Some of the better pharmacies are at DIT

II Shopping Centre in Gulshan. They're open until around 10 pm. There is a 24 hour pharmacy at Banani Mall on Kemal Ataturk Ave in Banani.

Old Dhaka

Sadarghat & Badam Tole If you have time to do only one thing in Dhaka, then take a small boat out on the Buriganga River from Sadarghat boat terminal. The panorama of river life is fascinating. In the middle of the river, which is roughly 500m wide, you'll see an unbelievable array of boats – uncovered and covered boats, cargo boats, speed boats, tugs and motor launches – going in every direction. You'll see crew painting boats, bathing, cooking or just resting and observing, while hordes of people cross the river in small canoes, and both large and small ships ply up and down the river.

If you look hard along the river's edge, you may also spot some of the ancient house boats called *baras*. These worn-out boats, some half a century old, are popular floating restaurants catering to the poorest of the poor, where meals are served from 8 am until midnight.

It costs Tk 2 to enter Sadarghat boat terminal. You'll find large ferries stationed there during the day, many heading south for Barisal in the evening. Among all the large ships are the tiny wooden ones which you

can hire for the trip or by the hour. Bargaining is difficult because the boat owner is unlikely to understand your itinerary. A reasonable price would be Tk 50 per hour, but to get that rate you may have to bargain awhile. Foreigners are rarely seen doing this, so not all boat operators will demand an outrageous fee. Still, expectations may be rising. If you overpay, you'll only be ruining it for future travellers.

Badam Tole, where the BIWTC Rocket ferries dock, is one km north-west along the river-side lane, Buckland Bund, which runs the length of the waterfront and is always packed with people, rickshaws and colourful trucks.

Walking from Sadarghat to Lalbagh Fort is a good way to get to know Old Dhaka, or at least to discover how easy it is to get lost in its winding lanes. Islampur Rd (which becomes Water Works Rd at the western end) is the major road connecting the two and runs parallel to the river, passing through Chowk Bazar and south of the large Central Jail.

Ahsan Manzil Around 600m west of Sadarghat is the Pink Palace, which is one of the most interesting buildings in Dhaka. The best feature is the interior – it's one of the few buildings furnished in the style of the era in which it was built. Dating from 1872, it was built on the site of an old French factory by Nawab Abdul Ghani, the city's wealthiest

---

Nawab Abdul Ghani

Nawab Abdul Ghani, born in 1830 of Kashmiri descent, was the most influential person in East Bengal in the last half of the 19th century. Unlike most zamindars, the nawab was Muslim. Ghani, his son Nawab Ahsanullah, and his grandson Salimullah Bahadur contributed greatly to Dhaka's development. Along with elephants, horses, boats and other materials donated to the British government, they also contributed large sums to local colleges.

As Ghani's land holdings grew to include most of Dhaka, he ruled like a king over the residents. He ordered them to settle their disputes in the arbitration court of his zamindar before going to the government courts. In effect, every conflict among his 'subjects' was settled at Ahsan Manzil.

Politically astute, he participated in both Hindu and Muslim festivals and both groups admired him. He also introduced professional horse racing to Dhaka. When he returned from a voyage to Calcutta by steamer, flags were flown along the river, a band played lively tunes and guns were fired.

The demise of the family occurred when Ahsanullah, for whom Ahsan Manzil (the Pink Palace) was named, died suddenly in 1901 without a will. Under Islamic law the monolithic estate was broken into nine parts and his son, Salimullah, received only one. Salimullah, although residing at the Pink Palace, was reduced to a relatively poor man. Nevertheless he contributed more to Muslim schools than anyone in the city's history, and founded Dhaka Medical School. Because of this he is revered today perhaps even more than his illustrious grandfather. ∎

zamindar (landowner). Some 16 years after the palace's construction, it was damaged by a tornado and in the reparation was substantially altered in appearance, becoming more grand than before. Lord Curzon stayed here whenever he came to visit. After the death of the Nawab and his son, the family fortune was dispersed and the palace eventually fell into disrepair. It was saved from oblivion by a massive restoration job in the late 1980s.

It's a magnificent pink-coloured building, with an imposing staircase leading to the 2nd floor, and is topped by a lofty dome. In each of the grand 23 rooms, there is a photograph of the room dating from around 1902. Having these photos allowed the accurate restoration of the furnishings and draperies of that year, so when taking a tour you'll be taking a walk back in time, to the high point in the palace's history.

The museum gives a good insight into the life of the ruling classes of Bengal during the Raj, with historical background to the building and period, and displays of items found on the site. There are also paintings of various Bengali notables and an excellent view over the river from the 1st-floor verandah. It's open Saturday to Wednesday from 10.30 am to 4.30 pm and Friday from 4 to 7 pm.

Shankharia Bazar Often called Hindu Street by foreigners, this is the most fascinating street in Dhaka and a must see. It's near Sadarghat and the Pink Palace, so a stroll down this narrow lane is easy to include in a visit to the area. It's the most densely populated area in Dhaka, and contains an interesting row of ancient houses sheltering countless Hindu artisans, most notably the conch shell bangle makers.

Shankharis first came here over 300 years ago, and their art is slowly dying out. If you pass a shop and hear some faint grinding sounds out the back, ask to see the tiny quarters where they make the jewellery; some owners will be delighted to show you around. There are machines which cut the shells into rough rings and bangles, and with these the crafts people initiate their carving. Other artisans along the street include drum makers, gravestone carvers, Hindu wedding hat vendors and paper kite sellers. Any day is good for visiting, including Friday which is a work day for Shankharis.

To find Shankharia Bazar head north along Nawabpur Rd from Sadarghat, after two long blocks you'll pass a small square on your right called Bahadur Shah Park, which has a cenotaph to commemorate the so-called Indian Mutiny of 1857. From the north-west corner, cross the street and head west, parallel to the river. After 100m you'll come to some small shops selling tombstones; that's the beginning, it continues for about 400m until it merges with Islampur Rd.

If you'd also like to see some rickshaws being made, head east of Bahadur Shah Park along Municipal St for about 150m and take a left (north) along a tiny lane, opposite St Gregory's Church. About 100m down that narrow, winding lane you'll find five or six shops.

Conch Shell Jewellery

To the Hindus, conch shells are a symbol of good fortune and purity. Hindu scriptures instruct married women to wear conch shell bangles on both wrists and to break them when the husband dies. Nowadays, Muslim and Christian women wear these bangles as well.

Three centuries ago, conch-shell artisans migrated from India to the Dhaka area, and Shankharia Bazar has been the centre of their trade since then. The conditions here are appalling. The tiny rooms are claustrophobic and the low ceilings allow little ventilation or sunlight. You have to stoop to enter the work areas. The artisans work hard and only earn Tk 80 a day. Many have moved on to other pursuits, such as making gold ornaments, stone spice-grinders or harmoniums and other musical instruments.

The craft faces an uncertain future. The shells come from the seas of India and Sri Lanka, and are not always available due to low import quotas. Also, more and more Hindu women are unable to afford these bangles, opting to buy the much cheaper plastic lookalikes. ■

Armenian Church One km north-west of Sadarghat and north of Badam Tole is an area called Armanitola, so named after the Armenian colony which settled here late in the 17th century. Even during the height of their influence in the mid-19th century, they numbered no more than about 40 families. However, because of their close business ties with the East India Company, many Armenians became rich zamindars with palatial houses.

The Armenian Church of the Holy Resurrection, which is on Armanitola Rd and dates from 1781, is fascinating and well worth a visit. Mr Martin (☎ 254-694, 253-116), one of five remaining church owners of Armenian descent, lives on the premises. He took over as caretaker in the mid-1980s and has done much to restore it, including throwing out the squatters. During the War of Liberation, the silver setting and organ were stolen and many of the graves were desecrated.

Now in reasonably good shape, the church is an oasis of tranquillity in the heart of the crowded city, and about twice a year the Armenian Archbishop from Australia comes here to hold ceremonies, which is by far the best time to visit. It is open every day except when the caretaker leaves the premises. Mr Martin speaks English and delights in giving personal tours. There's no fee for this but donations, which finance the restoration work, are most welcome.

The church is a small chapel with a balcony and the original wooden pews seat about 100 people. The building shows hints of Turkish architectural design. The grounds cover nearly a hectare and are paved with old gravestones, some quite ornately carved, with some fruit trees down the back. Judging by the ages of those buried here, the local climate didn't do the Armenians much harm.

From the intersection of Hindu St and Islampur Rd, head west along Islampur for about 700m until you come to Armanitola Rd (or Church Rd); head north one block (150m) along that road and the church is on your left. Alternatively, from Badam Tole, head north for two blocks to Islampur Rd, then left one block and right one block.

Sitara Mosque About four blocks (350m) north of the Armenian church, on the same street, you'll come to Sitara Mosque, popularly named Star Mosque. This picturesque mosque is one of the city's most popular tourist attractions because of its striking mosaic decoration of coloured glass set in white tiles. It is also distinctive for its low-slung style and the absence of a minaret. While the mosque is quite old, dating from the early 18th century, it has been radically altered. It was originally of the typical Mughal style, with four corner towers. Around 50 years ago, when mosaic decoration became popular in Bengali buildings, a local businessman financed its redecoration with Japanese and English china tiles and the major addition of a new eastern verandah substantially altering the overall structure. If you look hard, you can see tiles depicting Mt Fuji!

Bara Katra & Choto Katra These are two of the oldest buildings in Dhaka, which is why they're listed in most tourist brochures. However, these Mughal-era structures are very dilapidated, especially Choto Katra, which is in total ruins. Bara Katra (BORE-ah KAT-rah), which was once a palace with monumental dimensions, was built in 1644 and now has a street running through its once-magnificent arched entrance. It was originally quadrangular, with 22 rooms around a central courtyard, and gates to the north and south. While only a small portion of the original structure is still standing, the building is still occupied and has a small prayer room on top. If you walk up to the 3rd-storey roof, you can get some excellent views of Old Dhaka.

Choto Katra, which dates from 1663, was a caravanserai for visiting merchants. It was similar in design to Bara Katra, but there's not much left. However, if you go down the passage immediately before the south-east corner you'll come to a soap factory, with lakes of boiling soap in metal vats. Deeper in among the bowels of the ancient foundations are a maze of smoky rooms where the soap is moulded. By night it's like something out of Dante's *Inferno*.

Few locals know about Bara Katra, so don't expect help from them to find it. Head west along Water Works Rd (the continuation of Islampur Rd) for the landmark Chowk Bazar Shahid Mosque, which has a very tall red-brick tower – you can't miss it. Bara Katra is 100m south from the mosque, towards the river. Finding Choto Katra is more difficult. From Bara Katra head south and take the first left. Follow this road for a few hundred metres and the Choto Katra is along a street to your left.

Lalbagh Fort This unfinished fort is touted as Dhaka's premier tourist attraction, but if you're expecting another Red Fort you'll be disappointed. Regardless, it's definitely worth a visit and along with Sadarghat it's one of the two best places to begin a tour of the Old City. You'll find it near the intersection of Dhakeswari and Azimpur Rds.

Construction of the fort began in 1677 under the auspices of Prince Mohammed Azam, third son of Aurangzeb, who then handed it over to Shaista Khan for completion. The death of Khan's daughter, Pari Bibi (fair lady), was considered such a bad omen that the fort was never completed. However, three architectural monuments, all of the Bangla-Mughal style of architecture, were finished within the fort complex and remain in good condition – the Hall of Audience (or Diwan), the Mausoleum of Pari Bibi and the Quilla Mosque. The expansive complex, completed in 1684, and its serene formal gardens are enclosed by a massive wall.

On the eastern side of the fort, to your far left as you enter, is the residence of the governor containing the Hall of Audience. It's an elegant two storey structure with a symmetrical facade and a central hall. Inside, there's a small museum of Mughal miniature paintings and beautiful examples of calligraphy, along with the usual swords and firearms. Beyond, on the western side, a massive arched doorway leads to the central square *hammam* (a place for taking baths, body massages, keeping hot and cold water, and going to the toilet). In the winter it was heated from below. It's a low masonry structure with a glazed tile floor and topped by a dome. Adjacent to this chamber are the baths and toilets (not so very different from today's models).

The mosque on the western side of the complex is quite attractive but the middle building, the Mausoleum of Pari Bibi, is a unique and important structure. It's the only building in Bangladesh where black basalt and white marble (from Bangladesh) and encaustic tiles of various colours have been used to decorate an interior. At each corner are four graceful turrets capped by ribbed cupolas. The roof is covered with a false copper dome and crowned by a tall finial (ornament). Inside where Pari Bibi is buried, the central chamber is entirely veneered in white marble.

Admission to the fort is free. Entry to the museum and the hammam is Tk 1. Winter opening hours are Sunday to Wednesday from 10 am to 5 pm; Friday from 2.30 to 5.30 pm; and closed on Thursday and holidays. From April to October, opening and closing times are half an hour later.

Khan Mohammad Mirdha's Mosque Some 400m west of Lalbagh Fort, on Lalbagh Rd, is Khan Mohammad Mirdha's Mosque, one of the most beautiful in Dhaka. Erected in 1706, several decades after the fort, this Mughal structure is of similar inspiration and built on a large raised platform, up a flight of 25 steps. Three squat domes, with pointed minarets at each corner, dominate the rectangular roof, and the wall surface is profusely relieved with plaster panels. To get a good view of this walled mosque, you must enter the main gate, which is off the main road. Unfortunately, unless you're here during prayer times (eg around 1 pm), you'll probably find the gate locked.

Dhakeswari Temple About one km northeast of Lalbagh Fort, up a short alley off Dhakeswari Rd, is the city's main Hindu temple, dating from the 12th century. There are two sets of buildings. The one in the tourist photos consists of four adjoining

Durga Puja
This colourful festival occurs around the 2nd week of October and is a good time to visit Dhakeswari Temple. On the last day of the five day festival, devotees gather with their colourful goddesses made of bamboo and clay to pray to the goddess Durga. Around 5 pm they parade their effigies through the streets toward Sadarghat, arriving there at nightfall. Durga, seated on a lion with a long spear piercing Mahishasura, is then placed on a boat and sent to the middle of the Buriganga for immersion. This ends the simple but colourful ceremony. Foreigners, even those who just show up, are often treated as honoured guests and have an easier time amidst the throngs of people around the boat terminal.

Around Durga Puja, usually the last Saturday in September, there's a colourful boat race on the Buriganga near Postagola. It's quite a spectacle and is inaugurated each year by the President of Bangladesh. Each long boat is crammed with roughly 60 oarsmen and the competition ensues amidst continuous clapping by the spectators. Advance publicity is poor so foreigners never hear about it. Call Parjatan or the President's office for the details. ∎

rekha (buildings with a square sanctum on a raised platform with mouldings on the walls) temples covered by tall pyramidal roofs of the curvilinear bangla style. It's been modernised and is nothing special, but it is colourful and you are likely to find some long-haired *sadhus* (spiritual men) hanging around, smoking ganja.

Hussaini Dalan A block north of the Central Jail, on Hussaini Dalan Rd in Bakshi Bazar, is an historic building that looks more like a Hindu *rajbari* (zamindari palace) than a mosque. It was built in the 18th century near the end of the Mughal period as the house of the Imam of the Shia community; Muharram is celebrated here annually. The architecture of this Shia mosque, with its four large Doric columns supporting a grand porch, seems baroque in inspiration. The original building, however, was purely Mughal as it lacked the porch and had an elevated roof and minarets at all four corners. This changed during the 1897 earthquake when the roof collapsed – you can see a silver filigree model of the original building in the National Museum.

Baldha Gardens & Christian Cemetery One of the hidden gems of Dhaka are the Baldha Gardens in Wari, at the eastern end of Tipu Sultan Rd and a block south of Hatkhola Rd. The two walled enclosures, Cybele and Psyche, were once the private gardens of a wealthy zamindar Narendra Roy Chowdhury, whose grandson gave them to the government in 1962 as a silent tribute to the family.

Started in 1904, these botanical gardens house about 15,000 plants and 672 species. Many of these are exotic and rare plants procured from about 50 different countries, including an Egyptian papyrus plant used to make paper centuries ago and a century plant which apparently blooms once every 16 years. Check inside the buildings, which include an orchid house, a cactus house and a green house. The gardens are also a bit whimsical – you can't help wondering how all that Royal Doulton got smashed to make the free-form mosaic. Admission is Tk 2 and the gardens are open daily from 9 am to 5 pm, with a two-hour break at lunch. Keep your eye out for the resident mongoose.

Across the street to the east is the old Christian Cemetery, which dates from the mid-18th century. Dominating the whole cemetery is an interesting Mughal-inspired tomb of Columbo-Saheb. It's a high octagonal tower-like structure with eight arched windows surmounted by a dome. But no one has a clue as to who Columbo-Saheb was.

Rajbaris in Old Dhaka The largest concentration of Hindu rajbaris dating from the late 19th and early 20th centuries can be found in the east of Old Dhaka on Tipu Sultan Rd, which intersects with Nawabpur Rd and heads east. One of the most elegant is popularly known as the **Rose Garden**, and features four tall, graceful Corinthian columns, a semi-circular balcony on the 2nd floor and a dome on top. Another on this road is the **Sankhanidhi House**, which dates from 1921; the entire facade is liberally relieved with bands of floral plaster decoration.

A little further down the street is an ornate two storey **Radha-Krishna Temple**. This is a magnificent building; the entire facade is covered with profuse floral decoration in which the conch shell motif predominates. The windows in several places are still glazed with red and green coloured panes. Adjacent to the temple on the west is **Bhajahari Lodge**. Presently occupied by a school it features a grand frontage facing south and lovely 2nd-storey balconies.

You could also check out **Rupial House**, not far away near the Buriganga on the Buckland Bund in Farashganj. Of the late Renaissance style, this impressive mansion features a dance hall. Another fascinating structure is **Lalkuthi** (or Northbrooke Hall),

several blocks east of Sadarghat. Originally a town hall, it's a superb example of the European-Mughal style of the early 20th century.

Bangsal Rd For a souvenir of Bangladesh, you can't beat **rickshaw art**. The art is painted on strips of tin and vinyl which fits within most suitcases and costs only around Tk 40 each, sometimes more if it's special. Bargaining is required, of course. The place to find this art is on Bangsal Rd, popularly known as Bicycle Street. This is also the best place to buy a cheap Chinese bike (about Tk 4000), which you'll see everywhere in this country; there are lots of spare parts as well.

The street begins 700m south of the ever-crowded Gulistan Crossing near Banga Bazar. The rickshaw art and bicycle section

The elegant Rose Garden is one of several rajbaris on Tipu Sultan Road, Old Dhaka.

lasts only one block, starting just west of North-South Rd, one block south of the well marked Hotel Al-Razzaque International.

Central Dhaka
North of Old Dhaka is the old European zone, now the modern part of town.

Banga Bhavan & Baitul Mukarram Mosque
Banga Bhavan, the official residence of the President, the country's titular head, is just south of the modern commercial district of Motijheel. Photography, even of the gate, is forbidden.

Just west of Motijheel is the modern Baitul Mukarram Mosque. Designed after the holy Ka'aba of Mecca, this 'national mosque' is on most tourist routes. While it's the city's largest mosque, it's not very interesting except at night when it's lit up.

Dharmarajikha Buddhist Monastery Other noteworthy structures include the modern Kamalpur railway station and, beyond it, the Dharmarajikha Buddhist Monastery. It's the largest Buddhist cultural centre in the country and contains one huge bronze and one beautiful marble statue of Buddha. There's a peaceful pond; bring a book for reading.

Old High Court This imposing white building, once the governor's residence, is a good km west of Motijheel, just north of Dhaka University. It's the finest example in Dhaka of the European Renaissance style, with few or no Mughal features. Similar in size to the Pink Palace and also surmounted by a graceful dome, it features a prominent central porch with two wide verandahs on either side. Nearby is the newer **Mausoleum for Three Martyrs** and to the right is the better-maintained **Supreme Court**.

Suhrawardi Park Beginning near the Old High Court and stretching all the way up to the National Museum, the Suhrawardi Park covers an enormous area with quiet well maintained parkland. This was once the Race Course, where both the Bangladeshi Declaration of Independence and the surrender of

Pakistani occupation forces took place in 1971. The park is open daily between 6 am and 10 pm.

At the northern end is the **Shishu Park** amusement centre for children. Adults are allowed on most rides. Admission is Tk 2, and each ride costs an additional Tk 2. It's open daily from 2 to 7 pm, closes 4 pm Thursday and is closed Sunday. East of Suhrawardi Park is **Ramna Park**, which is well tended and has a boating lake.

Dhaka University & Curzon Hall Dating from 1921, Dhaka University (DU) has some fine old buildings spread over a large area to the north-west of Suhrawardi Park. In the same area is the **British Council Library** and immediately north of the university are the **Institute of Arts & Crafts**, which has an art gallery, and the Dhaka **Public Library** (☎ 503-242).

On the main campus, south of the Old High Court, is Curzon Hall, which houses the science faculty and is the university's architectural masterpiece. It's a fine example of the European-Mughal style of building erected after the first partition of Bengal in 1905. A red-brick building with many eye-catching details, it has an elegant facade with a central projecting bay and wide arched horseshoe-shaped portals.

Two blocks west, on Secretariat Rd and just north of the College of Medicine, is a modern monument, the **Central Shaheed Minar**, built to commemorate the historic Language Movement of 1952.

If you're looking for a place to meet DU students try Madhu's Canteen. It's a rustic yellow-coloured building where the political minds of the campus meet.

National Museum A visit to the National Museum (☎ 505-269) is a must. If you're short of time skip the top floor, which displays reproductions of western paintings (no nudes, of course) and portraits of historical figures. The displays are poorly executed and not all items are of museum quality, but you can learn a good deal about the country from a trip here.

There are displays from Bangladesh's Hindu, Buddhist and Mughal past, but the real value of the museum is the extensive collection of fine folk art and handicrafts. Check out the models of the many varieties of 'country' boats, most of which you'll still see on the rivers. There's also some interesting contemporary art, especially that of Shipacharya Zainul Abedin, and a simple but extremely moving display on the War of Liberation. Exhibits include the first, handmade Bangladesh flag and a Pakistani torture box, evil in its bland hi-tech design.

Admission is Tk 2; free on Friday. It's open daily from 10 am to 4.30 pm, Friday from 3 to 7 pm and is closed Thursday.

National Assembly Sher-e-Bangla Nagar, north of Dhanmondi, is where the striking National Assembly building, Sangshad Bhaban, is located. In 1963 the Pakistanis commissioned Louis Kahn, a world-renowned Jewish architect from the US, to design a regional capital for East Pakistan. Due to the liberation movement and ensuing war the building wasn't completed until 1982.

A typical Kahn structure, it's a huge

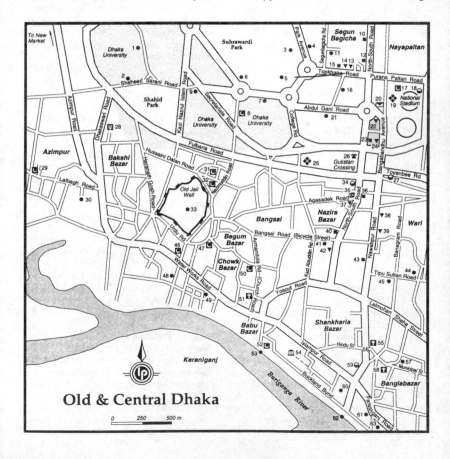

Old & Central Dhaka

0   250   500 m

assembly of concrete cylinders and rectangular boxes sliced open with bold, multi-storey circular and triangular apertures instead of windows. The marble strips between the concrete layers are 'like pinstripes on a finely tailored suit'. The interior, which includes an octagonally shaped Assembly hall, features bizarre Piranesi-inspired spaces. You can't take photos inside. Around the structure is a large lake, with red-brick apartments to one side where parliamentarians from outside Dhaka stay when the Assembly is in session.

Tours are only by special appointment but a few travellers have managed to arrange tours on the spot. Ask for a seat in the visitor's gallery; if Parliament is in session and you're lucky, you might be given one for a session several days later.

Sat Gumbad Mosque Dating from 1680, Sat Gumbad (Seven Domed) Mosque is the finest example of the pure Mughal style mosque in Dhaka. The mosque's most notable feature is its seven bulbous domes crowning the roof and covering the main prayer hall.

Not many years ago, the mosque's location was ideal, overlooking the Turag River, but the views are now completely blocked by ugly buildings. Try to come at prayer time (1 and 5 pm) when the gate is open.

Unfortunately, few travellers see Sat Gumbad because of its somewhat remote

PLACES TO STAY		
10 Hotel Pritom	2 Salimullah Muslim Hall	41 Shops with Rickshaw Paintings
12 Hotel Metropolitan & Fresh Pots Restaurant	3 Supreme Court	44 Sankhanidhi House Rajbari
15 Hotel & Restaurant Mrigaya	4 Ministry Of Foreign Affairs	45 Radna-Krishna Temple & Bhajahari Lodge Rajbari
23 Hotel & Restaurant Ramna	5 Old High Court	
	6 Shishu Acadamy	
36 Hotel Grand Palace International	7 Curzon Hall	46 Chowk Bazar Shahid Mosque
40 Hotel & Restaurant Al-Razzaque International	8 Musa Khams Mosque	47 Kartalab Khan's Mosque
	9 Shahid Minar	48 Bara Katra
43 Hotel Sugandha International	11 Passport & Immigration Office	49 Chota Katra
	16 Ministry of Home Affairs	50 Star Mosque (Sitara Mosque)
PLACES TO EAT	17 Baitul Mukarram Mosque (National Mosque)	51 Armenian Church
		52 River Mosque
13 New Cafe Jheel	18 BRTC Bus Station	53 Badam Tole Boat Terminal
14 Cafe Baghdad	19 Stadium Arcade	
22 Ruchita Restaurant	20 GPO	54 Ahsan Manzil Museum (Pink Palace)
24 Hotel Rajhani & Hotel Dawn	21 Osmani Auditorium	
37 Hamburger Restaurant	25 Banga Bazar (Gulistan Hawker's Market)	55 St Thomas Church
38 Cafe Al-Razib	26 Business Centre	56 Bahadur Shah Park
39 Hotel Nigar	27 Gulistan (Fulbaria) Bus Station (Local Buses)	57 Rickshaw Assembly Shops
42 Mili Restaurant (Tandoori Bread Oven) ·		58 St Gregory's Church & School
	28 Dhakeswari Temple	59 Baby Taxi Stand
OTHER	29 Khan Mohammad Mirdha's Mosque	60 Sadarghat Market
	30 Lalbagh Fort	61 Lalkuthi Rajbari (Northbrooke Hall)
1 Dhaka University & British Council Library	31 Hussaini Dalan	
	32 Tall Mosque	62 Sadarghat Boat Terminal
	33 Central Jail	
	34 Gulistan (Fulbaria) Bus Station (Inter-City Buses)	63 Ruplal House Rajbari
	35 Business Centre	

location in Jafarabad. Getting here is quite simple. As the crow flies, it's four km west of the National Assembly. Head north from Dhanmondi on Mirpur Rd to Asad Gate, take a left through it and go to the end of the road (two km), then take a right (north) and begin asking; it's nearby, towards the river.

Suburban Dhaka

Mirpur Zoo On the north-western outskirts of Dhaka, 16 km from the city centre, is Mirpur Zoo (☎ 382-020). If you want to see a Royal Bengal tiger, come here as you're unlikely to see one elsewhere in the country, including the Sundarbans. The zoo contains over 100 species of animals, including lions, leopards, monkeys, chimpanzees, African hippos, crocodiles, swans, bears, owls, wallabies, langurs and hyenas. The zoo has been improving slowly since opening in 1964. Unfortunately, there's a certain amount of tiger-taunting, monkey-mocking and the like by visitors, who number in the thousands each day. It's open daily between 6 am and 6 pm, and admission is Tk 5.

Some of the best wildlife here is the birds. There is a large lake within the northern perimeter of the zoo. During the winter, this area is a rich habitat for a great number of ducks, cranes and other waterfowl, both wintering and migrant species. Migratory birds such as bar-headed geese, shelduck, pintails, shovelers, cotton tils, widgeon and whistling duck are among the species you're likely to see at the lake. During the high season in January, the noise is deafening and the variety exciting.

To get here, take a bus from Farm Gate or Gulistan bus station to Mirpur via Begum Rokeya Sarani Ave. The route does not, unfortunately, run directly to the zoo, but stops short by a couple of km. Remind the conductor of your destination and take a rickshaw from the drop-off point (Tk 5).

Botanical Gardens Next to the zoo, these shady tranquil gardens stretch over 40 hectares and contain over 1000 species of local and foreign plants, including around 100 varieties of roses. If you're looking for respite from the city's mass of humanity, come and enjoy the serenity here. In the distance you'll see the Turag River. Before 7 am, you'll encounter virtually no one here other than, perhaps, some young men jogging or doing other exercises. It's open every day from dawn to dusk. The entrance is just next to the zoo's entrance.

These gardens are probably the best place in the city for bird-watching. The quiet early mornings are especially good. For bird-watchers keeping count, you can spot as many as 40 species in a single, three hour visit. Be forewarned though, if you happen to chat with the director of the gardens, don't mention bird-watching because it 'ruffles his feathers'. He'll adamantly declare that this is a 'botanical' garden and no place to come for viewing birds, and will send you next door to the zoo!

Art Galleries

For the country's best modern art, head for Gallery Tone (☎ 868-447) at House 29/B on Road 1 in Dhanmondi. Leading Bangladeshi abstract artists who exhibit here include Shahabuddin, who is best known for his bold drawings, Khalid Mahmood Mithu, a well known Dhaka photographer and artist, and Kanak Chanpa, a Chakma from the Chittagong Hill Tracts. Other leading artists are Mahbubur Rahman (sculpture) and Ranjit Das and Mahmudul Huq (abstract oils). It's open daily from 10 am to 8 pm, closed Friday.

You'll find lots of art galleries at the two storey DIT II Shopping Centre on Gulshan Ave. These include the Tivoli Art Gallery (☎ 601-847), Hoque Handicrafts (☎ 601-383), Saju Art Gallery (☎ 602-513), Yeart Art Gallery (☎ 606-944) and Nazart's (☎ 603-931); the quality of the art work is highly variable. La Galerie (☎ 600-589) at 54 Kemal Ataturk Ave in Banani, over La Dolce Vita Gelateria, is another gallery worth a look. For displays of work by students, check the Zainul Gallery at Dhaka University's Institute of Fine Arts.

Swimming

Non-guests can use the pools at the Sonargaon and Sheraton hotels for Tk 400.

Language Courses

The Heed Language Training Centre in Dhaka is the best place for lessons in Bangla. See the Language Courses section in the Facts for the Visitor chapter for more information.

Organised Tours

Parjatan's tour division (☎ 317-836, 817-855/6; fax 817-235), Airport Rd north of the intersection with Bijoy Sarani Ave in Tejgaon offers two city tours. The two hour tour includes Dhaka University, the Old High Court, Motijheel commercial district, the National Mosque and several gift shops. The three hour tour includes Sadarghat boat terminal, Bahadur Shah Park, Lalbagh Fort, Ashan Manzil Museum (the Pink Palace) and the National Museum. Each tour costs Tk 400 a person. For an extra Tk 200 per person (Tk 400 with lunch), you can extend the three hour tour to include some outlying areas such as Old Sonargaon to the south or Savar and Dhamrai to the north. You must have a group of at least 10 people, but individuals might be able to tag along with a group.

You can engage individual guides at Parjatan, usually on the condition that you hire a car and driver as well, but don't expect them to know much about the city's poorer districts.

There are several other companies offering city tours which don't require so many people. The company with the best reputation is The Guide (☎ 836-338), 47 New Eskaton Rd, Mogh Bazar. The minimum group size is four people and tours are offered on Saturday, Sunday and Tuesday. The price for a half-day tour is Tk 500 per person (Tk 850 for a full-day tour). The Travellers (☎ 814-493), 78 Kazi Nazrul Islam Ave, charges Tk 450 a person for a comprehensive half-day tour and Tk 750 for a full-day tour, including lunch (Tk 1050 for a tour including Old Sonargaon). You could also try Unique Tours & Travels (☎ 882-296; fax 883-392), 51/B Kemal Ataturk Ave, Banani.

Alternatively, hire a rickshaw and navigate your way around. The going rate is about Tk 40 per hour. Rickshaw wallahs who speak English can generally be found outside five-star hotels. Hotel Purbani in Motijheel is a good place to look because of its proximity to Old and central Dhaka. These guys charge around Tk 60 per hour and expect a tip. Convincing them that sex and drugs aren't on the itinerary can be difficult.

River Trips There are several companies offering trips on nearby rivers. The best trip is offered by The Guide. On Tuesday, Thursday and Sunday, it offers a 4½-hour cruise on the Sitalakhya River on its yacht, the *S B Rupshoi*, departing from Demra. The van from Dhaka leaves at 4 pm, returning around 10 pm. You'll get to stop at a village of *jamdani* (muslin cloth) weavers en route, and swimming is also possible. The Tk 800 per person cost includes dinner on board. This trip is also conducted during the day on Wednesday. The minimum-size group is four people. The Travellers arranges trips on the Buriganga River.

The tour division of the Parjatan (☎ 327-842, 817-855/6) offers a five-hour cruise on the *M L Shalook* on the Sitalakhya on Friday and Saturday, but only for groups of at least 10 people. The boat departs from Paglaghat (near Narayanganj) at 10 am and returns at 3 pm. Buses leave from the Sonargaon and Sheraton hotels at 9.10 and 9.15 am respectively. The tour costs Tk 500 a person and includes snacks, lunch and a cultural performance. When booking, which is necessary, you might ask how many people are signed up. When full, this small double-decker boat, which seats 72 people, has far too many people for comfort.

Places to Stay

Accommodation is more expensive in Dhaka than elsewhere in Bangladesh, but it's still cheap. The highest concentration of bottom-end and mid-range hotels is in the central area extending from Inner Circular Rd down to Old Dhaka. It's within walking distance of Motijheel, Old Dhaka and a number of parks and attractions. Unfortunately, most of the bottom-end hotels in this area don't accept foreigners, so finding a cheap place here can be quite frustrating.

Another major hotel area is further north, between New Elephant Rd and Farm Gate; the city's top three and several mid-range hotels are there as well as numerous restaurants. You'll get much better value, however, staying in the greater Gulshan area, where all the top restaurants are located. There are roughly 20 guesthouses there and most frequent travellers to Dhaka prefer them.

If you arrive late at night by plane, one option is to stay at the airport. Leave the arrival area (but not the building) and go upstairs to the departure area where you'll find a waiting room. Although there are only moulded plastic chairs, it gets you out of the crowds for the night. The cost is Tk 20.

Places to Stay – bottom end

Old Dhaka Most places in Old Dhaka refuse foreigners, including virtually all of the 10 or so hotels along Nawabpur Rd. One that bucks the trend is *Hotel Sugandha International*, 243 Nawabpur Rd, one km south of the stadium. The small, clean rooms cost Tk 75/120 for singles/doubles with fans, soft mattresses and attached bathrooms. The *Kauica Hotel* further north at 135 Nawabpur Rd has dreadful singles for Tk 60. It generally refuses foreigners but has been known to drop this policy.

The well marked *Hotel Al-Razzaque International* (☎ 244-424) at 29/1 North-South Rd, 600m south of Gulistan Crossing, is also friendly to foreigners. Small singles/doubles with attached bathrooms cost Tk 100/190. It's neat and has reasonably soft mattresses, plus it has one of the area's best restaurants.

For really cheap accommodation, typically Tk 50/70 for singles/doubles, there are a number of places you could try. They never see foreigners, so in their shock they might just agree to take you. These include *Hotel Al Mamun* at 31 Najin Ubidin Rd, near the north-east corner of the jail (no females); *Hotel Chan* in Chowk Bazar at 17 Water Works Rd (the continuation of Islampur Rd),

one block north and west of the Bara Katra; *Hotel Moir*, a few blocks north-west of Sadarghat at 77 Patuatuliy Rd near the corner of Simpson Rd; *Hotel Al Fazal*, east of Nawabpur Rd in a lane off Tipu Sultan Rd, and *Hotel Mesbah*, south of Baldha Gardens at 48 Narinda Rd.

Central Dhaka You'll find lots of cheap hotels along Topkhana Rd near the GPO but none of them, including the *Chand*, *Jewel* and *Mrigaya*, accept foreigners. If you're determined, try the *Asia Hotel* (☎ 240-709), up a side alley at 34/1 Topkhana Rd. It has singles/doubles for Tk 90/160 and on rare occasions has accepted foreigners.

Hotel Al-Belal (☎ 408-836) on Inner Circular Rd, just west of DIT Extension Rd, accepts foreigners. It charges Tk 100/150 for singles/doubles.

Women could try the *YWCA Hostel* (☎ 503-600) at 10 Green Square, Green Rd, next to its office at 13 Green Square.

If you arrive late at night at Gabtali bus station, you could stay at the well marked, six storey *Hotel Turag* across the street. It charges Tk 130/150 for singles/doubles, and is reasonably decent.

Places to Stay – middle

Central Dhaka It's hard to beat the well marked *Hotel Grand Palace International* (☎ 233-920) on North-South Rd, a block south of Gulistan Crossing. It's a clean new place with tidy, ventilated rooms for Tk 220, and they welcome foreigners. The entrance is on a side street.

Hotel Dawn is three blocks north on Bangabandhu Rd (the continuation of Nawabpur Rd) on the corner with Rajuk Ave. Professionally run, it has good ventilated rooms for Tk 300 with western-style toilets and hot-water showers. It even provides toilet paper, soap and towels! It's a seven storey building, and rooms high up are reasonably quiet.

A block west and 100m north along North-South Rd (the official address is 45 Bangabandu Ave), you'll find the popular *Hotel Ramna* (☎ 242-640). It charges Tk 150/260 for clean and well equipped singles/

doubles with hot-water showers, and has a large comfortable reception area with TV. Reception is on the 2nd floor and can be difficult to find in the maze of tailor shops – take the lift.

Hotel Pritom (☎ 250-380) and *Hotel Metropolitan* (☎ 257-357), a few blocks north over Topkhana Rd, are not highly recommended. Singles/doubles at the Pritom, which are fairly old and dark, cost Tk 225/380 and seem way overpriced. The Metropolitan is not as good but it's a better buy at Tk 170/285 for singles/doubles.

Further north along Inner Circular Rd, east of DIT II Extension Rd, you'll find several hotels which are far better value for the money. One is seven storey *Hotel Eastern* (☎ 410-090/1; fax 834-992) at 12 Inner Circular Rd (or Fakirapool Rd). The Green Line bus (to Chittagong) has its office here. This friendly new place has comfortable beds and new bathrooms. Singles/doubles cost Tk 140/230.

The popular *Hotel Parabat* (☎ 408-273) nearby has decent singles/doubles for Tk 150/250, while *Hotel Arina* (☎ 414-960) next door has singles/doubles for Tk 115/180 to Tk 200.

Hotel Blue Nile is on New Elephant Rd and not easy to spot; look for the well marked Coffee House across the street. For a double with attached bathroom it charges Tk 250, which may be negotiable. It's friendly and has a decent restaurant.

For a few more taka, you can get quite decent accommodation. In Motijheel, try the new *Hotel Pacific* at 120/B Motijheel, just north of Dilkusha II Circle. It'll probably be a very decent mid-range place when finished. *Hotel Midway International* (☎ 407-568; fax 835-360), one km north-west at 30 Inner Circular Rd (Nayapaltan), features parking and a doorman. It charges Tk 350/500 for new singles/doubles. The rooms are not spacious but they are spotless and have armchairs and desks, and there's a restaurant.

If you'd rather be further north, try the new *Hotel Super Star* (☎ 813-778, 328-789) at 44/A Kazi Nazrul Islam Ave in Kawran Bazar, one long block north of the Sonar-

gaon. A narrow six storey brick building with an elevator, it has air-con singles/doubles for Tk 500/900. Doubles are large rooms with satellite TV, armchairs, jute carpets and tiled bathrooms. There is also a restaurant.

The *MCC Guesthouse* (☎ 813-439), run by the Minnonite Central Committee on Mirpur Rd (☎ 310-486), is the best deal of all but it only has three rooms. It's located one km west of the National Assembly at 8/13 Sir Syed Rd in Mohammadpur near the office and is poorly marked. Rooms cost Tk 200 a person, plus there's a relaxing sitting area. Meals are Tk 50 (Tk 30 for breakfast).

Don't overlook the top-end hotels; many have 'economical' units and are excellent value for the price: the *Sundarban Hotel* (☎ 505-055/6; fax 863-341), just west of the Sonargaon, has units without a phone or TV for Tk 600/720 and the *White House Hotel* (☎ 834-601), 155 Shantinagar Rd, one km north of Motijheel, charges Tk 480/600 for units without TV.

Gulshan Area One of the cheapest guesthouses in Gulshan is the *Metro Guest House* (☎ 882-319) at House 46 on Road 29. It charges Tk 800/1000 for singles/doubles with satellite TV, air-con and full-size baths. The small sitting room serves as the dining area. The menu includes curries, Chinese dishes and a few sandwiches.

Cheaper still, but not as good, is the *Gulshan Guest House* (☎ /fax 886-451) at House 99 on Road 37, between DIT I and DIT II. It charges Tk 450/650 for carpeted singles/doubles with fans and Tk 800/950 with air-con and colour TV; the price includes breakfast but not tax (15%).

Places to Stay – top end
Central Dhaka Top honour goes to the 325-room *Sonargaon Hotel* (☎ 811-005, 812-011; fax 813-324), Mogh Bazar. It charges US$150/Tk 6000 plus 32.5% tax for deluxe rooms with cable TV. Amenities include a pool, tennis court, squash court, health club, car rental, disco and shopping arcade. Further south on the same road the older 256-room *Sheraton Hotel* (☎ 863-391; fax

832-915) has the same amenities except a disco. Its standard rooms cost US$182/Tk 7400, including tax.

The large Hotel Purbani International (☎ 955-2230/1; fax 956-2314) in the heart of Motijheel has singles/doubles for Tk 1800 to Tk 2200/2600 including tax (Tk 2600 to Tk 3000/3400 for superior/deluxe units with satellite TVs and minibars). Rooms include full-size baths. Built in the 1960s, it lacks the glitz of other top-end places but it's quite pleasant, accepts all credit cards, and features a bar and two restaurants.

The new *Hotel Razmoni Isha Kha* (☎ 400-140/1; fax 835-369) on Kakrail Rd, 1½ km north-west of Motijheel, charges Tk 1300 (Tk 1600 with a matrimonial bed) plus 5% tax for a carpeted room, including satellite TV, minibar, phone and modern bathrooms with tubs and showers. It is not as conveniently located as the Purbani but it's very presentable. At the time of writing a pool was under construction.

The five storey *Sundarban Hotel* (☎ 505-055/6; fax 863-341), just west of the Sonargaon, charges Tk 1000/1400 for singles/doubles and Tk 1400/1680 with air-con. All units are reasonably spacious and have small TVs, telephones, relaxing armchairs, carpets and large bathrooms.

For cheaper accommodation, try the *White House Hotel* (☎ 834-601) at 155 Shantinagar Rd, one km north of Motijheel. It has rooms with satellite TVs, a business centre and a restaurant; singles/doubles with air-con cost Tk 900 to Tk 1000/Tk 1100 to Tk 1200.

In Dhanmondi, your best bet is the *Ambrosia Guest House* (☎ 501-505), House 17, Road 3. It has singles/doubles for Tk 1200/1400 including tax, breakfast and laundry service. The homely *Care Guesthouse* (☎ 867-295), House 55, Road 5, is beautifully located overlooking Dhanmondi Lake. Run by Care, priority is given to workers of aid organisations. To enquire, call the Care office (☎ 814-195/6).

There are two possibilities on Mohakhali Ave: the Parjatan *Hotel Abakash* (☎ 607-085/6) at 83 Mohakhali, which has air-con rooms with TVs for Tk 1065, and the 100-room *Hotel Zakeria* (☎ 601-172), a block away at 35 Mohakhali, with rooms ranging in price from Tk 450 to Tk 1200 plus a bar and air-con Chinese restaurant. In nearby Gulshan you can find better guesthouses for only slightly more.

Gulshan Area The greater Gulshan area, including Banani and Baridhara, has a large number of guesthouses which offer a cosy ambience and much cheaper rates than the Sonargaon, and they are in the best restaurant area. Prices in this section include breakfast and tax.

One of the best run and best maintained places is the *Tropical Inn Guest House* (☎ 605-512, 604-145; fax 883-941), House 19, Road 96, Gulshan. Air-con singles/doubles cost Tk 2350/2875, including laundry, mineral water in the rooms and afternoon snacks. Rooms include phones, satellite TVs and VCRs. It has a good restaurant (curries, Chinese and western dishes) overlooking a garden area with a fountain and outdoor seating.

The *Green Goose Guest House* (☎ 608-222), House 30, Road 38, Gulshan, charges Tk 1725/2070 for air-con singles/doubles, including laundry. Rooms have satellite TVs, ceiling fans, minibars, sofas and armchairs. The outdoor garden area overlooking Banani Lake is well maintained, and there's a dining area with Chinese cuisine.

Eastern House (☎ 882-808; fax 886-298) at House 4, Road 24, between DIT I and DIT II, charges Tk 1610 to Tk 1840 which includes local calls, satellite TV and airport transportation. The restaurant features English, Chinese, Italian and Japanese cuisines.

The popular *Le Chateau* (☎ /fax 882-148) at House 10 on Road 62, charges Tk 1800/2000 for singles/doubles (Tk 2200 for suites), including dinner, machine-washed laundry, local phone calls, tea and coffee. Rooms have air-con, cable TV, minibars, phones and baths. Once called the 'White House II', it shouldn't be confused with the *White House* (☎ 601-566; fax 832-286) at House 5 on Road 68 behind the American

Club. It charges Tk 1400/1800 but is a bit dingy and not recommended.

In Banani, try *Sarothi Guest House* (☎ /fax 886-352) at House 49, Road 11. It has rooms for Tk 1250 (Tk 1800 for deluxe), but offers 15% to 30% discounts for stays of more than one day. Rooms have satellite TVs and minibars. It has a dining room with Bangladeshi and Chinese selections.

Rosewood Guest House (☎ 606-985, 886-327; fax 883-784), House 54, Road 16, Banani, has singles/doubles for Tk 1200/1700. Rooms are quite clean and have hot showers (Tk 2000 with full baths), air-con, satellite TVs, minibars and phones. The restaurant offers a wide selection of Chinese and western dishes.

In Baridhara, try the *Golden Inn* (☎ /fax 883-849), House 30, Road 10. For comfortable air-con singles/doubles with satellite TVs and minibars, it charges Tk 1200/1400 (Tk 1600 for super deluxe).

Places to Eat
Local & Fast Food In Old Dhaka, it's hard to beat the popular *Hotel Al-Razzaque International* at 29/1 North-South Rd, 600m south of Gulistan Crossing. There's no menu but some of the waiters speak English. You can get good rice chicken (or mutton or fish) for Tk 30, and biryani and other dishes. It has overhead fans to blow away the flies and freshen up the place. Women eat in separate cabins with curtains. You'll find cheap eateries along Nawabpur Rd to the east, in particular *Cafe Al-Razib*, which gets lots of customers.

In the modern section, try the *Hotel Rajhani* on the corner of Bangabandhu and Rajuk aves. It's a good-size place and very popular. Some travellers recommend the restaurant on the 7th floor of *Hotel Ramna* on North-South Rd as a good way to get away from the street noise and view the city. One block further north from Hotel Ramna and to your right is the *Ruchita Restaurant*, which has Bangladeshi, Chinese and English dishes, mostly in the Tk 30 to Tk 60 range, such as Chicken dopiaza (Tk 60) and vegetable chow mein (Tk 50). The

ambience here is a bit dark and dreary; however, it is reportedly possible to buy alcohol here, so it might be worth stopping by if you're thirsty – no promises. The bar is a meeting place for student politicians.

For good food and clean surroundings, it's hard to beat the popular *New Cafe Jheel* further north on Topkhana Rd, 200m west of North-South Rd. It has fresh hot Indian naan bread (Tk 3), chicken tikka (Tk 25), fried chicken special (Tk 30), rice (Tk 5) and beef kebabs.

There are numerous other late-night restaurants here worth checking, including *Cafe Baghdad* at 20 Topkhana Rd, which serves delicious hot kebabs right off the grill with sauce for Tk 6 each. *Fresh Pots Restaurant* around the corner on North-South Rd features primarily Chinese cuisine. Most dishes are in the Tk 50 to Tk 70 range, such as sweet and sour fish (Tk 60), but many dishes on the menu aren't available and the service is slow.

Over in Motijheel, there's another *Cafe Jheel* on the corner of DIT Extension Rd and Motijheel Ave. Two blocks down Motijheel is the *Crescent Garden Restaurant*. It's also very popular and a bit more upmarket, with chicken biryani (Tk 60), mutton curry (Tk 70) and chicken curry (Tk 52), among other dishes. *Hotel Park* just north of Dilkusha II Circle is another popular place and displays a menu outside, including chicken biryani (Tk 30), vegetable biryani (Tk 35) and chicken masala (Tk 35).

There's also cheap food to the north along Inner Circular Rd east of DIT Extension Rd where the Chittagong buses leave from, such as *Gausia Restaurant*. *Pizza Land*, a block further west on Inner Circular Rd, has pizza (pronounced 'peeja') for Tk 50 and Tk 75. As everywhere in Dhaka, they are ready-made and fairly dreadful.

In the Hotel Sonargaon area, try *Cooker's-7 Fast Food Restaurant*, 200m north of the hotel. It has lots of dishes in the Tk 20 to Tk 40 range, including hamburgers (Tk 25), chicken sandwiches (Tk 25), fried rice (Tk 20) and chicken and vegetables (Tk 25). *Pizza Garden* one block south of the Sonargaon has standard ready-made pizzas.

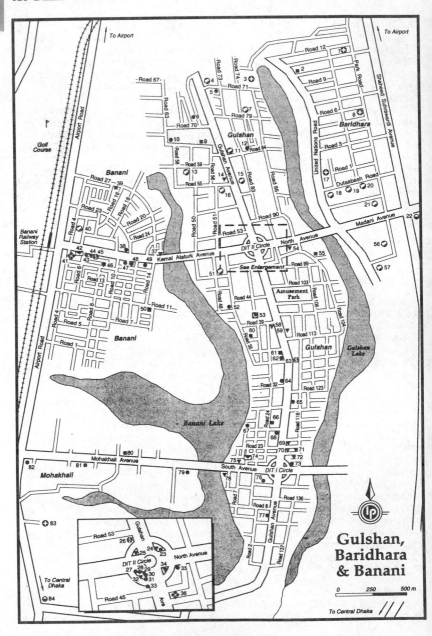

Gulshan,
Baridhara
& Banani

0   250   500 m

To Central Dhaka

Farm Gate and Mogh Bazar are also good areas for finding local restaurants and samosa stalls.

The Coffee House, on the 1st floor at 73 New Elephant Rd (as the sign says 'enter back side'), has relatively expensive fast

PLACES TO STAY		75	Sajna Restaurant	40	Myanmar (Burma) Embassy
		78	Aangan Restaurant (Indian)	41	UAE Shopping Centre/Banani Mall (24-Hour Pharmacy & Aarong Handicrafts)
2	Golden Inn Guesthouse				
9	Le Chateau	**OTHER**			
23	Hotel Regent				
39	Rosewood Guest House	1	Dr Wahab's Clinic	42	GPO & Petrol Station
50	Sarothi Guest House	3	Gulshan Hospital	45	Standard Chartered Bank & Chinese Laundry
55	Tropical Inn Guest House	4	Pakistani High Commission		
60	Green Goose Guest House	5	Bagha Club (British)	47	La Dolce Vita Gelateria
61	Gulshan Guest House	6	American Club	48	Banani Market
66	Eastern House	7	Italian Embassy	49	Saptagram Nari Swanirvar Handicrafts
80	Hotel Zakaria	8	British High Commission Medical Centre (Elizabeth House)		
81	Hotel Abakash (Parjatan)			51	Canadian High Commission & CIDA
		10	Japanese International Cooperation Agency (JICA)	52	University Press Bookshop & Cafe
PLACES TO EAT				53	Gulshan Central Mosque
14	Arirang Restaurant (Korean)	11	Australian High Commission	56	American Embassy & USAID
24	Leung Hung Chinese Restaurant	12	European Union (EU)	57	Nepalese Embassy
25	Ninfa's Restaurant & Landmark Shopping Centre	13	Thai Embassy	62	Kumudini Handicrafts
		15	German Embassy	63	ANZ/Grindlays Bank, British Airways & Rose Garden Guesthouse
		16	Danish Embassy & Danida		
29	Kintuki Restaurant, Newsstand & Pearl's Jewellery Shop	17	US Embassy Medical Unit (Suvastu House)		
		18	British High Commission & Club; ODA	64	Uttama Handicrafts
32	Don Giovanni's Sizzler Restaurant			65	Pollywog (Yoghurt, Brown Bread, Cookies, Peanut Butter)
		19	Japanese Embassy		
34	Pizza Palace, Plaza Restaurant & Zafrani Biriani Restaurant	20	Chinese Embassy		
		21	French Embassy	67	German Technical Cooperative Agency (GTZ)
		22	Baby Taxi Stand		
37	Kushum Restaurant	26	American Express & Singapore Airlines	68	Canadian Club
43	Sky Room Restaurant			73	Travel Channel
44	White Castle Restaurant	27	Lucky Enterprise Fax Centre	74	GPO
				76	DIT I Market
46	Shangri-La Restaurant	28	Monno Ceramics & Federal Express Couriers	77	IDEAS International Handicrafts & Bookshop
54	Seoul Garden Restaurant (Korean) & DHL Couriers	30	Fuji Color & Brightway Business Centre		
				79	BRAC Headquarters
		31	Kodak Photo Shop & Good Tailors	82	Dhaka District Forestry Office
58	King's Kitchen Restaurant	33	Sausly's (German Meat Shop)	83	ICDDRB Hospital & Traveller's Clinic
59	Wakhana Japanese Restaurant	35	DIT II Market		
69	Candy Floss	36	DIT II Shopping Centre	84	Mohakhali Bus Station (Mymensingh & Tangail Buses)
70	Mollika Snacks	38	Unique Tours & Travels		
71	Lemon Grass Restaurant				
72	Cathay Restaurant				

food – enormous 'jumboo burgers' are Tk 50 – and a fair approximation of cappuccino. It's open from 10 am to 9.30 pm.

In Dhanmondi, there are snack shops along Mirpur Rd, including *Coopers Pastry Shop* opposite Dhanmondi Lake. It has the usual breads, cakes and beef pies, and the standard pizza and hot dogs.

Chinese It doesn't take very long to become totally numbed by the array of Chinese restaurants serving almost exactly the same food at similar prices. They tend to cater to Bangladeshi tastes, so the food is a bit oily and salty – less so at the more expensive establishments. Many of these are in the Gulshan area.

In the city centre there are a number of Chinese restaurants along Inner Circular Rd.

One of the best for the price is *Nightingale Restaurant* (☎ 408-710) at 35/1 Inner Circular Rd, near North-South Rd. Most dishes are in the Tk 70 to Tk 100 range, including hot and sour chicken (Tk 80), fish with vinegar (Tk 95) and beef with vegetables (Tk 100).

The nicely decorated *Sicily Restaurant* (☎ 417-787), slightly further east next to the Midland Hotel, is also quite good and has similar prices, while the *Lan Hua* (☎ 488-886) across the street has a more plastic atmosphere.

Another street known for Chinese restaurants is New Eskaton Rd, a block south of the Sonargaon Hotel. From west to east these include the long-standing *Chop Sticks Restaurant* (☎ 405-245) at No 133, the *Mikado Restaurant* (☎ 404-245) and the *Tai King Chinese Restaurant* (☎ 400-194). Tai King is attractive inside and seems the best. The long menu includes chop suey (Tk 65), sweet and sour prawns (Tk 80) and shredded beef (Tk 100). Prices at the others are similar.

The best Chinese restaurant in this area is *Xian* (☎ 509-021) at 126 Elephant Rd. It features both Chinese and Thai cuisine, and dishes are generally in the Tk 100 to Tk 175 range. The place is a bit dark and there's classical music in the background.

Another area for Chinese restaurants is Dhanmondi, particularly along Mirpur Rd.

The best two are *Chilis Chinese Restaurant* (☎ 817-953), on Mirpur Rd just north of Dhanmondi Lake, and *Xenial* (☎ 818-149), House 365 on Road 16. Prices of dishes at both places are mostly in the Tk 120 to Tk 175 range. Both places are quite attractive, especially the Xenial, and the Chilis also offers a few Thai selections.

If price is your main concern, try these on Mirpur Rd: *Chung King Chinese Restaurant* (☎ 503-979) facing ANZ/Grindlays Bank; *Magdonalds* (☎ 505-891), which has numerous TVs playing while diners eat; *Ming House* (☎ 505-652), which at least doesn't have noisy TVs; and two km north in Mohammadpur, the *VIP Chinese Restaurant*. Most dishes are in the Tk 80 to Tk 100 range and the food is ordinary.

Gulshan Area Restaurants *Pizza Palace*, facing DIT II Circle, serves ready-made pizzas (Tk 50 and Tk 75), hamburgers, hot dogs and sandwiches. The food is far from tasty but the place is clean. On the same block you'll find the *Plaza* (ordinary Bengali restaurant) and *Zafrani Biriani* (mutton biryani, Tk 40). *Mollika Snacks* (superb chokputi, Tk 20, and lassi) and *Candy Floss* (sandwiches and decent cappuccino) are tiny places just north of DIT I Circle. There are also small places at DIT Mall and at Banani Mall on Kemal Ataturk Ave with snack food (samosas, Tk 8).

For a restaurant meal, try the popular *Kintuki*, which faces DIT II Circle. It has an extensive menu and all kinds of food, including good tandoori chicken. A full meal with drinks will cost you under Tk 100.

For grilled steaks, you can't beat the popular *Don Giovanni's Sizzler Restaurant*, which has a fairly rustic laid-back setting. Not cheap, it's just behind Kintuki and is upstairs. It's also the best place for pizza.

For mid-range meals, the city's best restaurants are in Gulshan and Banani, with new ones cropping up almost every month. The top three Indian restaurants are *Sajna* (☎ 603-507) at 10 South Avenue (200m west of DIT I Circle) followed by *Aangan* across the street and *Shehnai* (☎ 870-225) at 53

Kemal Ataturk Ave in Banani. A typical meal costs anywhere from Tk 250 to Tk 500 a person. You can also get good Indian food at *Ninfa's*, which overlooks DIT II Circle in Gulshan.

Among the Thai restaurants, the best is *Lemon Grass* (☎ 882-376), on the corner of Road 126 and Road 131, Gulshan. The menu is extensive and the food is superb. Prices are comparable or slightly higher than those at the Indian restaurants. The new *White Castle Restaurant* (☎ 605-914) at 20 Kemal Ataturk Ave in Banani, on the 15th floor, offers both Thai and Indian cuisine as well as Continental specialities. It's a very elegant and formal restaurant with good views of Gulshan.

The only place in the Gulshan area specialising in Bangladeshi food is the new *Kushum* (☎ 889-518) at 37 Kemal Ataturk Ave in Banani.

For Indonesian food, there's the *Sky Room* (☎ 882-648), 8 Kemal Ataturk, Banani, on the 12th floor of the ABC building.

The best Korean and Japanese food is served at *Arirang*, 12 Gulshan Ave. It's so popular with the local Korean community that it serves as their informal club. Expect to pay Tk 500 a person. For a change of scenery, try the *Seoul Garden Restaurant* (Korean) on North Ave, 150m east of DIT II Circle, or if you're after sushi, try the new *Wakana Japanese Restaurant* at 116 Gulshan Ave near DIT I Circle. Both have received good reviews.

Of the Chinese restaurants, the best are the long-standing *Shangri-La* (☎ 882-025), 35 Kemal Ataturk Ave, Banani (actually a block south of Kemal Ataturk), the *Cathay* (☎ 604-805), House 6, Road 133, Gulshan, and the colourful *King's Kitchen* (☎ 607-563) at 79 Gulshan Ave. Many good new ones, however, are popping up. For crispy noodles our noodle experts tell us the *Leung Hung Chinese Restaurant* is tops; this ordinary-looking place at DIT II Circle is not otherwise recommended.

Top-End Restaurants The fancy restaurants at the Sonargaon and Sheraton are very expensive. Both hotels have large buffet-style breakfasts for around Tk 350. You could eat enough to last until dinner. At the Sheraton, *Cafe Arami* is open around the clock – good for midnight snacks. Both hotels also have bars (as does the Purbani) and excellent but expensive pastry shops.

In Motijheel, the top place for Bengali food is the *Shahana Restaurant* at the Purbani. It features a lunch-time buffet (Tk 385) offering a wide selection of Bengali and Asian dishes. The decor is a bit worn but the food is fine.

The air-con *Kasturi* on North-South Rd opposite the Pritom Hotel is also noted for its Bengali food; a meal there will cost around Tk 100 to Tk 150. The menu includes curries made with a variety of local fish, including rui, koi, pavda, and king-size freshwater lobsters.

Entertainment

Traditional Music & Dance The best place for cultural performances is *Shilpakala Academy* (☎ 864-673/4), which is in the city centre in Segunbagicha, just east of the Supreme Court down a side street, next to the National Art Gallery. The major cultural event of the year is the month-long Asian Art Biennial, which occurs in November. The exhibition, which spills over into Osmani Auditorium and the National Museum, attracts top modern artists and the quality is very high.

For other events, consult the *Daily Star*; it sometimes announces events in advance. Generally, however, you cannot find out about upcoming events through the newspapers, so you'll have to contact them. The people at Shilpakala frequently have no idea of what's being presented that week, even that very night, and the receptionist may speak no English.

Cultural events are also held at *Shishu Academy*, which is south-west of the Supreme Court; the *National Museum* (☎ 505-269), one km north-west of the Supreme Court; *Osmani Auditorium* on Abdul Gani Rd, one km south-east of the Supreme Court; and Dhaka University. Finding out about events is very difficult.

For non-Bangladeshi cultural events

including films, contact the *British Council* (☎ 500-107/8) at 5 Fuller Rd, two km west of the Supreme Court; the *Russian Cultural Institute* (☎ 312-319) on Road 7 in Dhanmondi; the *Alliance Française* (☎ 504-732) nearby on Mirpur Rd, just north of Road 3 in Dhanmondi; the *Goethe Cultural Institute* (☎ 507-325) at House 23, Road 2 in Dhanmondi; and *USIS* (☎ 862-550/1) on the 4th and 5th floors of the Jiban Bima Bhaban building at 10 Dilkusha Rd in Motijheel, just east of the National Stadium.

Discos The city's only disco is at the Sonargaon Hotel.

Bars Various embassy social clubs in Gulshan have happy hours on Thursday nights and special events (usually open only to ticket holders).

Spectator Sport

There are often cricket, soccer or hockey matches at the National Stadium; the spectators are all males.

Things to Buy

Handicrafts The city has numerous handicraft shops, and they all offer a slightly different assortment of textiles (especially local clothing, robes, silk pillow covers and bedspreads), jute products and pottery. The leading handicraft shops are:

Aarong
  UAE Shopping Centre/Banani Mall, Banani (☎ 881-052)
  Corner Mirpur Rd & Manik Mia Ave (☎ 811-607)
  4 New Circular Rd, Mogh Bazar (☎ 401-605)
IDEAS International
  20 Gulshan Ave, Gulshan (☎ 881-383)
Karika Handicrafts
  Paribag Super Market, Kazi Nazrul Islam Rd, opposite Sheraton Hotel (☎ 504-362)
  Sheraton Hotel Shopping Arcade (☎ 863-391)
Kumudini
  97 Gulshan Ave, Gulshan (☎ 884-284)
  Sonargaon Hotel (☎ 811-005)
Saptagram Nari Swanirvar
  60E Kemal Ataturk Ave, Banani (☎ 603-689)
Uttama
  85 Gulshan Ave between DIT 1 and DIT II (☎ 610-596)

IDEAS International, which specialises in textiles, probably has the highest quality items and the widest selection, including the best book division and postcards. One of the cheaper shops is Karika Handicrafts, which has Bangladeshi fabrics and jute products such as wall pieces, bronze work, leatherwork, purses, handbags and jewellery.

Many shops accept credit cards. Most are open daily from 9 to 10 am and close between 7 and 9 pm, closed Friday. Many shops, including IDEAS, Kumudini and Saptagram are also non-profit organisations. Halima Handicrafts (☎ 314-996), 12/24 Sir Syed Rd in Mohammadpur, is a project to help abandoned and widowed women to support themselves and their children by producing goods such as wall hangings, bedspreads, cushions and tablecloths.

The Sonargaon and Sheraton hotels have handicraft shops in their shopping malls and are probably the best places for purchasing jute carpets. You can pay less elsewhere, including from the row of shops on New Elephant Rd, but the selection won't be as good. Kumudini specialises in jute products and Saptagram has clothes.

Other outlets include The Source (☎ 325-979), which features products made of water hyacinth; and Shetuli, which has outlets at the Sonargaon Hotel and at 91 Mohakhali Ave near Gulshan.

For modern ceramics, head for Monno Ceramics (☎ 501-599), which has an outlet at 334 New Elephant Rd in the city centre and at DIT II Circle in Gulshan.

For jewellery, consider items made of white conch shells, particularly bangles. They're made by Hindu artisans in Shankharia Bazar, and are sold at most handicraft shops.

Bangladesh is also noted for its pink pearls; you can find them sold individually and in jewellery all over the city. Reliable shops include Mona Jewellers (☎ 255-126), 28 Baitul Mukarram market in the city centre; Pearl Paradise (☎ 231-860), 20 Baitul Mukarram (and the Sonargaon); and New Pearls Heaven, upstairs at 62/7 Kemal Ataturk Ave in Banani. Baitul Mukarram

Suraiya Tapestries

Suraiya (sou-RYE-ah) tapestries are a unique Bengali art form of hand-embroidered cloth based on exclusive designs by Suraiya Rahman. Her inspiration comes from the traditional *kantha*, an embroidered quilt decorated with Bengali folk motifs. While her copyrighted patterns incorporate many of the traditional motifs, one of her innovations is to tell a story based on Bangladeshi legends, poetry and folklore; her colonial silk tapestries may contain polo players and British rhino hunters.

This unique art form began in 1980 when Suraiya started training women to do the embroidery. The women come from extremely poor backgrounds, and undergo extensive training before they may produce major compositions. They begin with home decoration items like pillow covers and eventually graduate to embroider fine tapestries. Quality control is the sole province of Suraiya, who gives big bonuses when there are no defects. Since she personally supervises the work, she can manage no more than 300 women. The Suraiya showroom is in a private house in Gulshan; call the CLO at the US Embassy (☎ 884-700/9) for directions. It's open Monday and Wednesday from 3 to 6 pm. ■

market is closed Thursday afternoon and all day Friday.

Banga Bazar Dhaka is a fantastic place for purchasing cheap ready-made garments, all of which are produced locally for export. Head for Banga Bazar; it's a block west of Gulistan bus station, at the dividing line between New Dhaka and Old Dhaka. It burned down in November 1995 but it's already back in business. Although some of the clothes are seconds, with small flaws, most are over-runs. The items include cotton shorts (Tk 40), dress shirts (Tk 80 to Tk 100), cotton pants (Tk 100), saris, colourful nylon jogging suits (Tk 260), winter jackets (Tk 300) and blue jeans (up to Tk 200).

Bargaining is required; you can usually get things for a third of the asking price. Speaking a few words of Bangla will help.

Banga Bazar is usually closed on Friday but ask around because schedules are frequently disrupted by strikes. Also, before holidays normal schedules may be disregarded.

New Market & Chandni Chowk Bazar The city's largest market is New Market at the southern end of Mirpur Rd. You can find a bit of everything, including maps of Dhaka and Bangladesh, material, saris and household items. Chandni Chowk, to the east across the street, is best for local fabrics, which vary extensively from the glittery to the more conservative. Both markets are closed on Monday afternoon and all day Tuesday.

Other Markets Stadium Arcade, which is just west of the National Stadium and the National Mosque, has a similar array of items including electrical items and cassettes of local music. It's closed Thursday afternoon and all day Friday.

DIT II Shopping Centre has about 10 antique shops, and DIT I Mall has a few more. Some items, particularly Hindu brass statutes, are small, portable and make good buys. Many items, such as clocks, large wooden chests made in Myanmar (Burma) and old Dutch 'country' china, come from old ships demolished at Chittagong. Asking prices tend to be ridiculously high so shop around and compare prices and variety before purchasing.

Getting There & Away

There are four major arteries leading out of Dhaka. Airport Rd becomes the road north to Tongi and Mymensingh, while Mirpur Rd becomes Aricha highway, leading northwest past Savar towards the Padma River crossing at Aricha. At the southern end of the city, the last roundabout you'll encounter is Jatrabari Circle. Heading south will lead you towards Comilla, Chittagong and Sylhet, while heading west over the Chinese Friendship bridge will bring you eventually to the Padma crossing at Mawa, 40 km to the southwest.

Land travel to western Bangladesh is complicated by ferry crossings; this will change a bit upon completion of the Jamuna Bridge. The main ferry crossing at Aricha adds about three hours to the trip as does the ferry crossing further south at Mawa. By rail a trip to Khulna Division involves an incredibly long circuitous route via Mymensingh.

Air Zia international airport (☎ 894-870), located on the northern outskirts of the city, 12 km from the city centre, handles both international and domestic flights on Biman Airlines. Recently upgraded, the airport has a bank, which is open for most arrivals, and a restaurant, and 'welcome offices' of the Sonargaon, Sheraton and Purbani hotels. There's no left-luggage facility at the airport but there is one at Kamalpur railway station.

Flights on Aero Bengal depart from the old airport on Begum Rokeya Sarani Ave, one km north-east of the National Assembly. Its flights to Barisal cost Tk 950 and are frequently cancelled during the monsoon because of inclement weather.

Offices and agencies for the major airlines include:

Aero Bengal
    House 17, Road 17, Banani (☎ 600-487, 881-145)
    Rajbithi Travels, 99 Karim Chamba, Motijheel (☎ 955-7896, 956-9182)
Aeroflot
    Borak Travels, 12 Dilkusha Rd, Motijheel (☎ 955-9111, 955-9930)
Air France
    Bengal Airlift, 54 Motijheel Rd, Motijheel (☎ 955-3050/9)
Biman Bangladesh Airlines
    Opposite Hotel Purbani, Motijheel; open 9 am to 7.30 pm every day (☎ 956-0151/2)
    Zia international airport (☎ 894-870)
British Airways
    Sena Kalyan Bhaban Bldg, Shapla Circle, 195 Motijheel Ave, Motijheel (☎ 956-4870/1)
    116 Gulshan Ave, Gulshan (☎ 881-154)
Dragon Air
    Between Farm Gate and Sonargaon Hotel, Kazi Nazrul Islam Rd (☎ 812-882, 311-630)
Druk Air (Bhutan Airlines)
    Vantage Travel, Sonargaon Hotel (☎ 817-134/5)
Emirates Air
    64 Motijheel Ave, Motijheel (☎ 956-3825/6)
Gulf Air
    Travel Trade, 10 Kawran Bazar, opposite Sonargaon Hotel (☎ 813-238/9)
    Bengal Airlift, 54 Motijheel Rd, Motijheel (☎ 955-3050/9)
Indian Airlines
    Sheraton Hotel (☎ 863-611, 256-533)
KLM
    4th floor, 10 Kawran Bazar, opposite Sonargaon Hotel (☎ 815-354)
Pakistan International Airways
    Sheraton Hotel (☎ 863-391)
Qantas
    Bengal Airlift, 54 Motijheel Rd, Motijheel (☎ 955-3050/9)
Singapore Airlines
    7th floor, Gulshan Tower, DIT II Circle, Gulshan (☎ 888-769)
Thai International
    Sheraton Hotel (☎ 834-711/2)

Bus There are four main bus stations. The largest is Gabtali bus station on the north-western side of town on Aricha Rd (extension of Mirpur Rd), about eight km from the heart of the city (Tk 5 by bus from Gulistan bus station). It serves destinations in the north-west and south-west, eg Savar, Aricha, Bogra, Pabna, Rangpur, Dinajpur, Rajshahi, Kushtia and Jessore. It's a mad house and you definitely must be on the guard for pickpockets, but in general people are very friendly and helpful.

An express bus costs Tk 5 to Savar, Tk 25 to Aricha and Tk 120 to Kushtia. Express/chair coach bus fares are Tk 100/120 to Bogra, Tk 120/150 to Rangpur, Tk 125/170 to Saidpur, Tk 135/180 Dinajpur, Tk 110/140 to Natore, Tk 120/150 to Rajshahi, Tk 110/160 to Jessore, Tk 130/180 to Khulna and Tk 110/140 to Barisal. The first bus leaves at 7 am. The last buses depart for Dinajpur and Saidpur at 5 pm; for Rangpur, Natore and Rajshahi at 7.30 pm; for Bogra at 8.30 pm; and for Barisal, Jessore and Khulna at 9.30 pm.

Most long-distance chair coaches leave in the evening, typically around 6 or 7 pm; a few also leave in the morning around 7.30 am or so. The ferry crossing at Aricha takes about two hours, and another hour for loading and unloading. One of the best bus companies serving Jessore, Khulna, Khustia and Barisal is Metro Paribahan, which is located at Gabtali, and has expresses and chair coaches including air-con chair coaches to Jessore (Tk 260) and Khulna (Tk 300). New Green Line, which serves Khulna, is another good line but it doesn't have air-con buses. Hasna Enterprise at Counter 41 (☎ 383-903) serves Rajshahi.

For destinations in the south and west Sayedabad bus station is on the south-eastern side of town on Hatkhola Rd, one km before Jatrabari Circle. Express/chair coach fares are Tk 35/55 to Comilla, Tk 70/100 to Maijdi, Tk 90/130 to Chittagong and Tk 110/140 to Sylhet. For Sylhet, check Romar line at Sayedabad bus station. Fares to Barisal, Jessore, Khulna and Kushtia are the same as those from Gabtali. Chair coaches to most destinations depart in the evening around 6 pm. For they depart Chittagong during the day between 7 am and midnight.

For Chittagong, the best chair coach companies are along a block stretch on Inner Circular Rd in Fakirapool, one km north-east of the national stadium. They all charge Tk 110 for chair coaches (Tk 230 with air-con). Green Line (☎ 416-905, 832-465, 409-575), 12 Inner Circular Rd, has departures at 7, 9, 10 am, 1, 3, 4, 5.30, 11.15 and 11.45 pm. The trip takes five hours. The last bus continues on to Cox's Bazar (Tk 350); it takes 10 hours; from Cox's Bazar, it departs at 4 pm.

Two comparable companies are Shahagh Paribahan Bus Lines on 2 Inner Circular Rd and Saudia Bus (☎ 415-581). Shahagh's buses for Chittagong depart at 8, 9.30, 11 am, 2.30, 3.30, 5 and 11.30 pm. Saudia has similar departures, the last being at 10.30 pm.

Many of the companies serving Chittagong also provide express service to Cox's Bazar. Fares are Tk 150 for an express and Tk 190 for a chair coach (Tk 350 with air-con).

Bilash, which serves Maijdi, is also on Inner Circular Rd and has chair coaches (Tk 100) departing at 9, 11 am and 3 pm.

Buses heading north for Gazipur, Mymensingh, Tangail and Jamalpur depart from Mohakhali bus station on Mogh Bazar Rd, Mohakhali, two km south of Banani. There are no chair coaches on these routes. Expresses charge Tk 30 to Tangail and Tk 50 to Mymensingh, and depart throughout the day.

Finally, there's Gulistan (Fulbaria) bus station in the heart of town on North-South Rd at Gulistan Crossing. Most buses depart

---

Leaving Gabtali for Dhaka
When taking a local bus from Gabtali bus station into Dhaka, don't just jump onto the first bus you see. Rather, go down the line until you find one which is nearly full. Buses depart only when full and choosing a near-empty one means you'll spend time waiting while the bus drives around the station looking for passengers – especially frustrating if you've just ended an all-night bus trip. ■

---

from a block east at the chaotic intersection of Bangabandhu Ave and Toyenbee Rd. It's extremely crowded and traffic jams in the area are constant. Most buses are local and people are stuffed into them like sardines. Destinations include greater Dhaka as well as many towns within 30 km or so of Dhaka, such as Mograpara (Old Sonargaon). The government BRTC also has a station (in Motijheel) but it's best forgotten as the service is far inferior to that of the private lines.

Train Dhaka's main railway station is the modern Kamalpur station in Motijheel. Buying tickets is easy and there's a large timetable in English. Double check it for accuracy because the schedules change slightly in the winter and the board may not reflect this. The enquiry counter, which is open until 11 pm, and the Chief Inspector are both helpful. See the Express Trains from Dhaka table for some examples.

Boat Book 1st and 2nd-class Rocket tickets at the well marked BIWTC office (☎ 239-779) in Motijheel, a block east of the Hotel Purbani. It's open Sunday to Wednesday until around 5 pm, Thursday until 2 pm, and is closed Friday and Saturday. There's little printed information in English.

The Rocket ferries usually depart from Badam Tole Ghat, one km north of Sadarghat. However, on occasion they leave from Sadarghat. The departure point will be written on your ticket, but it sometimes

Express Trains from Dhaka

Destination	Departure Time	Duration	Day Off	Fare (1st class/sulob)
Chittagong	7.40 am	6 hours	Wednesday	Tk 310/159
Chittagong	3.00 pm	7 hours	Sunday	Tk 310/159
Chittagong	11.00 pm	7 hours	Monday	Tk 485 (sleeper) Tk 310/147
Dinajpur	8.00 am	13 hours		Tk 410/130
Dinajpur	5.30 pm	14 hours		Tk 410/130
Jessore				Tk 483/160
Maijdi	12.30 pm	6 hours		Tk 240/82
Noakhali	7.20 am	6 hours		Tk 240/82
Noakhali	8.30 pm	8 hours		Tk 240/82
Rajshahi	8.40 am	13 hours		Tk 385/130
Sylhet	8.20 am	7 hours		Tk 274/135
Sylhet	2.35 pm	8 hours		Tk 274/135
Sylhet	10.00 pm	8 hours		Tk 445 (sleeper) Tk 274/135

changes, so get there in plenty of time. The trip to Khulna takes about 33 to 36 hours.

Those travelling deck class may want to ensure a good seat by hiring a boat to get out to the Rocket to stake a place before the hordes arrive. Others have been known to pay a local to occupy a place for them, sitting all day for a fee of around Tk 30.

Departure days (one boat a day) are Monday, Wednesday, Thursday and Saturday, and the departure time is 6 pm sharp. Fares to Khulna are 1st class, Tk 915; 2nd class, Tk 555; inter class, Tk 220; and deck class, Tk 135.

Private launches operate up and down the major rivers but most head south. A cartel of about 30 launch owners runs these services. The Sadarghat boat terminal is only about 200m long, but there are often so many launches docked there that you need to allow yourself some time to determine which one you want. Short-distance launches travel during the day. The large long-distance launches travel at night, arriving at Sadarghat in the morning and remaining there all day until departure around 6 or 7 pm. Tickets are usually sold on board on the day of departure. There are no launches to Chittagong.

Short-distance destinations reached by services from Dhaka include:

Bandura
    Many boats depart on the six-hour trip between 5.30 am and 2.10 pm daily. First/deck class costs about Tk 30/20.

Chandpur (60 km south-east of Dhaka)
    Boats depart hourly between 7 am and 1.30 pm and take five hours. Deck class costs Tk 25 or Tk 30. The best launch on this route is the yacht-like *Mayour* operated by the Flying Birds Corp. It departs from Sadarghat daily at 1.30 pm, and charges Tk 142 for an air-con 1st-class cabin, Tk 50 for 2nd class and Tk 25 for deck class. Another launch on this route is the *MV Matlab*, which departs daily at 12.30 pm and charges Tk 120 for a 1st-class cabin and Tk 60 for deck class.

Munshiganj (25 km south-east of Dhaka)
    There are frequent departures for the two-hour trip. Deck class costs Tk 8.

Srinagar (20 km south-west of Dhaka)
    At least one boat daily, at 11.30 am; it's a five-hour trip and costs Tk 25/15.

Long-distance routes from Dhaka include:

Madaripur (60 km south-west of Dhaka)
    Three launches daily at 8, 8.30, 9 pm. First/deck class costs about Tk 200/40.

Barisal (110 km south of Dhaka)
    Four or five launches leave daily between 6 and 7 pm; the trip takes 12 to 15 hours. Deck class costs Tk 60 but prices of 1st-class cabins, which usually have fans and common bathrooms, vary according to the boat, from Tk 250 to Tk 300 for a single and up to Tk 600 for a double. Two boats which make this run are the *MV Sadia* and the

Jalkaporte. Their 1st-class cabins are inferior to those of the Rocket, which also goes to Barisal four times a week.

Bhola (30 km east of Barisal)
Two launches *(Coco-1* and *Coco-2)* depart daily at 7 and 7.30 pm, and cost Tk 200 per person 1st class and Tk 50 deck class.

Patuakhali (40 km south of Barisal)
Two launches depart daily at 6 and 6.30 pm. First/deck class costs Tk 250/60.

Getting Around

The Airport The cheapest way to get to the city centre is by bus. They're extremely crowded, however, so this may not be a viable option if you have much luggage. You'll find buses out on the main highway, a five-minute walk from the airport. The fare is only about Tk 5 to most destinations, including Farm Gate. After 8 pm you may have difficulty finding one.

To get to the airport, buses and coasters leave Gulistan bus station throughout the day and cost Tk 5.

Baby taxis (auto-rickshaws) have no fixed rates, so you must bargain. Typical costs for most destinations are Tk 50 to Tk 100 (Tk 50 to Tk 70 to Gulshan or Banani). For getting to the airport, fares average about a third less. Rickshaws aren't allowed at the airport or on the major highway (Airport Rd) passing the airport.

The airport has taxis outside. The only other places you'll find them is at the Sonargaon, Sheraton and Purbani hotels, and near the GPO. Coming out of the airport you'll be surrounded by scores of young men offering you rides. This is not a dangerous situation, just a confusing one. Most are not the drivers; they simply help the drivers make the arrangements. There's a fixed-rate taxi booth just outside the airport but Bangladeshis never use it, preferring to bargain down the price with the drivers. Fares to most places in the city, however, are around Tk 400 for foreigners.

In the city centre, you'll find taxis stationed outside both the Sheraton and Sonargaon hotels. Expect to pay Tk 200 to Tk 300 to get to the airport. You can also arrange a car or van to or from the airport

with Parjatan. It offers transfer service between the Sheraton (☎ 509-479) and the airport (☎ 894-416) for Tk 400 (Tk 550 with air-con). Make sure, though, that it has the pick-up time and your address quite clear.

Bus Cheaper than cheap, buses have no signs in English and their numbering is in Bangla. Furthermore, they are always overcrowded so boarding between major bus stops is virtually impossible. Bus fares vary from Tk 0.50 to Tk 5. There are lots of double-decker buses – if you leap on one near the Gulistan bus station you might get an upper-storey window seat and a cheap tour of Dhaka.

The BRTC is now vastly outnumbered by private bus lines. It does, however, operate a number of female-only services. These are distinguished by the word *mohilla* মহিলা ; you can't just go by the number.

Buses to the towns of Narayanganj, Mograpara (Old Sonargaon), Murapara and other outlying towns and villages can be found at Gulistan bus station. If you're heading north-west for Savar and Dhamrai, you must go to Gabtali bus station.

Rickshaw You will find rickshaws everywhere and in crowded streets they're no slower than baby taxis. Aim for a basic fare of about Tk 5 for the first km, and Tk 4 per km after that.

Baby Taxis Although twice the price of rickshaws over short distances, baby taxis and mishuks (the slightly narrower ones without rickshaw art) cost little more for distances of five km or more and they're a lot faster. The baby taxi fare to Gulshan, including some searching for the address, should be around Tk 40 from the main GPO and Tk 50 to Tk 60 from Sadarghat boat terminal.

Tempo Fast and cheap, tempos are convenient if you aren't carrying much luggage and don't mind feeling like a sardine. The close quarters may make women feel uncomfortable. A trip from Gabtali bus station to Farm Gate is around Tk 5.

The Mustans
If you get a baby taxi from one of the larger taxi stands, you may see the driver give a young man a Tk 2 note before departing. This money ultimately goes to one of the *mustans* who wield Mafia-like power over their territories. Baby taxi drivers have to pay for the privilege of using a public space to park. A man carting cargo through a mustan's area may be stopped by one of his lieutenants and forced to pay a small fee for the right to pass on a public street. Roadside food vendors also have to pay regular tolls to mustans. These thugs levy similar tolls on slum-dwellers occupying public lands. Refusal often draws a beating.

Mustans operate all over the country. In Dhaka alone, the number of mustans is estimated to be anywhere between 300 and 1000. Their lieutenants collect money from a large number of sources and operate throughout the city, including Dhaka University. Popular belief is that the most powerful mustans are connected with the major political parties and, if true, this might account for much of the violence on campus. ■

Car A good way to do an all-day tour of the city would be to rent a car; you can do this for as little as Tk 800 (US$20). Renting them outside Dhaka costs only slightly more. All rental cars come with drivers, which is obligatory. Prices include everything except petrol; there are no hidden extras. Your driver can act as a guide as well but don't expect him to know much more than how to get where you want to go. If you go outside Dhaka, you'll have to pay the driver directly for his meals (Tk 50 per meal) and lodging (Tk 50 to Tk 100). All will offer a better deal if you rent for several days or by the month.

Parjatan (☎ 819-193, 319-561) has car rentals for Tk 65 per hour, plus Tk 7 per km and 10% tax (Tk 85 per hour and Tk 10 per km with air-con). It also has minibuses.

There are, however, other places offering better deals:

Max-Taxi
22/3 Block-B, College Gate on Mirpur Rd (☎ 319-107; fax 817-957); Tk 1000 a day, unlimited mileage, for a car or minivan without air-con (Tk 1200 outside Dhaka)
Limousin Rent-A-Car Centre
8/8 Mirpur Rd (☎ 312-667); Tk 1500/1200 for a van (with/without air-con), Tk 1700/1400 for a car. The vehicles are in good condition.
Bangladesh Tours
DIT Rd in Kawran Bazar, next door to the Sonargaon (☎ 313-094); Tk 1200/800 (with/without air-con) for a car (Tk 1500/1000 outside Dhaka) and Tk 1200/2000 for a minibus
Dhaka Tours
3 Link Rd, 1½ blocks south-west of the Sonargaon (☎ 500-979), Tk 1200/1000 for a car

(Tk 1500/1200 outside Dhaka) and Tk 1500/1800 for a minibus. It also has an office on Minto Rd opposite the Sheraton Hotel.

AROUND DHAKA
Many locations in Dhaka Division make good day trips from Dhaka. Here's just a few:

Tongi-Kaliganj Cycling Trail
The crowded town of Tongi (TONG-gee), which is 12 km north of Mohakhali bus station, is a good starting point for a cycling trip. When you cross the Tongi River bridge on the main road north to Mymensingh, go about one km further north into town and turn right. Head east from there. For the first km or so you'll ride past shops and at the three km point you'll cross over the railway tracks, where you'll leave the town behind. The road is good and follows the railway line, so you can cycle all the way to Kaliganj (20 km) on the Sitalakhya River. From there, the easiest solution is to return the same way. Alternatively, you could cross the river just south of town and cycle southward along the eastern bank towards Murapara and the Sitalakhya River bridge just south of Demra (about 30 km from Kaliganj). In the Murapara area the road follows the river closely but at other points it's a good distance from the river, so this trail is not the best. From Demra you can cycle into Dhaka – be prepared for heavy traffic – or catch a baby taxi.

Termouk Trail
A more adventurous back-road route that

connects with the same route (Tongi-Kaliganj Rd) is one via Termouk (tair-MOUK). Heading north towards Tongi, about a km before (south of) the Tongi River bridge you'll pass the last red-light intersection before the bridge. Take a right (east) there for Termouk (seven km), which is a major crossing point (not a village) on the Tongi River. The brick-road route is not direct, so you'll have to ask directions along the way. At Termouk, you can get a canoe to take you across the river; get off on the right (eastern) bank. From there, have someone point you towards Ulukala (ou-LOUK-ah-lah), which is on the same bank and several km to the north. From Ulukala you can continue northward, heading for the Tongi-Kaliganj Rd, which runs east-west. That portion will take about half an hour and you must ask directions (for the Tongi Rd). If you'd prefer to end up at Kaliganj, simply ask directions for that more north-eastwardly route (about 45 minutes). During the rainy season, either way could be slippery.

Tongi River Boat Ride

The Tongi is a great river for taking a boat ride and its proximity to the city makes logistics relatively simple. The Tongi splits off from the Turag River west of Tongi and heads eastward past Tongi to Termouk (six km from Tongi) and then south to Demra on the southern edge of the city just off the Chittagong highway. There, it spills into the Sitalakhya River which, in turn, continues south past Narayanganj.

Even though the Tongi is close to the city, you'll never sense it because of the rural scenery. The only signs are an occasional glimpse of tall buildings in the far distance. The flood season is June to October; during these months the river overflows its boundaries and becomes very wide. During the remainder of the year the river is quite narrow, which greatly facilitates viewing of

life along the river. During the dry season, you'll see irrigated paddy fields everywhere.

The best starting point is the bridge at Tongi. The motorised passenger boats plying the river are called *tolars* (toh-LARS) and can take up to about 50 passengers. The launching point for the tolars is on the northern bank, about 300m west of Tongi Bridge. Most tolars are headed to Ulukala, which costs Tk 5 and is a 1½ hour trip, and is 25 minutes past Termouk, where the river forks. The left fork (a tributary) heads north for Ulukala; the main river (the right fork) heads south for Hardibazar and Demra. From Ulukala, you can either return to Tongi by boat or take a rickshaw for Kaliganj on the Sitalakhya. This takes about 70 minutes (rough dirt roads but great scenery) and costs about Tk 50. At Kaliganj, your options include taking a bus back to Dhaka, the 2nd-class train back to Dhaka via Tongi (ride on top like some local men do), or another tolar to Demra (Tk 15) on the wide Sitalakhya, which takes about 4½ hours. You could shorten the journey, eg you could get off in Murapara (three hours, Tk 10) and catch a local bus back to Dhaka (one hour, Tk 10). Most tolars leave Kaliganj in the morning (just south of town on the western bank) before 9 am but there's also one in the afternoon at 2.30 pm.

Another possibility is trying to go from Tongi to Demra all the way via the Tongi River. This is quite difficult as there are no tolars direct to Demra and you may have to turn around for lack of connections. There are occasionally tolars from Tongi to Hardibazar; get to Tongi by 8 am as the best time to find one is in the early morning. They cost about Tk 7 and take about two hours from Tongi. From Hardibazar, it's very difficult to find onward connections but if you can get to the next few villages by any type of boat, you should eventually find one with onward connections to Demra.

Dhaka Division

Dhaka Division, the most densely populated division of the country, is surrounded to the west, south, and east by the other five divisions, with the Indian border to the north. Except for the Faridpur subdivision, which is west of the Padma, all of Dhaka Division lies east of the mighty Jamuna and Padma rivers and north of the wide Meghna. See the Khulna & Barisal Divisions chapter for information on Faridpur.

History

There are traces of ancient Buddhist settlements in the southern region around Savar and Vikrampur. When Muslim rule was established in northern Bengal in 1204, the Hindu Senas fled southward and settled in Vikrampur. Rivalry with their fellow-Hindu Devas in Sonargaon weakened their resistance against increasing Muslim attacks, and in 1278 Vikrampur fell. Sonargaon lasted another decade and continued as a subsidiary capital, with Gaud as the principal capital city.

In 1338 the Sultanate of Bangala was established, and as maritime trade with South-East Asia flourished, Sonargaon became the capital. According to some chroniclers, the city stretched for 60 km by 30 km at the confluence of the Meghna and the Sitalakhya rivers.

Early in the 17th century the Sultanate of Bangala collapsed under pressure from the Mughals. Sonargaon was taken in 1611 but it appeared too exposed to attacks and Dhaka was chosen as the site of the new capital.

In 1757 the whole of Bangala fell into the hands of the British. With the exception of Dhaka, the Mughal rulers had never attached much importance to this region. Nor did the British during their period of rule show any particular interest in developing it. That is, until jute became a commercially valuable commodity and the northern district of Mymensingh became the centre for growing this 'golden fibre'.

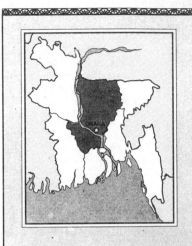

Highlights

- Sonargaon – remnants of an ancient city featuring Goaldi Mosque, and the unique village of Painam Nagar
- Atia Mosque – beautifully restored, with both pre-Mughal and Mughal features
- Mymensingh Rajbari – a truly outstanding rajbari built between 1905 and 1911
- National Martyrs' Memorial – a striking memorial to the millions who died in the struggle for independence
- Baliati Palace – one of the grandest rajbaris in Bangladesh, with over 200 rooms

SONARGAON

One of the best day trips from Dhaka is an excursion to Sonargaon (sometimes known as Old Sonargaon), the country's first capital from the 13th to the early 17th century. An hour away from Dhaka, it's just off the Dhaka-Chittagong highway, some 23 km south-east of Dhaka. In early times, it gained prominence with its ideal location at the confluence of two of the country's three largest rivers, the Meghna and Jamuna, and just up a channel from the Padma. Today these rivers with their gradual course changes no longer afford the site its once special advantage.

Many visitors to Sonargaon mistakenly believe that its buildings are remnants of the ancient capital city. Except for several mosques, a bridge, a few tombs and stupas, and some indistinguishable mounds scattered around the area, nothing remains of the original city.

The area now has two newer but much smaller villages: Mograpara and Painam Nagar. Unfortunately, the archaeological department has done little to preserve the buildings of Sonargaon. Reportedly, some of the poorer occupants sell the bricks from these ramshackle buildings to be broken into gravel for construction work. In the last 23 years, only Goaldi Mosque, a pre-Mughal bridge and a single *rajbari* (zamindari palace), Sardarbari, have been restored.

Mograpara

Located on the Dhaka-Chittagong highway and a thriving village, Mograpara claims most of the remains of the old capital, including the tomb of Sultan Ghiyasuddin Azam Shah (the oldest surviving Muslim monument in Bangladesh!), the Panch Pir Dargah tombs and Fetah Shah's mosque. Most of these are one or two km west of Mograpara. While these monuments are the most numerous remnants of the original capital, they aren't very impressive and most visitors, believing only Painam Nagar to be Old Sonargaon, don't even know they exist.

Folk Art Museum

Sadarbari, built in 1901, is a beautiful rajbari and an appropriate building for a folk art museum. About 50m in length and accommodating more than 50 rooms, this two storey building has two facades. Facing the street, ornamental verandahs, lined with columns and accented by a roof-top band of plaster floral relief overlook a bathing pond. This view, with steps leading down to the water and life-size English horsemen in stucco on either side, is one of the most picturesque in Bangladesh. The other facade, at the museum's entrance, is profusely embellished with a mosaic of broken china and stucco floral scrolls.

Most of the interior is exceedingly plain consisting of small unadorned rooms with various objects and handicrafts on display, including swords, waistbands, necklaces, anklets, beautiful beadwork, fishing baskets, Hindu statues and crude sickles. One room has a whole array of nutcrackers. The Tk 2 entry is a great bargain.

The museum is two km north-east of Mograpara down a narrow paved road, and

---

Sonargaon

The ancient capital of Sonargaon (Golden Town in Hindi) flourished as the region's major inland port and centre of commerce during the pre-Muslim period. By the 13th century it was the Hindu seat of power. With the Muslim invasion and the arrival of the Sultan of Elhi in 1280, its importance magnified as the region's de facto Islamic capital. Some 42 years later, the first independent Sultan of East Bengal, Fakhruddin Mubarak Shah, officially established his capital here.

For the next 270 years, Sonargaon, known as the 'Seat of the Mighty Majesty', prospered as the capital of East Bengal and the Muslim rulers minted their money here. Mu Huany, an envoy from the Chinese emperor, visited Sultan Ghiyasuddin Azam Shah's splendid court here in 1406. He observed that Sonargaon was a walled city with broad streets, great mausoleums and bazars where business of all kinds was transacted. In 1558, famous traveller Ralph Fitch noted that it was an important centre for the manufacture and export of *kantha* (traditional muslin) cloth, the finest in all of India. Ancient Egyptian mummies were reportedly wrapped in this indigo-dyed muslin exported from Bengal.

When the invading Mughals ousted the sultans, they regarded Sonargaon's location along the region's major river as too exposed to Portuguese and Mogh pirates. So in 1608, they moved the capital to Dhaka, thus initiating Sonargaon's long decline into oblivion. Yet its legendary fame for incredibly fine muslin fabric continued undiminished until foreign competition from the British and their import quotas ruined the trade. ■

has a small handicrafts shop. There is a larger display of local crafts at the Handicrafts Centre, 300m further down the same road, on your right.

Goaldi Mosque

Across from the Handicrafts Centre you'll find a winding dirt road heading west towards Goaldi Mosque, one km away. Built in 1519, it's the most impressive of the few extant monuments of the old capital city. A good example of pre-Mughal architecture, it's a graceful single-domed mosque measuring about 10m square, with some original

decorations surviving on the front wall, especially in the three *mihrabs*. The central mihrab (niche facing Mecca), constructed of black basalt, is beautifully embellished with carved floral and arabesque relief, while the side ones are decorated in red brick and fine terracotta work.

Some 50m beyond Goaldi is a second, and historically less important, single-domed mosque, built in 1704 during the Mughal period. Yet another single-domed mosque in the Mograpara area is Fateh Shah's Mosque, which predates Goaldi Mosque by 35 years. It has been renovated rather than restored and, consequently, is not so interesting.

Painam Nagar

Continue past the Folk Art Museum and Handicrafts Centre and you'll come to Painam Nagar. This town is unusual in that its layout suggests that it was planned to foster social cohesion. Constructed almost entirely between 1895 and 1905 on a small segment of the ancient capital city, this tiny settlement consists essentially of a single, long narrow street, less than 500m long, lined with around 50 dilapidated mansions, which were built by wealthy Hindu merchants. At the time of partition in 1947, many of the owners fled to India, leaving their elegant homes in the care of poor tenants who did nothing to maintain them. The remaining owners pulled out during the riots of 1964.

Today, Painam Nagar has a delightful ghost town quality, with its buildings choked with vines and their facades slowly crumbling away. One mansion, Awal Manzil, is a textile factory, while another near the far end, marked 'Sonargaon Art Gallery', is rented from the government by artist Aminul Islam, whose works are on display.

Places to Stay & Eat

There's only one place to stay in the area, the *Tourist Home* in Painam Nagar. No one ever seems to stay here and as a result the owner in Dhaka has clearly lost interest in this place. If you enquire of the caretaker, he may quote you an outrageous price of Tk 1000.

1 Tall Shiva Shrine	10 Danida Project
2 Tourist Home	11 Numerous Small
3 Old Rajbaris	Restaurants
4 Kashinath Bhavan	12 Ananda Sweets Shop
Rajbari	13 Tombs & Mosque
5 Old Rajbaris	14 Tomb of Sultan
6 Mughal-Era Mosque	Ghiyasuddin Azam Shah
7 Goaldi Mosque	15 Tombs of Panch Pir
8 Handicrafts Centre	Dargah & Mosque
9 Sadarbari Rajbari	
(Folk Art Museum)	

Sonargaon Area

With persistence you may be able to lower his sights and the price. There's only one room, which is spacious, with lots of furnishings, a fan and a western-style bathroom.

The caretaker might offer to arrange a meal for you. If not, you can always find food in Mograpara; there are a line of tiny, grubby-looking establishments on the Dhaka-Chittagong highway, just north of the intersection, plus the neater *Ananda Sweets Shop*, which is good for snacks. Most day visitors bring a picnic to enjoy on the lawn outside the museum. This is especially popular with Bangladeshis on Friday. You'll find soft drinks across the street from the museum and public toilets behind it.

Getting There & Away
Bus Buses for Mograpara depart from Gulistan bus station. Look for conductors yelling 'Meghna' (the river just beyond Mograpara); they can drop you off in Mograpara, which is three km before the Japanese Friendship Bridge. The fare is only Tk 10. If you're short of time, get a Comilla bus (about Tk 30) at the Sayedabad bus station (further south at the western end of Sayedabad Rd) and ask to be let off at Mograpara. This will cost you about Tk 30 but you'll find one departing almost instantly.

Car Mograpara is 20½ km south-west of Jatrabari Circle, the Dhaka junction for Comilla and Chittagong. About halfway to Mograpara you'll cross the Sitalakhya River; it's another 11 km to Mograpara, which is the first crowded settlement along the highway after the bridge. If you're lucky, you might see the small 'Folk Art Museum' sign.

MURAPARA
For a full-day outing you can combine a trip to Sonargaon with a visit to the rajbari at Murapara, which is 20 km up the Sitalakhya River from Narayanganj, on the eastern bank. Built in 1889 and now a small college, this rajbari is reasonably impressive, with a 65m frontage overlooking a spacious lawn with the river just beyond.

In the front of the main building, you'll see two small Hindu shrines, both marvellous gems and still in reasonably good condition. Built largely in carved red stone, the attractive stucco decorations and ornate roofs make good backdrops for photographs.

Getting There & Away
Bus Murapara is 26 km from Jatrabari Circle in Dhaka. Buses from Gulistan bus station cost Tk 10. Buses leave from Murapara just south of the college.

Car About 9½ km south-east from Jatrabari Circle, just over the Sitalakhya River, you'll come to a junction where you should take a left (the road to Sylhet) and continue 11 km to Murapara junction, the first major settle-

---

Cycling Around Old Sonargaon & Murapara
For a delightful bicycle day trip that combines peaceful rural scenery with some interesting historical sights and good river views, try the areas around Sonargaon and Murapara. Take your bike by baby taxi to Sayedabad bus station, in Dhaka and catch a Comilla bus (departing every five minutes). Tell the driver you want to get off at Mograpara – he will not know what you mean by Sonargaon.

As you pedal around the greater Sonargaon area, don't limit yourself to Painam Nagar.

Afterwards, head north along the Dhaka-Chittagong highway to the long bridge over the Sitalakhya River (11 km). Just before crossing it, turn right (north) onto the Sylhet road and peddle to Murapara junction (11 km). Cycle west to Murapara (five km) and south along the scenic eastern bank of the river, passing Murapara Palace, back to the junction with the Chittagong road (10 km more). If you can't find a Dhaka-bound bus there, go over the bridge and catch one at the crowded intersection just beyond.

The Chittagong and Sylhet roads can be hair raising with buses flying by, but otherwise there is not much traffic. ∎

ment on this highway. (If you pass a petrol station, you've gone too far.) Take a left (west) to the river, then south along the river through Murapara to the college just beyond.

NARAYANGANJ

If you're looking for a short river trip, consider coming to Narayanganj, which is just 17 km south-east of Dhaka connected by road and rail. Located at the mouth of the Sitalakhya River, it's an excellent place to begin or end a ferry trip. One possibility is catching a boat to Munshiganj, at the mouth of the Dhakeswari River, and another there

for the return trip to Dhaka. You can also catch a ferry all the way down (south) to Chandpur (50 km) on the mighty Meghna River or up the Sitalakhya to Rupganj (20 km, across from Murapara), or Ghorasal (40 km), and then take a train or bus back to Dhaka. The Sitalakhya is much narrower than the Meghna and allows you to see more activity on the banks along the way.

Narayanganj, once the business centre for Sonargaon, is not very interesting. It still maintains some sense of its former trading days, though the port is gradually silting up. Nowadays textiles are the main source of

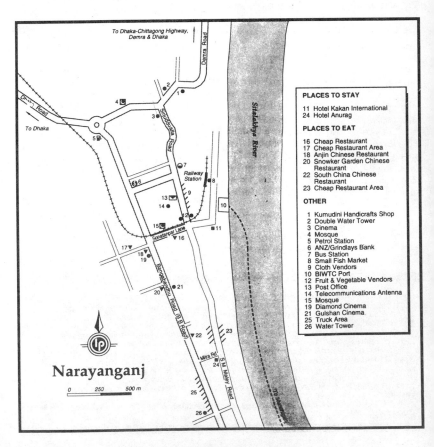

PLACES TO STAY

11 Hotel Kakan International
24 Hotel Anurag

PLACES TO EAT

16 Cheap Restaurant
17 Cheap Restaurant Area
18 Anjin Chinese Restaurant
20 Snowker Garden Chinese Restaurant
22 South China Chinese Restaurant
23 Cheap Restaurant Area

OTHER

1 Kumudini Handicrafts Shop
2 Double Water Tower
3 Cinema
4 Mosque
5 Petrol Station
6 ANZ/Grindlays Bank
7 Bus Station
8 Small Fish Market
9 Cloth Vendors
10 BIWTC Port
12 Fruit & Vegetable Vendors
13 Post Office
14 Telecommunications Antenna
15 Mosque
19 Diamond Cinema
21 Gulshan Cinema
25 Truck Area
26 Water Tower

Narayanganj

industry and the new buildings that house them often hide the remnants of architecture from more illustrious days. Narayanganj remains a major centre of the jute industry, and the handloom industry at Baburhat is known locally as the Manchester of the East.

The most interesting historical sights are two 17th-century Mughal forts along the Sitalakhya River – **Haliganj Fort** and **Sonak-anda Fort** – which were used to defend Dhaka from potential invaders. Both have impressively massive walls and are largely intact. Haliganj, which is on the western bank at Khizirpur, is hexagonal and features a large circular platform used as a cannon mount and a watchtower, while Sonakanda, which is across the river on the eastern bank and 1½ km further downstream (south), is rectangular. To get to either, go to the port in Narayanganj and hire a small motor boat.

Places to Stay & Eat

There are precious few places to stay in Narayanganj. On the corner of S M Maley and Mitra Rds you'll find the four storey *Hotel Anurag* (no English sign). It only accepts men and only has single rooms. They are reasonably clean and have fans and attached bathrooms, but are overpriced at Tk 100. The *Hotel Kakan International* near the BIWTC port does not accept foreigners.

For an inexpensive meal, one of the best areas is just up S M Maley Rd from Hotel Anurag; there are numerous small restaurants. You'll also find a number of inexpensive Bengali restaurants around the corner from, and east of, the Diamond Cinema, which is in the city centre on Bangabandhu Rd.

The city's best restaurants are Chinese and are all located fairly close to one another, on or just off Bangabandhu Rd. Try the *Anjin Chinese Restaurant* around the corner from the Diamond Cinema and one flight up. A block south you'll find the *Snowker Garden Chinese Restaurant* (2nd floor), and further south still, across the street, the *South China Chinese Restaurant*. A typical meal at these places costs around Tk 80. All are clearly marked with signs in English.

Getting There & Away

Bus Buses from Dhaka leave from Fulbaria station, and charge Tk 10 for the nerve-racking one hour trip. In Narayanganj, the bus station is on Sirjuddualla Rd, about 400 km north-west of the BIWTC port.

Train There are trains almost every hour in either direction between Dhaka and Narayanganj; the fare is just Tk 5 (2nd class only). From Narayanganj, the first train leaves at 6.14 am and the last at 9.10 pm; the trip takes an hour. The station is in the city centre, 100m north of the BIWTC port.

Boat The BIWTC port is near the heart of town. There are no direct ferry connections between Dhaka and Narayanganj; however, there are ferries to nearby Munshiganj every 30 minutes between 6 am and 9 pm; the fare is Tk 4. From there you can catch ferries upriver to Dhaka. Periodically throughout the day you can also find ferries heading south to Chandpur (Tk 35), but to ports further south (eg Barisal) you'll have to leave from Dhaka (Sadarghat).

You can also find motor passenger boats heading north up the Sitalakhya. Two of the major destinations are Rupganj (Tk 10) and Ghorasal (Tk 20). Getting back to Dhaka from either town is quite simple as there are numerous buses. The trip takes about 2½ hours to Rupganj and twice that to Ghorasal, and the morning is the best time to find a boat. It might be more fun, however, to catch one of the 2nd-class trains which pass through Ghorasal en route to Dhaka.

AROUND NARAYANGANJ
Munshiganj

Bound on the east and south by the Dhakes-wari, Meghna and Padma rivers, this busy port town is a tiny version of Narayanganj, with old and new buildings, quaint little arched bridges over small creeks and old temples fronted with ponds.

The **Idrakpur Fort** in Munshiganj is half-sunk in the ground but wholly intact. The curious 10m high circular platform may once have been a gun emplacement. Photography is restricted here as the compound houses the jail and the quarters for the Senior Sub-divisional Officer (SDO). Ask the SDO for permission.

Getting There & Away It costs Tk 4 for the 1½ hour launch trip from Narayanganj to Munshiganj. It only costs Tk 7 and takes two hours by boat from Dhaka, but the trip from Narayanganj is more scenic and picturesque than on the industrialised Buriganga. From the launch ghat it costs about Tk 10 by rickshaw to the Idrakpur Fort.

Vikrampur

This little village with traces of ancient Buddhist and Hindu palaces and temples is 12 km west of Munshiganj. It was once the domain of Rajah Chandragupta, king of Ujjain in India. It later became the seat of administration for a Brahmin-Buddhist king named Rampal, the son of Manipala who ruled this part of Bangala from 1084 to 1130. It was to here that Lakshamana Sena fled when his kingdom in Lakhnauti fell to the Khiljis Muslims.

There is a rajbari here, called Rampal, but it's not of major historical interest. There is also a *mazhar* (mausoleum) and the old six domed pre-Mughal mosque of Baba Adam (1483), complete with the usual architectural features of the period. It's a long and bumpy trip by rickshaw from Vikrampur, and will cost at least Tk 50.

SAVAR

A popular day excursion for Dhaka locals is a trip to Savar (SHAH-var). The town, called Savar Bazar, is on the Dhaka-Aricha highway, 15 km north of Gabtali bus station in Dhaka, but the main attraction is the historic Savar memorial, which is eight km further along this highway and just off the road. Tuesday is market day in Savar Bazar, which becomes very animated, especially along the banks of the Bangsi River just west of town.

National Martyrs' Memorial

Savar is home to the Jatiya Shaheed Smriti Sandha, the striking 50m high memorial to the millions who died in the struggle for independence. The beautifully kept grounds contain a number of grassy platforms which cover the mass graves of some of those slaughtered in the War of Liberation. This is a very important place for Bangladeshis and on weekends it gets very crowded. Just across the road there's a reasonable restaurant run by Parjatan and some souvenir stalls, and down the road towards Dhaka is the bus stand.

Snake Charmers' Village

The friendly group of Badhi river gypsies are famous as snake charmers. Their village, Bodapara (or Purabari), is on the outskirts of town along the river and to the north. A few speak English, so asking for a snake demonstration should be no problem. The rather unimpressive performance comes complete with a crowd of interested onlookers, but the

---

Centre for the Rehabilitation of the Paralysed (CRP)
CRP (☎ 06226) 464/5, Dhaka fax (2) 837-969) is an inspired organisation that has been operating since 1975, helping paralysed people develop skills that will enable them to become economically self-sufficient and to cope with life in general. The founder, Valerie Taylor, continues to keep the organisation going with money raised from donations. Today, the number of patients is about 80. There is a sizable Bangladeshi staff whose work is supplemented by volunteers from around the world.
Three of the centre's money-making projects are making crafts for Dhaka handicraft shops, fabricating wheelchairs for the local market and export, and selling milk and eggs. The centre, which is the only one of its kind in the country, is on the north-eastern outskirts of Savar Bazar on the Dhaka-Aricha highway. Visitors are most welcome at this sprawling complex; their various training sessions and workshops are held daily from 8 am to 1 pm and from 3 to 6 pm, closed Thursday afternoon and Friday. Purchasing a few handicrafts is usually possible. ■

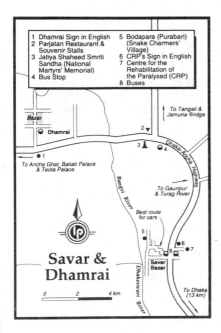

1 Dhamrai Sign in English
2 Parjatan Restaurant &
  Souvenir Stalls
3 Jatiya Shaheed Smriti
  Sandha (National
  Martyrs' Memorial)
4 Bus Stop
5 Bodapara (Purabari)
  (Snake Charmers'
  Village)
6 CRP's Sign in English
7 Centre for the
  Rehabilitation of
  the Paralysed (CRP)
8 Buses

To Tangail &
Jamuna Bridge

Bazar

Dhamrai

To Aricha Ghat, Baliati Palace
& Teota Palace

Bangsi River

Dhaka-Aricha Highway

To Gaunpur
& Turag River

Best route
for cars

Savar &
Dhamrai

Dhaleswari River

Savar
Bazar

To Dhaka
(13 km)

0   2   4 km

DHAKA DIVISION

will probably think you want to go to the memorial further on.

To get to the snake charmers' village, go to the centre of Savar Bazar along the Dhaka-Aricha highway, take the crowded road west through the heart of town towards the Bangsi River as far as you can (1½ km) and then take a right (north) along a dirt track for another 1½ km to Bodapara. If you're driving, the only route available is more complicated but it's paved and quite passable; see the Savar & Dhamrai map for more details.

DHAMRAI

If you're in the Savar area, make a side trip to Dhamrai, which is only five km west of the monument and one km north off the Dhaka-Aricha highway. Known for its brass artisans and *jamdani* (embroidered muslin or silk) cloth weavers, it's a predominantly Hindu town with a friendly atmosphere. Old Hindu homes dress up the place a bit and, unlike Sonargaon with its Raj-era buildings in ruins, most of these, though fewer in number, are in good shape and inhabited by some of the town's wealthier citizens.

On market days, including Saturday, the main drag is lined with vegetable stands. Behind these are where the artisans have their shops. Further on sits the town's multi-storey wheeled Jagannath, which has Hindu myths painted on the sides and is paraded down the street during the *mela* (festival) held here during the full moon in late June/early July. See Hindu Festivals under the Special Events section in the Facts for the Visitor chapter for more information.

variety of snakes is interesting. For this Bangladeshis probably wouldn't pay more than Tk 10, but foreigners will be expected to pay much more. Try to keep the amount to a reasonable Tk 50, so as not to ruin things for future visitors. For a more elaborate performance with dancing, you'll have to pay more but it might be more memorable.

Places to Eat

There is a well marked *Chinese Restaurant* on the main drag in the centre of Savar Bazar.

Getting There & Away

Buses for Savar leave from Gabtali bus station. The fare is Tk 5 by bus and Tk 50 by baby taxi to Savar Bazar (15 km), and Tk 10 by bus to the memorial (23 km). You could also take an Aricha-bound bus from Gabtali or Farm Gate and get off at Savar, but you'll pay slightly more. If you want Savar town, ask for 'Savar Bazar', otherwise the driver

Places to Stay & Eat

If you are looking for a small town to spend a week or more getting to know the people, this would be a good choice. There aren't any hotels, but some family might offer you a room. Finding food isn't the easiest either, but along the main drag amidst a predominance of sweet shops is a restaurant or two.

Getting There & Away

Buses to/from Dhaka cost Tk 15 and depart

in Dhaka from Gabtali bus station. The trip takes about an hour.

MANIKGANJ

If you have the means to explore further, you could check two rarely visited rajbaris further west in the Manikganj district, roughly 30 km beyond the Savar memorial. The first, **Baliati Palace**, is one of the finest rajbaris in Bangladesh. It's also the largest, with a frontage of approximately 125m, and occupies an area of about eight hectares, with over 200 rooms! Originally owned by descendants of Govinda Ram Saha, the impressive Renaissance frontage, with its attractive array of tall fluted Corinthian columns lining a wide corridor, is reminiscent of a Georgian country house in England.

Further west, on the banks of the Jamuna River, is **Teota Palace**, which dates from the mid-19th century and was built by the zamindars of the Joy Sankar estate. The highlights are the large Hindu temple and the smaller family shrine. The well preserved temple, built in 1858, resembles the impressive Shive Temple in Puthia. The nearby family shrine has five embellished semi-circular arched doorways as its entrance.

Getting There & Away

Baliati Palace is about halfway between Savar monument and Aricha Ghat. Turn left (south) at Kalampur, which is about eight km before (east of) Manikganj on the Dhaka-Aricha highway. Teota Palace is 30 km or so further west at Sivalaya, which is several km south of Aricha Ghat by tarred road and along the Jamuna River.

BHAWAL NATIONAL PARK

Located at Rajendrapur, and only one hour north of Dhaka, Bhawal National Park is far less interesting than Madhupur Forest. Its accessibility ensures it is more frequented, especially as a picnic spot on weekends.

There's angling and boating on the long meandering lake, ponies to ride and pleasant walking through stands of young *sal* trees, but it's no wilderness. Although, virgin forests until a few decades ago, the trees

you'll see are regrowth, and they're still not very tall or interesting. In a country with so few forests, however, it's a welcome sight. Admission to the park is Tk 15 per person.

Places to Stay & Eat

There is a small *Forestry Guest House* which can be reserved through the Dhaka District Forestry Office (☎ 602-709) on Mohakhali Rd in Mohakhali, Dhaka for about Tk 500 a night. Camping requires permission from the same office but is not recommended because it would attract numerous onlookers. Instead, try the boy scouts' camp inside the Baptist Mission compound, two km beyond the BRAC training centre, which is a few km from the park entrance and to your left down a tarred back road towards Tangail.

Snack food and drinks are available at the park.

Getting There & Away

The park is on the Dhaka-Mymensingh highway, 38 km north of Dhaka and 15 km beyond Shandana (shan-dah-NAH), the four-way intersection for Gazipur. Express buses headed for Mymensingh from Mohakhali bus station in Dhaka run right past the well marked park entrance, which is on your right. The trip takes an hour by car or express bus.

TANGAIL

Getting to Tangail, some 85 km north-west of Dhaka, is tough on the body and nerves because the road is in poor condition and crowded with speeding buses and trucks. During the 2½ hours from Dhaka, you'll average no better than 35 km/h and will cross six or seven single-lane bridges. This road will most likely be upgraded with the completion of the Jamuna Bridge.

Tangail has, without question, one of the country's real gems – Atia Mosque. Other than the mosque, however, there is nothing to see. The city itself is singularly unattractive, with incredible traffic jams for its modest size.

If you're heading north to Madhupur Forest (45 km) and want to camp or stay at the guesthouse there, Tangail is a necessary stopover. You can only get the required permission (routinely granted) from the director of the District Forestry Office (☎ 3524, 4129; fax 4254) here in Tangail; you cannot obtain permission in Madhupur, Mymensingh or even Dhaka. The office is on the 3rd floor of the well marked Water Development Board building, a block north of the post office, which is on Victoria Rd. Rooms at the Madhupur Forest Guesthouse cost Tk 500.

Atia Mosque

Built in 1609, this fascinating transitional-phase mosque, depicted on the 10 taka note, shows a happy blend of pre-Mughal elements with imperial Mughal architectural features. Beautifully restored to its former glory, it's a four domed mosque, with a large hemispherical dome over the square prayer hall and three small domes in front, just behind the entrance way. Turrets at all four corners are relieved with plaster panels and give the building a fortress-like appearance.

The textured exterior walls, which are relieved with plaster panels fused harmoniously with terracotta floral scrolls, are unique and exceptional. It's as though the entire building was draped with a textured Indian material. Entering through one of the three arched openings in front, you'll see more terracotta work in the closed rectangular verandah area, which leads into the large prayer hall.

This well known mosque is located five km south of Tangail on the tarred road to Nagarpur. Coming from Dhaka, you'll have to go completely through town, along Victoria Rd and the crowded Six Annas Market Rd, before coming to the intersection of Delduar and Nagarpur Rds on the southern edge of town. Veer to your right into Nagarpur Rd and continue for around four km. The turn-off on your left is marked by a sign in Bangla; the mosque is several hundred metres down that dirt road.

Places to Stay & Eat

Tangail supports only several hotels. The best is the *Polashbari Hotel* (☎ 3154), which is a new four storey establishment on Masjid Rd, near the heart of town and east of the market, with a sign in Bangla. It's decent enough, with singles/doubles for Tk 70/100 to Tk 120. The rooms are small but they're clean and have fans, reasonably comfortable single mattresses and attached bathrooms.

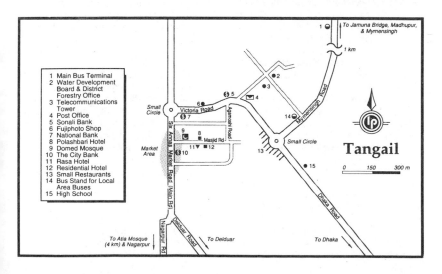

1 Main Bus Terminal
2 Water Development Board & District Forestry Office
3 Telecommunications Tower
4 Post Office
5 Sonali Bank
6 Fujiphoto Shop
7 National Bank
8 Polashbari Hotel
9 Domed Mosque
10 The City Bank
11 Rasa Hotel
12 Residential Hotel
13 Small Restaurants
14 Bus Stand for Local Area Buses
15 High School

Tangail

If it's full, try the two storey *Residential Hotel* (Bangla sign only) just across the street. It's quite clean and has similarly priced rooms. Cheaper places apparently don't exist, though, try the area around Atia Mosque; there is reportedly a small hotel.

For a meal, you could try the friendly *Rasa Hotel* (Bangla sign only), a small clean restaurant across the street from the Polashbari. Meals of rice with chicken, fish or mutton are Tk 22. You'll find three or four more restaurants serving similar food at the intersection of Dhaka and Mymensingh Rds.

Getting There & Away

Ordinary buses to Dhaka, Mymensingh and Jamalpur all cost Tk 30. Chair coaches, which cost Tk 40, exist but are harder to find. They all leave from the main bus station on Mymensingh Rd, two km north of the intersection with Dhaka Rd. Buses for Tangail depart from Mohakhali bus station in Dhaka.

MYMENSINGH

The northern part of Dhaka Division reaches the Indian border at the low, wooded chain of hills called the Meghalaya. It is the largest district of Bangladesh, located in the heart of the deltaic region of the Brahmaputra/Jamuna and the Meghna rivers. The finest jute is produced here along with high quality rice, both of which thrive in the permanently swampy region below the Meghalaya.

The five domed **Qutb Mosque**, remotely located in Ashtagram near Bhairab Bazar, is ornately embellished with terracotta art work and is the most notable structure from the 16th-century pre-Mughal period. In the village of Egarasindur are two fine Mughal mosques – the **Saadi Mosque** of 1652 and the **Shah Mohammed Mosque** of 1680.

Neglected by its Mughal overlords, the region boomed under the British when jute was an important crop. The whole region became one vast jute plantation; it grew better and was of a higher quality than anywhere else.

The outskirts of Mymensingh are slightly deceptive, with many modern buildings housing various colleges and the Kumudini

Hospital greeting the newly arrived visitor. The further one goes into the town, however, the more the original impression diminishes: the scene reverts back to the usual chaos of Bangladeshi urban life. Despite this, the town has a comfortable, unhurried atmosphere.

Information

The central section of the city, the *sadar*, is hidden by trees and walls from the main road, with bumpy lanes winding past the occasional painted exhortation to 'Cust your voot for Nazim' or whomever. Some pleasant Raj buildings also adorn the city centre. A minaret, enlarged and modernised, towers over it all. The railway station is here, just near a small church. Numerous post-independence structures mixed with the old contribute to the hotchpotch nature of the sadar.

An old channel of the Brahmaputra River separates the city from the jute plantations and mills of the village of Samoganj, 2½ km away. Near the river is a picturesque old Siva (Shiva) temple, looking much more at home than the nearby huge Boro Mosque.

In the Sonali Bank compound is one of Bangladesh's few remaining Raj-period wooden buildings. Unless you really want to see it don't bother coming here – it doesn't change money.

Mymensingh Rajbari

This well kept palace, built between 1905 and 1911, is a truly outstanding rajbari situated in the middle of city overlooking the Brahmaputra River. It's now a Women's Teachers' College, but much of the original structure has been left as it once was, complete with crystal door handles, marble floors, etched glass door-panes and ornate chandeliers. An ornamental marble fountain with a classical statue of a semi-nude nymph lies just beyond the arched gateway entrance. Behind the main building is the Jal-Tungi, a small two storey bathhouse at the edge of a large tank once used as the womens' bathing pavilion. Visitors are allowed to roam the grounds, but permission to enter the building must be obtained from the registrar's office in the west wing of the main building.

Harijan Poly

This is a community of the Hindu untouchable caste, known today as harijan (meaning God's children) due to Gandhi's effort to lessen their 'untouchable' status. It's an interesting area to walk through, if only to feel the difference in being among Hindus after so many Muslims. By following the main track leading into the community to the end and taking a left, you'll come to a small Hindu shrine and see a red metal gate opposite. Behind the gate lies the Harijan Primary School, founded and run by an unflagging Clara Biswas. The school provides basic education and skill training to about 400 children between the ages of four and 13 years.

Agricultural University

Two km south of the city centre lies the well known Agricultural University on sprawling, landscaped grounds. The country's only agricultural college, it is a peaceful environment

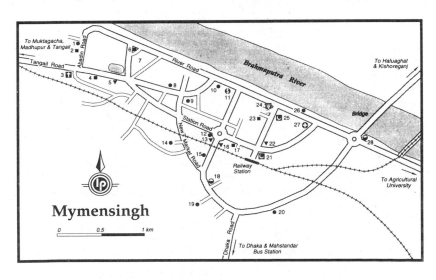

Mymensingh

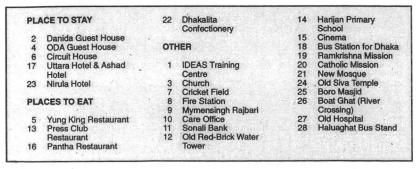

PLACE TO STAY		22	Dhakalita Confectionery	14	Harijan Primary School
2	Danida Guest House			15	Cinema
4	ODA Guest House	**OTHER**		18	Bus Station for Dhaka
6	Circuit House			19	Ramkrishna Mission
17	Uttara Hotel & Ashad Hotel	1	IDEAS Training Centre	20	Catholic Mission
23	Nirula Hotel	3	Church	21	New Mosque
		7	Cricket Field	24	Old Siva Temple
PLACES TO EAT		8	Fire Station	25	Boro Masjid
		9	Mymensingh Rajbari	26	Boat Ghat (River Crossing)
5	Yung King Restaurant	10	Care Office	27	Old Hospital
13	Press Club Restaurant	11	Sonali Bank	28	Haluaghat Bus Stand
16	Pantha Restaurant	12	Old Red-Brick Water Tower		

IDEAS International

Many visitors to Bangladesh quickly discover that IDEAS International in Dhaka is a great place to buy quality handcrafted items. Few realise that behind it all is a remarkable programme which has contributed to the development of crafts and people in Bangladesh.

The IDEAS project identifies marketable crafts and provides low-income groups with the skills to produce them. The products are then marketed through in-country sales and exports. We specifically target destitute women, tribal people and young men living in slums for group training based on their existing skills, education and family circumstances. After a comprehensive skills' course at our Mymensingh Training Centre, the group undergoes an 'apprenticeship' where we strictly monitor the work for quality. After training, the group returns to their home village where a small workshop area is set up by a parent aid organisation. We feel that coming daily to a specific workplace develops group identity and provides a sense of responsibility for the production. When the products are sold, the proceeds go to the group.

Generally our products are a combination of traditional and introduced crafts, ranging from handloom weaving and embroidery to wooden and papier mache items, mostly depending on the resources available in the country and current craft trends. Our aim is to provide people with a skill that will enable them to become economically viable. Once a group has been trained, IDEAS commits to providing orders, marketing the products and creating new designs.

Training is our biggest task; for some this is the only formal instruction they've ever received. Moreover, we face constant production obstacles. Months of monsoon rains hinder drying paint, handmade paper and papier mâché. Non-toxic paint must be specially ordered from a company that wants to sell 20 gallons at a time, can't always provide the required colours and takes forever to deliver.

At IDEAS, the trade-off for all the production headaches is a positive one. As we get to know the craftspeople, we can see these young men and women, once destitute, looking healthier and happier, with a real sense of self-worth.

Of the many widowed/divorced women trained by IDEAS, Rekha is one of our success stories. She lives in a slum near the training centre, and when IDEAS first set up shop she came to us for help. During the time it took us to actually begin the training, we would often see Rekha collecting firewood, trying to eke out an existence as best she could. Eventually she joined a group of women learning woodcutting skills. At that time, in late 1990, they were probably the first group of women in Bangladesh to be employed in what was traditionally a man's domain.

Within weeks, the women looked different. They projected a certain air of success and their self-esteem had improved considerably. For Rekha, her health was no longer a source of complaint and she has since seen her older son graduate from secondary school with a viable future of his own.

Lyn & Lee Morris, IDEAS Training Centre, Mymensingh

---

for roaming around, even a quiet picnic is possible here. There is a bricked trail which starts at a public park near the university and goes for about 800m along the banks of the Brahmaputra River – great for peaceful walks.

Places to Stay

On Station Rd not far west of the railway station, the *Uttara Hotel* is not very clean and has singles/doubles, with attached bathroom, for Tk 60/120. The *Asad Hotel* just around the corner is slightly better and offers claustrophobic singles for Tk 45 and roomier doubles for Tk 80. Neither of these have signs in English, and both can be quite noisy from the street traffic below.

The *Nirula Hotel* (no English sign), is a five storey building in Chowk Bazar near the Boro Masjid. Cleaner, though windowless, singles/doubles with attached bathrooms cost Tk 50/80. The smelly bathroom problem has been solved by putting them on the balcony.

The government-run *Circuit House*, down a small lane off River Rd, sits on the edge of a spacious green park area where locals practice football and cricket. The government rate is Tk 16 per person, higher for foreigners. Permission to stay is granted by the district commissioner, whose office is nearby.

The British *ODA Guest House* on Tangail Rd comes closes to providing western comfort, with clean rooms, air-con and a dining/sitting room for Tk 200 per person. Reservations should be made in advance through the ODA office in Dhaka (☎ 318-489, 325-347), but the manager is flexible. Inexpensive western meals are available with short notice. There is no sign outside, look for a white, two storey residence next to a vacant lot.

There is also the Danish-operated *Danida Guest House* tucked away on Abadin Rd, but at the time of writing it had been temporarily closed. If it's up and going again, it's a decent place to stay.

Places to Eat

There's a small restaurant at the railway station, supposedly only for 1st-class ticket holders but no one checks. Behind the old red-brick water tower off Station Rd, the *Press Club Restaurant* on the 2nd floor serves a set meal of chicken biryani and a variety of snacks. It is open for lunch and dinner from noon to 9 pm.

The *Yung King* Chinese restaurant on Shehora Rd is a little expensive but the food is good and the place is reasonably clean. The *Pantha Restaurant*, two blocks south of Station Rd, offers good local food and is open for lunch and dinner.

Opposite the mosque on Station Rd is *Dhakalita Confectionery* (no English sign), with a good range of cakes and bread; it has ice cream even in winter.

Getting There & Away

Mymensingh is quite isolated from the rest of Bangladesh by the Jamuna and Meghna rivers but this will change to some extent with the completion of the Jamuna Bridge. Train connections to Rajshahi Division are quite good but they involve a three hour ferry crossing. This lengthy route eventually snakes down to Khulna Division.

There are three main roads out of Mymensingh that eventually end up in or near Dhaka. The buses take the shortest route which goes directly south, passing west of Gazipur and more or less parallel with the railway line. The old Dhaka highway through Tangail is more circuitous, but offers interesting side trips along the way, including Madhupur Forest. When the Jamuna Bridge is completed, connections with the western zone will be quite good and traffic on the Tangail road may increase.

Bus As the bus stations are widely scattered, it's simpler to go to one of the private bus depots which operate in an area about one km south of the city centre. There are frequent departures. From the main bus station at Mahstandar, south-west of the city centre on the Dhaka road, buses leave for Dhaka every 40 minutes from 6 am to 6 pm, and cost Tk 30/50 for local buses/expresses. There are no chair coaches on this route. For buses south-west to Madhupur and Tangail (Tk 30), head for the Stadium bus stand.

The route to Sylhet or Comilla is circuitous and runs south via the ferry crossing at Bhairab Bazar, where buses leave from the old bus station. It's simpler to take a train to Comilla or Akhaura (there's a rail bridge at Bhairab Bazar) or to go via Dhaka.

Train Mymensingh is on the Dhaka-Rangpur route and there are four IC trains which operate six days a week (with different days off for each train) in either direction. Two of the northbound trains connect with Bogra; the fare is Tk 325/76 for 1st class/sulob. To Dhaka departures are at 4.10 and 6.10 am, and 4.10 and 5.10 pm, and cost Tk 44 for economy class (no 1st class) for the two hour trip. To Rangpur it's Tk 375/86. There are also several mail trains. The daily IC train to Comilla costs Tk 233/70.

AROUND MYMENSINGH

To the north, the Indian border and the hill country of the Meghalaya beckon enticingly, but there is no border crossing here. The area may be divided politically, but culturally it shares a common heritage among the tribal hill people – Mandi (also known as Garos), Hanjongis and Kochis who are ethnically distinct from the others around them.

Haluaghat

This is the end of the line, so to speak; the metalled road ends here, but a number of potholed dirt roads take off in various directions for smaller villages along the Indian border. Haluaghat, one of the tribal centres for the area, is a typical bustling town less than two hours north of Mymensingh. It's one big market, with vendors selling a variety of rice, dried peppers, melons in season and so on. Blacksmiths work in small shops next to silversmiths and cloth dealers.

Oxford Mission The Oxford Christian Mission, founded in 1910, welcomes visitors and can provide a place to stay. Padre Babu is in charge and speaks a little English. The mission operates a boys and girls high school, with a combined enrolment of about 1000. If you're interested in getting out further into some of the smaller Mandi villages, such as Askipara, Padre Babu may be able to help with directions or provide one of the children as a guide.

The spacious compound is tucked away off the main street of town. Many locals don't seem to know where it is: asking directions may prove futile. Basically, follow the main road north through town past some modern-looking buildings (grain storage warehouses) on your left (west). About 50m further is a large mosque, take the narrow road leading west and follow this road for about 300m. The red metal gate on your left past the grain warehouses is the entrance to the mission.

Getting There & Away Buses from Mymensingh leave for Haluaghat frequently from the bus stand near the Brahmaputra Bridge. The fare is about Tk 15.

Askipara

This Mandi village is in a beautiful area north of Haluaghat, near the Indian border, and about as remote as you can get in Bangladesh. The predominantly tribal area is officially 'restricted', requiring permission from the district office in Haluaghat but you may be able to get around that. A local guide could be your 'host', or you could get lucky and not be checked going into the area. There are no official checkpoints, only an occasional roaming police troupe. At worst, without permission, you would only be turned back.

In Askipara, you might to be able to stay with the 'richman' – a well-to-do Mandi who

welcomes visitors. There are wonderful walks in the area, and some distance away right on the border is 'Pani Hata', an Anglican Mission surrounded by beautiful teak trees. On the hilltop above the mission is a wonderful view looking out over the Indian plains to the hills of the Meghalaya.

There is no public transport to Askipara, but a rickshaw can be hired from Haluaghat for the two hour trip (Tk 100).

Muktagacha

Twelve km west of Mymensingh on the old Tangail-Dhaka road is the little village of Muktagacha. It is said that sometime during the early 18th century, a local smith named Muktaram presented the eldest son of the region's ruler with a brass 'gacha', or lamp, as a sign of loyalty. In recognition of the gift, the son named the town Muktagacha.

The rajbari here draws the occasional visitor, but the town is best known throughout Bangladesh for its famous sweet shop, **Gopal Pali Prosida Monda**, which makes the best *monda* in the country. Two hundred years ago, the Pal family cooked these delicious sweetmeats for the zamindar who liked them so much that he employed the family. When the landowner's family left during Partition, the Pal family opened up shop and have been in business ever since.

The western palate may not appreciate the subtleties of this famous monda, which, to the uninitiated, tastes a bit like a grainy, sweetened yogurt cake. Still, if you're in town, stop by and try one. The shop, with a lion motif over the door, looks more like a sitting area than a sweet shop, as there is no display area or cash counter.

If arriving from Mymensingh on the Tangail road, take the second road leading north-east (right) into Muktagacha. Go down about three blocks and the shop will be on your right.

Twenty feet past the shop, to the left, are old concrete pillars marking one of the entrances to the **Muktagacha Rajbari**. The rajbari is definitely worth seeing if you're heading to Madhupur Forest. This early-to-middle 19th-century palace, now mostly in ruins, includes several different blocks and spreads over ten acres. It is a very special estate, even in disrepair, bedecked with Corinthian columns, high parapets and floral scrolls in plaster. The Rajeswari Temple and the stone temple, believed to be dedicated to Siva, are two of the finer temples within the complex.

Madhupur Forest Reserve

Some 50 km south-west of Mymensingh on the road to Tangail, Madhupur (MODE-uh-poor) town is nothing special but the surrounding area is definitely unique. The biggest attraction is Madhupur Forest, a tract of land roughly 50 sq km just north-east of town. About eight km from Madhupur town, on the highway to Mymensingh, you'll arrive at the forest's south-western edge. It continues for around eight km along both sides of the highway, but the principal section lies to the north. There are some secluded spots that are perfect for camping.

This is the last remnant in Bangladesh of moist deciduous old growth forest, which at one time extended for hundreds of kms. Unfortunately, government conservation efforts are ineffective and there has been considerable cutting in the area. Before long

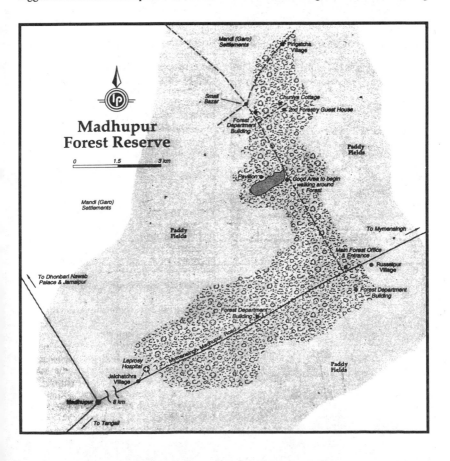

Madhupur
Forest Reserve

0   1.5   3 km

Mandi (Garo)
Settlements

Pingatcha
Village

Small
Bazar

Chuniya Cottage

2nd Forestry Guest House

Forest
Department
Building

Paddy
Fields

Pavilion

Good Area to begin
walking around
Forest

Mandi (Garo)
Settlements

Paddy
Fields

To Mymensingh

Main Forest Office
& Entrance

Russelpur
Village

To Dhonbari Nawab
Palace & Jamalpur

Forest Department
Building

Forest Department
Building

Mymensingh-Madhupur Road

Leprosy
Hospital

Jalchatchra
Village

Paddy
Fields

Madhupur   8 km

To Tangail

the last remaining old sal trees will be history, altering this forest's distinct character forever.

Mandi Settlements

Far into the forest where there are fewer trees, are some small Mandi settlements. The atmosphere of these enclaves is quite distinct from that of Muslim villages. A matrilineal group, the Mandi, or Garo as they are commonly called by outsiders, may have originally migrated from Myanmar (Burma). They are peaceful and accustomed to living in a spacious forest. Primarily Christians or animists, they seem to be at ease with foreigners.

Unfortunately for the Mandi, neighbouring Muslims are slowly encroaching on their lands and cutting down their forests. Accustomed to having their own space, the pressured Mandi, who were the original inhabitants of this region, are selling off their lands and heading to more remote areas further north. The rate of deforestation is high and poorly paid forestry officials are turning a blind eye to the destruction. If something doesn't change, this reserve is doomed. ■

A Mandi woman.

An exploration of the forest will likely turn up some rhesus monkeys and plenty of golden-coloured capped langurs, which look like bushy-tailed monkeys. There are also three species of civets, including the endangered large Indian civet. Many years ago this area was also famous for tigers.

Madhupur is also very good for birdwatching. There are numerous species but serious bird-watchers will be most interested in spotting the dusky owl, the brown fish owl, the spotted eagle owl and the famous brown wood owl, which is a speciality of the forest. During the winter some of the trees shed their leaves, making it easier to spot birds. This time of year is also more favourable for hiking when the lower swampy areas dry up after the monsoon.

While you're in the Madhupur Forest Reserve area, you might consider a short visit to Pirigatcha, which is 1½ km beyond the Forestry guesthouses, to your right at the intersection. A Jesuit priest Father Homerick has been living in that village for many years. Well known and liked, he has helped the Mandi build a large school and he has all kinds of activities underway, including small-scale industry, and fruit and vegetable projects.

Places to Stay In addition to camping, you can stay at the Forestry Guesthouse in the forest. The setting is lovely. Visitors use *Chuniya Cottage*. It has three bedrooms, common areas and a caretaker. The other similar guesthouse appears to be reserved exclusively for forestry personnel. During the winter, the reserve is quite popular. Camping, which is only allowed in this area, may be less than peaceful on weekends. Potable water is available.

Permission to camp or stay at Chuniya Cottage is obtained from the District Forestry Officer in Tangail (see the earlier Tangail section for more information). The cost is Tk 500 for a room, and although it's possible that with advance warning the caretaker might provide food, bring your own to be on the safe side.

The Rubber Tree Fiasco

Some years ago, the forestry department received a grant to help farmers in the Madhupur forest area supplement their incomes by planting rubber trees. The intention was for farmers to plant trees wherever the land was already cleared, thus filling in open patches and easing the pressure to cut down more existing forests.

What happened, however, was the farmers began clearing new patches in the forest, claiming them as old clearings, and requesting assistance. Initially, forestry officials turned a blind eye to this. When the facts were uncovered, the foundation terminated its assistance. As you go through forested areas you may see rows of rubber trees planted during that time. ■

Getting There & Away Madhupur is about halfway between Mymensingh and Tangail and there are frequently buses (Tk 80) between the two. By bus or car, it takes about 45 minutes from Mymensingh and a bit longer from Tangail. From town, the entrance is about 15 km to the north-east along the Mymensingh highway. Take a tempo or hop on any bus heading for Mymensingh.

The main entrance to the forest is on the northern side of the Mymensingh-Madhupur road at the eastern end of the forest, just before it abruptly ends and paddy fields begin. At the entrance you'll find the main forestry headquarters; those driving must register their vehicles here. Chuniya Cottage and the camping area are about six km up the road on your right.

Dhonbari Nawab Palace

Some 15 km north of the town of Madhupur, is the old Dhonbari Nawab Palace, which is well worth visiting. The property was originally owned by a Hindu Dhanwar Khan, but eventually fell into the hands of Muslims, which explains why this rajbari has, most unusually, a mosque. Within the complex there is also a main palace and a large *kutchery* building, in poor to fair condition, but still intact. One is being used as a school.

The main building has an impressive 65m long facade, with an arched entrance and 10 pairs of Corinthian columns. What's most impressive about the long kutchery nearby is the very fanciful *do-chala*, or hut-shaped pavilion, on top.

The interior of the elegant three domed mosque, which was renovated in 1901, is marvellous – the inner walls are covered profusely from floor to ceiling with mural decorations made from broken china pieces in a floral motif.

To get here from the town of Madhupur, take the tarred road north towards Jamalpur and after about 15 km you'll see the palace on your right, just off the highway.

Gauripur Rajbari

Eighteen km east of Mymensingh across the Brahmaputra River and a few km off the Kishoreganj road is the town of Gauripur. Here the Gauripur Palace, built in the last century, serves as the headquarters of the *upazilla* (local-level government) of the Mymensingh district. This palace was the seat of the famous Gauripur zamindars in the last century, and the scattered remains of their palaces are still visible amidst the overgrown jungle thickets.

Egarasindur

Further south along the Mymensingh-Kishgoranj route, some 15 km beyond (south of) Kishgoranj on the Narayanganj fork, lies the small town of Pakundia. Here a side road toward the river leads to the village of Egarasindur, about three km away. The village claims two lovely old mosques that are well worth checking out.

The **Sadi Mosque** of 1652 is a grand building with a large dome towering over two smaller ones. The **Shah Mohammed Mosque** of 1680 has a single dome and one wall sparsely relieved with terracotta panels of geometric and floral patterns. It is fronted by a brick structure considered to be the real attraction, which resembles a common reed hut and served as a *dachala*, or gatehouse.

Khulna & Barisal Divisions

Of all the divisions of Bangladesh, Khulna is most marked by the fingers of the Ganges which sluice down into the Bay of Bengal, creating a vast maze of waterways. Two-thirds of Khulna Division is marshland or dense jungle and a haven for wildlife. In the south are the Sundarbans ('beautiful forest'), a huge, almost untouched tract of water-logged jungle.

Khulna is in the south-west of Bangladesh and borders the state of West Bengal in India. In the north, the Padma (Ganges) River slices it off from Rajshahi Division, while the new 'breakaway' Barisal Division (included in this chapter) forms the eastern boundary.

The dense jungles and numerous rivers formed natural barriers to any invasion from the west or east. Even after its late settlement Khulna Division remained relatively neglected by the Mughals, and it was not until the arrival of the British that it started to be developed.

Nowadays it remains the centre of the declining jute industry, once the backbone of the economy, and the fish and shrimp processing industry, which continues to thrive. Several large match factories and the only newsprint mill in the country have been set up in this division as well. Except for matches, all of these products are shipped out through the international port of Mongla.

JESSORE

If you've crossed from India at the Benapol border, you'll arrive almost immediately at Jessore (JOSH-or) on your way to Dhaka, Khulna or points north. The Bhairab River, which runs through the heart of town, and the city's impressive court building, which dates from the British Raj, add charm to this otherwise fairly ordinary city. Once you're beyond the congested central area, the town, which has many shady streets, takes on a more tranquil air.

Of the country's modern cities, including Khulna, Dhaka and Sylhet, Jessore is the

Highlights
- Bagerhat – one of the cradles of Islam in Bangladesh; it has numerous historical monuments, including the famous Shait Gumbad Mosque
- Sundarbans National Park – where you'll see the largest coastal mangrove belt in the world, some of the last remaining stands of Gangetic-plain jungles and, if you're lucky, one of the few royal Bengal tigers surviving in the wilderness
- Chanchra Siva Temple – one of the best examples of the 'composite style' of Hindu architecture in Bangladesh, dating from 1696

oldest. As a district headquarters outreach from Calcutta, it was far more prominent than Khulna during the Raj era, and the huge court here obviously handled cases from far and wide. There are still train connections to Calcutta but they're not used. Jessore Zilla School is the country's oldest high school, built around 1860.

Jessore's high concentration of development projects attracts a number of foreign visitors, including Hillary Clinton who visited the area in 1995. The world-famous Grameen Bank, the Janama Centre, and the country's two largest development organisations, Bangladesh Rural Advancement Committee (BRAC) and Banchte Shekha manage a number of notable projects. Care, Danida and UNICEF head the list of foreign aid organisations which have offices here. Activities of most of these organisations are concentrated primarily in villages outside Jessore. The Janama Centre (☎ 5838), however, which fosters women's legal rights, is based in town, next to the Catholic Church.

Orientation & Information

To the north, the Bhairab River meanders through town, and the city's principal bazar begins just east of the intersection. A further 1½ km down Municipal Rd is the Moniher Cinema intersection, where all the bus stations are located. Between these two intersections is where you'll find most hotels, restaurants and banks.

Biman and most of the development organisations, on the other hand, are west of the heart of town towards the airport, including Care, UNICEF, the Janama Centre, Danida and Banchte Shekha. The latter two

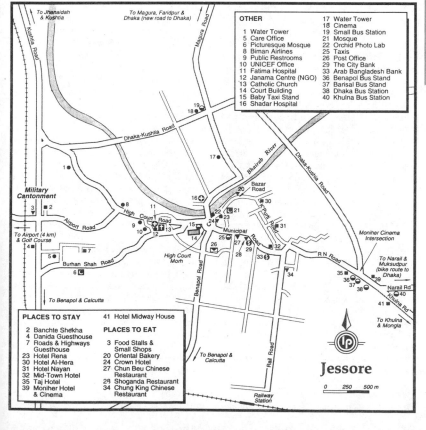

OTHER

1 Water Tower	17 Water Tower
5 Care Office	18 Cinema
6 Picturesque Mosque	19 Small Bus Station
8 Biman Airlines	21 Mosque
9 Public Restrooms	22 Orchid Photo Lab
10 UNICEF Office	25 Taxis
11 Fatima Hospital	26 Post Office
12 Janama Centre (NGO)	29 The City Bank
13 Catholic Church	33 Arab Bangladesh Bank
14 Court Building	36 Benapol Bus Stand
15 Baby Taxi Stand	37 Barisal Bus Stand
16 Shadar Hospital	38 Dhaka Bus Station
	40 Khulna Bus Station

PLACES TO STAY

2 Banchte Shekha
4 Danida Guesthouse
7 Roads & Highways Guesthouse
23 Hotel Rena
30 Hotel Al-Hera
31 Hotel Nayan
32 Mid-Town Hotel
35 Taj Hotel
39 Moniher Hotel & Cinema
41 Hotel Midway House

PLACES TO EAT

3 Food Stalls & Small Shops
20 Oriental Bakery
24 Crown Hotel
27 Chun Beu Chinese Restaurant
28 Shoganda Restaurant
34 Chung King Chinese Restaurant

Jessore

0   250   500 m

KHULNA & BARISAL DIVISION

have guesthouses and are the best places to stay.

There's no tourist information office, so the above mentioned organisations are probably your best source of information about the area. The people at Care (☎ 3429), on the western side of town near the Danida Guest House, are knowledgeable and always friendly, as are the people at BRAC (☎ 4124).

Places to Stay – bottom end

Most hotels are in the centre of town, east of High Court Morh, and further east around Moniher Cinema intersection. One of the best for the money is *Hotel Al-Hera* (no English sign), a two storey establishment on K'Purti Rd. It has reasonably clean and spacious singles/doubles with fans, mosquito nets and common bathrooms for Tk 35/55 (Tk 60/100 with attached bathrooms). It's run by strict (but friendly) Muslims who may not accept women. Even if they do, unmarried couples will be refused unless they say they are married.

Another possibility is *Hotel Nayan* (☎ 6535), which is two blocks away on the same street and well marked in English. It's overpriced at Tk 90/150 for small singles/doubles with attached bathrooms, fans and mosquito nets (Tk 70 for tiny singles with common bathrooms), but it's clean enough. You might also check *Hotel Rena* nearby on Bazar Rd, close to the Morh. It's priced midway between the Al-Hera and the Nayan, but is a better deal than the Nayan.

Taj Hotel (☎ 6532) on RN Rd, 100m or so west of the busy intersection with Dhaka-Kushtia Rd, is dirt cheap. Singles/doubles with common bathrooms cost Tk 35/50 (Tk 60 with attached bathroom). From the outside this place appears to be a complete dump, but the rooms, which are reasonably clean and have windows, are better than you'd expect. It's a lot better than *Hotel Midway House* nearby, across from Khulna bus station. Rooms here cost Tk 40/70 with attached bathrooms, and are cramped and dirty, with tiny windows.

Places to Stay – top end

The city's top hotels are mediocre and without restaurants, which is why most travellers in the know stay at guesthouses. The only two top-end hotels are the *Mid-Town Hotel* (☎ 6501/5731) on Municipal Rd and *Moniher Hotel* (☎ 4150) at the huge landmark Moniher Cinema. The six storey Mid-Town is reportedly not very friendly but does a booming business with Bangladeshis. Standard singles/doubles (Tk 80/120), with fans, mosquito nets and attached bathrooms, are bright and roomy with lots of windows. The air-con rooms on the lower floors (approximately Tk 350 for a double) are far nicer and in a totally different class. Unmarried couples will be forced to take separate rooms unless they say they're married.

The air-con rooms at the newer Moniher are of similar quality and price as those at the Mid-Town. A 'luxury' air-con double costs Tk 350. The cinema, however, may make it a bit noisier than the Mid-Town.

Most of the guesthouses are on the western side of town towards the airport. *Banchte Shekha* (BACH-tah SHAY-kah) (☎ 6436) on Airport Rd (just east of the bypass road to Benapol) is a favourite. Coming from the airport you'll pass the centre's sign on your left, 150m after crossing the railway tracks. One of the country's largest PVOs (private voluntary organisations), it offers destitute women a wide range of training programmes aimed at helping to empower them socially and economically. The staff here are exceedingly friendly, which makes staying here all the nicer.

The huge complex has over 70 rooms for housing trainees and visitors. At Tk 80 a person, rooms are spotless and well lit, with fans and carpets, and the large bathrooms have hot-water showers. Advance reservations are advisable but if you just show up, chances are good you'll get a room, provided there's space. If you let them know in advance, you can join in their family-style meals – typically fried fish, rice and dahl (watery lentils). There's also food at the busy intersection nearby.

For the money, it's hard to beat the tranquil, single storey *Roads & Highways*

Guesthouse (☎ 6632), which is about one km away, 300m east of the Care office on a paved back road and unmarked. There are three spacious guest rooms, two with twin beds and fans for Tk 75 per room and a third room with a single large bed and air-con for Tk 100. Getting a room is not difficult provided you call ahead. You can also eat here as well if you order in advance.

The most expensive guesthouse, and the one with the nicest facilities, is the attractive well marked *Danida Guesthouse* (☎ 6402), which is 200m west of Care, on the busy bypass road to Benapol. It has four air-con rooms and a total of seven beds. There's also a sitting room and dining room, and meals are available if ordered in advance. It's very popular with expatriates, so advance reservations are strongly advisable.

Another cheaper option is the government *Circuit House* (☎ 4002/3999), closer to the town centre, with rooms for Tk 16. It's almost always fully booked because of the city's political importance, so the chances of getting a room are remote.

Places to Eat

Two inexpensive places in the centre serving typical Bangladeshi food are the clean *Crown Hotel* on Bazar Rd just east of High Court Morh and the *Shoganda Restaurant* (no English sign) on Municipal Rd, 1½ blocks east of the same circle. At the Crown you can get a cold Coke, two portions of dahl, and one portion each of spinach, rice and salad for just Tk 14! Make sure your order is clear, however, as it has a habit of bringing dishes not ordered. For a good

range of biscuits and cakes, try the *Oriental Bakery* on Bazar Rd, a block beyond the Crown Hotel.

The two best restaurants are both Chinese and near the centre of town – the *Chun Beu Chinese Restaurant* (☎ 6141) on Municipal Rd and *Chung King Chinese Restaurant* (☎ 4057), several blocks further east on Rail Rd. The attractive air-con Chun Beu, which is poorly signed, is on the 2nd floor (up a flight of smelly stairs) of a building at an intersection. Open every day from 11 am to 4 pm and 6 to 11 pm, this friendly establishment offers a wide range of dishes, including Chinese chop suey (Tk 70), Mandarin fish (Tk 90) and chicken fried rice (Tk 60). The colourfully painted two storey Chung King is hard to miss and similar in most respects.

Getting There & Away

Air There are several flights a day to/from Dhaka, including one in the evening. The fare is Tk 631. Biman (☎ 5023) has an office in town on the road leading to the airport and at the airport (☎ 5026). Reconfirmation of return flights, though usually not required, is advisable since most flights are fully booked.

Bus There are buses to Dhaka all day, from around 6 am to 10.30 pm. Druti Paribahan (☎ 4105), which offers chair coach service, has departures at 9.30 am and 9.45 pm; the trip often takes no more than seven hours (about 2½ hours to the ferry crossing), but sometimes up to 10 hours if there's a long wait for the ferry across Padma River. Druti charges Tk 160 compared to Tk 110 for

---

Buses & the Ferry Crossing

The main ferry crossing across the mighty Padma River en route to/from Dhaka is at Aricha, 2½ hours by bus from Dhaka. At the ferry ghat you'll leave your bus behind (take your luggage with you) and get a different one (same company) on the opposite side of the river. It gets confusing as there are lots of ferries headed in different directions. Flashing your bus ticket should get you pointed to the correct boat, or stick with your ticket collector who continues on with the new bus. The ferry crossing itself often takes up to two hours, though the entire process with the unloading and loading of buses, usually takes about three hours or more. On the other side someone should lead you to the correct bus, but in all the chaos it's helpful to memorise some of the people from your boat. ■

ordinary buses. Druti's office is just east of Moniher Cinema intersection.

In Dhaka, buses for Jessore leave from Gabtali bus station. Buses for Khulna (Tk 20 for chair coach and Tk 15 for ordinary) leave from the same general area about every 15 minutes and take 1¾ hours.

Minibuses for Benapol (Tk 12) also leave periodically from 6 am. The trip takes one to 1½ hours. There are also cheaper local buses to Benapol (Tk 6), leaving from the western outskirts of Jessore, but by the time your rickshaw has found the right place you'll have paid almost as much as you would have for a faster and more comfortable minibus. If you're headed to Calcutta, count on about six hours for the entire trip.

Buses for Barisal cost Tk 105 (Tk 140 for a chair coach) and depart from Moniher Cinema intersection between 6 am and 12.15 pm. Because of numerous ferry crossings, the trip takes at least nine hours. There are also several buses a day to Rajshahi (Tk 70/80) and Bogra (Tk 80), departing mostly in the morning and early afternoon.

Train The railway station (☎ 5019) is two km south of the central area at the end of Rail Rd. Train connections to Dhaka are complicated. The 'direct' IC express to Dhaka can take up to 24 hours as you must go far north to Sirajganj and Jamalpur, then south to Mymensingh and Dhaka. Fares in 1st class/sulob are Tk 483/160. There are also even slower mail trains.

If you're determined to travel to Dhaka at least part of the way by train, take the 12.45 pm express to Rajbari and Goalundo Ghat, then the ferry across the Padma River and a bus from the other side. The 1st class/sulob fare to Goalundo Ghat is Tk 230/76. You can do it in 12 to 14 hours, depending mainly on the wait for the ferry.

The express to Rajshahi departs at 5 pm and costs Tk 230/76 in 1st class/sulob. It's usually quicker, however, to take the next train to Ishurdi (five daily) and change trains there. Most trains for Ishurdi (Tk 180/62 in 1st class/sulob) continue on to Saidpur (Tk

340/110); the express, which departs from Jessore at 10.45 am and 10.15 pm, is the best.

It's simpler to travel by bus on the short journey to Khulna. Although for the experience of taking a train in Bangladesh, this would be a good opportunity as there are six departures daily. The trip takes just 1½ hours and costs Tk 72/24 in 1st class/sulob.

AROUND JESSORE
Chanchra Siva Temple
The Chanchra Siva Temple is an elegant brick structure and one of the best examples of the 'composite style' of Hindu architecture in Bangladesh, combining various forms of Hindu designs with the sloping-roof Bengali hut form. Dating from 1696, this oblong shrine, measuring about eight metres across, features ornamental arched entrances and is crowned by a short dome-shaped spire. The entire outer surface is profusely embellished with beautiful terracotta panels depicting rosettes and other floral designs.

The temple is south of Jessore. From Jessore, travel along Khulna Rd for just a few km until it intersects with the tarred road south to Keshabpur and start asking directions from there. It's not well known, so finding it may be a bit tricky.

You could combine this with a trip further south to Shagardari, the home of Michael Madhusudhan Datta, one of the country's greatest poets. His two storey home was once in near ruins but it has now been restored and can be visited. To get there, continue south to Keshabpur, which is 30 km from Jessore or a one hour drive, and then another eight km or so south-west to Shagardari.

Baro Bazar Mosque
This old pre-Mughal mosque, dating from the 15th or early 16th century, is a good example of a single-domed mosque following the traditional Khan Jahan style, with thick walls, arched doorways, a square shape, sparse exterior embellishment and a low semicircular dome. Also not well known by the locals, it's about 18 km north-east of Jessore on the Jessore-Magura highway at Baro Bazar.

Sonabaria Temple

The Sonabaria Shyam Sundar Temple, built in 1767 some 15 years after the magnificent Kantanagar Temple of Dinajpur, is of the same *nava-ratna* (nine towered) style as that terracotta masterwork. Like Kantanagar, it's a square structure, rising in three diminishing storeys and is extensively decorated with terracotta art. It's only about half the size of Kantanagar, however, and not as beautiful or well preserved.

As the crow flies, it's about 30 km southwest of Jessore, near the Indian border. To get there from Jessore, take the road west towards Benapol for 25 km to the tiny village of Navaron (about two-thirds the distance to Benapol), where you'll find a country road heading south. It's about 15 km down that road.

BENAPOL

Benapol is the border town on the overland route from Calcutta. The border officials see quite a few travellers crossing here and things are relatively efficient. Travellers report being surprised by the friendliness of Bangladeshi border officials after dealing with their Indian counterparts, but watch out for minor rip offs when changing money. The town itself is as ugly as they come – a single road, one or two km long, lined from end to end with huge trucks waiting to cross the border. Coming from Dhaka, you should obtain a 'road transit permit' to cross the border. Although some travellers have succeeded in getting across without one, don't take the risk.

Crossing the Border

The border is officially open between 7 am and 8 pm but the form filling can take hours, so get there early.

Changing Money There are 'authorised' moneychangers on the Indian side. If you have taka, don't flash wads because the rule about not bringing in more than Tk 100 is given at least lip service. Currency declaration forms are no longer used in Bangladesh.

If you're departing from Bangladesh, sell your excess taka on the black market before crossing. Rates are not the best, so don't try to change large amounts. As for changing other currencies into Indian rupees, you'll do better waiting to change your money on the Indian side where you'll get better rates.

Entering & Exiting Be sure to arrive at the border in plenty of time. With so many people passing through here, the formalities can easily take up to two hours. From the railway station at 'Bonga' (short for Bongapore) in India to the border is Rs 30 by baby taxi. By rickshaw (Rs 10 per person), the trip takes about 30 minutes.

After the immigration checkpoint, don't take the first bus on the right for Jessore (Tk 6) unless you want to be crammed in with all the luggage. Instead, go to the bus stand, which is one km away (Tk 6 by rickshaw) and get a minibus (Tk 12); these are faster and cleaner, and well worth the extra hike and cost. Even if you have reserved a seat, grab it immediately as it is very difficult to evict local passengers once they have settled in your seat. There are minibuses every 20 minutes to Jessore, the major transit point for Dhaka, Khulna and points north.

Leaving Bangladesh for the Indian border (Haridaspur), procedures are the reverse. From Bonga (five km) you can take the train to Calcutta; the trip takes 2½ hours to Sealdah railway station and costs Rs 13 (2nd class only).

Places to Stay & Eat

Benapol supports only one small *residential hotel*. Heading towards India, you'll find it on your right along the main drag, not far from the centre of town. This grubby hovel is unmarked and has no name, so you'll have to ask for directions. The single storey building consists of only several windowless bunk rooms, each with five or six beds crammed one against the other. The cost is about Tk 20 per bed or about Tk 60 for the entire room. The beds are a bit hard but the room has a fan and the common bathroom is reasonably clean, including the shower. A woman travelling with a man can stay here, possibly single women travellers as well. Regardless, you're far better off staying the night in nearby Jessore, where you can still get to the border at 7 am when it opens by taking the first morning bus from Jessore.

There's one reasonably decent restaurant in Benapol, a well marked *Chinese Restaurant* on the same side of the road as the hotel, several hundred km further east. It has air-con, cold drinks and an extensive menu; a meal will cost you Tk 60 or so. You'll also find some small ordinary *restaurants* along the road where you can get a meal for Tk 20 or so.

Getting There & Away

Coming from Jessore, ask for both 'Benapol' and 'the border' to avoid any possible confusion. It's worth waiting for one of the minibuses that ply between Benapol and Jessore; the fare is Tk 12 and the trip takes one hour, sometimes 1½ hours. They take the main road, use the main bus station area in Jessore (Moniher Cinema intersection), and pass some old mosques and Hindu temples on the way. Local buses are cheaper (Tk 6), slower and crowded, and they depart and arrive in Jessore on the western edge of town instead of the main bus station area.

KHULNA

The British used the ancient port of Chittagong and developed Calcutta into a great city port, leaving Khulna to its own devices.

Today, Chittagong port, unable to handle all of the trade that has come its way, has given Khulna's river ports on the Rupsa (ROOP-sha) River and at Mongla a considerable amount of business. Modernisation of these ports has attracted industry and commercial development to Khulna, which is now the country's third-largest city.

Despite the development of Khulna as a port, the Rupsa is not deep enough to handle ocean-going vessels. Mongla, 40 km to the south, has been developed as the modern port for Khulna.

Khulna is the major starting point for trips to the Sundarbans, which start about 50 km to the south.

Orientation & Information

Most hotels and restaurants are located in the city's heart. Khan A Sabar Rd, also known as Jessore Rd, is the main drag through the city, and KDA Ave is the major thoroughfare on the western side. The main bus station is two km north-west of the city centre and the new GPO is similarly a long way north along Khan A Sabar Rd. The old GPO and the telephone and telegraph offices, however, still operate in the city centre, just past Hadis Park. If you take the narrow lane that follows the river south from the BIWTC office (and the railway station just opposite) near the city centre, you'll pass through a bustling bazar.

Changing money in Khulna can be a problem. The best place is probably at ANZ/Grindlays Bank in KDA Ave near Shiv Bari Circle, but it charges Tk 300 per transaction. AB Bank may be better for changing travellers cheques in US dollars; the transaction fee is Tk 110 compared to UK£10 for pound sterling travellers cheques!

For medical emergencies, there's Sadar hospital (☎ 20133). For general tourist information and arranging car rentals (and trips to the Sundarbans), the best place is the Hotel Royal International but only if you have a bit of money to spend because it's likely to try to sell you an expensive package tour. Reception staff speak good English and the manager is used to dealing with foreign aid-organisation visitors. Travellers on the cheap might do better talking with the manager of the Park Hotel, who is also articulate and helpful, and won't push to sell you something.

Travel Permits to the Sundarbans

The Divisional Forestry Office (☎ 20665, 21173), which issues permits to the Sundarbans, is on KD Ghosh Rd (on the corner of Circuit House Rd) and is open from 10 am to 5 pm Saturday to Thursday. The staff are very helpful but they have virtually no information and no booklets on the Sundarbans. Permits are issued on the spot and cost Tk 2.5 per person per day. The magic words to write on the application are: 'I will avail the Port Authority vessel' (to get to Hiron Point

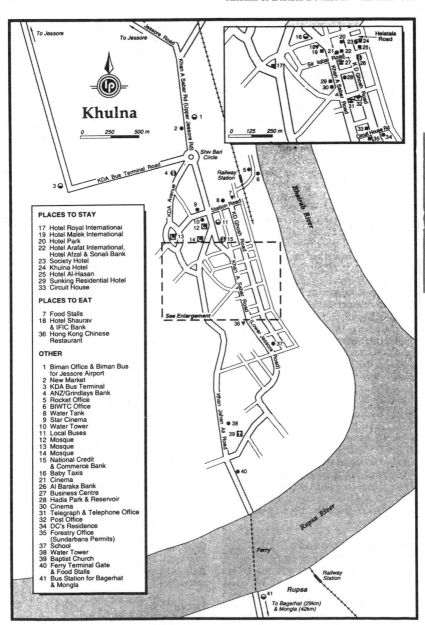

Khulna

0   250   500 m

PLACES TO STAY

17 Hotel Royal International
19 Hotel Malek International
20 Hotel Park
22 Hotel Arafat International,
    Hotel Afzal & Sonali Bank
23 Society Hotel
24 Khulna Hotel
25 Hotel Al-Hasan
29 Sunking Residential Hotel
33 Circuit House

PLACES TO EAT

7   Food Stalls
18 Hotel Shaurav
    & IFIC Bank
36 Hong Kong Chinese
    Restaurant

OTHER

1   Biman Office & Biman Bus
    for Jessore Airport
2   New Market
3   KDA Bus Terminal
4   ANZ/Grindlays Bank
5   Rocket Office
6   BIWTC Office
8   Water Tank
9   Star Cinema
10 Water Tower
11 Local Buses
12 Mosque
13 Mosque
14 Mosque
15 National Credit
    & Commerce Bank
16 Baby Taxis
21 Cinema
26 Al Baraka Bank
27 Business Centre
28 Hadis Park & Reservoir
30 Cinema
31 Telegraph & Telephone Office
32 Post Office
34 DC's Residence
35 Forestry Office
    (Sundarbans Permits)
37 School
38 Water Tower
39 Baptist Church
40 Ferry Terminal Gate
    & Food Stalls
41 Bus Station for Bagerhat
    & Mongla

To Jessore
To Jessore
Jessore Road
Khan A Sabar Rd (Upper Jessore Rd)
KDA Bus Terminal Road
KDA Avenue
Shiv Bari Circle
Railway Station
Station Road
K D Ghosh Road
Khan A Sabar Road (Lower Jessore Road)
Bhairab River
See Enlargement
Khan Jahan Ali Road
Rupsa River
Ferry
Railway Station
Rupsa
To Bagerhat (29km)
& Mongla (42km)

Helatala Road
Sir Iqbal Road
Khan A Sabar Road
K D Ghosh Road
Circuit House Rd

0   125   250 m

KHULNA & BARISAL DIVISION

and back) – you risk not getting a permit otherwise. Guides are compulsory and cost Tk 50 a day.

For more information on arranging trips to the Sundarbans and accommodation, see the Sundarbans section later in this chapter.

You might also check the Sundarbans Tourist Complex (☎ 21731/2, 23-24) at 17 BK Roy Rd in the Sheikh Para district.

Places to Stay – bottom end

Cheap hotels are concentrated in the heart of the city in an area one km south of the railway station. Most are well marked in English. One of the best places for the price is the *Society Hotel* (☎ 20995) on Helatala Rd; it has singles/doubles with attached bathrooms for Tk 50/70. Singles are tiny, but doubles are a bit more spacious and reasonably clean, with fans and mosquito nets. The *Khulna Hotel* (☎ 24359) is 30m away on the same alley. Fairly clean singles/doubles with attached bathrooms cost Tk 70/100 (slightly less with common bathrooms).

A block south on Sir Iqbal Rd you'll find the friendly *Hotel Afzal*, which has singles/doubles with common bathrooms for Tk 45/70. You get what you pay for. The *Sunking Residential Hotel* (☎ 25262) on Khan A Sabar Rd is overpriced at Tk 70/120 for similar-quality rooms.

Another great place for the price is the poorly marked *Hotel Malek International* (☎ 22226) in the heart of the city on Khan A Sabar Rd across from the Eastern Bank. It's on the 3rd floor and unusually tidy, with a carpeted sitting room with TV and comfortable seating, and hallways lined with potted plants. Singles are small but have fans, mosquito nets and western toilets, while doubles are a bit more spacious. A good place to eat is just next door.

Places to Stay – top end

One of the best mid-range establishments is *Hotel Arafat International*, which is down a lane just west of the Afzal Hotel. It's a nice place, with large, well furnished rooms with attached bathrooms for Tk 120/180, though the gaggle of excitable room boys might get on your nerves. Before booking a room here, check the *Hotel Golden King International* (☎ 25917), which is on the same street at 25 Sir Iqbal Rd; its room rates are in the same range or slightly higher.

Hotel Park (☎ 20990/25677), which is around the corner at 46 KD Ghosh Rd, is a notch better and neater than the Afzal. It has 44 rooms, laundry service, and a small comfortable reception area that features a TV, numerous relaxing chairs and a refrigerator with cold drinks. It charges Tk 115/160 for singles/doubles (Tk 180/240 for deluxe units and Tk 550 with air-con). The standard rooms are a much better buy; the only differences between the two categories is that the deluxe rooms are slightly larger and have western toilets.

The friendly *Hotel Royal International* (☎ 21638/9; fax 61266/77), at the southern end of KDA Ave, is the city's top hotel. Singles/doubles cost Tk 450/500 (Tk 600 with twin beds). Rooms are reasonably spacious, with fans, full carpeting, good-sized bathrooms with western toilets and hot water. There's also a large lobby, a travel agency, where you can make arrangements for car rentals and guided trips to the Sundarbans, and even an elevator! The restaurant, which is one of the city's best, features European and Chinese cuisine, and the menu offers many selections, including beckti sweet and sour fish (or grilled) and chow mein, both for Tk 75.

If you're not satisfied with the Royal or it's full, try *Hotel Tiger Garden*, a new 60 room establishment also on KDA Ave.

Staying at the government *Circuit House* (☎ 20314/20466), next to the stadium, will require permission from the District Commissioner (☎ 25233), across the street. Ask for Mr Chofik at the Circuit House, who is very friendly and will help you get permission. The guest rooms here (only Tk 16) are wonderful and spacious, and the two club-like sitting rooms are grand. You can also get meals here.

Places to Eat

For really cheap food, head for the area

around the railway station; there are several local food stalls nearby. An excellent place in the centre of the city is the well marked *Hotel Shaurav*, an air-con restaurant just above IFIC Bank on Khan A Sabar Rd. The friendly owner speaks English and is helpful in making selections from the Bangla menu. The place is very neat and prices are quite reasonable.

The city's top restaurants, all expensive in comparison, are the *Royal Deck* at Hotel Royal International, the new air-con *Howang Ho Chinese Restaurant* nearby, the rooftop restaurant at *Hotel Park*, which serves local dishes, and *Hong Kong Chinese Restaurant* on Khan A Sabar Rd, a block south of the stadium. The latter is poorly lit and nothing special.

Getting There & Away
Air The nearest airport is at Jessore. Biman (☎ 60940/9) provides direct bus service from Jessore airport to Khulna (two hours, Tk 20). You can take this same comfortable bus back to Jessore, departing from the Khulna office about three hours in advance of every flight.

Bus The main bus station is KDA bus terminal (also known as Sonadanga bus terminal), two km north-west of the city centre on the newer of the two entrance roads north into Khulna. A rickshaw costs about Tk 10 from the city centre and Tk 20 from Tupsa ghat. This station serves all points except Mongla and Bagerhat; buses for those towns leave from south of the city, just across the river. Inside KDA terminal, each company has its own ticket office, and bus companies with common destinations are grouped in the same area.

Buses to Dhaka leave all day until early evening. New Green Line, which is recommended, has departures in the morning at around 8.30 am and again in the evening at 8 and at 9 pm, arriving in Dhaka about eight hours later, sometimes longer if the ferry crossing is extra busy. The fare is Tk 130 for a chair coach and Tk 100 for an ordinary bus. Buses for Barisal leave mostly in the early

morning and again in the early evening.'SM Enterprise, for example, has departures for Barisal at 6.30 am (arriving around 2.30 pm), and at 7 and 7.30 pm. Modu Sanda also serves Barisal. The fare is Tk 120.

Buses for Jessore leave frequently until the early evening; the fare is Tk 20 for chair coaches and Tk 15 for ordinary buses, and the trip takes 1¾ hours. There is a direct bus to Bogra (Tk 90) at 7.30 am, and possibly one in the late afternoon. It is also possible to find a direct bus or two for Faridpur (Tk 60). In general, however, Bogra and Faridpur are easier to get to from Jessore.

Buses headed south to Mongla and south-west to Bagerhat depart throughout the day from the southern side of the city, across the Rupsa River and just beyond the ferry ghat. Most people take the ferry, which departs about every 20 minutes, but those in a hurry sometimes take one of the smaller boats. The fare for either is only about Tk 1. By direct coaster, Mongla (42 km) is Tk 15 and just over an hour away. The road is in superb condition. The turn-off east for Bagerhat (29 km) is nine km down this same highway; the fare is Tk 10 and the road is also in excellent condition.

Train The main railway station (☎ 23232) is just off the river near the city centre. There are four IC expresses a day to Jessore (8.30 and 11.15 am, and 3.30 and 9 pm) and two mail trains (9.50 am and 10 pm). The trip takes 1½ hours. The 8.30 am and the 9 pm express trains continue on to Ishurdi and Saidpur (the morning train requires a change at Jessore), while the 3.30 pm express continues on to Rajshahi. The 1st class/sulob fare is Tk 72/24 to Jessore, Tk 280/92 to Rajshahi and Tk 380/120 to Saidpur. It's far simpler to take the bus to Jessore, but with six trains daily, this would be a good opportunity to experience the Bangladeshi railway.

If you prefer to travel to Dhaka mostly by train, take the 11.15 am express which continues on to Rajbari and nearby Goalundo Ghat (Tk 285/94 for 1st class/sulob), then take the ferry across the Padma River and catch a bus to Dhaka on the other side. The entire trip including the ferry crossing can be done in 13 to 15 hours, depending mainly on the wait for the ferry.

The Bagerhat train terminal is across the Rupsa River, just left (east) of the ferry ghat. Departures are at 7, 11.45 am and 4 pm, and the fare is Tk 6 (Tk 10 for the faster 4 pm train which doesn't stop at Bagerhat College). There are frequent derailments, so the normal 1½ hour trip may be longer.

Car If you're driving to Mongla or Bagerhat, you'll have to take the Rupsa ferry (Tk 32), which departs every 20 minutes. The road is excellent.

You can rent a car at the Hotel Royal International; the cost is Tk 900 a day, including the driver but not including petrol or the driver's meals (Tk 50 a day if you leave town). The manager is sometimes misinformed about retail details, so deal directly with the driver when setting the terms. You could also enquire at Rent-A-Car (☎ 24857).

Boat The BIWTC office (☎ 20423, 21532) is near the city centre, just behind the railway station. The house-like office for the Rocket ferries, which opens every day at around 9 am, is just beyond BIWTC. Between Dhaka and Khulna there are four Rockets per week in each direction. These ferries also call at Mongla, Barisal, Chandpur and several smaller ports. The schedules have changed

very little over the years. Departures from Khulna are at 3 am every Monday, Wednesday, Friday and Saturday (Monday, Wednesday, Thursday and Saturday from Dhaka). Fares in 1st/2nd/inter/deck class on the *Ghazi* and the *Masood* are Tk 915/555/220/135 to Dhaka, Tk 430/280/120/75 to Barisal and Tk 130/80/52/20 to Mongla. Fares on the *Moti Moti* and the *Tal* are 15% less – Tk 778/472/185/115 to Dhaka. To be assured of a 1st class cabin, you should reserve at least several days in advance, although it is sometimes possible to get one even on the day of departure.

BAGERHAT

Don't miss Bagerhat. It has far more historical monuments in the surrounding area, mostly mosques, than any other town in Bangladesh, except Dhaka, and it also has one of the most famous – Shait Gumbad Mosque.

Bagerhat was also home to one of the most famous men in Bangladesh history, Khan Jahan Ali, and is one of the cradles of the Muslim religion in this country.

The principal mosques, all built during the middle of the 15th century, are in one large area about three km long, starting four km west of Bagerhat, which nestles tranquilly on the Bhairab River. The beautiful countryside is a joy to walk through. The main Hindu temple, Khodla Math, built roughly 175 years after all the mosques, is eight or so km

---

Khan Jahan Ali

Khan Jahan was a Muslim mystic who settled in Bagerhat in the middle of the 15th century after decades of wandering. Like Sheikh Shah Jalal-ud-din who immigrated to Sylhet, this Sufi mystic became widely known as a holy man. And like most of the Sufis who settled in the subcontinent in medieval times, he came from Turkey. Sufis are Muslim mystics, the counterparts of the Hindu sadhus or yogis of India.

Upon arriving in Bagerhat with thousands of horsemen, clearing the jungle and founding Khalifatabad, the town's original name, this warrior-saint quickly initiated an incredible construction programme. He adorned his capital city with an incredible number of mosques, bridges, brick-paved highways to neighbouring regions, palaces and other public buildings in an astonishingly short span of time – just a decade or two. Large ponds of water with staircase landings were built in various parts of the township to provide salt-free drinking water in this predominantly saline belt. No walls were necessary as Khan Jahan would simply retreat into the swamps if attacked.

When he died, a mausoleum was raised to his memory, which you can see, along with some of the major mosques still standing. Today Khan Jahan is the patron saint of the area and his name equates with a major pre-Mughal architectural style in Bangladesh. ■

to the north along a twisting road. The equivalent of some six storeys high, it's one of the tallest Hindu structures ever built in Bangladesh, so don't miss it. There's more jungle in this area than paddy and there are lotus-filled ponds, some ancient, which support a variety of bird life. With the Sundarbans so close there are reportedly occasional attacks by crocodiles in the waterways around Bagerhat.

Shait Gumbad Mosque & Surrounding Mosques

Built in 1459, the same year Khan Jahan died, the famous Shait Gumbad Mosque, with its numerous little domes and four short towers at the corners, is the largest and most magnificent traditional mosque in the country. 'Shait Gumbad' means 'the temple with 60 domes' but this is a misnomer because in reality it is roofed with 77 domes. Some 60m long, with 35 arched doorways, countless domes and corner towers topped by cupolas, this single storey fortress-like structure is quite impressive from a distance. Inside, it's equally fascinating, with a single huge sanctuary dominated by a forest of slender stone columns, 60 in all, from which rows of arches spring to support all the domes. The long aisles of pillars and arches emphasise just how big the building is.

Well maintained and typical of the pre-Mughal 'Khan Jahan style', it's a heavy brick building with two metre thick walls and a dark veneer of age, and is the more impressive for its rustic surroundings.

Around Shait Gumbad, there are three other mosques worth checking, all single domed and in reasonably good condition. These are **Bibi Begni's Mosque**, which is about 500m behind Shait Gumbad and across a large pond; **Chunakhola Mosque**, which is in a paddy field behind Bibi Begni's by about the same distance; and **Singar Mosque** across the highway from Shait Gumbad.

Mazhar Khan Jahan Ali

About two km east of Shait Gumbad is Khan Jahan's tomb. Overlooking a pond known as Thakur Dighi, the squat, quadrangular brick

structure, which is of the same basic design as all the mosques in this area, has a single dome and 2½ metre thick walls which are relatively unadorned. It's the only monument in Bagerhat which still retains its original cupolas.

The cenotaph, seen right at the entrance, is apparently covered with tiles of various colours and inscribed with Koranic verses, but is usually covered with a red cloth embroidered with gold threads. The mausoleum and the nearby single-domed Dargah Mosque are enclosed by a massive wall with short towers at each corner and archways on the front and back. There is a tiny bazar with teashops which caters to pilgrims who come to buy rosewater in bottles and joss sticks as offerings at the cenotaph.

As you enter the premises the fakirs will stir on sighting you and commence calling on Allah. They're close relations of the spiritual mendicants, both Hindu and Muslim, you find all over the subcontinent. The main entrance to the shrine faces an archway where stone steps lead down to a fairly large pond, where the faithful bathe before entering. You'll be invited inside for a look and then for a small contribution; a few taka will suffice. The interior at one time was quite beautiful, with multicoloured tiles and moulding around the doorways, but most of that is gone. You'll also probably be implored by the locals to take a walk to the other side of Thakur Dighi to see some crocodiles that inhabit the pond.

Nine Domed Mosque

Check out the nine domed mosque, which is on the western bank of the same pond. Recently repaired, it's an impressive elegant structure of the same period, with three arched entrances on each side, massive walls and nine low hemispherical domes supported on four slender stone columns. The *mihrabs*, or central doorways, are embellished with terracotta floral scrolls and foliage motifs, with a prominent chain-and-bell terracotta motif in the centre. You might also check the **Zinda Pir Mosque** just north of nine domed mosque.

Ronvijoypur Mosque

Across the main highway from Khan Jahan's tomb is the splendid Ronvijoypur Mosque. Quite beautiful, it's one of a number of single domed brick mosques in the area. It is singularly impressive, however, with the largest dome in Bangladesh, spanning some 11m and supported by three metre thick walls. Each side has three arched doorways, and at each corner is a circular tower which, like most single-domed mosques here, misses its crowning kiosk.

Khodla Math

This Hindu structure is more remote but well worth the effort of getting to. As you get near the temple, you can't help but spot the 20m high spire as it rises above the trees. This truly impressive brick tower looks rather like a giant beehive. Built in the early 17th century during Mughal times by a Brahmin, it was by legend a memorial to a court adviser. The entrance facade is thought to have been profusely decorated with moulded terracotta art, but it's now badly weathered. The best preserved side is that with no entrance; on the false doorway you can still see some delicate terracotta artwork. The other sides all have entrances with arched doorways, leading through the three metre thick walls to the square sanctum.

Getting There & Away Khodla Math is on the old road to Khulna, just outside the village of Ayodhya, at least eight km north-west of Bagerhat and near the railway line to Khulna. During the rainy season, this narrow winding back road is sometimes cut off. From Bagerhat, you can take rickshaws or baby taxis. Muslims in town aren't very knowledgeable about this, so you'll do better saying you want 'Ayodhya'. If that doesn't work, mention 'Jatrapur station' on the Rupsa-Bagerhat line; they'll certainly know that. It's the closest railway station to the temple (three km south-east), and from there people should be able to guide you to Ayodhya with no problem.

Places to Stay & Eat

The best value in town is undoubtedly *Hotel Suktara*, which is near the railway station. Its large, clean rooms with attached bathrooms (Tk 60) are arranged around a sunny courtyard, and the manager couldn't be friendlier. It's a lot better than the nearby *Hotel Momotaj*

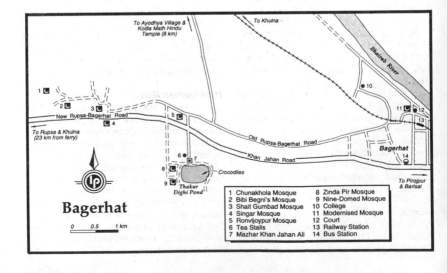

Bagerhat

0   0.5   1 km

To Ayodhya Village & Kodla Math Hindu Temple (8 km)

To Khulna

Bhairab River

New Rupsa-Bagerhat Road

To Rupsa & Khulna (23 km from ferry)

Old Rupsa-Bagerhat Road

Khan Jahan Road

Bagerhat

To Pirojpur & Barisal

Thakur Dighi Pond

Crocodiles

1 Chunakhola Mosque
2 Bibi Begni's Mosque
3 Shait Gumbad Mosque
4 Singar Mosque
5 Ronvijoypur Mosque
6 Tea Stalls
7 Mazhar Khan Jahan Ali
8 Zinda Pir Mosque
9 Nine-Domed Mosque
10 College
11 Modernised Mosque
12 Court
13 Railway Station
14 Bus Station

on Rail Rd, which is priced reasonably (Tk 45 for a single with attached bathroom), but at the time of visiting the manager was not very friendly.

The Suktara has no restaurant but staff will bring in local food for very little mark-up. There is also a Chinese restaurant, the *Maryona*, but the food is very disappointing. Otherwise, your only option is to try one of the basic local restaurants in the central area.

Getting There & Away
Bus Buses from Rupsa (Khulna) to Bagerhat cost Tk 12, and the trip takes about 45 minutes. The bus passes Shait Gumbad (six km before town) on your left and this would be a good place to get off, but you might have trouble catching a bus back to Rupsa from here as they're very full. The Bagerhat bus station (a stretch of road) is about one km from the centre of town on the Bagerhat-Khulna highway (which joins with the Khulna-Mongla highway nine km south of Rupsa). The road is excellent and buses for Khulna leave fairly frequently all day.

If you're headed to Mongla, it may be faster to take a bus to the Khulna-Mongla Rd intersection and hail another there. You may have to stand but the 33 km trip from the intersection takes less than an hour. Buses from Khulna headed east to Pirojpur and Barisal also pass through Bagerhat, but finding a seat on one might be very difficult.

Train The train departs from Rupsa (Khulna) at 7, 11.45 am and 4 pm, and from Bagerhat at 9.30 am, 2 and 6 pm. Coming from Rupsa, you could get off at the Shait Gumbad halt (Tk 5) or at Bagerhat, the final stop. Getting off at the former won't save you much time because the road from the halt to Shait Gumbad is so much more inferior.

MONGLA
Mongla, 42 km south of Khulna, is a surprisingly small and isolated town for a major port. Arriving from Khulna, you'll have to catch a tiny sail boat or public ferry to the other side. If you have a car, you'll have to

leave it at the bus stand as the ferry does not take vehicles.

Despite being about 80 km upriver from the Bay of Bengal, the port on the vast confluence of the Pusur and Mongla rivers has a string of freighters riding at anchor waiting to be loaded/unloaded at the new dockyards, off limits to the west of town. It's a spectacular sight, especially towards the southern end where dense jungle lines the banks. The vast Sundarbans national park begins only five km south.

Despite its small size and there being no transport other than rickshaws (no cars or baby taxis!), there's a hint of city atmosphere about Mongla.

Some of the locals have crewed foreign ships, and there are smuggled goods available for sale in the market, sometimes alcohol. If you bring out a bottle of beer or scotch in at least one hotel restaurant no one will bat an eye as some of the locals may be doing the same. This is the one place where people won't assume that you work for an aid organisation – if you're a man, they'll assume that you're a crew member from one of the ships in the harbour.

A hospital (☎ 393) is available for medical treatment.

Boat Cruise
'The' thing to do in Mongla is to hire one of the picturesque boats at the port for a ride out on the river and to some neighbouring villages. If it were not for their sails, these boats, each steered from the back by a standing oarsman, would remind you even more of their famous Venetian counterparts. If you sail southwards to the confluence of the two rivers, you'll come to where all the ocean-going vessels are anchored.

Places to Stay
If you're desperate for a free place to stay, try the Bangladeshi-run *Church of Bangladesh* in the residential quarter.

The most convenient of the hotels is *Hotel Singapore* (☎ 209), a well marked two storey building in the heart of town on the short lane leading to the main ferry ghat. Consequently, getting a room isn't guaranteed. They're reasonably clean but very small, and cost Tk 45/90 for singles/doubles with common bathrooms and Tk 75/120 with attached bathrooms.

To save money, head north to the market area. Beyond this, along Madrasa Rd, you'll find two more places. The first you'll pass is *Mongla Boarding*, with a Bangla sign, while the second, the two storey *Hotel Sundarban*, 200m beyond, is well marked in English. Both places are dumpy and charge Tk 35/50 for singles/doubles with common bathrooms.

The city's top establishment is the *Port Authority Guest House* (☎ 399), which is roughly 200m south of the main ferry ghat on the main drag, and can be reserved only through the Mongla Port Authority Chairman in Khulna (☎ 62331). It's not marked and is easy to miss. Singles/doubles, which cost Tk 120/240, are unusually large and freshly painted, with nice wooden furnishings, various reading chairs, twin beds with mosquito nets, overhead fans and large bathrooms with western toilets. Unfortunately, you may be told the rooms are all taken, though that won't be the case.

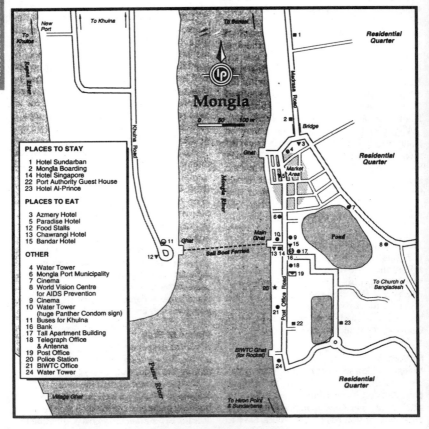

PLACES TO STAY

1 Hotel Sundarban
2 Mongla Boarding
14 Hotel Singapore
22 Port Authority Guest House
23 Hotel Al-Prince

PLACES TO EAT

3 Azmery Hotel
5 Paradise Hotel
12 Food Stalls
13 Chawrangi Hotel
15 Bandar Hotel

OTHER

4 Water Tower
6 Mongla Port Municipality
7 Cinema
8 World Vision Centre
  for AIDS Prevention
9 Cinema
10 Water Tower
   (huge Panther Condom sign)
11 Buses for Khulna
16 Bank
17 Tall Apartment Building
18 Telegraph Office
   & Antenna
19 Post Office
20 Police Station
21 BIWTC Office
24 Water Tower

The popular, well marked *Hotel Al-Prince* (☎ 454), 150m east as the crow flies, facing another paved street, has a restaurant and lots of rooms. The charge is Tk 70/120 for singles/doubles with attached bathrooms. The units aren't nearly as nice, but they're spacious by Bangladeshi standards, with fresh sheets (two if you ask), fans, hard mattresses, mosquito nets, walls with peeling paint and bathrooms with Asian-style toilets. For lunch or dinner, you could try the fried fish and chips or rice (Tk 55) along with a cold drink, among other choices. You can drink your own alcohol here without problems.

Places to Eat

There's not much choice here. If the *Hotel Al-Prince* is beyond your price range, try one of the eateries near the ferry ghat. The best appears to be *Bandar Hotel*, which is on the main drag across from Hotel Singapore. There's also *Chawrangi Hotel* at the main ghat. Rice, dahl and curry are the mainstays; Tk 20 will buy you a filling meal at either place. Two similar places in the market area, both on the main drag, are *Paradise Hotel* and *Azmery Hotel*, several blocks further north.

Getting There & Away

Bus There is no chair coach service to Mongla. An express bus from Rupsa (Khulna) costs Tk 15 and takes a little over an hour. Local buses are cheaper but much slower. Buses and cars do not cross the river. There's a small public barge (50 paisa) but most people take the small Venetian-like boats with sails, which are a lot more fun. The crossing takes 10 to 15 minutes and costs Tk 1 (Tk 12 for a boat to yourself).

Boat The BIWTC office is 150m south of the ferry ghat, and the Rocket ghat is 100m further south, opposite the Port Authority Guesthouse. You may have difficulty booking 1st and 2nd class Rocket tickets here, so if possible book in Khulna or Dhaka. Departures for Dhaka are at 6.10 am on Saturday, Monday, Wednesday and Friday.

Departures to Khulna are on Saturday, Monday, Wednesday and Thursday at 5.20 pm according to the schedule, but later in practice. Fares in 1st/2nd/inter/deck class are: Dhaka Tk 875/540/200/135; Barisal Tk 375/230/100/60; and Khulna Tk 130/80/52/20. By the time Rockets from Dhaka reach Mongla they're often late, so if you think you've missed the boat for Khulna it's worth checking anyway. See the following Sundarbans National Park section for details on travel to Hiron Point.

AROUND MONGLA
Dhangmari Forest Station

This forestry station, which is on the northern fringes of the Sundarbans and has good maps of the area, is only about four km south-west of Mongla, across the Pusur River and in an inlet at Dhangmari.

To reach Dhangmari the round trip takes about 2½ hours by row boat (Tk 90 plus *baksheesh*, or tip). The assistant manager at the Hotel Al-Prince can help you make arrangements. Alternatively, try for a boat at one of the little boat builders' yards on the waterfront near the BIWTC office. (For a longer motorised excursion into the Sundarbans, expect to pay about Tk 600 plus Tk 50 baksheesh for a five hour trip.)

SUNDARBANS NATIONAL PARK

The Sundarbans is the largest littoral mangrove belt in the world, stretching 80 km into the hinterland from the coast. The forests aren't just mangrove swamps, they include some of the last remaining stands of the mighty jungles which once covered the Gangetic plain.

The Sundarbans cover an area of nearly 3600 sq km in Bangladesh and another 2400 sq km in India. Six 'ranges' make up the region. At partition, Bashirat and Namkhona went to India, while Chandpai, Sharankhola, Hulna and Satkhira went to Bangladesh. About one-third of the total area of this forest is covered in water – basically by river channels, canals and tidal creeks varying in width from a few metres to five km in some places. Even the land area is subject to tidal inundation during spring tides. The Sundarbans are bound by the Bhaleswari River in the east, the Bay of Bengal to the south, Khulna Division to the north, and the Raimangal and Haringhata rivers to the west. At one time the mangrove forests extended even further.

The impenetrable forests of the Sundarbans begin about five km south-west of Mongla, along the Pusur River. For about 60 km to the south there are no settlements of any kind. There are no permanent settlements within the forest apart from a few government workforce camps housing the labour force for the extraction of timber. These camps are all either built on stilts or 'hang' from the trees because of the soft ground and the two metre tides that course through the coastal areas. The ground is all bog, down to a depth of about three metres. The workforce numbers about 20,000, although that number more than doubles during April and May.

The ecological balance is extremely delicate and is influenced greatly by tidal shifts which affect the salinity, and hence the growth rates in the surrounding vegetation. Deer, pigs and even crabs are predators of young trees, and cyclones wreak havoc.

The first historical record of any society inhabiting the region is from the 13th century, when many Hindus, fleeing the Muslim advance, sought refuge among the forests. They settled here, building a number of temples. They were later joined by the Khiljis who were fleeing the Afghans. There are no other signs of early civilisations. In the 17th century the Portuguese-Mogh pirates probably caused the population to leave the area, although the lack of fresh drinking water and the unhealthy climate must have been the other contributing factors.

Since 1966 the Sundarbans has been a wildlife sanctuary. The government recently set aside three specific areas as tiger reserves. Besides its wildlife, the Sundarbans has great economic potential. The Divisional Forestry Office keeps a close watch on the region and supervises activities to protect the delicate ecological balance. Hunting is prohibited.

Travel Permits

Permits are required to visit the Sundarbans, and are issued by the Divisional Forestry Office in Khulna. Guides are required and cost only Tk 50 a day. See Travel Permits in the Sundarbans in the Khulna section earlier in this chapter for further information.

Life in the Sundarbans

From November to mid-February thousands of fishermen from Chittagong converge on

---

Honey & Tigers

The Sundarbans are one of the country's richest sources of honey (madhu or mau), producing over 550,000 pounds annually. About 90% comes from the far western area called Satkhira (or Buri Goalini), where flowering trees thrive on the higher saline.

During the short honey season from April to May, the honey farmers (maualis), mostly destitute day labourers, work in small groups from dawn to dusk searching for bees. After locating the hive, they smoke out the bees and carry away the honey and beeswax in earthen jars. At night they sleep in their boats, only to be at it again the following day.

Locals say that each season some five to 10 maualis are attacked and eaten by tigers. Indeed, they are far more vulnerable to tiger attack than anybody else. The maualis carry no protection and in the frenzy of following the bees to their hives, they can't possibly keep an eye out for tigers as well. Royal Bengal Tigers always attack from the rear, and in a matter of seconds can crush a victim's head or break his neck. On the Indian side of the Sundarbans, the forest department has developed iron head masks for the maualis which have proven quite effective. But in Bangladesh, honey collectors continue unprotected.

Most of the honey is sold at Gabura, just north of Buri Goalini, and most is purchased by pharmaceutical firms. The remainder goes to local merchants, who often adulterate it by adding liquid glucose, making it heavier. In Mongla and Khulna you may see some of this honey for sale. To verify if it's pure, try this: take a thin piece of cotton, dip it in the honey and set fire to it. It'll burn very quickly if it's pure and much more slowly otherwise. ∎

the island of Dhubla, on the mouth of the Kung or Masjat River, a Sundarbans estuary. They come with about 40 trawlers, each with 30 to 40 small boats in tow. During this period fishing is carried on ceaselessly, day and night. They reap the rich harvest of the schooling shrimps who come here to breed, but also catch fish and sharks.

During the same period, thousands of low-caste Hindus from Khulna, Barisal and Patuakhali come to the island for a three day festival. They set up statues of deities in makeshift temples, bathe in the Ganges, and release or sacrifice goats. During the *mela* (fair), sweetmeats, dried fruits, toys, hookahs, wooden clogs and religious paraphernalia are sold in the market. A few weeks after their departure, the fishermen also head back to Chittagong, and for the next nine months the island is deserted.

Fishing families who live like sea gypsies can also be seen in the Sundarbans. They have large boats with thatched roofs and cabins, and they catch fish using trained otters. Nets are placed at the mouths of streams or creeks, and the otters are released upstream and chase the fish down into the nets. Woodcutters also work in the Sundarbans during much of the year. They build temporary dwellings on the edge of the forest to a height of three metres or so for protection from tigers; others live in boats.

Besides producing fish in great quantities, the region produces the sundari tree, which is in demand for shipbuilding, railway sleepers, lightpoles etc. Other forest products include honey, *gol* leaves (from a local shade tree of that name), reeds and snails for lime. The people who gather honey, known as *maualis*, occasionally constitute a part of the diet of the royal Bengal tiger. The unfortunate maualis are a particular favourite of the tigers because they're always looking up at the trees.

There are many other animals in the forests, including the beautiful spotted deer. Not surprisingly, bird life matches the lushness of the jungle in its variety and numbers.

The Sundari Tree

The region derives its name from the sundari

trees that grow here to about 25m in height. These trees are very straight, have tiny branches and keep well in water – they become rock hard when submerged for a long time and are thus very suitable for building. Sundaris are felled mainly for shipbuilding, electric poles, railway sleepers and house construction. Its wood has a purple lustre and accounts for about 75% of total wood extractions. The *gema* wood, also felled in the Sundarbans, is mainly pulped for the Khulna newsprint factory. Timber workers here are called *bawalis*.

Royal Bengal Tigers

The royal Bengal tiger is the pride of Bangladesh. It was aptly named by the British as has been known to grow to a body length of more than two metres, has extraordinary strength and agility, and is considered to be the most majestic of tigers. It has a life span of 16 years and preys on deer, boars and fish stranded on riverbeds at low tide. It is only in old age, when it has lost its physical agility and its canine fangs, that it sometimes preys on workers in the area.

There are thought to be roughly 400 tigers remaining in the Sundarbans, but your chances of seeing one are extremely remote. Every year there are reports of people in the area getting eaten by tigers, so the locals are terribly afraid of them and with good reason. In 1994, for example, a Dhaka newspaper reported that more than 10 people had been killed by human-eating tigers over the past year. Although they may not admit it, most guides, despite carrying rifles, are terrified of the tigers. Consequently, they'll make considerable noise during excursions, scaring them off and virtually ensuring that you won't encounter one. Nevertheless, there are just enough sightings to encourage visitors that they might be lucky. One group reported seeing a tiger swim right by their boat. Try to remember that it is the pristine environment rather than the wildlife that is the attraction of the area.

Other Wildlife

Wildlife in the Sundarbans also includes

deer, wild boars, clawless otters, monkeys, crocodiles and some 50 species of reptiles, including snakes and eight species of amphibians, and numerous river dolphins. Spotting animals in these thick mangrove forests is very difficult, however. Most visitors return reporting having seen very little wildlife, but those who enjoy unusual scenery still find the trip interesting. Some more elevated viewing towers have been constructed to help visitors spot more wildlife.

There are an estimated 30,000 spotted deer in the Sundarbans; they're among the most beautiful in the world. They are easy to find for they come down to a clearing or to the riverbanks to drink. There are also monkeys. Curiously, they have been observed dropping *keora* leaves whenever the deer appear on the scene.

Not surprisingly, the Sundarbans is one of the best areas for bird-watching. Over 270 species have been recorded here, including about 95 species of water birds and 35 species of birds of prey. Bird life includes snipes, white and gold herons, woodcocks, coots, yellowlegs sandpipers, common cranes, golden eagles and the *madan-tak* (adjutant bird), which always looks worried and dejected. Migratory birds are mainly Siberian ducks.

Organised Tours

The dry season, November through April, is the most popular season for visiting the Sundarbans. Parjatan conducts three-day guided package tours from Dhaka, mostly during this season. Call the Parjatan general manager's office (☎ 327-842, 817-855/6) for

information, not its other offices. For an all-inclusive three day trip, including airfare from Dhaka to Jessore, it costs Tk 7000 (Tk 12,000 for a five day trip), though this cannot be arranged for parties of less than 10 people. Taking the first plane in the morning to Jessore, then a van to Mongla and a boat from Mongla to Kotka, you arrive at Kotka by nightfall for dinner and lodging at the Forestry Rest House. The 2nd day is spent exploring the Sundarbans and the third day is spent returning to Dhaka.

The best private tour operator in Dhaka is The Guide (☎ 400-511; fax 833-544) at 47 New Eskaton Rd, a block south of the Sonargaon Hotel. (It's a bit hard to find; see the travel agency section in the Dhaka chapter for details.) It's very professionally run and offers similar tours, except guests sleep on board the motor boat and there's no minimum group size requirement; however, the price per person varies considerably. For example, three day trips cost Tk 17,000 (two people), Tk 12,000 (three to five people), Tk 8000 (six to nine people) and Tk 6400 (10 to 15 people). For each additional day the cost increases about 25%.

In Khulna, you can also arrange trips with Mohammad Faruk, the manager of the Hotel Royal International (☎ 21638/9). He runs about 20 trips a year and visitors have reported satisfactorily. He charges Tk 5000 a person for an all-day excursion from Khulna to the Sundarbans and back by speed boat, and Tk 12,500 a person for a two day trip, staying overnight at Kokta. Prices per person reduce considerably as numbers increase. For 15 people, the price for a four day/three night all-inclusive excursion from Jessore airport is Tk 5500 per person; this

Environmental Destruction

Two of the primary economic activities in the Sundarbans National Park are logging and shrimp farming. Most of it is done illegally, although it is meant to be strictly controlled by the forestry department, which has sufficient boats to patrol the waters. In 1995, after an extensive study, an independently funded report was issued suggesting that the rate of forest destruction in the Sundarbans was higher than previously suspected, and that due to the forestry department's lacklustre performance, management of the area would be placed with an independent body. The government's reaction to this will indicate its commitment to preserving the area. Meanwhile, the destruction of the Sundarbans continues. ■

price does not include the airfare to Jessore. You can arrange trips on the spot upon arriving in Khulna, but it would be better to call Mr Faruk in advance. You might also call the Sundarbans Tourist Complex (☎ 21731/2, 23024) to see what it can offer.

Places to Stay

Most visitors stay at the large *Mongla Port Authority Rest House* at Hiron Point (also called Nilkamal). This four storey hotel-like building is run by the Mongla Port Authority and is principally for their staff. It has very decent rooms, a dining hall, a bar and recreation facilities for the staff of about 30, and for visiting pilots. Tourist rates for the rooms are around Tk 240 for a double room with fan (more with air-con), and space is limited. Only the Chairman of the Mongla Port Authority, Reginald Haq, whose office is in Khulna (☎ 62331), can book you a room.

The only alternative is the small *Forestry Rest House*, which is at Kotka, about 30 km north-east of Hiron Point, just off the Bay of Bengal. It has two bedrooms with four beds each plus common areas. Expect to pay about Tk 500 for a room. The only person who can give permission is the Divisional Forestry Officer in Khulna (☎ 20665). All the major tour agencies use this guesthouse on their all-inclusive tours.

Apart from birds, your chances of seeing much wildlife at Hiron Point or Kotka are poor. If you mount one of the observation towers at night, however, and bring a torch, there is a very slight possibility that you might spot a tiger, especially if there's a full moon; it's worth the effort.

Getting There & Away

Hiron Point and Kotka are about 80 km south of Mongla with nothing in between. A trip by motor launch takes six to 10 hours from Mongla depending on the tide direction. Getting there and getting around on your own may be more expensive than visiting with a tour. The best place to look for a boat is Mongla, not Khulna. If you don't have much success, try the Port Authority. There is a very slight chance that you might be able

to hitch a free ride on one of its boats but don't count on it. You could also try hiring a boat from the Dhangmari Forest Station nearby. See the earlier Mongla and Around Mongla sections for travel to these alternatives.

If you cannot get right down to Hiron Point, you can take local country boats about halfway down. They carry large earthen pots of freshwater for the settlements on the edges of the dense jungle. The boats are pretty fast, speeding down with the ebb tide current early in the morning and bringing back a load of gol leaves, or bundles of reeds, with the incoming tide in the afternoon. The main problem is communicating with the boatmen who speak little English.

Getting Around

Once you get to Hiron Point, you still have the problem of getting out into the forest. The only means of transportation inside the forest is by boat (usually row boats) as there are no roads and very few forest paths. Walking around is virtually impossible because the ground is so muddy and slippery due to regular inundation by tidal waters. If you want to try, you'll have to wait until the tide goes out. When the tide comes in (at 50 km an hour!), the forest almost floats on water.

BARISAL

The capital of the new Barisal division, Barisal (BORE-ee-shal) is a major port city largely isolated from the rest of Bangladesh. It's fairly large, has a busy central area and lots of quiet back streets, with a number of buildings, of no major significance, that date from the Raj era. An exception is the intriguing Pakistani-era mansion on Sadar Rd across from the pond. The most interesting area is perhaps the port, which is always teeming with activity. Finding a place to stay around this area can be difficult as some of the hotels do not accept foreigners.

There are also a couple of old Hindu temples in the city centre, including a Krishna temple on Chowk Bazar Rd. On the main drag is a Sonali bank which changes travellers cheques.

KHULNA & BARISAL DIVISION

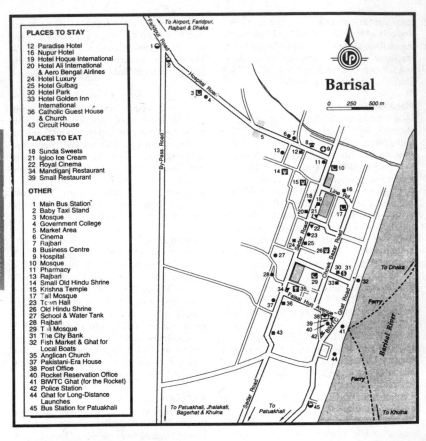

Barisal

0   250   500 m

PLACES TO STAY

12 Paradise Hotel
16 Nupur Hotel
19 Hotel Hoque International
20 Hotel Ali International
   & Aero Bengal Airlines
24 Hotel Luxury
25 Hotel Gulbag
30 Hotel Park
33 Hotel Golden Inn
   International
36 Catholic Guest House
   & Church
43 Circuit House

PLACES TO EAT

18 Sunda Sweets
21 Igloo Ice Cream
22 Royal Cinema
34 Mandiganj Restaurant
39 Small Restaurant

OTHER

1 Main Bus Station
2 Baby Taxi Stand
3 Mosque
4 Government College
5 Market Area
6 Cinema
7 Rajbari
8 Business Centre
9 Hospital
10 Mosque
11 Pharmacy
13 Rajbari
14 Small Old Hindu Shrine
15 Krishna Temple
17 Tall Mosque
23 Town Hall
26 Old Hindu Shrine
27 School & Water Tank
28 Rajbari
29 Tall Mosque
31 The City Bank
32 Fish Market & Ghat for
   Local Boats
35 Anglican Church
37 Pakistani-Era House
38 Post Office
40 Rocket Reservation Office
41 BIWTC Ghat (for the Rocket)
42 Police Station
44 Ghat for Long-Distance
   Launches
45 Bus Station for Patuakhali

To Airport, Faridpur,
Rajbari & Dhaka

Faridpur Road

Hospital Road

By-Pass Road

Line Rd

Sadar Road

Chawk Bazar Road

Faisal Huq Avenue

BIWTC Ghat Road

To Dhaka

Ferry

Barisal River

To Khulna

Ferry

To Patuakhali, Jhalakati,
Bagerhat & Khulna

To
Patuakhali

On the city's western side is a bypass road headed south to Patuakhali. At the intersection on the northern end are lots of baby taxis (fairly rare here) and the main bus stand. Near the bus stand, in an idyllic jungle-clad surrounding, is the Rama Krishna mission and a large Hindu temple.

Places to Stay – bottom end

For the money, you can't beat the *Catholic Guest House* (☎ 3354) at 5 Sadar Rd towards the southern end of town, half a km north of the Circuit House. The German parish priest, Philip Rozario, has two guest rooms, with a common bathroom, available for visitors. There are four beds per room and the beds are hard, but at Tk 20 a person it's hard to complain.

The *Oriental Institute*, now run by Caritas, a Christian organisation, costs a bit more but is much better. The rooms are a bit spartan, with twin single beds, fans and common bathrooms, but they're very decent and cost only about Tk 50 a room. Moreover, the setting is very tranquil with lovely grounds. Meals are rarely served but you may receive breakfast. This centre seems under-utilised, so getting a room is usually not a problem.

The major drawbacks are the location, on the western outskirts of town beyond the medical college, and that men and women are lodged separately, even if married.

Two of the cheapest places are three blocks to the north, in the heart of town on Sadar Rd: *Hotel Gulbag*, a block south of the Royal Cinema, and the *Hotel Luxury* across the street. The Gulbag has singles/doubles for Tk 40/80 with shared bathrooms, but it's a bit grubby. The Luxury is equally dirty, but its rooms are larger and cost more (Tk 60/110 for singles/doubles with attached bathrooms). Check out time is 24 hours after check-in time.

You'll find several more hotels two blocks to the east, just before the BIWTC Ghat Rd. Several do not take foreigners. A good hotel that accepts foreigners is the *Hotel Golden Inn International* (☎ 3161). Singles/doubles cost Tk 80/150, which seems a bit high for such small rooms, but they are clean and have fans, mosquito nets and decent bathrooms. Across the street is the *Hotel Park* (☎ 2678), which has slightly darker rooms with attached bathrooms for approximately the same price.

Places to Stay – top end

The new *Hotel Ali International* (☎ 4122), which has a friendly English-speaking manager, is in the heart of town on Sadar Rd, on the 3rd and 4th floors of the building where Aero Bengal is located. Singles/doubles (Tk 160/240) are large and spotless, and feature comfortable armchairs, fans, coffee tables, comfortable beds and modern attached bathrooms with western facilities. Deluxe singles/doubles cost Tk 220/270 (Tk 700/800 with air-con) and are even larger, with wide beds.

Alternatively, try the new *Hotel Hoque International* (sign in Bangla) at 54 Sadar Rd. It charges Tk 130/230 for superb and clean singles/doubles, although it's often full. One traveller reported that in five months of travelling in South-East Asia this was the best hotel he found! There's also the older *Nupur Hotel* (☎ 3377) on Line Rd; however, it's also frequently full and over-

priced at Tk 125/230 for singles/doubles with attached bathrooms.

The city's top address is the *Paradise Hotel* (☎ 2009) on Hospital Rd. Deluxe air-con rooms with double beds and attached bathrooms cost Tk 650, and it's only three blocks from the heart of town. A cheaper alternative, and an equally nice place to stay, would be the *Circuit House* (☎ 6464), on the main drag on the southern side of town. It is in an attractive old single storey building and has a relaxing atmosphere, with a large comfortable sitting room. You must first reserve, however, with the District Commissioner (☎ 2040), and getting a room could be difficult as it's well used by government officials.

Two final places you might try are the *WAPDA Guesthouse*, run by the Water Power Development Authority, and the *BIRI Guest House*, run by the Bangladesh Irrigation Project Office.

Places to Eat

For cheap food, try the BIWTC ferry *ghat* (landing); there's a small restaurant just north of this and possibly others in the area. Some of the cha stalls here and elsewhere around town specialise in 'red tea' – cardamom tea without milk. If you head from here towards the centre of town along Faisal Huq Ave you'll come to *Mandiganj Restaurant*, just before Sadar Rd. Its most popular dish is two slices of good bread and hot milk (no sodas) for Tk 8.

The city's best restaurant is unquestionably at the *Royal Cinema* on Sadar Rd. The fare and prices are standard, and the quality is decent enough. For ice cream, there's an *Igloo Ice Cream Outlet*, 30m to the north, and for sweets and snacks, try the small clean *Sunda Sweets* half a block further.

Getting There & Away

Air Aero Bengal, which has offices in Barisal (☎ 2304) on Sadar Rd in the same building as Hotel Ali International and in Dhaka (☎ 881-145), has flights everyday, departing from Dhaka for Barisal at 9 am and 4 pm, and departing from Barisal an hour later. The fare is Tk 950 (high by Biman standards) and departures are from the old airport in Dhaka, a block north-east of the National Assembly. During the monsoon season flights are cancelled very frequently because its 17-seater planes are too small to tolerate bad weather. If the late afternoon return flight to Dhaka is cancelled, you could take the Rocket, which usually arrives from Khulna around 6.30 pm, headed for Dhaka.

The airport is a 20 minute ride north of town. Aero Bengal provides free bus service to and from town, departing from its office on Sadar Rd about an hour before the scheduled departure hour. Biman, which recently initiated Sunday flights here (Tk 600), may provide the same service. You can also get to the airport by baby taxi for Tk 60.

Bus The principal Dhaka-Barisal overland route now passes via Mawa (the Padma River crossing) and Madaripur, but you can still also take buses via Aricha and Faridpur, which is longer. Either way, there are three ferry crossings, two just north of Barisal. Day coaches depart from either end, mostly in the morning starting around 6.30 am, while night buses depart mostly between 6 and 9 pm. The trip takes eight to 10 hours, and costs Tk 110 (Tk 140 by chair coach). Buses depart from the northern entrance to Barisal, four km from the town centre.

There are also direct connections west to Khulna; the fare is Tk 90 for an ordinary bus and Tk 120 for a chair coach. The trip, which involves two ferry crossings, is via Pirojpur and Bagerhat, and takes at least eight hours. SM Enterprise and Modu Sanda both have chair coaches on this route, with departures in the morning and at around 7 pm.

Buses travelling south to Bakerganj (18 km) and Patuakhali (40 km) cost Tk 7 and Tk 15 respectively. From Patuakhali there are buses to Barguna, Galachipa and Kalapara.

Boat There is a Rocket to Dhaka, via Chandpur, on Monday, Wednesday, Friday and Saturday, arriving from Khulna usually between 5.30 and 6.30 pm, and departing from Barisal 45 minutes later. The journey

supposedly takes 12 or 13 hours, but 15 or 16 is more typical during the high-water (monsoon) season. Fares to Dhaka are Tk 435/267/95/60 in 1st/2nd/inter/deck class. To Chandpur it's eight to 10 hours, and Tk 230/155/50/35 in 1st/2nd/inter/deck class. At Chandpur you can connect with the train to Chittagong.

The Rocket from Dhaka arrives here on Tuesday, Thursday, Friday and Sunday, usually between 5 and 6 am, and continues to Khulna, arriving there in the early evening. Fares are Tk 375/230/100/60 to Mongla and Tk 479/290/125/78 to Khulna.

For information and reservations in Barisal for the Rocket, see the BIWTC office at the harbour. For a 1st-class compartment you must reserve at least one day in advance (preferably earlier), otherwise you will have to wait until the boat arrives to see whether any of the eight compartments are unoccupied. There is likely to be a vacancy.

There are also large launches plying nightly between Barisal and Dhaka, including the *Jalkaporte* and the *MV Sadia*. Their 1st-class compartments are smaller and definitely inferior to those of the Rocket but they are decent enough, while deck class is just as good. There are four such launches departing every evening at 5.30, 6, 7 and 7.30 pm from either end. The departure points are Sadarghat terminal in Dhaka and the large terminal just south of the BIWTC terminal in Barisal. On the *Jalkaporte*, which departs at 6.30 pm, deck class costs Tk 50 and air-con singles/doubles cost Tk 300/600. On the *MV Sadia* the fares are Tk 60 and Tk 250 respectively. The trip by launch takes the same length of time as the Rocket. There are no launches plying between Barisal and Khulna, only the Rocket.

BIWTC also provides service to/from Chittagong three times a week, departing from Chittagong at 9 am on Monday, Thursday and Saturday, and returning the following day. The trip takes around 24 hours. The fare in 1st/2nd/deck is Tk 768/509/108. If you want a 1st-class cabin, you should reserve at least a day or two in advance, even up to a week to be sure.

AROUND BARISAL
Agailjhara
About 50 km north-west of Barisal, Agailjhara is of no particular note, but if you should be in the area a great place to stay is the *MCC Guesthouse*. It's a very nice relaxing place with several guest rooms, and the cost is only Tk 100 a person plus Tk 50 for meals (Tk 30 for breakfast). The people here are very friendly. In Dhaka you can reserve by calling the Mennonite Central Committee (☎ 815-625, 310-486).

Madubashah
Further from Barisal, about 10 km away, is the village of Madubashah, where you'll find a lake that is known for attracting birds.

Mosques & Temples
There are two pre-Mughal mosques much further from Barisal in the outlying districts. **Qasba Mosque**, in the village of Guarnadi, has nine domes. The other, about 15 km south-east of Patuakhali, is the **Masjidbari Mosque**, which is the more significant of the two. Built in 1465 and fairly well preserved, it is typical of the single-domed Khan Jahan style and similar in inspiration to the numerous single-domed mosques in Bagerhat to the west, for example. Other historical monuments include some newer Buddhist temples in **Bakerganj** and **Patuakhali**, and some medieval Hindu temples in the villages of **Madubashah**, **Goyllah**, **Badajur** and **Bangaparipara**. The latter are most likely in various advanced states of decay.

Kuakata
Even further south, about 100 km from Barisal, are some fine beaches in the village of Kuakata on the Bay of Bengal. Getting there, however, is an all-day journey. You can take buses as far south as Kalapara, which is near Kuakata, and probably a small launch from there. There are also reportedly launches direct from Barisal to Kuakata, apparently taking around nine hours.

KUSHTIA
Kushtia, just south of the Rajshahi Division,

is a poor, neglected town with a long, straight main street, Nawab Sirajdula Rd. The only 'sights' are a lively Hindu Jagganath temple on Nawab Sirajdula Rd and Tagore Lodge outside of town.

Tagore Lodge
Perched on the south bank of the powerful Padma River, this picturesque bungalow was built in the mid-19th century as an ancestral home of the world famous Bengali poet, Rabindranath Tagore. From 1880 Tagore lived here for over 10 years, composing some of his immortal poems, songs and short stories. He returned in 1912 for several years, translating his works into English and earning the Nobel Prize (1913) in the process.

One of the nicest features of this well maintained estate is the tranquil rural surrounding. The 15 room two storey building itself is quite elegant, with open terraces on the ground floor covered partially with a sloping tiled roof, and a central portion covered by a pitched roof with gables.

The estate is located outside Silaidaha (near the Padma River), eight km east of Kushtia, across the Gorai River.

Sailkupa Mosque
Extensively renovated, this six domed mosque, which dates from the late 15th or early 16th century, is one of the better preserved examples of architecture from the pre-Mughal period in Bangladesh. The building is largely unadorned, with plain exterior walls and entrances. Although the main entrance with three arched doorways was originally decorated with terracotta panels, they're now heavily covered with plaster.

It's located in Sailkupa, as the crow flies about 28 km south-east of Kushtia and 16 km north-east of Jhenaidah. From Kushtia, head south on Jessore Rd for about 20 km until you reach Garaganj, then east for about 10 km to Sailkupa. It's in that vicinity.

Places to Stay & Eat
The *Hotel Diamond* has desperately bad doubles with common bathrooms for around Tk 40. The old *Azmiree Hotel* (AJ-mee-ree)

(☎ 3012) at Court Para near Kushtia Halt is better. It has big, dim, damp-ravaged singles with common bathrooms for about Tk 50, and doubles with attached bathroom for Tk 80. The shutters and bars look as though they could withstand a siege. Forget *Hotel Jubilee* (☎ 3318) on the main drag; it looks better but it definitely doesn't accept foreigners.

The best place to stay is unquestionably the large attractive old *Circuit House* out of town. It has spacious well maintained rooms with twin beds, fans and attached bathrooms, but you'll have to make yourself presentable for the District Commissioner to have a shot at a room here. It serves good meals also and, as with most of the circuit houses, the cost is quite cheap, including the rooms.

There are the usual local eating places, although not many, and one Chinese restaurant, the *Tai Shun* (run by a moonlighting college professor), in a compound off the main road. It's pricey but not bad.

Getting There & Away

Bus Those travelling north must cross the Padma by ferry between Bheramara and Paksey. The ferry (Tk 17 for cars) takes only 20 minutes and runs next to Harding Bridge, the longest railway bridge in Bangladesh. To Ishurdi, a local bus costs about Tk 15. There are a few direct buses to Jessore but you'll probably have to change at Jhenaidah, which is to the south, about halfway. If you're headed back to Dhaka, you'll pass through Jhenaidah and Faridpur en route to Daulatdia Ghat for the crossing to Aricha. The road between Jhenaidah and Faridpur is one of the best in the country.

Train An IC train runs east from Kushtia to Rajbari (for Goalundo Ghat or Faridpur), and costs Tk 70/23 in 1st class/sulob for the 1½ hour journey. It departs at 8 am from Kushtia Halt, near the bus station, not the main Kushtia railway station. There's also a local train departing at 9 pm which takes three hours for the same journey.

Trains to Jessore run far more frequently from Poradaha, the junction town 10 km south-west of Kushtia.

FARIDPUR

Technically in the Dhaka Division, Faridpur is geographically more a part of the Khulna Division, west of the Padma River. There are a couple of important Hindu temples in Faridpur district, but the only reason you're likely to pass through this backwater town is if you're attempting to travel between Barisal and the western part of Khulna Division. Still, it's a pretty place, with leafy suburbs and picturesque old ponds (or 'tanks') scattered about.

There's a Rama Krishna Mission on the north-west outskirts which may have information on Hindu sights and festivals, although it's not too keen on foreigners.

Faridpur is the home town of the father of the nation, Sheikh Mujib Rahman. On his birthday each year he was presented with 30,000 to 40,000 cattle, making him one of the wealthiest men in the land.

Places to Stay & Eat

Hotel Luxury, near the bus stand, is a so-so place with singles/doubles with attached bathrooms for Tk 50/90.

The best place to eat is the *Peking Restaurant*, which is some way from the town centre (a pleasant Tk 5 rickshaw ride); though the food is just ordinary.

Getting There & Away

If you're headed east to Dhaka, take a bus to Rajbari (Tk 10) and Goalundo Ghat for the river crossing to Aricha. Buses south to Barisal cost around Tk 45.

AROUND FARIDPUR

In the village of Khalia, the **Raja Ram Temple** is an early 18th century *mandir* (Hindu temple) built exactly in the form of the Jagannath Temple in Puthia.

In Ujani Gopalpur, the 17th century **Math Shrine** is a fine example of the *chau-chala* hut design, characterised by a corniced, brick hut-shaped roof. The design, which imitates bamboo rafters and a thatched roof in brick, is purely decorative.

Rajshahi Division

As the north-western division of the country, Rajshahi's borders are, as one would expect, the major rivers: the Jamuna separates it from Dhaka Division, while the Ganges/Padma borders Khulna Division. The Ganges becomes very wide where it enters Bangladesh, stretching almost 20 km from bank to bank.

Rajshahi is one of the largest divisions in Bangladesh, with 16 districts and 25% of the country's population. It stretches from the wooded Terai region at the foothills of the Himalaya to the north, right down to the broad Gangetic valley to the south.

History

With the emergence of the Mauryan Empire in the 3rd century BC, and its expansion under the Buddhist Emperor Ashoka, the region became Buddhist. Brick buildings, mainly of a religious character, were introduced, and Pundravardhana (now known as Mahasthangarh) became the capital of Bengal. Pundravardhana was not only a Buddhist centre but also an important commercial entrepot of the silk trade. Chinese visitors in the 5th and 7th centuries were impressed by the large monasteries, the soaring temples and the Ashoka stupas. When the Gupta Empire, which emerged in the 4th century, disappeared, the Palas took control, making this region the last stronghold of Buddhism on the subcontinent.

The Pala kingdom eventually fell into poverty and, with the arrival in the 12th century of the Hindu Senas, Pundravardhana declined. The Senas adopted the traditional *bangla* temple design (sloping roof style associated with pre-Mauryan and Mauryan architecture), which the Muslims adopted as a principal feature of their mosques when they came to power a century later.

When the Mughals shifted to Dhaka, the region declined in importance, but with the arrival of the British in the 18th century, Rajshahi was quickly turned into a sugar and

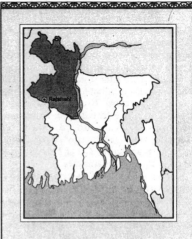

Highlights
- Mahasthangarh Ruins – remains of the oldest city in Bangladesh, with an impressive site museum
- Kantanagar Temple – a spectacular Hindu temple profusely decorated with sculptured terracotta plaques
- Somapuri Vihara at Paharpur – the most impressive archaeological site in Bangladesh
- Sura Mosque – a fine example of pre-Mughal architecture

cotton-producing region. Today, it's also the centre of the silk industry and produces 53% of the total wheat grown in Bangladesh, and almost half the country's mangoes for which the region is famous. As a result, it's one of the country's better off areas. For travellers, the region offers the opportunity to see a remarkable variety of historical monuments, including numerous mosques, Hindu temples, *rajbaris* (palaces built by the zamindars) and British-era buildings.

BOGRA

Bogra (BOGE-rah) is a major crossroads and

a bustling city with a compact commercial centre and a vibrant market. There are also some outlying residential areas which are pleasant, shady and fairly tranquil, and the people here seem a bit more relaxed, and stare less at foreigners, than in many areas.

The heart of town, Sat Mata, is a small traffic circle and a good place to begin exploring the central area. It's so crowded here during the day that walking is often faster than taking a rickshaw, at least for distances up to a km. Chandi market is full of life, and lying to the east is the Karatuya River, which is mostly blocked from view by numerous multistorey buildings. Walking around, you'll see numerous tea houses; many of them offer sweet yoghurt *(misti doi)* and sweetmeats, which are popular in this area.

A km north of Sat Mata, along busy Kazi Nasrul Islam Rd, off to the east (right) just before the water tower, you'll find an old Hindu quarter including some Hindu ruins. If you're really lucky, you might see a ceremony or other activities taking place. In January and early February, for instance, you can watch the mass production of life-size statues of Swarvati.

Bogra also makes a good base for visiting two of the country's most famous archaeological sites – Mahasthangarh and Paharpur. The former is just 10 km north of town, while the latter, which is more impressive, lies further to the north-west, over two hours by bus or car.

Information

To change money, head for Janata Bank on Kazi Nasrul Islam Rd, about 600m north of the city centre. Other banks include Rupali, on the same road near Sat Mata, Sonali, in an ornate Raj-period building, and Shilpa, on Nawab Bari Rd. These banks don't always change money though.

Nawab Chowdhury Museum

Nawab Syed Abdus Sobhan Chowdhury Memorial Museum, two blocks east of Sat Mata, is very interesting because it's one of only several rajbaris in Bangladesh that is furnished and, uniquely, the furnishings are all original. The elaborately carved wooden chairs and tables, the wall mouldings, the high ceilings and the original glass lighting fixtures combine to give the huge reception room and adjoining dining room a grand and authentic appearance. You'll also see a portrait of the original owner's heir, Jackie Chowdhury. A very friendly man, he lives in Dhaka but on weekends he sometimes comes here to relax since part of the building, which is maintained by the government, is still considered his personal residence. If you're lucky he might be around to give you a personal tour.

Surrounding this single storey structure are some gardens which afford a good view of the Karatuya River just beyond. Just next to the museum's entrance is an unusual small zoo called a *carnapuli* (car-NA-pou-lee), made of painted cement animals. Especially popular with children, it attracts a lot more Bangladeshis than the museum.

The museum is open from 5 to 7.30 pm every day except Friday, when it's closed. If you can't visit during these hours or you arrive on a Friday, come anyway as chances are very good that the caretaker will offer to take you on a short tour. Make sure the caretaker introduces you to the crafts people out the back who are reproducing some of the statues which used to grace the estate.

Places to Stay – bottom end

If low price and a central location are your main considerations, try *Hotel Marlin Residential* (☎ 5366), which is at the northern end of Nawab Wari Rd, one block east of the tall landmark mosque, or *Hotel Metro* next door, which is virtually identical in all respects. Only the Metro has a sign in English. Singles/doubles with fans, mosquito nets and common bathrooms cost Tk 40/50. Rooms at both places are dark and tiny, and not particularly clean, but the management is friendly enough and they're both superior to the similarly priced *Janata Hotel*, a run-down grubby place in the depths of Shaptobari market.

A better place is the three storey *Bogra Boarding* (☎ 5609), nearby on Nawab Wari

Rd; there's a sign in English. The rooms are tiny and some are reportedly infested with crickets, but they are nevertheless a bit cleaner, and come with fans and mosquito nets. The common bathrooms are also quite clean. Singles/doubles cost Tk 35/60, and the management, which is usually but not always friendly, has cold drinks available for guests.

Much better still is the *Mandolin Hotel & Restaurant* (☎ 5176) on the top floor of Shaptobari market. It has a pleasant reception area with comfortable sofas for relaxing on. In addition, it has one of the better res-

taurants in town; it's carpeted and has bright red tablecloths and a TV, which distracts from the otherwise warm ambience. There are only 12 rooms, one with air-con (Tk 300) and several windowless singles with common bathrooms (Tk 50). The remainder are singles/doubles with attached bathrooms (Tk 80/130); they are reasonably clean and roomier than normal, with lots of light, fans and mosquito nets.

The best deal is the *YMCA Hostel* (☎ 5242). To get there from Sat Mata, take Sherpur Rd south and immediately after passing the small Bhai Paglar Majar cemetery on your

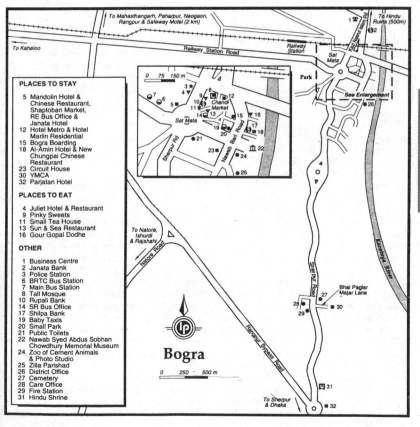

PLACES TO STAY

5 Mandolin Hotel & Chinese Restaurant, Shaptobari market, RE Bus Office & Janata Hotel
12 Hotel Metro & Hotel Marlin Residential
15 Bogra Boarding
18 Al-Amin Hotel & New Chungpai Chinese Restaurant
23 Circuit House
30 YMCA
32 Parjatan Hotel

PLACES TO EAT

4 Juliet Hotel & Restaurant
9 Pinky Sweets
11 Small Tea House
13 Sun & Sea Restaurant
16 Gour Gopal Dodhe

OTHER

1 Business Centre
2 Janata Bank
3 Police Station
6 BRTC Bus Station
7 Main Bus Station
8 Tall Mosque
10 Rupali Bank
14 SR Bus Office
17 Shilpa Bank
19 Baby Taxis
20 Small Park
21 Public Toilets
22 Nawab Syed Abdus Sobhan Chowdhury Memorial Museum
24 Zoo of Cement Animals & Photo Studio
25 Zilla Parishad
26 District Office
27 Cemetery
28 Care Office
29 Fire Station
31 Hindu Shrine

Bogra

RAJSHAHI DIVISION

left (roughly two km), take the next left (east) down Bhai Paglar Majar Lane. There's a sign on Sherpur Rd at the entrance to the lane. If you pass a fire station on the right, you've gone too far. The 'Y', which runs a primary school and a vocation education programme, is in peaceful quiet surroundings, with friendly and helpful staff. There are three clean and comfortable guest rooms (16 more are being added), with twin beds, writing tables, fans, balconies, attached bathrooms and clean towels. The price is Tk 80 for a bed or Tk 150 for the room. There's no kitchen, but the staff can arrange for meals to be brought in from the outside.

Places to Stay – top end

The best hotel in the centre of town is the new *Al-Amin Hotel* (☎ 4345), which opened in 1995. A pale-yellow, six storey building overlooking the Karatuya River, with a sign in Bangla, it has three room categories. All 42 units are the same size and have attached bathrooms; only the furnishings differ. The standard units, which cost Tk 100/200, are a great deal, with carpeting, small sofas, fans and balconies, and there's a satellite-TV viewing area on each floor. The more deluxe rooms (Tk 200/400 and Tk 400/700) are of course even nicer. The hotel features a decent Chinese restaurant on the top floor and a 1600 seat cinema; the screen and speakers of which can be seen and heard by diners as they eat – a major potential detraction if you want peace and quiet or don't like Hindu films.

Bogra's top hotel is the three storey *Safeway Motel* (☎ 6087/4652) on the north-western outskirts of town on the highway to Santahar, just off Rangpur Bypass Rd. A grass yard with chairs and a small pond provide a restful and, for Bangladesh, an unusual respite. Singles/doubles, which cost Tk 500/650, are spacious and have full carpeting, fans, air-con that frequently cuts off during the night, bureaus with dressing mirrors and large bathrooms with hot-water baths. There are also cheaper Tk 50 rooms for clients' chauffeurs. The Safeway also has one of the best restaurants in town.

Alternatively, try the *Parjatan Hotel* (☎ 6753) at the southern entrance (circle) to town, four km from the town centre. Similar in most respects, it has spacious ventilated rooms with firm stuffed-cotton mattresses and cold-water showers for Tk 312, and air-con rooms with softer mattresses and hot-water showers for Tk 520, plus cheap lodging for drivers. The government's modern brick *Circuit House*, which is in the heart of town on Nawab Bari Rd, costs far less but with a Parjatan here, the District Commissioner is unlikely to consent.

A final possibility is the *Archaeology Department Rest House*, which is at the Mahasthangarh ruins, across from the museum overlooking a winding river. It has no phone but you can reserve a room by calling the Director of Archaeology in Dhaka (☎ 326-708) or the regional office in Bogra (☎ 6527, 6071/2). Since few people stay here, if you just show up, the likelihood of getting a room seems high. The rest house has three doubles; they cost Tk 50 and come with twin beds, fans and attached bathrooms. You can also get meals here if you order in advance.

Places to Eat

An excellent inexpensive place to eat in the heart of town is the popular *Sun & Sea Restaurant*, which is 75m or so north-east of Sat Mata. Marked in English, it's an unusually tidy restaurant with typical Bangladeshi fare at popular prices, and cold soft drinks. Three similar places in the town centre which seem more ordinary are the well marked *Juliet Hotel & Restaurant*, around the corner on Kazi Nasrul Islam Rd, *Gour Gopal Dodhe* (no English sign), on Nawab Bari Rd a block north of Bogra Boarding, and an unmarked restaurant two blocks south on the same street. At all of these places, two parathas and a small dish of vegetables will cost you about Tk 15.

For Chinese fare, one of the best places in the centre of town is the friendly *Mandolin Hotel & Chinese Restaurant*. It's a cosy carpeted restaurant in an unlikely place – the top floor of Shaptobari market. The TV, however, is a distraction. The management is friendly, and selections are numerous and moderately priced. You could also try the relatively posh *New Chungpai Chinese Restaurant* on top of the Al-Amin Hotel, off Nawab Bari Rd. The menu has over 250 selections, mostly in the Tk 60 to Tk 100 range.

The city's best restaurants by reputation are at the *Parjatan Hotel* and the *Safeway Motel*. Both are carpeted and have air-con. The chicken 'cheezling special' (No 69) at the Safeway is highly recommended by one long-time Italian guest; it costs Tk 125. Most other selections are less expensive, eg Chinese mixed vegetables (Tk 64) and beef with Chinese vegetables (Tk 78). The restaurant at the Parjatan offers a variety of Chinese, western and Bangladeshi dishes, and it's slightly cheaper than the Safeway, but the ambience is a bit gloomier.

Getting There & Away

Air The closest airports, both three hours away, are Rajshahi (daily flights) and Ishurdi (Wednesday and Sunday).

Bus Most bus offices are west of Sat Mata, but there are also some just to the east. One of the best deluxe buses to Dhaka is RE, which is located inside Shaptobari market (facing Sat Mata) on the ground level. It has four chair coaches a day to Dhaka; the first departs at 7 am and the last at 9 pm. Ordinary Dhaka buses charge between Tk 110 and Tk 120, including Palque and SR. The journey to Dhaka is via the Nagarbari-Aricha crossing of the Jamuna and normally takes around nine hours (3½ hours to Nagarbari Ghat, three hours for the ferry crossing and 2½ hours to Dhaka), or more if the ferry crossing is longer. With the completion of the Jamuna Bridge, the travel time via Sirajganj and Tangail should be much less.

There are buses throughout the day to Natore (Tk 25) and Rajshahi (40) but much fewer to the Khulna division. There's a direct bus to Kushtia (Tk 60) at noon, for instance, and several around 9 am to Khulna (Tk 110).

Northbound buses to Rangpur (Tk 40) depart frequently starting around 6 am, with the last departure around 6 pm; the trip takes 2½ hours.

Travellers to Paharpur can take regular buses throughout the day to Jaipurhat; the trip takes 1½ hours and costs Tk 20. From there you can take a tempo to Paharpur. You can also take a dilapidated BRTC bus at 7 am daily to the Indian border at Bholahat; the fare is Tk 80.

RAJSHAHI DIVISION

Jamuna Bridge

The most controversial, and expensive, project that the government has ever undertaken is the construction of the Jamuna Bridge, scheduled for completion by the end of 1997. The $700 million price tag is staggering. Even with loans from the World Bank and Japan, resources are being siphoned from other sectors. At a time when the country has so many unresolved problems, most notably education, the question arises whether a single bridge could be worth so much.

There are also serious social and environmental complications. By the time the project is completed, more than 72,000 people will have been moved from their land. And, because land in Bangladesh is flat, river courses are in a state of flux. Indeed, the Jamuna only came about in 1762, when the mighty Brahmaputra changed its course. For this reason, ongoing maintenance upstream is necessary to ensure that the river doesn't end up skirting around the new bridge. To allow for some shift, a 16 km approach road on either side of the 4.8 km four lane bridge will have to be built. Even if the government can afford the hefty annual maintenance the question remains whether successive governments will have the commitment to do so.

Two economic side-benefits tipped the scale for the World Bank to vote 'yes' to the Jamuna Bridge: it would permit transmission of electricity, natural gas and telecommunications, which would have cost $100 million otherwise, and it would allow the easy future addition of a railway line.

However, as one journalist put it, the Jamuna Bridge 'stands as a confluence of hopes and aspirations of the entire nation'. The project was such a high priority of the government that donors, in order to maintain their good relations with the government, may have found it too hard to resist. ■

Train There's an express every day except Tuesday to Dhaka via Mymensingh, departing from Bogra at 8.35 pm and arriving at Mymensingh at 5 am and Dhaka at 7 am. The 1st/sulob class fares are Tk 325/105 to Dhaka and Tk 280/90 to Mymensingh. There is also a slower mail train, which departs from Bogra at 5 pm and arrives at Dhaka at 9 am. The fare to Dhaka is Tk 325/76 in 1st/2nd class.

From Dhaka, the Ekota Express departs in the late afternoon and gets into Bogra at around 4.30 am. You won't get much sleep on this trip as there's a three-hour ferry crossing in the middle of it. (This will change with the completion of the Jamuna Bridge, still several years away.) Still, the train is comfortable and the ferry, which sometimes runs aground, serves meals. If coming from Dhaka, when you catch the train waiting at the other side of the river make sure you get into a carriage that goes to Bogra, as the rest of the train goes to Dinajpur.

You can also get to the Paharpur ruins by train. There are three trains daily to Jaipurhat (with bus connections to Paharpur), departing from Bogra at 3.35 am, 1.05 (mail train) and 4.55 pm. This requires a change at the junction town of Shantahar (to change from the small gauge to broad gauge), and costs Tk 80 in 1st class and only Tk 15 in 2nd class to Jaipurhat. There are no direct trains to Dinajpur or Rajshahi; trains to these and other towns in Rajshahi and Khulna divisions run from Shantahar.

AROUND BOGRA
Sariakandi
For a bit of good adventure, consider heading east via Gabtali (General Zia's home town) to Sariakandi (20 km) and hiring a motorised boat there to take you out on to the Jamuna River. This is most interesting during flood season as you can see all the broken embankments and people living on tiny islands created by the massive annual flooding.

Hat Bazar
Every Friday in a tiny village just south of Bogra there's a *hat bazar*, a local market that attracts so many people that it literally swells

onto the highway, often causing a major traffic jam. These bazars can be extremely interesting and roaming around this one can be lots of fun. Look for the reed fish traps; very intriguing, they come in many shapes and styles.

MAHASTHANGARH
The oldest known city in Bangladesh, dating back to at least the 3rd century BC, Mahasthangarh (formerly known as Pundravardhana) is today an archaeological site consisting largely of foundations and hillocks hinting at past riches. There isn't a lot to see, but the scale is impressive and the countryside is good to wander in.

The principal site, called the Citadel, contains traces of the ancient city, but many other sites in the vicinity are usually lumped together under the name Mahasthangarh. This whole area is rich in Hindu, Buddhist and Muslim sites, most of which have all but vanished:

The Buddhists were here until at least the 11th century AD, their most glorious period being from the 8th to the 11th centuries AD when the Buddhist Pala emperors of North Bengal ruled. It is to this period that most of the visible remains belong. So while there are Hindu and Muslim structures here and there, most are Buddhist.

Site Museum
Although quite small, this is one of the better site museums in Bangladesh, with some interesting pieces, mostly Buddhist, from the 6th to 13th century AD. It consists of one very long room, with displays all around. On weekends there are always lots of visitors here, sometimes big groups of school children.

Upon entering, to the left you'll find lots of old Buddhist terracotta pieces from the Vasu Bihar excavations, as well as some gold ornaments and coins recovered here dating back to the 3rd century BC. The terracotta pieces were used to decorate Buddhist shrines, where they were discovered; some date back to the 2nd century BC. Excellently preserved, many of them depict a female figure with an elaborate headdress and richly bedecked with ornaments. The motifs represent human and semi-divine beings, animals and plants of various kinds, and composite animals or beings. Among the metal objects on display are copper rings, copper medallions, knives and an embossed gold amulet.

There are also some well preserved bronze images from Vasu Bihar, mostly from the Pala period (8th to 11th century AD), representing Buddha and other Buddhist deities in different forms and sizes. Of the female figures, different varieties of Bodhisattva Tara far outnumber others. Unlike the terracotta pieces, which were all discovered at the shrine area, the Vasu Bihar bronzes were all found in the monasteries, mostly inside the cells, and undoubtedly represent cult images for the private worship and ritual purposes of the resident monks.

Also on display, mostly to the right as you enter, are some large black-stone carvings of various Hindu deities, including Vishnu, Ganesh, Siva (Shiva) and Saraswati.

The museum is open daily from 10 am to 5 pm except Friday when it's closed. The fee is Tk 2 and at the entrance there are archaeological books for sale, which are fairly inexpensive and quite informative.

The Citadel

The Citadel, adjacent to the museum, forms a rough rectangle covering more than two sq km. More impressive is the fact that the remains of the fortified city rise around 4½m above the surrounding country – in Bangladesh that almost qualifies it as a mountain range. It was surrounded by a moat on three sides, with the once mighty Karatuya River guarding the fort.

Probably first constructed under the Mauryan Empire in the 3rd century BC, the site shows evidence of various Hindu empires and Buddhist and Muslim occupations. It finally fell into disuse around the time of the Mughal invasions, although Hindus still make an annual pilgrimage to the Karatuya River in mid-April. Most of the visible brickwork dates from the 8th century

AD Buddhist Pala Empire, apart from that added in the current restoration programme.

Outside the Citadel, opposite the museum, the remains of a 6th century AD Govinda Bhita Hindu temple overlook a picturesque bend in the river.

Lakshindarer Medh

Near Gokul, a couple of km south of the Citadel, this large mound is the partially excavated site of an ancient Siva temple, over which a Buddhist stupa was constructed in the 7th century AD. Local legend associates it with the snake goddess Manassa or, alternatively, with a dalliance between a wandering prince and a temple dancer.

Vasu Bihar

This Buddhist archaeological site is situated on low hills seven km to the north-west of the village of Mahasthan (MOSH-than). In the 7th century AD, the traveller Xuan Zhang wrote that this site accommodated 700 Buddhist monks in its monasteries, and also noted the gigantic Ashoka stupa. Many of the items on display in the museum came from here. Today, all that remains of the temple and monasteries are the brickwork foundations of the complex, which consist of five mounds. Unless you have an interest in archaeology, the trip along village tracks to get here will be the highlight of a visit.

Places to Stay & Eat

The *Archaeology Department Rest House* is across the road from the museum, overlooking the Karatuya River. You need permission from the Director of Archaeology in Dhaka (☎ 326-708) to stay here. You could also try contacting the regional office in Bogra (☎ 6527, 6071). If you just show up, however, chances are fairly good that you'll be allowed to stay if one of the three rooms isn't being occupied, which is usually the case. The man at the museum ticket booth can point you to the responsible person. The cost is only Tk 50 per room with two beds, and the guesthouse, which has flowers outside and a well maintained lawn, is quite nice and beautifully located overlooking the river.

You can eat there as well if you order well in advance. Otherwise, bring your own food or head for Mahasthan where you'll find a few basic restaurants.

Getting There & Away

Buses run from the Bogra bus station north to Mahasthan, and cost about Tk 4 for the half-hour trip. From here take a rickshaw or walk the 1¾ km to the Citadel and the nearby museum and guesthouse.

Vasu Bihar is seven km to the west of the museum, and by rickshaw it's a long and expensive ride (at least Tk 20 each way) over bumpy little roads and brick-paved paths. You might be able to take a tempo most of the way here from Mahasthan. When asking directions use the local name of the site: Narapatir Dhap.

PAHARPUR

The Somapuri Vihara at Paharpur was formerly the biggest Buddhist monastery south of the Himalaya and dates from the 8th century. It is by far the most impressive archaeological site in Bangladesh, so impressive that it was declared a protected archaeological site in 1919, although the scholar-traveller Dr Buckman Hamilton had shown his interest in it as far back as 1807.

Somapuri Vihara

Although in an advanced state of decay, the overall plan of the temple complex is easy to figure out. It is in the shape of a large quadrangle covering 11 hectares, with the monks' cells making up the walls and enclosing a courtyard. From the centre of the courtyard rises the 20m high remains of a stupa that dominates the countryside. There's a good view from the top. Its cruciform floor plan is topped by a three-tier superstructure with the first tier raised just slightly above ground level. The second rises almost three times higher; and the third level soars up to be topped by a large, hollow, square cubicle somewhat similar to the hollow tower structure of Mohenjo Daro in Pakistan.

This *mahavihara*, or large monastery, has slightly recessed walls embellished with

well preserved terracotta bas-reliefs of rural folk and wildlife in their local settings. The clay tiles are not sequentially arranged – they were really meant to be admired individually as decorative pieces, not to tell a story. Some of them depict an animal that just might be the variety of rhinoceros which is extinct in Bangladesh.

Lining the outer perimeter are over 170 small monastic cells. There are ornamental pedestals in 72 of them, the purpose of which still eludes archaeologists. It is possible they contained the remains of saintly monks who had been in residence in these cells. The cells have a drainage system with 22 outlets to the courtyard, marked by stone gargoyles.

There are points of interest on each side of the courtyard. On the east side, you can make out the outline of what was once a miniature model of the temple. On the western wing of the north side are the remains of structures whose purpose continues to baffle archaeologists. On the eastern wing of the south side is an elevated brick base with an eight-pointed, star-shaped structure which must have been a shrine. To the west lie the remains of what appear to have been the monks' refectory and kitchen.

Except for the guardhouse to the north, most of the remains outside the courtyard lie to the south. They include an oblong building, linked to the monastery by a causeway, which may have been the wash house and latrines. In the same area is a bathing ghat, probably of Hindu origin. Only 12m south-west of the ghat is the rectangular Temple of Gondeswari, with an octagonal pillar base in the centre and a circular platform to the front.

The monastery is thought to have been successively occupied by Buddhists, Jains and finally by Hindus. This explains the sometimes curious mixture of artwork, although the basic structure has remained unaltered. The Jains must have constructed a *chaturmukhar*, a structure with all four walls decorated with stone bas-reliefs of their deities. The Hindus made alterations to the base walls to replace the Buddhist terracotta artwork with sculptural stonework of their own deities, and with terracotta artwork representing themes from the *Mahabharata* and the *Ramayana*. Artefacts discovered at the site range from bronze statues and bas-reliefs of the elephant-headed Hindu god Ganesh, to statues of the Jain god Manzuri; from bronze images of the Buddha, to statues of the infant Krishna.

Museum

The small museum houses a representative display of the many domestic and religious objects found during excavations. It gives a good idea of the range of cultures which have used this site. Stucco Buddha heads unearthed here are similar to the Gandhara style. Sculptural work includes sandstone and basalt sculptures, but the stonework of Hevagara in passionate embrace with Shakti is the collection's finest item. The most important find, a large bronze Buddha, is usually away on tour. The museum is open from 9 am to noon and 2 to 5 pm daily, from 10 am to 5 pm Friday, and closed on Thursday. The museum and rest house are both in the Department of Archaeology compound, which also encloses a well kept garden.

Satyapir Vita

This complex originally contained the Temple of Tara. Approaching the site on the Jamalganj road, you first come to the ruins 400m east of the Somapuri Vihara. It is trapezoidal in shape, measuring about 75m by 40m by 85m, and was walled up except on the northern side, although the main entrance appears to have been from the south. The main temple is an oblong building, 24m by 12m, composed of three parts – the sanctum in the north, a pillared hall with a circumambulatory passage in the south and a shrine. Today, only scant ruins remain. A square-based stupa, three metres on each side, has a small reliquary which was full of tiny clay stupas when discovered, apparently offerings by pilgrims as tokens of reverence.

Places to Stay

If you plan to spend a day at Paharpur, start early as the place is extensive and fascinating. There is an *Archaeology Department Rest House*, but you have to book it at the Archaeology Department in Dhaka (☎ 326-708) or Bogra (☎ 6527, 6071). As at Mahasthan, however, if you just show up there is a good chance that you may be allowed to stay if you're friendly and there's space available. The cost is only Tk 50 per room. Meals may be available if you order well in advance, but it's advisable to bring supplies with you.

Getting There & Away

From Bogra Paharpur is 56 km north-west of Bogra. First take a bus to Jaipurhat, 44 km away. It is a 1½ hour trip costing Tk 20 by direct bus. The bus station in Jaipurhat is on the outskirts of town. From there you have two options. The first is to take a rickshaw from the bus station to a crossroads (Tk 3) and catch a crowded little tempo (Tk 6) from there to Paharpur village (nine km). The road is narrow but sealed all the way. Taking this option, you should be able to get from Bogra to Paharpur in 2½ hours.

A slower option is to walk or take a rickshaw the km or so to the Jaipurhat railway station. There, take one of the infrequent trains which cost Tk 2 and take 15 minutes to Jamalpur. This train is often hours late so see if there's a bus waiting across the tracks; it costs Tk 3 for a bumpy 40 minutes. From Jamalpur, it's a 45 minute walk to Paharpur or a short ride by rickshaw. Either way, on the trip back to Bogra don't count on getting a bus from Jaipurhat to Bogra after 6 pm.

From Rajshahi It is also possible to get to Paharpur from Rajshahi, which is almost 100 km to the south via Naogaon. From Naogaon, it is 20 km to Badolgazhi, though there is no transport for the final eight km to the site. This is not a good route unless you plan to overnight at Paharpur.

NAOGAON

While you're in the area, you could also check the old **Dubalhati Palace**, which is about 30 km south-west Paharpur as the crow flies, about eight km south-west of Naogaon. The main building, which has a 65m long facade, features a central block with Corinthian columns. If you look above them you'll see an unusually ornate parapet on top, with highly ornate plaster decorations consisting of floral patterns and sculptures of classical Greek male and female figures, plus an English insignia. The rajbari is now abandoned, so you can wander freely inside, visualising the splendour that the original owners (the Dubalhati Raj family, one of the oldest families in the district) lived in.

RANGPUR

Rangpur is a major transit point in the north and is the site of the Research Centre for Leprosy and several historic public buildings of the Raj era, including Carmichael College.

It's a large spread-out town, although most places of interest to travellers lie between Nawabganj Bazar, the centre of town on the corner of GL Roy and Station Rds, and the railway station, three km south at the end of Station Rd. If you're arriving by bus from Saidpur, you can get off at the first circle (Medical Morh) or at the bus station. The first is closer to the central market area and most lower-end hotels, while the latter is closer to the railway station.

The Sonali Bank, in an impressive Raj-period building, will change travellers cheques. It's on Station Rd, 500m south of Nawabganj Bazar. Care has an office here but no guesthouse. Its friendly staff may be a good source of information.

Tajhat Palace

Tajhat Palace, now the High Court Division of the Supreme Court, is one of the finest rajbaris ever built in Bangladesh. Indeed, it's so large and impressive that one immediately assumes it was always a public building. In the 19th century, a Hindu Manna Lal Ray was forced to emigrate from the Punjab and found his way to Rangpur. He became a successful jeweller and eventually acquired a lot of land, his crowning achievement being the construction of this huge mansion during the mid-19th century.

This magnificent edifice, which is structurally intact but deteriorating fast, is similar to Ahsan Manzil in Dhaka. It has a frontage of about 80m and, like the Pink Palace, is crowned by a ribbed conical dome and features an imposing central staircase made of imported white marble (the various marble sculptures of classical Roman figures along the balustrade having long since disappeared). The balcony roof is supported by four Corinthian columns, which are featured again on each of the projecting ends of the building. It's five km south of Nawabganj Bazar and two km south of the railway station, outside the defacto city boundaries.

Carmichael College

This famous old college, which dates from 1916, has a picturesque appearance and is worth checking out in conjunction with the High Court, two km to the south-east. Similar in inspiration to Curzon Hall in Dhaka, this structure, with a grand frontage of over 100m, represents a splendid fusion of classical British and Mughal architecture. Its mosque-inspired domes rest on slender columns and there are a series of arched openings on all sides which add to the mosque-like appearance. The campus, which is on the outskirts of town, is spacious and rural, with cows grazing on the main lawn. Coming here might be a good opportunity to meet some students, but you'd have to come on a week day.

Places to Stay – bottom end

Some 200m north of the railway station along Station Rd on your right, the unmarked single-storey *Nashirabad Hotel* should be avoided unless you're really low on taka or arrive very late at night by train. Small dirty rooms with common bathrooms cost Tk 35/60, which you may be able to bargain down Tk 5 or so.

In the town centre, a long block east of Nawabganj Bazar, *Al Sans Hotel* (☎ 3768) on Jaragosh Rd has singles/doubles with attached bathroom for Tk 60/100. A better choice would be the *Dhaka Hotel* on GL Roy Rd, which has singles/doubles with fans and attached bathrooms for Tk 60/120, and one of the better restaurants in this area. Next

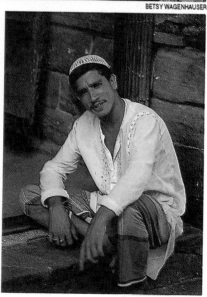

Top: Mourners in a Muslim cemetery at Dinajpur.
Bottom Left: Harmonium artisan in Dhaka.
Bottom Right: Devotee at Khan Jahan Mausoleum, Bagerhat.

JON MURRAY

GREGORY WAIT

IAN LOCKWOOD

Top Left: Swarighat fish market, Dhaka.
Top Right: Potter at the wheel.
Bottom: Mandi workers transplanting rice, Madhupur Forest.

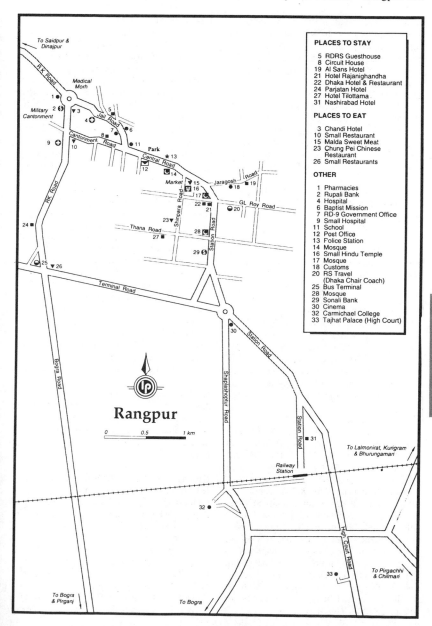

PLACES TO STAY

5 RDRS Guesthouse
8 Circuit House
19 Al Sans Hotel
21 Hotel Rajanighandha
22 Dhaka Hotel & Restaurant
24 Parjatan Hotel
27 Hotel Tilottama
31 Nashirabad Hotel

PLACES TO EAT

3 Chandi Hotel
10 Small Restaurant
15 Malda Sweet Meat
23 Chung Pei Chinese
   Restaurant
26 Small Restaurants

OTHER

1 Pharmacies
2 Rupali Bank
4 Hospital
6 Baptist Mission
7 RD-9 Government Office
9 Small Hospital
11 School
12 Post Office
13 Police Station
14 Mosque
16 Small Hindu Temple
17 Mosque
18 Customs
20 RS Travel
   (Dhaka Chair Coach)
25 Bus Terminal
28 Mosque
29 Sonali Bank
30 Cinema
32 Carmichael College
33 Tajhat Palace (High Court)

Rangpur

0   0.5   1 km

RAJSHAHI DIVISION

door, on Station Rd, is the six storey *Hotel Rajanighandha* (☎ 2669), which is even better. It has big, clean singles/doubles with attached bathroom for Tk 70/120.

Places to Stay – middle

The *Hotel Raj* (☎ 4202), 1½ blocks south of the market, has singles/doubles for Tk 80/150. The rooms have several chairs, tables with mirrors, fans, mosquito nets and decent bathrooms, but they're nothing special. It does have one of the best restaurants in town, however, and features Chinese cuisine.

Around the corner on Thana Rd you'll find *Hotel Tilottama* (☎ 3482), which is the best hotel in this category. It also has a restaurant and the ambience is a lot better, and the friendly English-speaking manager is very helpful. Singles/doubles, which cost Tk 100/160, have thin carpets, chairs, reasonably comfortable beds and bathrooms with western facilities.

Places to Stay – top end

The top hotel is the *Parjatan* (☎ 3681) on RK Rd, just north of the bus station. It's a modern establishment and features a spacious lobby with comfortable seating and cable TV. The standard rooms, which cost Tk 573, are ventilated and roomy, and come with carpets, nice furnishings and attached bathrooms with western facilities. There is also a restaurant.

The beautiful *Circuit House* (☎ 3095) on Cantonment Rd has lovely gardens in the front and singles/doubles for Tk 100/150. The District Commissioner (☎ 2111), however, will probably just refer you to the Parjatan.

You could also try the *RDRS Guesthouse* (☎ 2767) near RD-9, an unmarked three storey building just north of the Baptist Mission and 100m off Jail Rd. RDRS, a local developmental organisation, has very decent and comfortable guest quarters available to all, but at Tk 500 a room they're no bargain. Set meals here cost Tk 80 except for breakfast (Tk 60). To reserve, you must call here, not its office in Dhaka. On weekends the office closes on Thursday at noon.

Places to Eat

One of the better places in the centre of town for Bangladeshi food is the *Dhaka Hotel* on GL Roy Rd. It also has Chinese fare but it's reportedly mediocre. Or check to see if the nearby *Mitaly Restaurant* (no English sign) is still open. It's down an alley off GL Roy Rd near the south-east corner of the intersection with Station Rd. The chicken fry is reportedly good and it serves coffee. Another place close by is *Malda Sweet Meat*, on Central Rd at the market. You can get a Bengali meal, such as curry and rice, for around Tk 15 to Tk 20.

In the Medical Morh roundabout area, try the *Chandi Hotel*, which is just south of the roundabout. It's a friendly and relatively neat place. You can order tasty chicken, dhal (watery lentils) and rice for Tk 20, plus a very small plate of misti doi for Tk 6.

One of the best restaurants in town besides the tourist-oriented *Parjatan* is the *Chung Pei Chinese Restaurant* on the ground floor of Hotel Taj. It's a comfortable air-con place with low lighting and a long selection of Chinese dishes, including chicken and vegetables (Tk 45), fried prawns (Tk 75) and Mandarin fish (Tk 80). You could also try the restaurant at the *Hotel Tilottama* around the corner; it's likely to be a cut above the rest.

Getting There & Away

Air Biman (☎ 3437) flies every morning to Saidpur, which is 40 km to the west. Most people take a bus from there to get here, but an expensive taxi from the airport is an option.

Bus The bus station is on RK Rd (or Bogra Rd), three km south-west of the central area (at least Tk 10 by rickshaw). Buses for Bogra depart every 20 minutes from 7 am to 5.30 pm, and the fare is Tk 40. There are no direct buses to Dinajpur, Thakurgaon or Chilahati. For these towns, you must change at Saidpur. Buses for Saidpur leave every few minutes and charge Tk 28 for the 1¼ hour ride; the last bus departs around 7 pm. Trips to Dinajpur take around 2½ to three hours. Only a few buses make the five-hour, Tk 60 journey to Rajshahi, and the last leaves at 3 pm. There are no chair coaches on any of these routes.

Chair coaches for Dhaka all leave from around 5 to 7 pm; the trip normally takes about 11 hours. Many companies, such as Royal, leave from the bus station but for guaranteed seating you'll do better going to their offices and reserving a seat there. RS Travels, for example, is in the town centre on GL Roy Rd, 70m or so east of Station Rd. Its buses all leave between 5.30 and 6.30 pm, and the fare is Tk 140. Other companies offering chair coach services leave from the same area. Some Rajshahi buses apparently leave from there too.

Train IC trains to Dhaka via Mymensingh depart at 8.30 am and 7.45 pm, and 1st/sulob class fares are Tk 321/98 to Dhaka and Tk 233/70 to Mymensingh. It takes at least 12 hours to get to Dhaka, including a lengthy ferry crossing and a change of trains. A mail train for Mymensingh departs daily at 1.40 pm, and costs Tk 233/49 in 1st/2nd class. If you're headed south, you should take a bus west to Saidpur and catch one there.

AROUND RANGPUR
Sura Mosque

Built between 1493 and 1538 this small brick-and-stone structure is one of the oldest mosques in Bangladesh, and is a fine specimen of the pre-Mughal period. Highly ornate and in good condition, it features a long corridor in front, a square central prayer hall topped with a bulbous dome and walls covered with geometrically designed stone carvings, one of which is relieved with terracotta ornaments.

Finding this mosque is difficult at best. From Rangpur, head for Pirganj, which is about 40 km south of Rangpur on the Rangpur-Bogra highway. From Pirganj, head south-west.

SAIDPUR

Saidpur is a quiet little backwater shaded by enormous trees, and the atmosphere of the Raj lingers. Near the quaint old railway station is one of Bangladesh's few surviving English-style churches, and the neat back streets are lined with old cottages.

Although Saidpur is fairly small, it nevertheless rates an airport, the only one in northern Bangladesh. Consequently, it serves much larger cities, including Rangpur, Dinajpur and Thakurgaon, and is fairly busy as a result.

The City Bank and Sonali Bank both have branches in the central area and might be persuaded to change cash at bad rates, but you'll have to continue on to Rangpur or Dinajpur to change travellers cheques.

Places to Stay & Eat

Haque Boarding, in the heart of town on Dinajpur Rd, 250m west of the intersection with Station Rd, has tiny ventilated singles/doubles for Tk 25/40 and filthy common bathrooms. Rooms are reasonably clean and have fans, mosquito nets and tiny attached bathrooms.

The best place to stay is the *Bengalipur Concern Guesthouse* (☎ 2103), which has spotless facilities. Well known by rickshaw drivers, it's in the Bengalipur area, ½ km east towards town from the bus station, 150m south of the highway. The price is Tk 120 a person but you may have to share your room with others. It's a relaxing place, with a spacious living area with comfortable chairs and reading material, and you get meals as well. Reserve by calling Project Concern's office in Dhaka (House 63, Rd 15A, Dhanmondi, ☎ 812-795/6), but if you just show up, the friendly caretaker will most likely give you a bed if there's one available. Coming from the bus station towards town, take your first left immediately after you pass the paddy fields and ask for directions. From the airport it's a 12 minute rickshaw ride.

Saidpur has only very ordinary restaurants, including one on Station Rd just before the post office and two others 200m to the east, across the railway tracks. Each of them serve typical Bangladeshi meals (curry, bhoona etc) for about Tk 20.

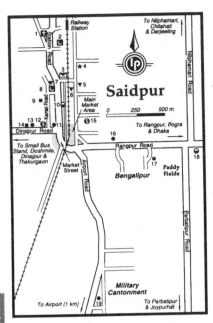

RAJSHAHI DIVISION

Getting There & Away

Air The airport (☎ 2006) is two km to the south, beyond the attractive old administrative area and next to the military cantonment. The Biman office (☎ 2007) is on Dinajpur Rd, 200m west of the city's main intersection. There are flights to/from Dhaka every morning; the fare is Tk 816 plus Tk 50 airport tax. There are lots of rickshaws and a few unmarked taxis for taking travellers into town but no baby taxis. The rickshaw fare is Tk 10 into town but you'll probably have to bargain hard to get this price. The taxis are impossible to distinguish from private cars so you'll have to ask someone at the airport to point one out.

Bus The main bus station is on the eastern side of town, about 1½ km from the town centre. There are departures every few minutes for Rangpur (1¼ hours), Dinajpur (one hour) and slightly less frequently for Thakurgaon (1½ hours). You can also get buses to Chilahati and Parbatipur. The last buses for all these towns depart around 7 pm. If you're headed south for Jaipurhat (near the Paharpur ruins) you may have to wait so long for a direct bus that you'll be better off taking a series of buses.

You can get buses here for Dhaka, but you'll do better going to their offices in the centre of town along Station Rd and reserving a seat there. Chair coaches all leave around 5 to 6.30 pm, and the trip usually takes about 11 hours, more if the ferry crossing is unusually slow. The Motibar Rahman Dular coach, for example, departs daily at 5 pm.

You'll also find a small bus stand on the western edge of town where some local buses heading for Doshmile, Dinajpur and Thakurgaon leave from. It's about one km from the town centre and beyond the bridge.

Typical fares are Tk 6 to Doshmile, Tk 15 to Dinajpur, Tk 23 to Thakurgaon, Tk 28 to Chilahati, Tk 28 to Rangpur and Tk 120 to Dhaka (Tk 140 for a chair coach).

Train Trains to Khulna run via Ishurdi. The IC Rupsa Express departs at 8 am and 8.40 pm, and fares are Tk 385/84 in 1st/sulob class. The fares to Jessore are Tk 345/115. A mail train for Ishurdi departs at 7.30 am.

Two express and two local trains a day (including one at 3 pm) make the two-hour trip north to Chilahati. The fare is Tk 70/23 in 1st/2nd class.

DINAJPUR

Dinajpur, 50 km south of Thakurgaon and 70 km west of Rangpur, is the largest city in north-western Bangladesh and is famous for its rice. There are some interesting old buildings in town, the most famous being the Dinajpur Rajbari, one of the country's finest monuments. It includes an adjoining Krishna temple. There are also some interesting buildings in the surrounding rural areas, including another of the country's real gems – the much photographed Kantanagar Temple, which is in all the Bangladesh tourist brochures. In winter the area is slightly cooler than the country's southern region and there are lots of good back roads for cycling.

In short, Dinajpur, which is perhaps a bit more relaxed than its size would suggest, is a good destination if you're interested in old structures, or would like to cycle or drive around rural areas.

Orientation & Information

The railway station is the heart of town. Just north is the market and most hotels and restaurants. South of the railway station is the administrative area, including the Circuit House, a large compound of some imposing Raj-era buildings (the GPO, tourist office, mapping office, etc) and a grass *maidan* (parade ground) where sports people play and demonstrators congregate.

Don't expect much of anything from the tourist and mapping offices. The Sonali Bank, on the other hand, changes travellers cheques and is in a marvellous old rajbari about a km north of the railway station.

If you want to check out the local Indian-movie scene, try one of the three cinemas along Station Rd. Kutibari Hall Cinema reportedly frequently screens movies in English.

Rajbari

The Dinajpur Rajbari is dilapidated but it's still one of the country's most picturesque, and it's worth exploring the buildings and grounds. To the left of the entrance is a daintily painted Krishna temple. The rajbari itself lies through a second gate, facing another courtyard. Both structures date from the 1890s when the 18th-century palace was rebuilt after the great earthquake of 1897.

As with many of these magnificent 18th and 19th-century rajbaris, this one and the Krishna temple reflect the cosmopolitan tastes of their owners. Florid oriental designs blend with European-inspired proportions and neo-Renaissance features, including ornate gateways and many beautifully carved stone columns. The single-storey flat-roofed Krishna temple, for example, is decorated with attractive stucco floral motifs. The front verandah is supported on four semi-Corinthian pillars and the main hall on another set of similar columns. The main two storey rajbari has a broad frontage of about 45m, with a series of tall Ionic columns, and on either side of the balcony is a broad spiral masonry staircase leading to the upper storey. Inside, there's a 15m long, eight metre high hall.

The Krishna temple is open only from 8 am to 1 pm and 5 to 8 pm. Hindus still worship here, so the cows that wander among the ruins are probably as safe as their ancestors were when the terracotta scenes of Krishna and the gopis were made.

The rajbari is about four km north-east of central Dinajpur and a rickshaw will cost at least Tk 15. Don't bargain a round-trip fare as there are plenty of rickshaws available nearby.

Places to Stay – bottom end

Most of the lower-end hotels are near the railway station in the centre of town. The cheapest is *Arab Boarding*, just west of the station. Its singles/doubles, which are tiny and filthy with common bathrooms, cost Tk 24/45.

Hotel Rehana (☎ 4144), which is 1½ blocks up Station Rd (no English sign), is next in line, with singles/doubles for Tk 35/60. It's friendly, a little better, with attached bathrooms and fans. Avoid rooms in the back which are adjacent to a large cinema. The *Nabina Hotel* (☎ 4178) is half a block west and of comparable value. It has ventilated singles/doubles and beds with mosquito nets for Tk 40/50 (Tk 50/70 with attached bathrooms).

Hotel Conica (☎ 4148), around the corner on Station Rd, is much better and is highly recommended, with doubles for Tk 80 but only a few singles (Tk 50), and they're usually all taken. One traveller, who noted that rooms have a button for ringing room service, said that it was the best hotel he stayed at in Bangladesh. Its rooms have fans, mosquito nets and attached bathrooms, and there's a restaurant. Equally good, however, is the *New Hotel* (☎ 4155), which is across the road and has singles/doubles for Tk 50/80. It's clean, with decent attached bathrooms and rooms with fans and mosquito nets. The hotel's restaurant is the best Bangladeshi eatery in the centre of town.

Places to Stay – top end

Hotel Al-Rashid is a km north of the railway station, a block east of Station Rd. It's a very clean, well run establishment. The small rooms have attached bathrooms and are worth the Tk 70/150 for singles/doubles. There's a local restaurant nearby.

Even better, drop by the CDA office (☎ 4764) on the eastern outskirts of town on Fulbari Rd. The attached *CDA Guesthouse* has several rooms, with four beds per room. They are spotless and cost Tk 60 a person; guests can eat here as well.

For the price and quality, you can't beat the *Circuit House* (☎ 3122), which has the best accommodation in town. It overlooks the grassy maidan behind the railway station. It has eight modern guest rooms and, therefore, space is often available. You need permission from the District Commissioner, whoᵉ office is on the other side of the maidan. The rooms, which cost Tk 30, are relatively new and spacious, with twin beds, fans, mosquito nets and spotless attached

bathrooms. You can also eat here, but you must order in advance. If it's full, try the government housing office; it has a *guesthouse* here too.

The *Ramshagar Lake Guesthouse*, beautifully located on a hill overlooking Ramshagar Lake, is 11 km south-east of town on Pulhat Rd. It has two spacious rooms and they cost around Tk 120. The rooms have two or three beds, overhead fans, old frayed carpets, mosquito nets and attached bathrooms with western-style toilets. Meals are not available. Not many people stay here overnight, but on weekends the lake attracts numerous residents of Dinajpur.

Places to Eat

New Hotel has the best Bangladeshi restaurant in the town centre and is highly recommended. Very popular and open almost to midnight, it's one of the rare places where you can get vegetarian dishes. Two spicy vegetable dishes plus rice costs just Tk 13 and makes a very filling meal. The *Hotel Conica*, which also has a restaurant, is just across the street.

The small unmarked *Slim Hotel* just east of the railway station looks grubby but may be cheaper. There's also *Padma Sweets* around the corner from Hotel Conica; it's clean and better for snacks. If you're in the area around Hotel Al-Rashid you'll find a few more small restaurants, including the unmarked *Dinajpur Brahamian Sweets*, which is two blocks north-east on a corner and better for snacks.

The city's top restaurants are both Chinese and have air-con: the *Puffin Restaurant*, which faces the railway station, and *Martin Chinese Restaurant* (☎ 4074), which is almost a km to the north along Station Rd. Dishes at both places are mostly in the Tk 60 to Tk 80 range. The Puffin's rundown appearance is misleading because the restaurant inside, on the 3rd floor, is quite attractive, light and airy, with a menu in Bangla. The well marked Martin is dimly lit inside and features an extensive menu in English.

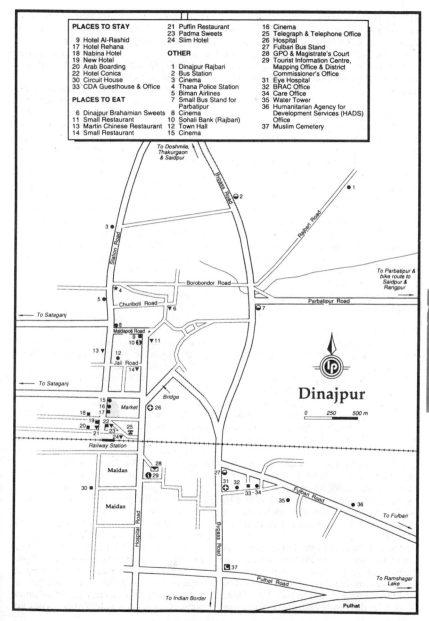

PLACES TO STAY

9 Hotel Al-Rashid
17 Hotel Rehana
18 Nabina Hotel
19 New Hotel
20 Arab Boarding
22 Hotel Conica
30 Circuit House
33 CDA Guesthouse & Office

PLACES TO EAT

6 Dinajpur Brahamian Sweets
11 Small Restaurant
13 Martin Chinese Restaurant
14 Small Restaurant

21 Puffin Restaurant
23 Padma Sweets
24 Slim Hotel

OTHER

1 Dinajpur Rajbari
2 Bus Station
3 Cinema
4 Thana Police Station
5 Biman Airlines
7 Small Bus Stand for Parbatipur
8 Cinema
10 Sonali Bank (Rajbari)
12 Town Hall
15 Cinema

16 Cinema
25 Telegraph & Telephone Office
26 Hospital
27 Fulbari Bus Stand
28 GPO & Magistrate's Court
29 Tourist Information Centre, Mapping Office & District Commissioner's Office
31 Eye Hospital
32 BRAC Office
34 Care Office
35 Water Tower
36 Humanitarian Agency for Development Services (HADS) Office
37 Muslim Cemetery

To Doshmile, Thakurgaon & Saidpur

Bypass Road

Rajbari Road

Station Road

To Parbatipur & bike route to Saidpur & Rangpur

Borobondor Road

Churiboti Road

To Sataganj

Parbatipur Road

Maldapoti Road

To Sataganj

Jail Road

Bridge

Dinajpur

0   250   500 m

Market

Railway Station

Maidan

Hospital Road

Maidan

Fulbari Road

To Fulbari

Bypass Road

Pulhat Road

To Ramshagar Lake

To Indian Border

Pulhat

RAJSHAHI DIVISION

Getting There & Away

Air The nearest airport is outside Saidpur, from where flights to/from Dhaka (Tk 816) leave every morning at 11.20 am. There's a Biman office (☎ 3340) in Dinajpur, on Station Rd about two km north of the railway station.

Bus The bus station is on the north-eastern side of town on Rangpur Bypass Rd. The bus fare is Tk 14 to Saidpur (one hour) and Tk 20 to Thakurgaon (1⅔ hours). If you're headed east to Rangpur or north to Chilahati, you'll have to change in Saidpur as there is no direct service to those towns. The trip to Rangpur takes between 2½ and three hours.

Buses direct to Dhaka and Bogra cost Tk 65 to Bogra and Tk 135 to Dhaka (Tk 170 by chair coach). Chair coaches all depart between 5 and 7 pm, and some of them have offices in town. Buses take 12 to 14 hours to Dhaka, depending on the wait at the ferry crossing across the Jamuna River. The time should lessen once the Jamuna Bridge is completed.

Train A number of useful trains serve Dinajpur, although there are better connections available at the nearby junction town of Parbatipur.

IC trains for Khulna via Ishurdi, Kushtia and Jessore depart from Dinajpur daily, except Monday, at 6 am. On Sunday, Tuesday and Thursday a carriage connects with Rajshahi. To Khulna, the 1st/sulob class fares are Tk 400/130; and to Rajshahi they're Tk 213/68.

The *Uttara Express* is a mail train running from Parbatipur to Rajshahi daily at 4 am. Fares are Tk 213/68 in 1st/sulob class. The *Ekota Express* runs from Parbatipur to Bogra, from where you can catch trains to Dhaka. The 1st/sulob fares to Dhaka are Tk 420/135.

If you're headed to the Indian border at Chilahati, you can take the 5 am train east to Parbatipur and connect with trains to Chilahati, arriving there around 1 pm. The total fare comes to Tk 42 in 2nd class. There is also a decrepit 2nd-class train for Thakurgaon and Panchagarh, departing daily around 7 am. The trip takes about five hours to Panchagarh but delays are common.

AROUND DINAJPUR
Ramshagar Lake
Beyond Pulhat is a large picturesque lake, about 350m long, that is popular with Dinajpur residents as a picnic spot on Friday. If you're looking for a place to get away from it all, this would be a good spot to come, especially during the week when it's all but deserted. Some 11 km south-east of town, the lake is only about 250m off the tarred Pulhat Rd, to your right, but it's surrounded by paddy fields and not visible from the road. There's an entrance fee of Tk 10 per vehicle. You can get a regular bus here for Tk 5. You'll find a guesthouse overlooking the lake (see Places to Stay – Top End in the previous Dinajpur section) and possibly several small boats for hire.

Kantanagar Temple
One of the most spectacular monuments in Bangladesh, this Hindu temple should not be missed. Built in 1752 by a renowned maharaja from Dinajpur, Pran Nath, it is the country's finest existing example of the brick and terracotta style. Its most remarkable feature, typical of the late Mughal-era temples, is its superb surface decoration, with endless panels of sculptured terracotta plaques, depicting both figural and floral motifs. The interior and exterior walls are simply amazing. Every available space, including the archways, vaults and columns of all three storeys, are profusely decorated with tiny figures and motifs in terracotta. The most prominent panels over the archways depict scenes from the great Hindu epics, particularly battle scenes.

Certainly the folk artists did not lack imagination or humour. Demons are depicted biting deep into the heads of the faithful (monkeys); one demon can be seen swallowing monkeys whole, that promptly reappear from his ear. Amid this confusion a pair of monkeys may be seen carrying off a demon, like a chicken on a pole. Other scenes are more domestic, including a wife massaging her husband's legs and a lady busy combing lice from another's hair. Another portrays a river cruise on a long boat overcrowded with merrymakers around a troupe of dancers, while amorous scenes are often placed in obscure corners. Overall, the effect of these intricate harmonious scenes is like a richly embroidered carpet. And the predominantly red colour contrasts sharply with the deep green surrounding landscape.

The temple, a 15 sq metre three storey edifice, was originally crowned with nine ornamental, two-storey towers, giving it a more temple-like appearance. They collapsed during the great earthquake of 1897, however, and were never replaced.

Getting There & Away The temple is 26 km north of Dinajpur on the road to Thakurgaon. Tell the bus driver where you want to go and remind him after about 20 km. Get off the bus in Kantanagar village, which is the first village (about five km) beyond Doshmile; sometimes this is a regular stop, sometimes not. From the highway a dirt track goes left (west) for about 200m through the village and down to the river, from where you can barely see the temple's rooftop. A boat will be waiting there to take you across. It's then a 10 minute walk to the temple – up a small hill, then left at the first fork and then follow the winding path.

Buddhist Ruins of Sitakot Vihara Monastery

Some 46 km south-east of Dinajpur, about six km north-east of Charkai railway station and three km north-west of Nawabganj, are the Buddhist ruins of Sitakot. Excavations here in 1968 exposed a Buddhist monastery dating from the 7th to 8th centuries. There are some 50 similar ancient mounds in the area, but little remains of them as they have been the target of vandalism by the neighbouring villagers searching for building materials.

The Sitakot monastery was built on a square plan and the 40 living spaces for monks once overlooked a central courtyard. Unlike the more important Paharpur and Mainimati monasteries, this monastery bears no evidence of having any central temple in the inner courtyard. Instead, there were cell-like shrines in the centre of each courtyard, with deities apparently located inside. Several Bodhisattva images were uncovered during excavations, but nothing remains except for traces of the foundations. The lack of any archaeological finds or objects of daily use, such as coins or icons, suggests that the monastery here was abandoned peacefully.

Overall, unlike the Buddhist monasteries of Paharpur and Mainimati, this small isolated monastery doesn't have enough complexity or archaeological finds to warrant a special trip. If you're in the area, however, it's probably worth a short stop. Buses from Dinajpur to Charkai cost about Tk 20.

THAKURGAON

Thakurgaon is one of the more pleasant towns in northern Bangladesh and a good travel destination, especially if you are interested in cycling. There are lots of back roads in the area with relatively few motor vehi-

Kantanagar Temple was Bangladesh's major nava-ratha (nine towered) shrine until all nine towers collapsed during the Great Indian Earthquake of 1897.

cles, and the scenery is beautiful in the country. One interesting trip would be north to Panchagarh via Atwari, and then further north to the Indian border at Tetulia (where there's a guesthouse available) and Bangla-bandha. Alternatively, from Atwari you could take a narrow back road south-west to Baliadangi, then either east back to Thakur-gaon or further south all the way to Haripur at the Indian border and, from there, south-east to Dinajpur.

It's relatively cool here, so in December and January you will definitely need a jumper at night. The town is small enough to cover on foot provided you like to walk, but rickshaws are everywhere and at night you'll be charmed by the tinkling of their lanterns as they run along the dark streets.

If you're interested in seeing what some of the local nongovernment organisations (NGOs) are doing, visit the office of the Humanitarian Agency for Development Services (HADS) in town and its farm on the south-western edge of town. It has a number of small-scale activities in operation, including a small dairy. The Swiss-supported Rangpur Dinajpur Rural Services Project (RDRS) is another possibility.

Places to Stay

The best cheap hotel is *Tangon Boarding*, a two storey structure on the western end of Hospital Rd, one long block west of the heart of town, near the Tangon River. It has small singles/doubles with overhead fans and attached bathrooms for Tk 30/40. *Noor Hotel* (☎ 3543), which is just off the Dinajpur-Panchagarh highway, a block north of the intersection with Hospital Rd, is much poorer value. It's a dirty hole and charges a ridiculously high Tk 75 for a grubby venti-lated room with three beds and a filthy attached bathroom.

The friendly *HADS Guesthouse & Office* (☎ 3513) is on Sirajuddowlah Rd, north of the hospital. The rooms, which cost Tk 400, are spacious and airy, with fans, comfortable twin beds that have mosquito nets, drinking water and spotless attached bathrooms. Staff can also arrange for meals to be brought to your room. Reservations are advisable since there are only three guest rooms. Call the HADS office at 3/8 Humayun Rd, Moham-madpur, Dhaka (☎ 813-758; fax 813-014).

Or try the *RDRS Guesthouse* (☎ 3670), which has comparable rooms for Tk 400. They are spacious, with comfortable twin

RAJSHAHI DIVISION

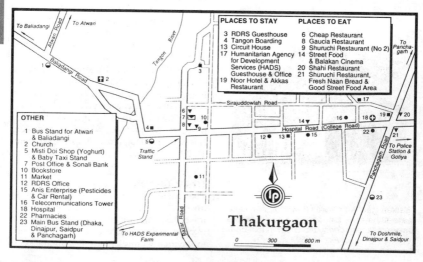

PLACES TO STAY
3 RDRS Guesthouse
4 Tangon Boarding
13 Circuit House
17 Humanitarian Agency
for Development
Services (HADS)
Guesthouse & Office
19 Noor Hotel & Akkas
Restaurant

PLACES TO EAT
6 Cheap Restaurant
8 Gaucia Restaurant
9 Shuruchi Restaurant (No 2)
14 Street Food
& Balakan Cinema
20 Shahi Restaurant
21 Shuruchi Restaurant,
Fresh Naan Bread &
Good Street Food Area

OTHER
1 Bus Stand for Atwari
& Baliadangi
2 Church
5 Misti Doi Shop (Yoghurt)
& Baby Taxi Stand
7 Post Office & Sonali Bank
10 Bookstore
11 Market
12 RDRS Office
15 Anis Enterprise (Pesticides
& Car Rental)
16 Telecommunications Tower
18 Hospital
22 Pharmacies
23 Main Bus Stand (Dhaka,
Dinajpur, Saidpur
& Panchagarh)

Thakurgaon

beds, carpets, mosquito nets, emergency lights, drinking water, desks and clean attached bathrooms that have hot-water showers and western-style toilets. It serves meals as well. To reserve, call the guest-house, not RDRS in Dhaka.

If these guesthouses are full, the chances are good that the District Commissioner will allow you to stay at the government *Circuit House*, which is on Hospital Rd and much cheaper.

Places to Eat

The best place for a meal is the *RDRS Guest-house* (Tk 60 for breakfast and Tk 80 for lunch or dinner), but meals are not generally available to non-guests unless you order in advance.

The best local restaurant is *Shuruchi Restaurant No 2* on Hospital Rd; the fare is Bangladeshi, inexpensive and a notch better than at other establishments.

Other places to eat, all similar, are the *Gaucia Restaurant*, around the corner, and several restaurants along the Dinajpur-Panchagarh highway at or near the intersection with Hospital Rd, including *Shuruchi Restaurant No 1* and *Shahi Restaurant*. You can also get snack food at a small restaurant next to Balakan Cinema on Hospital Rd, opposite Anis Enterprise, and sweet yoghurt at a misti doi shop at the western end of Hospital Rd, across from Tangon Boarding.

Getting There & Away

Bus Buses for Atwari and west to Baliadangi depart from a small bus station at the western end of town. All other buses depart from the main bus station on the Dinajpur-Panchagarh highway, a half km south of Hospital Rd. Buses south to Dinajpur and north to Panchagarh cost Tk 20/12 and depart from around 7 am to 7.30 pm. The trip takes approximately 1¾ hours to Dinajpur and about half that to Panchagarh. Buses to Saidpur cost Tk 23 and depart between 6.30 am and 5.30 pm; the trip takes just under two hours. The trip to Bogra via Saidpur takes five hours and costs Tk 75.

If you're headed to Dhaka, you have a choice between a normal bus (Tk 140) and a chair coach (Tk 180). The trip takes 12 to 14 hours. Chair coaches depart at 5.30 am and at 2.30 pm, while normal buses depart at all hours of the day.

Train The railway station is on the western edge of town. The 2nd-class train connecting Dinajpur and Panchagarh departs from either town around 7 am and passes through Thakurgaon several hours later.

Car For a rental car, see Anis Enterprise, a pesticide store across from the Balakan Cinema on Hospital Rd. A minivan and driver can cost as low as Tk 600 a day plus petrol if you bargain real hard or a local friend arranges it, but most travellers should expect to pay 25% to 50% more.

AROUND THAKURGAON
Singra Forest Reserve

Just north of town is a 200-hectare protected forest which is definitely worth a trip. Singra (SHENG-grah) is fairly uniformly planted in sal trees, with some areas of mixed woodland on the edge of the reserve. The forestry official here is welcoming. For bird-watching, the best time to come is during the winter months when you'll spot a fair number of winter migrants. On one visit, a well known bird-watcher from Dhaka spotted 20 or so pairs of Indian pitta, many spangled drongo and a few black ones, lesser scaly breasted woodpeckers and orange-headed thrush (both common here), Indian cuckoo and a jacobin cuckoo, several paradis flycatchers and a changeable hawk eagle.

Getting There & Away To get here, starting from the main junction on the Dinajpur-Panchagar highway, go approximately one km north where you'll find a driveable dirt track on your left (west) and a small sign in English, Singra Picnic Centre. The gated picnic area is 1½ km down that track and the small reserve is just beyond.

Biganj Forest Reserve

About 23 km south of Thakurgaon and 28 km

north of Dinajpur, just east of the Dinajpur-Thakurgaon highway near Biganj, is a small forest reserve similar to Singra but more degraded. It attracts basically the same birds as Singra. You might also spot wood swallows, lesser whistling duck and, if you're really lucky, grey-breasted prinia, which were first recorded in this area in 1995.

PANCHAGARH

Some 40 km north of Thakurgaon, Panchagarh is the site of a largely disappeared mud fort (Bhitar Garh) built in the 14th century by the Hindus as defence against the encroaching Mughals. It's on the main road which heads north to the Indian border crossings at Tetulia and Banglabandha. You cannot cross the border at either town, but the paved route north of Panchagarh is very scenic and perfect for cycling because of the few vehicles that use.

Places to Stay & Eat

The best place to stay is the government *Circuit House* (☎ 348), which costs Tk 16 a room and possibly more for foreigners. Located on Tetulia Rd in the northern outskirts of town on the left (west), it's a two storey building with a garden in the front. It has six spacious standard rooms which have carpets, fans, attractive furnishings and spotless bathrooms with showers and western-style toilets. To stay here, you must get permission from the District Commissioner, whose office is a stone's throw away. Guests can also eat here.

If you can't get a room at the Circuit House, try the *Diabetic Association of Bangladesh*, which is a pale yellow two storey building on the same road closer to the town centre, just north of the bridge. Well marked, this complex has eight decent guest rooms (about Tk 60) with fans and attached bathrooms.

Much further north in Tetulia there's another government *Guesthouse*, is beautifully located on a hill overlooking a nearby river and India. To stay and eat there, you must reserve a room at the government engineer's office (☎ 223) on Tetulia Rd, just south of the bridge. For food in Panchagarh,

look for food stalls near the main intersection and around the market.

Getting There & Away

Buses to Panchagarh cost Tk 12 from Thakurgaon and Tk 32 from Dinajpur. For fun, you could also take the old 2nd-class Dinajpur-Panchagarh train, which leaves daily at 7 am from either town, and stops at Thakurgaon en route; the fare is Tk 20 and the trip takes about five hours.

CHILAHATI

Chilahati is the main crossing point in northern Bangladesh for India. Before heading from the railway station to the last Bangladeshi checkpoint at the border (four km), or when arriving in Chilahati from India, you must pass through immigration and customs at the far end of the railway platform. It is open until 6 pm, and procedures are usually, but not always, straightforward and hassle free.

Places to Stay & Eat

If you're caught here for the night, you'll find a very basic *guesthouse*, which has rooms with attached bathrooms for just Tk 25, and you can eat at one of the incredibly cheap local restaurants, which serves rice for Tk 2!

Getting There & Away

From Bangladesh Travelling north from Bangladesh into India, you can take a local train from Saidpur to Chilahati. There are two daily, the last departing at 3 pm and arriving at 6.15 pm. When passing through immigration, you may be hassled to no end if you tell officials that you are carrying more than Tk 100, the official maximum. One traveller who told them he possessed Tk 450 reported being severely hassled, having his bags searched in a truly painstaking manner and then being forced by customs officials to pay Tk 100 to the rickshaw driver who was taking him to the final checkpoint. (The normal fare is much less, although the distance is quite long.) So don't come here with more than Tk 100!

Procedures at the last Bangladeshi checkpoint at the border, about four km from Chilahati (up to two hours if you chose to walk), are usually straightforward and hassle free. You can change money here as well, and Bangladeshi officials are fairly lax in searching for taka when you leave. It's then a short walk to the first Indian border post at Hemkumari and procedures on the Indian side are usually straightforward.

From Hemkumari you can take a slow bus to Haldibari or an even slower rickshaw (two hours), where you then have the option of taking a train or bus. The train to Siliguri costs about Rs 8 and departs at 7.30 am. Change trains at New Jalpaiguri, where you also have to register at the Foreigners' Registration Office. You can catch the toy train to Darjeeling from any of the three railway stations in Siliguri – there are two or three departures daily.

From India Travelling from Darjeeling to Siliguri takes 10 hours by the toy train. A train from Siliguri to Haldibari is a two-hour trip and costs about Rs 8 in 2nd class. It is advisable to take the early train as Haldibari is not a great place to stay. If you do have to stay there, the only place you may find is a Dak Bungalow.

There is a bus from Haldibari to Hemkumari, a border village, but it's slow and often late. An alternative is a rickshaw trip which takes two hours. From Hemkumari it's a four km hike along a dirt road to Chilahati, where you'll find immigration. Keep a few rupees to change to takas at the Indian border point for the train fare to Rangpur or Dinajpur, where you can cash travellers' cheques.

RAJSHAHI
Built on the northern bank of the Padma River, Rajshahi is a big town, laid-back and relatively prosperous.

Unlike most riverbanks in Bangladesh, the Padma River is somewhat elevated (partly natural and partly as a dyke for flood control) and thus affords one of the best river views in the country. Sunsets here are particularly worth seeing. The thing to do in

Rajshahi in the late afternoon is to walk south from the Parjatan Hotel towards the river and then stroll along the river. It's almost carnival like, and obviously a place to be seen, with people strolling and chatting, children playing, and small-time vendors selling ice cream and other snack food.

Looking across the vast flood plain to the opposite bank you'll see India, where the river is called the Ganges. India's Farakka Dam regulates the flow of the Ganges. In 1995 this area was probably the worst hit by flooding in the country. Yet in the dry season very little water comes down to Bangladesh these days – a major cause of friction between the two governments.

The presence of Rajshahi University (RU), which also has a large campus on the north-eastern outskirts of town, a medical college, an engineering college, a zoo, a sericulture institute, a Christian mission hospital, a Parjatan tourist hotel, an airport and two museums, adds to the relatively sophisticated atmosphere of town. If you come during the first half of the year through early July, you'll get to sample some of the area's famous mangoes.

Orientation & Information
The Parjatan Hotel has the usual brochures but no tourist information. If pressed, the staff will send you to the District Information Office in the cantonment area, where you might get tea and biscuits but you won't get any information – their job is collecting government statistics. You'll have better luck introducing yourself to the friendly expats at the Christian mission hospital; they may be able to help out.

The Sonali Bank will reluctantly change money, but you'll get better rates and service at the nearby Agrani Bank in Saheb Bazar. The post office is on Greater Rd on the western side of town.

The British Council Library, a pale single storey building lined with columns near the heart of town on Emaduddin Rd, has books in English and friendly staff who can help with local information. It's open between 2 and 7 pm, closed Friday. Because of the colleges in town, there are quite a few book-shops in New Market and to the north of Saheb Bazar. They sell mainly academic texts, but the odd novel is available.

With the Indian border so close, there is a huge local trade in smuggled goods, most evident in Saheb Bazar. Indian beer can sometimes be found at very high prices.

Varendra Research Museum

Founded in 1919 with the support of the Maharaja of Dighapatia who granted the land, the Varendra Research Museum is the oldest museum in the country and is definitely worth visiting. The building, which is predominantly British in style, has some interesting Hindu-Buddhist features, including a trefoil arch over the doorways and windows, and a small *rekha* temple forms on the roof.

Inside, artefacts from all over the subcontinent are on display, including some rare examples from the ancient city of Mohenjo Daro in Pakistan. Other displays include a superb collection of local Hindu sculpture (in stone imported from Bihar), which shows how Bangladesh influenced that culture. Tantric motifs are evident, and the figures are more relaxed, giving them a more natural appearance.

The museum is open daily from 10 am to 5 pm, except Friday when it's only open from 2.30 to 5 pm, and Saturday when it's closed.

Martyrs' Memorial Museum

The collection of Liberation War mementoes at the Shaheed Smriti Sangrahashala (Martyrs' Memorial Museum) at RU is a good reminder of the dreary days of the 1971 war. Unfortunately, the miserable state of the museum, with its dusty collection of war artefacts, is more likely to make one feel that the country has forgotten its heroes. Among the exhibits are blood-stained uniforms, a pen used by a fighter to write his last love letter, the deed papers of surrender by the Pakistani forces, remnants recovered from a mass grave of victims, which included intellectuals from RU, and weapons used by the freedom fighters. Photographs serve as testimonials to the Pakistani army's torture,

murder and rape, and the burning of thousands of homes.

Buildings of the British Raj

Near the centre of Rajshahi are some Raj-era buildings. Rajshahi Government College, which dates from 1873 when several maharajas donated money for its establishment, is an elegant two storey edifice with beautiful semi-circular arched windows. Others nearby include Collegiate School (1836), which consists of two single-storey structures to the east of the college, with verandahs running along the facades, and Fuller House (1909), a large two storey red-brick building which is somewhat similar in appearance to the college.

Baro Kuthi

A block south-east of Rajshahi Government College on a high bank of the Padma River is an historic structure known as Baro Kuthi. Reasonably intact, it's one of the last remaining examples of the indigo *kuthi* (factories) which once flourished in the region. They were, like Baro Kuthi, simple buildings of no architectural interest except for their defensive arrangements.

The history of the kuthis is fascinating, however. Baro Kuthi was built by the Dutch in the early 19th century for the silk trade. Seconding as a fort in times of emergency, this massive building had about 12 rooms, those on the ground floor being comparatively unventilated and dark. These were probably used as a prison and for mounting cannons. After 1833, when the kuthi was taken over by the East India Company, the British owners used Baro Kuthi for the infamous indigo trade, which lasted for about 25 years. Today, it has the reputation, probably justifiably so, of having once been the scene of countless crimes, including murder, torture and rape, during that period.

Sericulture Centre

Rajshahi is at the heart of Bangladesh's silk-producing area, and the Sericulture Centre has a showroom of silk fabrics where you can pick up some fair bargains, or order lengths and colours to your specifications. If you aren't interested in buying, there isn't much else to see here. The small showroom is in a walled garden of mulberry trees, south-west of the railway station on Railway Station Rd.

Zoo

Just west of the Parjatan Hotel is a zoo, which has entrances on both the northern and western sides. It's small but there are enough animals to entertain young children for a while.

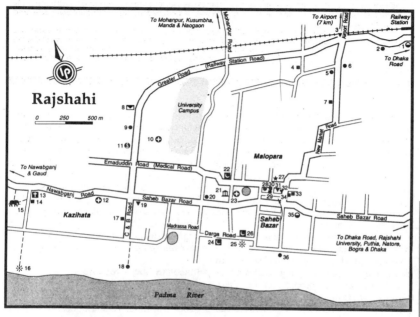

PLACES TO STAY

4	Hotel Al Misfalah
7	Hotel Metropolitan
14	Parjatan Hotel & Biman Airlines
17	Circuit House
29	Sky Hotel
30	Hotel Parijat
33	Hotel Raj Mahal
34	Memory Hotel

PLACES TO EAT

3	Khan Hotel & Restaurant
19	Monibazar & Nanking Chinese Restaurant
31	Red Dragon Restaurant
32	Roochita Confectionery & Ranmania Restaurant

OTHER

1	New Bus Station
2	Sericulture Centre
5	New Market
6	Photo Lab
8	Post Office
9	Court
10	Hospital
11	Agrani Bank
12	Christian Mission Hospital
13	Rajshahi City Church
15	Zoo
16	Sunset Promenade Point
18	Simla Park & Picnic Spot
20	Fire Station
21	Varendra Research Museum
22	Main Mosque
23	Hospital
24	Small Mosque
25	Good View of River
26	Dargapara Mosque
27	Police Station
28	British Council
35	Buses for Dhaka
36	Baro Kuthi

The Infamous Indigo Kuthis
In the 18th and early 19th centuries the indigo trade was highly profitable. By the mid-1800s, the Rajshahi region alone had more than 150 indigo factories in operation. The local zamindar owners even loaned money to the peasants so that they would plant more indigo. Indeed, trade was so lucrative and the kuthis so numerous that factory labourers had to be imported from outside. The farmers, however, didn't profit at all and began changing crops. Using oppression and torture to keep the peasants growing indigo, angry zamindars sometimes went as far as to commit murder and burn whole villages. A common adage held that 'no indigo box was despatched to England without being smeared in human blood'.

In 1859, the peasants revolted against the brutal repression. The Indigo Revolt, which lasted two years, brought the cultivation of indigo to a halt. Eventually the government had no choice but to decree that the peasants could no longer be forced to plant indigo. As a result, by the end of the century the indigo trade had completely disappeared. Some of the kuthis were converted into silk factories; most, however, simply fell into ruin. ■

Places to Stay – bottom end

Most of the lower-end establishments are in the central Saheb Bazar area. The *Memory Hotel* (☎ 4742) will be just that for India buffs. Marked Padma Boarding and located on New Market Rd next to the AB Bank, this awful place has tiny, damp, windowless singles/doubles (Tk 30/60) and dirty common bathrooms. They do have fans and mosquito nets though.

Hotel Parijat (☎ 3434), a poorly marked two storey building facing the police station on Emaduddin Rd, is small and cleaner, with ventilated singles (common bathrooms)/doubles (attached bathrooms) for Tk 40/80. *Hotel Al Misfalah* (☎ 2357) has identically priced rooms, which are reasonably clean and have attached bathrooms, but it's not conveniently located. It's 300m or so northwest of New Market and about two km from the centre of town.

The well marked *Hotel Metropolitan* (☎ 2861), on New Market Rd, slightly closer to the town centre, has singles/doubles with fans, mosquito nets and attached bathrooms for Tk 50 to Tk 60/110. The rooms are not cramped and the hotel features a 2nd-floor reception area which is breezy and has lots of comfortable chairs – good for relaxing.

Places to Stay – middle

Two very decent mid-range hotels in the town centre are *Hotel Raj Mahal* (☎ 4399), just east of New Market Rd, and *Sky Hotel* (☎ 2060), 1½ blocks to the west. The Raj Mahal has freshly painted singles/doubles with carpets, fans, mosquito nets and attached bathrooms for Tk 80/110. There are also larger doubles for Tk 150, which have sofas, and Tk 200 rooms that are almost like suites.

The spotlessly clean five storey *Sky* is equally nice, with singles/doubles for Tk 70/180, and unusually spacious open hallways that give the place a very breezy atmosphere. Rooms are bright and fairly large by local standards, and the doubles have mirrors and comfortable reading chairs.

Places to Stay – top end

The *Parjatan Motel* (☎ 5492), which has large singles/doubles with twin beds for Tk 320/425 with fans and Tk 580/740 with air-con, features a carpeted reception area with comfortable cane furnishings and a carpeted dark restaurant.

For a room at the government *Circuit House*, call the District Commissioner's office (☎ 2050) or home (☎ 2040) in advance to reserve a room. Located on C & B Rd, not far from the Parjatan Motel, it's a very attractive place with spacious rooms that are frequently available. Rooms cost only Tk 16 a night (Tk 8 a person), and you can eat here as well.

Places to Eat

The *Khan Hotel & Restaurant* is at the intersection of Airport and Railway Station Rds. A typical Bangladeshi meal will cost you Tk 15 to Tk 20. Before ordering, check to see if the restaurant next door has anything better to offer.

In the heart of town around Saheb Bazar you'll find similar places. For snacks, sweets and tea, try *Roochita Confectionery* on New Market Rd. There's also the *Red Dragon* Chinese restaurant around the corner on Emaduddin Rd; however, the food is fairly ordinary.

For better Chinese food, head for the *Nanking Chinese Restaurant* at Monibazar crafts centre at the intersection of Nawabganj and Greater Rds; it's one of the city's best eateries.

The city's best restaurant is probably that of the *Parjatan Hotel*. It features Bangladeshi, Chinese and Continental cuisine. The selections are extensive, and include chop suey (Tk 55), sweet and sour chicken (Tk 60) and Italian fish (Tk 80).

Another possibility would be to take a picnic out to the well marked Simla Park and picnic spot, which is beyond the Circuit House on C & B Rd, overlooking the Padma River.

Getting There & Away

Air The airport is 10 km from the centre of town. To get to and from the airport, hail a baby taxi. There are daily flights between Dhaka and Rajshahi, departing from Dhaka at 7.15 am and from Rajshahi at 8.20 am. If you call the Parjatan, staff will arrange for you to be picked up; the cost is Tk 200 a person.

Bus Most buses, except those to Dhaka, depart from New bus station across from the railway station. You can get ordinary buses here to Bogra (Tk 42) from 6.30 am to 3 pm, Jessore (Tk 85) from 6.30 am to 5.45 pm and to Rangpur (Tk 75) and Nawabganj. Buses for Dhaka leave from the town centre on Saheb Bazar Rd, a block east of the intersection with New Market Rd. Ordinary buses, such as Rupali Lines, charge Tk 110. Modern Enterprise's fare (Tk 140) and schedule (departures at 7.30 am and 7 pm) are typical of those of most chair coaches. The trip normally takes about 8½ hours.

Train IC trains depart from the railway station (☎ 4060) for Dhaka daily at 6 pm, and cost Tk 385/127 in 1st class/sulob. The journey takes about 11 hours. Cheaper mail trains leave daily at noon. To Jessore and Khulna, there's an express every day at 8 am; the fare is Tk 230/76 and Tk 280/92, respectively, for 1st/sulob class. There's also a slightly cheaper mail train at 10.15 pm.

Rail connections with the north are more frequent from Natore, which is on the main north-south line and only an hour's bus ride away. From Rajshahi, there's a daily express to Saidpur, except on Friday; it departs at 2.15 pm and costs Tk 205/67 in 1st/sulob class (Tk 210/69 to Dinajpur). There's also a mail train to Saidpur at 10.45 am.

Car Most people arrange car rentals through the Parjatan, however, all it does is call a local agency (☎ 2971) and then take half of whatever price you happen to bargain for. This way, it will cost you at least Tk 1000 a day plus the driver's food (Tk 50 a day outside Rajshahi). If you call the agency yourself, your bargaining should result in a much lower price, typically around Tk 700 a day plus petrol. The vehicle is usually a minivan.

AROUND RAJSHAHI
Kusumbha Mosque
The Jami Mosque in Kusumbha, 42 km due north of Rajshahi by tarred road, was built in 1558, just prior to the Mughal era. Attractive, well maintained and nicely located, this very traditional structure features black-stone walls, three arched *mihrabs* (doorways facing Mecca) at the front, six domes and, somewhat unusually, a womens' gallery on the upper storey.

Buses from Rajshahi depart for Kusumbha and Manda (15 km further north) from the bus station across from the railway terminal. The fare is Tk 20.

PUTHIA
Puthia (POU-tee-ah) has the largest number of historically important Hindu structures in Bangladesh. It also has one of the country's finest old rajbaris, although it's in bad

condition. In short, this town is a must see. Only 23 km east of Rajshahi (16 km west of Natore) and one km south of the highway, it's also very accessible. Coming from the highway, you'll pass a tall Hindu shrine to your left. Continue past it to the heart of the village, which is a large grassy field, with the rajbari just beyond. You can start your tour from here. As you walk around, ask for *mandir* (temple), which may lead you to the discovery of some lesser Hindu structures in the area besides the ones mentioned here.

Puthia Palace

This two storey stately edifice was built in 1895 by Rani Hemanta Kumari Devi in honour of his illustrious mother-in-law, Maharani Sharat Sundari Devi. She was a major benefactor in the Rajshahi region, having built a boarding house for college students and a Sanskrit college, for which she was given the title maharani in 1877. Very imposing, the building is in just good enough condition today to serve as a college.

Its grand appearance is due to the 13 huge round columns lining the 60m long facade, with symmetrical projections on either end of the facade. The central part has an imposing portal at the front, capped by a triangular pediment, with a parapet tastefully decorated with floral plasterwork. Inside, there are 16 rooms, including two fairly large halls.

The Kusumbhu Mosque, dating from the Turkistan Khiljis period (13th to 15th century), is somewhat unusual in that it features a women's gallery on the upper storey.

Govinda Temple

The most amazing of the village's monuments is the Govinda Temple, which is to the left of the rajbari. Erected between 1823 and 1895 by one of the maharanis of the Puthic estate, it's a large square structure with incredibly intricate designs in terracotta embellishing the entire surface. In this sense, it's very similar in inspiration to the Kantanagar Temple north of Dinajpur, which is about a century older. Both have the appearance of being covered by red oriental carpets. Most of the terracotta panels depict Radha-Krishna scenes and scenes from the Hindu epics. The building's structure is also interesting, rising in two storeys and crowned by a set of miniature ornamental towers.

Siva Temple

Built in 1823, this photogenic Siva temple at the entrance to Puthia, overlooking a pond, is an imposing square structure and an excellent example of the *pancha-ratna* (five-spire) Hindu style of temple, common in northern India. It's very ornate, with three gradually tapering tiers, and is topped by four spires plus a much larger central one. Unfortunately, many of the stone carvings and sculptural works were disfigured during the 1971 War of Liberation. There's still an impressive intact *lingam* (a phallic image of Siva) of black stone, however, which the cheerful informative caretaker will undoubtedly show you.

Jagannath Temple

One of the finest examples in the country of the hut-shaped temple is the Jagannath Temple, which is about 150m to the right (west) of the rajbari. Dating from the 16th century and nicely restored, this elegant little temple, measuring only about five metres on each side, features a single tapering tower which rises to a height of about 10m. The temple's western facade is finely adorned with terracotta panels of mostly geometric design.

Tahirpur Palace

If you're really into exploring old rajbaris, you could also check Tahirpur Palace, which is in Tahirpur, 18 km due north of Puthia up a back road, along the Baralai River. Rebuilt after the great earthquake of 1897, it's an imposing two storey structure which, despite the collapse of its roof, remains largely intact. There are 16 rooms, including a large central hall, and chances are good that you can roam freely inside.

Getting There & Away

There are numerous buses between Rajshahi and Natore throughout the day; the fare is about Tk 15. The 23 km trip from Rajshahi takes only half an hour. Upon leaving Puthia, you can easily hail a bus on the main highway.

NATORE

Located on the Rajshahi-Dhaka highway, some 40 km east of Rajshahi and 75 km south-west of Bogra, Natore (NUT-or) is most noted for having two of the most outstanding rajbaris in the country. So you'll definitely want to stop here. There's also a regional Care office here, and if you need any information you can count on the staff being friendly and receptive.

Otherwise, there's not much reason to stop in this busy crossroads town, the main drag of which runs east to west. A bus station, Care and several cheap hotels are at the eastern end, at a three-way intersection, with major highways heading east to Pabna and Dhaka and north to Bogra. The railway station is at the city's opposite end, on the road west to Rajshahi.

Uttara Gano-Ghaban (Dighapatia Palace)

Once the palace of the Dighapatia maharaja, the region's governor, Uttara Gano-Ghaban, as the palace is called today, is now a government building and serves as one of the President's official residences. Three km north of town off the road to Bogra, this beautifully maintained complex, occupying an area of some 15 hectares of land and enclosed within a moat and a high boundary wall, is approached from the east through an imposing four storey arched gateway. The main single storey palace presents a beautiful 50m long frontage, relieved with plaster floral decorations and a series of pointed arches. The incongruous mosque-like dome covering the central hall was added in 1967.

Inside, you'll find a huge domed reception hall, a large dining room, a conference room and nine bedrooms. Furnishings include marble-top tables, life-size bronze figures, chandeliers, carved wooden chairs, tables and beds. Visiting hours are Saturday to Thursday from 10 am to 4 pm.

Natore Rajbari

One of the oldest rajbaris in Bangladesh, dating from the mid-1700s, the magnificent but dilapidated Natore Rajbari is actually a series of seven rajbaris, four of which are notable and remain largely intact. The main block, called Baro Taraf, consists of three separate palaces and is approached by a long avenue lined with impressively tall imported bottle palms, the white trunks of which resemble temple columns.

The very classical looking principal rajbari has a frontage of about 35m, with an elegant central porch supported by a series of Corinthian columns and semi-circular arches. Inside you'll find a large reception hall which rises to a height of 10m and is lit by 18 clerestory windows, originally fitted with coloured glass panes. At the back there's a verandah supported on 20 pairs of Corinthian columns. You'll find some stairs there leading to the roof, from which you can get a fairly good view of the entire 15-hectare complex.

Also facing the main block are a 65m long palace lined with columns and a smaller rajbari lined at the front with a series of paired Doric columns. Next to the latter, which is inhabited, you'll see the family's shrine, a small Krishna temple whose deity has been destroyed.

To the rear of the main block is a second block called Chhota-Taraf, consisting of two rajbaris. The principal one faces a pond and is unquestionably one of the most beautifully proportioned buildings in Bangladesh. Entering through the front triple-arched portico, you'll find a reception hall with a lofty ceiling crowned by a pyramidal roof with clerestory windows. Much of the palace's black and wh.'t: marble floor has been ripped up, but this imposing 15-room structure is otherwise largely intact. There are stairs out the back leading to the roof, where you can peak down into the main hall.

Getting There & Away Natore Rajbari is at the northern edge of town. To get here, you can head northward from the heart of town, but to avoid getting lost, it may be easier to take the Natore-Bogra road and, one km before the turn-off for Dighapatia Palace, take a left on an unmarked paved road which leads westward towards the complex. It's 1½ km down that road, just beyond a school on your right. You can wander around at will.

Rani Bhawani Gardens

For over half a century until she died in 1791, Rani Bhawani, wife of the owner of the Natore Rajbari, managed the huge estate after her husband's death and became a legendary figure because of her boundless charity. Many organisations were the recipients of her largess, and even today her name is recognised by many Bangladeshis. A garden bearing her name is now a popular picnic spot. To get there, take a right (north) at the thana office on the main east-west drag through town and begin asking directions.

Places to Stay & Eat

One of cheapest places to stay is the *Hotel Rat* (☎ 660), at the eastern end of town, 200m north of the three-way intersection. Unmarked in English, it has a small lobby with TV. Tiny singles/doubles with fans, mosquito nets and attached bathrooms cost Tk 35/70.

The *Uttara Motel* (☎ 519), on the 3rd floor of a building overlooking the intersection, is better value. It charges Tk 50/70 for singles/doubles. Doubles are spacious with lots of light, and have tables, mosquito nets, fans and attached bathrooms. The inviting

reception is a spacious airy balcony, with a TV viewing area and a fridge with cold drinks, and just below is the Care office.

In the centre of town try *Natore Boarding*, which is very basic but has friendly staff. Its singles/doubles with attached bathrooms cost Tk 35/70.

The main drag is the best place for finding street food and perhaps a restaurant or two.

Getting There & Away

Bus Buses headed north and east leave from the intersection at the eastern end of town, while those for Rajshahi leave from the west. Buses for Rajshahi cost Tk 15 and take about an hour, while those to Pabna cost Tk 20 and take about 1½ hours.

Train The railway station is on the western side of town. Trains from the nearby junction of Ishurdi run through Natore northward to Jamalpur (stop for the Paharpur ruins), Saidpur, Dinajpur and Chilahati at the Indian border.

PABNA

Located between Rajshahi and Dhaka, Pabna, which dates from medieval times, features some fine old buildings, including a superb Hindu temple, as well as two well known rajbaris. Outside of Pabna there's also the Shahzadpur Mosque (1528), which is a splendid 15 dome pre-Mughal mosque in traditional bangla style, with thick walls and various arched entrances.

Jor Bangla Temple

Built in the 18th century in the form of two traditional village huts intertwined and standing on a platform, this temple, two km east of the town centre, is the best remaining example of the *jor bangla* (twin-hut) style. Before construction was completed something sacrilegious occurred on the site, so the temple was never used. While the building is not large and imposing, it is extremely elegant and has been beautifully restored. Like all the hut-style temples, it features an exaggerated arched roof, and the entrance's facade is enriched with intricate terracotta panels depicting several scenes from Hindu mythology.

Taras Rajbari

The Taras Rajbari, viewed from the street through an unusually impressive archway flanked by huge Doric columns, is a few hundred metres south of the town centre on the main road. Dating from the late 19th century, it was evidently once an elegant palace, but it's now all too obviously the drab home of government offices. The building's most prominent feature is its two storey front portico supported by four tall columns, resembling that of a pre-civil war *Gone with the Wind* mansion in southern US.

Sitlai Palace

Picturesquely situated on the banks of the Padma River, to the east of town, Sitlai Palace, dating from 1900, is a grand imposing rajbari that's still fairly well preserved. Today, it's occupied by a drug company, EDRUC, so you can't see the 30-room interior. The exterior is interesting, however, with a broad staircase flagged with white marble, leading to a 2nd-storey arched portico. Like so many zamindars, the Maitra family received extensive properties in the area and were successful in business, eventually becoming philanthropic as well and thus acquiring the title *raja*.

Places to Stay

On Cinema Rd, west of the town centre, the *Bhubasi Hotel* (no English sign) has reasonable singles/doubles with common bathroom for about Tk 30/40, and with attached bathroom for Tk 50/60. Opposite, the *Eden Hotel* is newly renovated and slightly more expensive. Neither of these hotels is keen on accommodating foreigners.

In the town centre, on Hamid Rd, the *Hotel Prince* (☎ 5451) has fair rooms with common bathroom for Tk 30/50. Towards the northern edge of town at Radhanagar, on the main road, *Hotel Tripti Niloy* is good value with singles/doubles, including attached bathrooms, for about Tk 60/85.

Places to Eat

The *Midnight Moon* is a tiny, basic restaurant serving expensive and unappetising Chinese food. It's in the Huq Supermarket Arcade off Hamid Rd. Your only other choices include the restaurant at the *Hotel Tripti Niloy* and a few reasonable local restaurants.

Getting There & Away

Most buses leave from the main road just south of the town centre. There are buses to Dhaka via Aricha, although the expresses which originate in Rajshahi will probably be full.

Buses run west to Natore (Tk 20, 1½ hours) and Rajshahi (Tk 30, 2½ hours), and north-west to Ishurdi (Tk 7, 45 minutes), which has better bus and train connections. You have to go to Ishurdi to get to Kushtia in Khulna Division; the bus leaves from the town centre with the other buses.

GAUD

A site of great historical importance, Gaud (or Gaur) has more historic mosques than any area in Bangladesh, except Bagerhat. Unfortunately getting here is so difficult that it attracts virtually no visitors. It's over 100 km west of Rajshahi and the last few km, which are not accessible by car, may be spent on an oxen cart. It's situated right on Bangladesh's disputed western border – some of the sites are in India, and the rest are across the river in Bangladesh.

The Hindu Senas established their capital here and called it Lakhnauti, after which the Khiljis from Turkistan took control for three centuries, to be followed in the late 15th century by the Afghans. Under the Afghans, Gaud became a prosperous city surrounded by fortified ramparts and a moat, and spread over 32 sq km. Replete with temples, mosques and palaces, the city was visited by traders and merchants from all over central Asia, Arabia, Persia and China. Today, a number of mosques are still standing and some have been restored, but none of the buildings from the earlier Hindu kingdoms remain.

It was never very easy to get to Gaud, and the current touchy political situation regarding the ill-defined border with India makes it more difficult. Permission from the Deputy Police Commissioner in Rajshahi is required, and on arrival in Gaud you must report to the border police.

Chhota Sona Masjid

Built from 1493 to 1526, the well preserved Small Golden Mosque is the most impressive structure in the area and a fine specimen of pre-Mughal architecture. Rectangular in plan, it originally had 15 gilded (sona) domes, from whence its name is derived. The mosque's chief attraction, however, is the superb decoration carved on its black-stone walls. On both the inner and outer walls, ornate stonework in shallow relief covers the surface. It also features an ornate ladies' gallery, arched gateways and lavishly decorated mihrabs.

Khania Dighi Mosque

Also known as Rajbibi Mosque, this single-domed mosque, built in 1490, is in Chapara village and is in reasonably good condition. It too has some ornately decorated walls, but here they are embellished primarily with terracotta floral designs. As at Chhota Sona, it also features some highly ornate stonework, primarily on the three arched entrances on the western wall.

Darasbari Mosque

Built around 1470, Darasbari Mosque is not in as good condition as Khania Dighi Mosque and is missing some of its original domes. It has two sections: a long oblong prayer hall measuring 30m; and a wide verandah on the east. The walls are two metres thick, and on the interior western wall of the prayer hall you'll see nine doorways relieved with some superb terracotta ornamentation of various floral and geometric patterns.

Monuments in Firozpur

Nearby, at Firozpur, you'll find several interesting structures which are all fairly well preserved and close to one another. One is the picturesque **Shah Niamatullah Mosque**, or Three Domed Mosque, which was built in 1560 and is beautifully located overlooking a large pond. About 100m away is the **Mausoleum of Shah Niamatullah Wali**; it has three domes and four squat towers.

The third structure, a bit north of the mausoleum, is **Tahkhana Palace**, which was built by Shah Shuja in the early 17th century and is the area's major Mughal-era building. A large two storey brick edifice, it has a flat roof, which in those times was virtually unheard of in Bangladesh.

Places to Stay

The *Archaeology Department Rest House* in Gaud is fairly basic but decent, and the cost is only Tk 50 a room. You should book a room via the Archaeology Department in Dhaka (☎ 326-708), but if you just show up, chances are good that you'll be allowed to stay here because there may be no other accommodation in Gaud. Staff can probably help you out with food as well, but bring some just in case.

Getting There & Away

Getting to Gaud requires a near heroic effort. The route is via Nawabganj, 48 km north-west of Rajshahi. At Nawabganj, there's a ferry crossing which takes 20 minutes or so. From the other side you can take a tempo west to Shibganj (20 km), then a bus north to Kansat (eight km). The last remaining stretch to Gaud (11 km) can only be done by a slow horse cart (Tk 100 to Tk 200 return trip) because of the road's incredibly poor condition. Count on sleeping in Gaud as you won't be able to get back to Kansat (which has no hotels) in time for the last return bus to Shibganj at 3 pm.

Chittagong Division

Chittagong Division shares borders with Sylhet Division to the north, India and Myanmar (Burma) to the east, and Dhaka Division along the Meghna River. Around Chittagong, particularly in the Chittagong Hill Tracts and south to the Myanmar border, hills are the dominant feature. The Pathua Hill chain averages 650m, with Keokradong, the highest peak in the country, towering above at 1320m. The only plains are at the base of this chain.

The coastal strip from Chittagong is very narrow, crowded in to the sea by the hills to the east. This is the only coastal region of Bangladesh where the land is not fragmented by river deltas. The beaches are long and broad, and extend from Sitakunda to Patenga, where the estuary of the Karnapuli River cuts them off, then continue to Teknaf. This last uninterrupted stretch (120 km) is said to be the world's longest beach!

History

Comilla, particularly the Mainimati archaeological site, is probably the oldest inhabited area. In the 7th century, the area was a small part of the kingdom of Samatata, ruled by a line of Buddhist kings known as the Khadgas, who were eventually overthrown by a new Buddhist dynasty, the Devas. According to the famous Chinese traveller Xuan Zhang, Buddhism flourished during this period. From his visit during 637-639 AD, he reported 30 monasteries with a population of 2000 monks.

The history of the area is most notable for the Buddhist resistance against the invading Muslims who settled in and around Chittagong in the 12th century. Not until the latter part of the 17th century did the Mughals extend their empire this far and supersede the Buddhist Arakanese kingdom of Burma in Chittagong. With the collapse of Mughal power, it was the British who finally overran the various local rulers, although

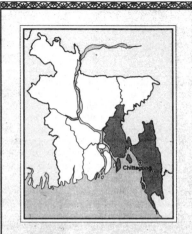

Highlights
- Mainimati Ruins – more than 50 Buddhist sites which were an important centre of culture from the 6th to 13th century.
- Chittagong Hill Tracts – home to tribal people struggling to maintain their traditional homes and identity.
- Ethnological Museum – located in Chittagong and featuring displays on the people and culture of the hill tribes.
- Cox's Bazar – the gateway to an enormous expanse of shark-free beach.
- Ramu & Lama Khyangs – would be more at home in Myanmar than Bangladesh.

Portuguese pirates had long preyed upon the rich maritime trade of the region.

The two main racial types in the Chittagong area are the Tibeto-Burmese tribal people and the more numerous Dravido-Aryan Bengalis. For centuries, the tribal people have lived in the hills, attempting to maintain their religious and cultural identity.

There are 13 tribal groups, with a total estimated population of around 600,000. Most are Buddhist, and are estimated to total about 400,000 in the district. Their *khyangs* (temples) and stupas (pagodas) date mostly from the 18th and 19th centuries. Despite Muslim control, the atmosphere as you move south is quite different – quieter, gentler, more languid – more like Myanmar or Nepal than the subcontinent.

CHITTAGONG

Chittagong city, the second largest in Bangladesh, has a population approaching 2.5 million. The climate is pleasant year-round – it becomes cool in winter and only slightly humid in summer, and the annual rainfall is 2400 mm (twice that of Dhaka).

The city, 264 km south-east of Dhaka, is on the Karnapuli River and its port is the country's busiest. There's an international airport, though the term 'international' belies the tiny arrival hall where the immigration counter is also the bank. Chittagong is the jumping-off point for the Chittagong Hill Tracts to the east and for Cox's Bazar to the south.

The Chittagong dialect of Bangla is somewhat different than in other parts of the country, and travellers who have picked up a smattering of the language may find it more difficult to understand here.

History

Locals will say the word Chittagong originated from 'chattagram', meaning small village, though it more likely comes from the Arakanese phrase *tsi-tsi-gong* inscribed on a tablet of the Buddhist invaders. It means 'that war should never be fought'. Chittagong appears to have been thriving as a port as early as Ptolemy's era (2nd century AD). He described it as one of the finest ports in the east. Xuan Zhang, the Chinese traveller, records the city as a 'sleeping beauty emerging out of the misty water'.

Despite its name, Chittagong has been fought over in a fairly consistent fashion. In 1299 Muslims occupied the city, until the Arakanese retook and retained it up to 1660. The Mughals took possession next, only to be expelled by the Arakanese in 1715. Finally, in 1766 the British raised their flag.

By this time, the Burmese had subdued the hill area of Arakan (now known as Rakhine),

and many Arakanese fled into the British-occupied territory south of Chittagong. Continuing friction between the British and the Burmese led to the first Anglo-Burmese war in 1824, and resulted in the British annexing Arakan. The Burmese thus were forced to give up any claims they previously had to the region around Chittagong.

The evolution of the city followed a similar pattern to Dhaka, except that the oldest parts, where Sadarghat now stands, were completely wiped out during the British and postindependence periods.

Orientation

Station Rd is more or less the centre of town and it forms a good reference point. Towards its eastern end, on the corner of Jubilee Rd, is the large New Market building (Riponi Bitan). Jubilee Rd continues south over Station Rd to merge with Sadarghat Rd, the main artery of the Old City. Sadarghat Rd officially begins on an offshoot near the GPO, rather than at its apparent beginning at the intersection near New Market.

The New Market is a modern shopping centre with sections for textiles, jewellery, books, stationery, watches, photographic goods (check used cameras carefully!) and pharmaceuticals. Other shopping centres include Reazzudin Bazar, Anderkilla Bazar, places in the Chandanpura area and Chowk Bazar.

Aarong (☎ 209-061) has an outlet on Nizam Rd near Prabartak and the Meridian Hotel (1367 CDA Ave), which offers a wide range of handicrafts along with books, postcards and ethnic clothing, such as *salwar kameez* and punjabi suits.

Maps The best map available is the Chittagong City Guide Map published by Kathakali. It costs Tk 30 at the bookshop near the Hotel Meridian on CDA Ave and Tk 50 at Hotel Agrabad's bookshop.

Information

The Tourist Information Centre is at Parjatan's Shaikat Hotel on Station Rd, and as usual staff hand you a brochure and deny any further knowledge.

Money Most convenient to the Station Rd area is ANZ/Grindlays, just down a small street running north off Station Rd, west of the intersection with Jubilee Rd. There's another branch in Agrabad, although it charges an exorbitant Tk 300 for cashing travellers cheques. American Express (☎ 501-045/6) is off Sheikh Mujib Rahman Rd, Agrabad. Standard Chartered across from New Market charges Tk 65/90 for travellers cheques of US$50/100 denominations. Most banks want to see proof of purchase in addition to a passport.

Post & Communications The GPO is just behind the New Market on Suhrawardi Rd (the continuation of Station Rd). It is open from 8 am to 8.30 pm, except Friday when it is open from 3 to 9 pm. The international telephone office is on Buddhist Temple Rd, in the same area.

Film & Photography For same-day colour film processing, try Quick Service on the ground floor of the New Market.

Old City

As in Dhaka, the city's oldest area is the waterfront area called Sadarghat. The early arrival of the Portuguese is evinced by the proximity of the Paterghatta district, just next to Sadarghat. Here the Portuguese had their enclave, and it remains a Christian area. There isn't much to see in Paterghatta, but it's a quiet, clean place to walk around – until you get into the slums of prawnshellers near the waterfront, which will leave a stench on your shoes that will take days to wear off. A rowing boat back to Sadarghat costs anything from Tk 5.

Across the river is the fish harbour and you can hire a local boat from the boat terminal to go across (10 minutes, Tk 20) and wander around the fish market. There's a big fish processing plant, and 50m from the fish market is the Marine Fisheries Academy housed in a new building with a small museum. It has a few fish specimens to look at, if you need to add a little excitement to your day and think this will do it.

Shahi Jama-e-Masjid This *masjid* (mosque) in Anderkilla (inner fort) was built in 1670 on a hillock and hence looks a bit like a fort. It has a tall minaret, Saracenic or Turkish in design, which looms up out of the press of shops that have since surrounded it. In the early 1950s it was greatly enlarged and most of its original features altered, though a number of original inscriptions are still embedded in the thick walls.

Chilla of Badar Shah West of Bakshirhat, is this *chilla*, or place of meditation, which derives its name from a Sufi who came to Chittagong in 1336. It is a modest-sized place with a courtyard and worship area built around the grave of Badar Shah, and is walking distance from the Shahi-Jama-e-Masjid, though with several *mazars* (graves) in the same area check to be sure you're directed to the right one. On the same road are several interesting shops that make traditional tablas.

British City

The British originally occupied the area just north-west of Sadarghat, a slightly hilly section, where they built their usual collection of administrative and cultural edifices: a hospital; the Secretariat; and the High Court. Station Rd, with its brightly lit stalls, forms the boundary with the Old City.

The British City, again like Dhaka, has become the central business district of the city. The area retains its colonial air and comparative sense of order and cleanliness.

Zia Memorial Museum On a knoll on Shahid Saiffuddin Khaled Rd, one of the most attractive structures left by the British, the Chittagong Circuit House, was where Zia Rahman was cut down by a group of soldiers in May 1980. Built in 1913 in the typical style of a British manor house, it originally stood amid thirty-five acres of landscaped gardens and lawns. Its one of the few remaining timber structures in the country, and is constructed predominantly of wood with a brick masonry foundation. Now a museum commemorating the death of President Zia, it is open daily from 4 to 7 pm. On the front lawn, there is a *shishu* (children's park) which also opens at 4 pm.

Chandanpura Mosque Near Dewan Bazar, this mosque is north of the city centre on the road to Kaptai. It has no historical importance but is an attractive sight with its delicate design.

Fairy Hill This area is said to be named for the fairies and genies that were believed to occupy this hill when the Sufi saint Badar Shah first came to Chittagong. Legend says that he had to make a number of requests to the fairies before they would allow him to build a place of worship. Views from the top are good, especially at sunset, when you might catch a cooling breeze as well. It's behind the GPO and New Market – climb the path leading off Jubilee Rd just north of the pedestrian bridge near New Market. Ask directions for the High Court, the building on top of the hill – Fairy Hill was the

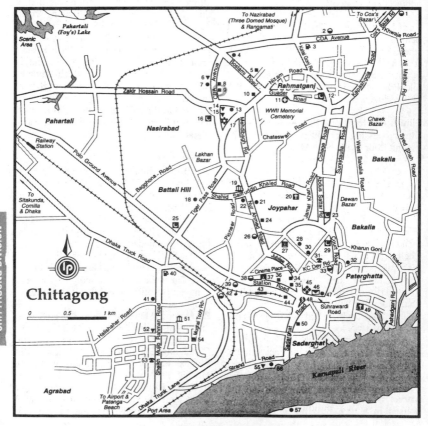

common name during the Raj era and is rapidly being forgotten.

DC Hill Atop this hill is the District Commissioner's residence, but the surrounding area is open to the public. A neglected helicopter pad sits at the top and from here there is a commanding view of Chittagong. It is a pleasant place with many old trees. The views are just as good as from Fairy Hill, but DC Hill is less crowded in the evenings.

WWII Memorial Cemetery This peaceful well maintained cemetery on Fazul Rd contains the graves of soldiers from both the Allied and Japanese forces who died on the Burma front.

Modern City
Agrabad, the modern commercial section, with its banks, large hotels and corporate offices, is quite in keeping with the trends of a 20th century city. Not surprisingly, this

development has brought all the problems already faced by Bangladesh: a maelstrom of rickshaws, innumerable beggars and roads potholed beyond belief. The outer reaches of the city have become industrialised; the only steel mill and oil refinery in Bangladesh are in Chittagong.

Ethnological Museum Around the corner from the Hotel Agrabad, this interesting museum has displays on Bangladesh's tribal people and is well worth visiting. The museum's assumption that these cultures are doomed is depressing, but probably accurate. It's open during the winter from 10.30 am to 5.30 pm Saturday to Wednesday, from 3 to 6 pm on Friday and is closed on Thursday. In summer it opens and closes a halfhour later. There is a 30 minute break for lunch at 1 pm year-round. If you find it closed, due to hartaals etc, it's worth walking around the back to talk with the enthusiastic director, Mr Bhattacharjee. He will show you photographs

PLACES TO STAY		3	Petrol Station	32	British Council Library
		4	Biplob Uddyan	33	Society Market Bus
5	ABWE Guesthouse		(Revolution Park)		Station
8	YMCA	7	Aarong Handicrafts	37	Chateswari Temple
9	Meridian Hotel	11	Medical College	38	BRTC Bus Station
10	Hotel Deen Luxury		Hospital	39	Bus Station for Dhaka
24	Hotel Bandagaon	12	Qadam Mubarak	40	Petrol Station
34	Hotel Al-Amin		Mosque	41	Karnafuli Market
35	Hotel Safina	13	Chittagong Public	42	Kadamtale Bus
36	Hotel Dream & Other		Library		Station
	Hotels	16	Mosque	43	Central Railway
44	Shaikat Hotel &	17	Blossom Garden		Station
	Parjatan Tourist	18	Battali Hills Park	45	New Market
	Information Office	19	Zia Memorial	46	GPO
50	Hotel Shahjahan		Museum	47	Fairy Hill & High
54	Hotel Agrabad	20	Church		Court
		21	Biman Airlines	48	Standard Chartered
PLACES TO EAT		22	Stadium		Bank
		23	Chandanpura Mosque	49	St Placid (Old
6	Phuket Restaurant	25	Mosque		Portuguese
14	Sarina's Restaurant	26	Cinema Palace Bus		Church)
15	Sayeman Restaurant		Station	51	Ethnological Museum
52	Chungking Restaurant	27	Nandankanan	53	Telephone &
55	Hong Kong		Buddhist		Telegraph Office
	Restaurant		Monastery	56	Sadarghat (BIWTC)
		28	DC Hill		Boat Terminal
OTHER		29	Shahi Jama-e-Masjid	57	Fish Market
		30	Forestry Department		
1	Cox's Bazar Bus		Office		
	Stand	31	International		
2	Bardarhat Bus Station		Telephone Office		

of tribal groups from the Hill Tracts and happily discuss his ethnological studies in lengthy detail.

Qadam Mubarak Mosque
Built in 1719 in the Rahmatganj area, the late-Mughal Qadam Mubarak ('footprint') mosque derives its name from a slab which bears an impression of the Prophet's foot.

Chittagong Port
The port of Chittagong is on the west bank of the Karnapuli River, 15 km from its confluence with the Kapurtali River. Chittagong now has 20 berths and handles bulk cargoes and container ships – up to 900 vessels and 5.5 million tonnes annually. The port has made Chittagong the commercial centre of Bangladesh, but the rail, road and river transportation facilities from Chittagong are barely able to cope with the port's cargo-handling facilities. The port area is closed to all but permit-holders due to strict security measures.

Mazar of Sultan Bayazid Bostami
This shrine is in the Nasirabad area, five km north-west of the city centre. A great *mela* is held here during the Muslim festival of Shab-e-Barat.

The shrine isn't especially impressive, and women might not be allowed inside; but it's a peaceful place, and worth visiting to see the pond full of turtles which legend says are evil spirits, turned into turtles by the curse of a saint over 1000 years ago. Judging by their size they could well be that old. They like to be fed bread, which you can buy at the stalls near the entrance.

The easiest way to get there is to take a rickshaw or tempo to the corner of CDA Ave and Bostami Rd. From there you can take any bus or tempo (Tk 3) heading along Bostami Rd; they all stop near the shrine. The key word to emphasise is 'Sultan' – Bostami gets you directed to a post office. If you see a sign saying 'Chittagong Cantonment' on the left, you've just passed the mazar. Tempos run between here and Station Rd for Tk 6.

Pahartali Lake
More often known as Foy's Lake, this area has boating facilities and is a popular picnic spot; things get hectic on weekends. Earlier in the morning is a nice time to visit. On a cool day, walking is pleasant in the denuded hills around the lake. Additionally, there are some grand views of Chittagong and the Bay of Bengal from a high hill near the lake's edge. You can get there by rickshaw (Tk 10) or tempo (Tk 3) from the junction of CDA Ave and Zakir Hossain Rd.

There is a zoo on the way to the lake. It's a rather pitiful place but marginally interesting for the examples of wildlife that inhabited the area only 40 years ago. A few of the more significant cast of characters include two royal Bengal tigers, black bears, one lonely hoolock gibbon (the only ape found in the Indian subcontinent) and the elegant Great Pied Hornbill.

Organised Tours
Green Channel Tours (☎ 225-775, 504-126; fax 225-544; Dhaka ☎ (02) 860-455, 506-087; fax 867-129), 5th Fl, 95 Agrabad C/A, can put together trips in the Chittagong and Cox's Bazar areas. They offer a sea-cruise every Friday during winter. This 'novel and thrilling' excursion is a day-long affair and includes breakfast, lunch, music, raffle drawing and fun. Cost is Tk 500 for adults and Tk 250 for children.

Places to Stay – bottom end
The cheapest deal in the city are the series of 'boarding shacks' across from the central railway station on Station Rd. These are basically covered shop fronts with several beds crammed together. Out the back are common toilets and bathrooms. There are no mosquito nets but they do have fans. All this costs only Tk 16, though there is absolutely no privacy and you could end up knowing your neighbour more intimately than you might like. For more 'worldly' lodgings read on.

One of the best hotels in this category is the *Hotel Safina* (☎ 614-317) on Jubilee Rd. It's a labyrinthine place from the British period, but the staff are friendly and knowledgeable about local sights, and some of the rooms are quite OK. Singles/doubles with short beds and common bathrooms cost Tk 60/100 (Tk 80/140 with attached bathrooms). You can watch the BBC on the TV in the reception area.

Around the corner from the Safina, tucked away upstairs in a complex of shops, *Hotel Al-Amin* (☎ 614-417) is a run-down place with singles/doubles for Tk 51/60 with attached bathrooms. The *United Hotel* (☎ 618-563), 149 Golap Shingha Lane, up a quiet lane opposite the Safina, is worth checking out. It has singles/doubles with attached bathrooms for Tk 80/130, and singles with common bathrooms for Tk 70.

Right across from the railway station, *Mrs Iqbal Boarding* is conveniently located, but the rooms are not especially clean. Singles/doubles with attached bathrooms cost Tk 65/120 and with common bathrooms are Tk 45/60.

In Feringee Bazar, where Kazi Nasrul Islam Rd (often called just Nasrul Rd) turns north to meet Station Rd (Suhrawardi Rd), *Hotel Al Farooq* at 256 Nasrul Rd (no English sign) is an extremely basic old place but women may get turned down. Airy doubles with attached bathrooms cost Tk 60, and singles with common bathrooms are Tk 35. It sits left of a beautiful, decaying mosque near the beginning of Nasrul Rd.

The *YMCA* on CDA Ave still has no accommodation.

The central railway station is somewhat unique for having *retiring rooms*. There are several very large two or three-bed rooms for Tk 68 per person. They're often full, but it's worth a try.

Places to Stay – middle

There are quite a few mid-range hotels along Station Rd, all large and reasonably run. At No 91, *Hotel Dream* (☎ 619-401) is cleaner than many and is one of the best bets in this category. The friendly staff are accustomed to foreign travellers. Although the stairs aren't for the weak of knee, the high building allows for airy rooms; best are the corner

doubles. Singles/doubles with attached bathrooms cost Tk 90/146. There's also a restaurant.

Hotel Mishka (☎ 223-756) at No 95, next to Hotel Dream, is reasonable at Tk 110/150 for singles/doubles with attached bathrooms, but no mosquito nets (Tk 250 for renovated doubles). There's a very good restaurant and an extremely helpful manager.

At No 85, *Hotel Midtown* (☎ 617-236) has not-so-clean singles/doubles/triples with attached bathrooms for Tk 75/125/180, but no mosquito netting. *Hotel Manila* (☎ 614-098) is expensive for what you get, with singles/doubles with attached bathrooms for Tk 70/120, and more cockroaches than people in the street below.

At 3A Sadarghat Rd, near the corner of Suhrawardi Rd and opposite the GPO, *Hotel Hero City* (☎ 221-221) has small, clean rooms for Tk 90/130. The lack of an English sign makes it a little difficult to find. It has a restaurant.

Hotel Bandagaon (☎ 228-811), No 875 Nur Ahmed Rd, the northern continuation of Jubilee Rd, has singles/doubles with attached bathrooms for Tk 90/160, which would be reasonable if it had mosquito netting

Hotel Raj (☎ 617-547) at 154 Nasrul Rd, near the corner of Sadarghat Rd, is a big place which was once good value but the prices have gone up – singles/doubles start at Tk 130/200. Rooms with air-con start at Tk 500. Also just off Sadarghat Rd, but on the opposite side, *Hotel Naz* (☎ 617-162) is quiet and friendly, and has singles/doubles with attached bathrooms for Tk 70/110.

The *Hotel Shahjahan* (☎ 616-543) on Sadarghat Rd is a big, bland place with a restaurant. It has very large, clean singles/doubles with attached bathrooms from Tk 125/300, and deluxe doubles with air-con for Tk 650. Guests are 'requested not to strike the staff'!

Places to Stay – top end

Parjatan's *Shaikat Hotel*, on Station Rd east of the railway station, is centrally located, but otherwise there's not much to recommend it. Doubles cost from Tk 650/500 with/without air-con. On the same road, about 300m west of the station, *Hotel Golden Inn* (☎ 220-023; fax 610-683) is a clean place managed by friendly staff. Its glossy brochure describes the 'modern, mini shopping corner' as a place 'for meeting your petty needs.' Economy singles/doubles cost Tk 275/450, and singles/doubles with air-con and TV are Tk 495/700.

Hotel Agrabad (☎ 501-199; fax 710-572), in the Agrabad section, is Chittagong's top hotel, with singles/doubles from US$91/101 plus 35% tax. It has a couple of restaurants and one of the few bars in the city. There is a swimming pool which nonresidents can use for Tk 110. Rickshaws from here are very expensive – walk up the street a little.

Hotel Hawaii (☎ 504-057), nearby on the same road as the Ethnological Museum, has larger versions of the standard hotel room from Tk 312/372 for singles/doubles with attached bathrooms (including a bath). Service is lackadaisical and the place looks a bit rundown, but the price is right.

The *Meridian Hotel* (☎ 210-371) at 1367 CDA Ave is nearly as good as the Agrabad and better value. It's conveniently located to the city's better restaurants and shops.

On Nizam Rd, *Hotel Deen Luxury* (☎ 212-563) is on the expensive side, with air-con singles/doubles for Tk 650/850.

Near the old British city, *Arabian International Hotel* (☎ 613-246) is next door to United Hotel, conveniently located off Jubilee Rd. Rooms are a little stuffy, but the staff are friendly. Rooms with attached bathrooms cost Tk 150/250 for singles/doubles; deluxe doubles with air-con and TV is Tk 400.

If you want to mingle with English-speakers, try the *ABWE Guest House* (☎ 210-245) run by the Association of Baptists for World Evangelism at 22 Panchlaish Rd near the Medical Centre off Nizam Rd. Rooms are Tk 200 per person for non-missionaries. Breakfast, lunch and dinner are also available for Tk 85/95/125. Advance reservations are not required, but can be made through its Dhaka office (☎ (02) 884-699).

Places to Eat

Jubilee Rd is one of the best restaurant areas. Even the cheap eateries are pretty good by Bangladesh standards. There are a number of good local places around Hotel Safina. The *Mitan Biriani Restaurant* to the right as you leave the hotel has excellent kebabs.

Eating places in the bazar near the Hotel Al-Amin are good value, especially for the popular Chittagong beef. There are also a few good local food joints across from Hotel Dream.

On Jubilee Rd, upstairs opposite New Market, *Chimbuk Restaurant* has an upbeat atmosphere and a balcony, although its local food is nothing special. In the same area, the canteen-like *ABP Biryani* serves excellent beef kebabs for very little taka. *Cafe de Grand* on Nandankanan St, north of Hotel Safina, is a bright and bustling biryani restaurant with friendly service. There are also a couple of biryani places in BRTC Market at the BRTC bus station on the corner of Baitul and Station Rds.

The *Chin Lung* Chinese restaurant, opposite the GPO on Suhrawardi Rd, is just above average in quality and prices. The *Tai Wah* Chinese restaurant on Jubilee Rd next to the Broadway Hotel has reasonable food, although you have to wonder why all those stuffed animals are lurking behind the curtain. There's a Thai restaurant at 1376 Nur Ahmed Rd (also known as Asian Highway Rd).

While waiting for your bus to Cox's Bazar, have breakfast at the cafe in the *Hotel Islamia* at 22 KC Dey Rd, where you can also get coffee. There's a restaurant upstairs. The restaurant at the railway station is recommended, and is usually open long hours.

The restaurant at *Hotel Mishka* on Station Rd isn't bad. Across the road, the *Shipsa Restaurant* in the Shaital Hotel is good, if a little expensive, and has a variety of dishes.

There are expensive restaurants at *Hotel Agrabad*. Nearby, *Curry House* at Hotel Hawaii has reasonably priced Bangladeshi food, and there's also a Chinese restaurant. *Chungking Restaurant*, in the same area on Sheikh Mujib Rahman Rd, is one of the oldest Chinese establishments and is reputed to have the best Chinese food in town. The *Shangrila Chinese Restaurant*, 39 Agrabad C/A, off Sheikh Mujib Rahman Rd, serves very large quantities.

The best, more expensive restaurants are on CDA Ave around the Zakir Hossain Rd junction.

Locals consider the restaurant at the *Meridian Hotel* to be the city's finest; it serves Bengali and Chinese food. On the same street, *Sarina's* serves Indonesian, Thai, Chinese, Mughali and Bengali dishes for reasonable prices, while Indian rock videos pulse enticingly on the TV. Next door, the *Sayeman* is Chittagong's best known Mughal restaurant. Meals range from Tk 100 to Tk 200 per person.

South of these restaurants, the similarly priced *Blossom Garden* sits on the edge of a hill and offers outside garden dining, with the option of indoor dining. It serves Mughlai, Chinese and Bengali dishes. In the same area, next door to Aarong Handicrafts, is *Phuket Restaurant*, a recommended Thai and Chinese eatery, though one local remarked, 'It was a much better place before the manager was busted for smuggling'.

On Strand Rd down from the BIWTC, *Hong Kong Restaurant* has a limited Chinese menu, but is one of the last surviving bars in the city. Housed in a bright, tomato-red, fort-like building from the Raj era, it is hard to miss. Upstairs it is dark and shady, but you can buy beer (Tk 110) and hard drinks, except on Friday.

Getting There & Away

The Dhaka-Chittagong highway is the best in the country, but travel by train, which is only marginally slower than by bus, is far less nerve racking.

Air Biman has three to four flights daily to Dhaka (Tk 948), the last one departing at 7.15 pm. Afternoon flights to Cox's Bazar depart on Monday and Saturday (and Thursday during winter) for Tk 312. There are also flights to Calcutta, India, and, on Thursday, to Yangon (Rangoon), Myanmar.

Airline offices in Chittagong include:

Air India
    Hotel Agrabad (☎ 504-767)
Biman
    120 Nur Ahmed Rd (☎ 651-890)
Indian Airlines
    Hotel Agrabad (☎ 504-830)
Pakistan International Airlines
    6th Floor, Hotel Agrabad (☎ 501-993)

Bus The largest bus station is Bardarhat, four km north of the city centre. To get there, take a local bus (Tk 2) from Station or Jubilee Rds. Most buses for Cox's Bazar and Kaptai leave from there. Saudia is one of the better companies serving Cox's Bazar (four hours); the standard fare is Tk 65. Buses for Rangamati (three hours) now leave from Modapur bus station on CDA Ave.

Most Dhaka-bound private bus companies operate out of the old BRTC bus station on Station Rd. An air-con chair coach to Dhaka takes five hours and costs Tk 230. Green Line (☎ 221-531, 224-589) buses leave from 3 Railway Mans Store on Station Rd almost hourly up to midnight, and has the best reputation on this route. It now has some stiff competition from Shahagh Paribahan, Borak and Saudia, which you should find in the same area. The air-con bus service of these lines is run like an airline. They offer magazines and headphones with three channels to choose from. Chair coaches without air-con to Dhaka cost Tk 130 (Tk 90 for an express). For chair coaches, it's best to book a day ahead.

Some buses for Dhaka, Cox's Bazar and other towns leave from a bus station on Jubilee Rd in front of Hotel Safina, but it's difficult to get timetables. The Cox's bus seems to depart early in the morning. Nearby, buses leave for Dhaka from the bus station on KC Dey Rd.

Another departure point is Cinema Palace bus station on Nur Ahmed Rd, next to Cinema Palace; it has a few Dhaka-bound buses. Buses returning from Cox's Bazar usually continue on to this more convenient station after stopping briefly at Bardarhat.

For express buses to Comilla (Tk 55) and

CHITTAGONG DIVISION

Chandpur (Tk 55), head for Kadamtale bus station just over the railway lines at the west end of Station Rd. There are no direct buses to Sylhet; you must change in Comilla.

Train There are three trains a day to Dhaka, and the trip takes six or seven hours. Snacks and soft drinks are available during the journey. Fares to Dhaka, normally Tk 310/159 for 1st class/sulob and Tk 485 for a sleeper (night train only), are being reduced by a third to compete with bus fares. According to the schedule, trains depart at 7.20 am, 3 and 11.30 pm for Dhaka, and arrive at 2.25, 9.05 pm and 6.10 am respectively. The morning train is supposedly slightly nicer. The fare to Comilla is Tk 49 in sulob class.

IC trains also run to Sylhet via Comilla in the morning, departing at 10.30 am, and cost Tk 298/92 in 1st class/sulob. Daily Noakhali trains go via Laksham and to Chandpur as well.

Boat There are no direct launches to Dhaka from Chittagong. To get there partially by launch, you should take the train or bus to Chandpur and catch a launch there. Some large launches ply between Chittagong and Barisal, also between Chittagong and the islands of Hatiya and Kutubdia. If you want a 1st-class cabin, you should buy your ticket a day or two in advance. For Barisal, purchasing tickets even a week in advance is recommended.

The BIWTC terminal is at the end of Sadarghat Rd, a few hundred metres to the west along the riverbank. The administration office is clearly marked in English, but the tickets are sold from a nondescript building just before the office. Launches leave for Barisal on Saturday, Monday and Thursday at 9 am, and the 24 hour trip costs Tk 768/509/108 in 1st/2nd/deck class. These boats also travel to Hatiya, which is an 11 hour trip. The fare is Tk 430/286/62.

There are daily private launches for Kutubdia Island, a six to seven hour trip, plus a BIWTC ferry on Wednesday at 9 am. The BIWTC fare is Tk 221/149/36 in 1st/2nd/ deck class. There's a government rest house on Kutubdia which you might be able to use. You can continue on to Cox's Bazar by private launch (at least one a day).

Getting Around
The Airport There isn't always a bus to meet incoming flights and the airport is a long way out from town – baby taxis cost around Tk 60. At the T-junction, 500m from the airport, you can catch a bus (Tk 5) to New Market. To get to the airport, a Biman staff bus leaves the Biman office daily at 12.30 pm and generally has room to give travellers a free ride.

Local Transport Rickshaws and baby taxis are plentiful, and cost roughly the same as in Dhaka. Tempos and buses are cheaper, but they are cramped and crowded and can be quite frustrating if you don't speak Bangla. The route is also not well established.

AROUND CHITTAGONG
A couple of sites are difficult to get to but are worth making the effort.

Shatpura
This small village, 24 km south of the city, has Buddhist and Hindu temples. The Nindam Kanon Temple is a meditation centre. There's little or no public transport in this direction.

Patenga Beach
This public beach, 24 km south of Chittagong via the airport road, was severely damaged during the 1991 cyclone, and there's some construction going on, so it's hard to recommend. Also, getting here is quite difficult as rickshaw and baby taxi drivers don't want to make the journey and are likely to refuse unless you guarantee the return fare. The fare is over Tk 100 by rickshaw and over Tk 200 by taxi. You might try finding a public bus (BIWTC Bus No 1 reportedly travels there), or hitching a lift on the Biman staff bus to the airport and walking or taking a rickshaw from there (six km).

Bird-watching enthusiasts will find the mudflats near Patenga Beach an excellent high-tide roost for waders, the occasional

Top: Ornate rajbari, Sonargaon.
Bottom: Tank on the fringes of the Sunderbans.

IAN LOCKWOOD

JON MURRAY

JON MURRAY

Top: Women planting trees near Madhupur Forest.
Bottom Left: Painam Nagar's ghost town main street, Sonargaon.
Bottom Right: Village street in Rajshahi.

spoon-billed sandpiper, Nordman's green-shank, and good numbers of great knot and grey-rumped tattlers. The best time of year is winter, but bird-watching is good from August to May. A mid/late morning high tide is the best time of day; you'll need tide tables to figure out when to go. Look for a schedule at the BIWTC terminal.

Getting to the mudflats is not much easier. Try the Biman bus or take a baby taxi to the Steel Mill Colony (housing development) on the way to Patenga. From there walk to the beach and head north a short distance to the mudflats.

Fouzdharat Beach

For similar reasons of difficulty with transport, this beach, 16 km north of Chittagong along the Dhaka Rd, is equally deserted.

SITAKUNDA

Some 36 km north of Chittagong, this sleepy little town has a major attraction – the historic Hindu **Chandranath Temple**, six km away on top of a hill, an hour's hard climb. There are great views from the top, which can be a real treat in flat Bangladesh. Unless you have a particular interest in Hindu temples, however, the only time it's really worth visiting is during the Siva Chaturdasi Festival, held here for 10 days in February when it attracts thousands of Hindu pilgrims. Sitakunda's Buddhist temple is just a ramshackle wooden building, not worth the effort.

Getting There & Away

Take a bus for Feni from the Kadamtale bus station in Chittagong; the trip takes 45 minutes and costs around Tk 12.

RAMGARH

It's a little known fact that there are tea estates in the Chittagong area which are as large as those in Sylhet. One of the best places to see them is north-east of Ramgarh. Two of the country's largest tea estates are located here, and you can walk around them at leisure. As they are located just outside the Hill Tracts no permit is required.

CHITTAGONG HILL TRACTS

Decidedly untypical of Bangladesh in topography and culture, with steep, jungled hills, Buddhist tribal people and a relatively low population density, the 13,180 sq km of the Hill Tracts are an idyllic place to visit. The region comprises a mass of hills, ravines and cliffs covered with dense jungle, bamboo, creepers and shrubs.

The Chittagong Hill Tracts are a restricted area and, unfortunately, getting a government permit to visit the area takes 10 to 14 days, which is often prohibitive for short-term visitors. For diplomats who do not go through a travel agency, the process takes at least 21 days! Continuing military operations to subdue the tribal people's Shanti Bahini (Peace Army) are, at least theoretically, the reason for the restriction, but the lengthy process of approval, which is always

CHITTAGONG DIVISION

Ship Breaking

Ten km north of Chittagong lies an expanse of coastal mud flats where ships are scrapped. Though not your normal tourist attraction, it could make for an interesting afternoon. Huge ships, bought in Singapore, are brought here and run aground. Armies of workers then use blow torches, sledge hammers and plain brute force to tear them apart. Supervisors don't seem to mind visitors, but it's best to ask permission first. Once you've received permission and there is a high tide, you can get out on top of the ships, some of which are five to seven storeys high. Be advised, however, that this is not an entirely safe undertaking and can be a dirty process.

To get to the ship-breaking area, simply take a local bus (Tk 5) towards Feni/Comilla. About eight km out of Chittagong you'll begin seeing the ships to the left above the coastal villages and farms. Ask the driver to stop at any of the places where scrap metal is sold on the roadside and follow one of the semi-tarred roads toward the sea. There are numerous access roads into this area. At any given time there are 20 to 30 ships (or parts thereof) beached along about five km of mud flats.

Ian Lochwood

Tribal Dress

The dress of the hill people varies considerably. Chakma women wear a *thami*, a long skirt made of a rectangular piece of hand-woven bluish coloured cloth, with bold red stripes on all four sides. They also wear a blouse, a breast cloth called *khadi* and a white turban. The men wear lungis and a white turban. The Marma males also wear lungis, while the women wear a red striped shirt called a *thabain*. The Murung men wear only a loin cloth or *dawng* around the waist, with the two ends hanging to the front and back. Occasionally they also wear a head-dress called a *khebang*. The women wear a handwoven black skirt, 20 to 30 cm wide, called a *wanclai*, around the waist which remains open at the left side. These short skirts are beautifully embroidered with various designs and usually bordered in red. This skirt is also sometimes decorated with a kind of grass seed. ■

forthcoming if you have the time to wait, makes a mockery of the government's brochures enticing foreigners to visit the region. Permits must be obtained in Dhaka. For information see Travel Permits in the Visas & Documents section of the earlier Facts for the Visitor chapter.

The troubles stem from the cultural clash between the various tribal groups, who are the original inhabitants of this region, and the plains people, who are desperate for land. Centuries ago, the tribal people's ancestors wandered into the teak forests of the Chittagong Hills, mostly from the Arakan hills in Myanmar. Predominantly Buddhist, they are Sino-Tibetan in origin and appearance: short in stature, wheat-coloured or brownish complexions, black hair, broad faces, short wide noses, high cheekbones and mostly brown eyes.

About half the tribal population are Chakma, and most of the remainder are either Marma, who represent about a third, or Tipera. Among the 10 much smaller groups (Murung, Tengchangya, Khumi, Lushai, Pankhu, Sak, Bowm, Mogh, Kuki and Reang), the Murung stand out as being the most ancient inhabitants of the area.

Like the general population, most tribal people are poor and illiterate, but their culture and way of life are very different from those of the Bengali farmers of the plains. Some of the tribes are matriarchal and all of them have similar housing – made entirely of bamboo, raised on a bamboo platform about two to five metres high and covered by thatched roofs of dried leaves.

In most other respects, the tribes are quite different. Each tribe, for instance, has its own distinctive rites, rituals and dress; the Chakma women, for example, all wear indigo and red-striped sarongs. Each tribe also has its own dialect.

The women, who are known to be hard workers, are particularly skilled in making beautiful handicrafts, while some of the men still take pride in hunting with bows and arrows. And both women and men love music and dancing.

Under the British, the Hill Tracts had special status and only tribal people could own land there, but the Pakistani government abolished the special status of the Hill Tracts as a 'tribal area' in 1964. The construction of the Kaptai Lake for hydroelectricity in 1963 was another blow, submerging 40% of the land used by the tribal people for cultivation and displacing 100,000 people. The land provided for resettlement was not sufficient and many tribes fled into neighbouring (Indian) Assam and Tripura.

During the War of Liberation, the Chakma king sided with the Pakistanis, so when independence came the tribal people's plea for

Tribal Agriculture

Most tribal people are farmers, practising shifting cultivation called *jhum*. They slash-and-burn the slopes between January and April, then sow the seeds with the first rains. While these hill people's staple is rice (which their favourite intoxicant beverage is prepared from), they also plant other crops, including cotton, maize, sesamum, pumpkin, yam and melon. By tradition, the Jhumias, as the farmers are called, often plant various seeds together. The following year they plant elsewhere, allowing the land to recover for a year or two. By lowland standards this seems wasteful, but the lands here lack the constant replenishment of rich nutrients from the rivers. ■

special status, not surprisingly, fell on deaf ears. Meanwhile, more and more Bengalis were migrating into the area, usurping their land. The tribal people, with no legal recourse, did not take this lying down. In 1973, they initiated an insurgency which continues to the present day. To counter it, the government, for six years starting in 1979, issued permits to landless Bengalis to settle there, with title to tribal land, resulting in the mass migration of approximately 400,000 people into the area – almost as many people as all the tribal groups combined! One noticeable result is that the tribal people are now beginning to forsake some of their customs. Sadly, their culture may be subsumed in the blander Muslim majority.

With tensions on the wane, the entire Rangamati district is now open to foreigners with permits, but not to foreign journalists! This includes Kaptai Lake, Manikcheri (capital of the Murung tribe), Penchuri (accessible by paved road), and Suvalung and Balukali (accessible by boat).

The other Hill Tract areas, such as the Kassalong and Sajek valleys – inhabited by the Lushai tribe (once headhunters but now Christians and westernised) – remain off limits. Government officials in Rangamati can give permission to visit them, but they rarely do.

The Insurgency of the Hill Tract Tribes

In 1973 the tribal groups, led by the Chakmas, united to form the Shanti Bahini, with the aim of protecting their culture, language and way of life, and to strive for political autonomy. Inevitably, intertribal rivalry shattered the union, leaving the problem to simmer until 1978, when 200,000 ethnic Indian Muslims were expelled from Burma (Myanmar). These refugees began to establish colonies in the Matranga region of the Chittagong Hill Tracts. The tribes, again threatened by the encroachment of foreigners, attacked and destroyed several of the settlers' villages. As a result, the district was put under military administration and skirmishes between Shanti Bahini and the Bangladesh military became almost routine. As murders increased, many tribes were forced to move across the border into India.

The disruption escalated when oil was discovered in the Hill Tracts and the Shanti Bahini, outlawed by the government, began guerrilla operations. In 1984, after the abduction and release of foreign oil workers, talks between the Shanti Bahini and the government commenced. Concessions were made and it appeared that the situation might return to normal, though this has proved impossible.

The Indian government now insists that Bangladesh resolves the situation so that tribal people can return to Bangladesh. Conditions in the Tripura Indian refugee camps are intolerable, with many tribal people, especially children, dying every day of disease. The Indians, tired of these tribal people on their hands, are pressuring them to return – sometimes, allegedly, against their will. On the other hand, the tribal people rightfully fear that if they don't return soon, the settlers will steal their land. In recent years, more than 400,000 settlers have swarmed into the hill tracts from the flood-prone lowlands.

The 50,000 tribal people remaining in the Indian refugee camps are also wary of the reception awaiting them back home. They hear tales of Jumma massacres carried out by the Bangladeshi in league with armed gangs of settlers. Despite a ceasefire in 1992, there have been many violations. On 17 November 1993 in Naniachar, tribal eyewitnesses said that the army fired into a crowd of Jumma students. When the youths tried to escape by diving into a nearby lake, they were hacked to death by settlers with machetes. The army dismissed it as a clash between tribals and settlers, even though only one of the 35 victims was a settler. There are also ongoing reports of Bangladeshi soldiers entering tribal villages at night and burning down bamboo houses. In retaliation, the Shanti Bahini periodically carry out violent attacks on government posts and tribal 'collaborators'. The Shanti Bahini, with its estimated 2000 trained and armed soldiers, is not without resources but support from India, which has its own tribal uprisings to contend with, is now waning.

The Bangladesh government defends its position by claiming that people of Bengali origin have been in the hill tracts since time immemorial. In early 1991, however, it gave local tribal-dominated councils control for the first time over primary education, health, and family welfare. In 1994, each returning tribal refugee was promised a gift of several kilos of rice and over Tk 10,000. There were also assurances that settlers had been ousted and that the land would be returned to rightful tribal owners. While many Jumma militants are suspicious, the return of tribal people to Bangladesh is increasing and tensions are decreasing. Whether the Bangladesh government honours its promises and the settlers return to the plains without a fight remains to be seen. Clearly any lasting solution must fully take into account the traditions and ancient rights of the tribal peoples. ■

Rangamati

The town of Rangamati, 77 km east of Chittagong, is nothing special but the location is nice. It's on a small isthmus on the shores of Kaptai Lake and joined to the mainland by a small causeway. The countryside is lush, undulating and verdant. The outlying areas around Rangamati are the lands of the Chakma tribe, so virtually all of the tribal people you meet here will be Chakma.

In Rangamati, there is a **Tribal & Culture Institute Museum**, and a basic government handicraft display centre near the GPO. The best place to see and buy tribal textiles is at the Bain Textile Handicraft Centre near the Parjatan Hotel. The display is quite good and prices are fair, and, strangely, finding these textiles in Dhaka is extremely difficult.

A good place to visit is the Buddhist monastery, **Jawnasouk Mountain Vihara**, across the lake from Rangamati. The **Long Gordu Meditation Centre**, in a forest reserve 20 km from Rangamati, is closed to foreigners.

Also on the lake are two sites which can only be visited by boat. The **Raj Bana Vihara** (the King's Forest Temple) is a Buddhist temple on Ranga Pani Island, about eight km from Rangamati. The Chakma king, a barrister in Dhaka, has his *rajbari* on another island not far away. The traditional residence is nothing special but it does have interesting old furnishings.

Places to Stay & Eat Rangamati has only several budget hotels, in the Tk 50 to Tk 120 range. The cheapest and most basic place is the *Boarding House* at the town's port, Tobolchuri Ghat. The more pleasantly situated *Al Mahmud Hotel*, near the bus station, and the *Gulistan Hotel* are other options. For a place with food, try *Hotel Hiramund*, opposite the New Court building and close to the bazar.

Most visitors here are Bangladeshis. Those on economical organised tours usually stay at the *Shapla Hotel* in town; its ventilated units cost about half as much as those at the Parjatan.

The *Parjatan Hotel* (☎ 3126; Dhaka ☎ (02) 819-192) is in a choice location out of town on Deer Hill, offering beautiful views of Lake Kaptai from rooms with balconies. The charge is Tk 400 for ventilated rooms (Tk 650 with air-con). It also has three cottages for families (Tk 550), with three to four beds each, and two dormitories for youths, with eight beds each. Unfortunately, the restaurant here is not very good. Travel between the Parjatan and Rangamati is either by foot (about an hour) or baby taxi; there aren't many rickshaws in this hilly area.

Getting There & Away Buses from Chittagong to Rangamati (three hours, Tk 30) depart, periodically, from Modapur bus station on CDA Ave. You'll pass two security posts en route; the second one, just outside Rangamati, is where you'll have to complete a large form in duplicate (no photo required). Passage is fairly easy so long as you have the required permit.

Rental cars (taxis) from Chittagong cost around Tk 1500 a day (Tk 2000 with air-con). The only 'extras' are the driver's lodging (about Tk 60 a day) and food (Tk 50 per meal). The drive takes 2½ hours. This option usually works out cheaper than an organised tour.

Kaptai Lake

A boat trip on Kaptai Lake, the country's largest artificial lake, with stops at tribal villages along the way, is the highlight of a trip here. The lake was formed by the damming of the Karnapuli River and is ringed with thick tropical and semi-evergreen forests dominated by tall teak trees – a scene like nowhere else in Bangladesh.

While the lake itself is beautiful, the villages you'll see around the lake really make the trip special. Bring your binoculars for bird-watching and better viewing of some of the thatched villages and fishing boats (also the military speed boats and camps) you'll see along the way. The tourist boats usually stop at villages, allowing you to see traditional bamboo houses.

Tourist boats from the Parjatan Hotel

charge Tk 200 per hour for the boat and take up to about 10 passengers. The Parjatan also has smaller faster speed boats for Tk 500 an hour. You can go anywhere around the lake but there are enough interesting villages within a half-hour's distance that there's really no need to go further. Villagers may stare a bit at you but they generally do not ask for *baksheesh* (tip) – a welcome relief. Bring your swimming gear because you can take a plunge anywhere.

There are also two public launches a day leaving Rangamati for the town of Kaptai; they depart at 8.30 am and 3.30 pm but verify the schedule beforehand to be sure. The trip takes 1½ hours (four hours round trip). There is also a speed boat that does the round trip in two hours. These boats leave from the main port in Rangamati, Tobolchuri Ghat, near the bazar.

Kaptai

Once a hunting ground for wild animals, Kaptai is 60 km east of Chittagong and at the southern end of Kaptai Lake, 1½ hours by boat from Rangamati. Today it's the site for a 50m dam and a hydroelectric plant, and the atmosphere is rather oppressive: no photography or 'unauthorised movement'. The Kaptai ghat looks quite picturesque at night, however. Some three km west of town on the road to Chittagong you'll find the ancient **Chit Murung Buddhist Temple**, which houses some statues of Buddha.

Kaptai is a flat town with one main street consisting of a long row of low structures; this is the bazar where you'll find all the eating places, hotels and boarding houses, tea houses and general stores.

Places to Stay There's a government *Circuit House*; as always you'll need to seek permission from the District Commissioner to stay here. His office is nearby. The *Kamal Boarding House* is clean and cheap. Other places to stay, such as *Sat Khana Boarding House*, are very basic.

Getting There & Away Direct buses from Chittagong's Bardarhat bus station leave throughout the day and cost about Tk 20. There security posts on this route.

Chitmorong

This is a Buddhist village of the Marma tribe, five km from Kaptai on the road to Chandraghona, 26 km further south.

Part of the attraction of Chitmorong is the languid, serene atmosphere. Amongst the bamboo and thatched village huts you can purchase a cup of the local palm wine, *tari*. The village contains some richly adorned Buddhist sculptures, and the monastery is presided over by an English-speaking head monk. On the hilltop is a huge stupa with a temple to one side. Here you may come across the head monk, who will chat with you over a cup of tea (your donation). A Buddhist festival is held here every Bengali New Year, around mid-April.

Getting There & Away The bus will drop you off at a bus stop with a milestone; there is no village in sight, but the rooftop of the stupa-like monastery can be seen above the trees. There is a footpath on the left which ends at the top of a rather steep, concrete stairway; at the bottom, you hope, waits a boat to ferry you across to the village.

Organised Tours

Most foreigners come with The Guide (Dhaka ☎ (02) 400-511; fax 833-544), which takes groups of two or more. A four day/three night tour includes Rangamati and environs, the Buddhist monastery and Chakma King's rajbari, a boat trip on Kaptai Lake including a stop at a Chakma village, swimming, hiking, the Bain Textile Handicraft Centre and the Tribal & Culture Institute Museum.

The Guide's cost per person, including airfare from Dhaka, for a three day/two night trip is Tk 10,800 (two people), Tk 10,400 (three to five people), Tk 7400 (six to nine people) and Tk 7000 (10 to 15 people). Four day trips cost about 25% more.

Parjatan (Dhaka ☎ (02) 327-842, 817-855/6; fax 817-235) requires a minimum of 10 people for its tours. For a visit of four days and three nights, the charge per person is Tk 6500

CHITTAGONG DIVISION

(economy) and Tk 10,000 (deluxe, ie staying at the Parjatan Hotel), including airfare from Dhaka. Once you sign the permit application form (one photo is required), Parjatan handles the rest. Approval normally takes seven to 10 days. Hayat Ali Khan, the general manager in charge of tours, is the person to see.

COX'S BAZAR

This area, adjacent to the Chittagong Hill Tracts, runs south down the coastline to the Myanmar border. The population of the region is about one million and is a mix of Muslims, Hindus and Buddhists. The culture here is less overtly Muslim, or even Hindu for that matter, having a more Burmese-Buddhist atmosphere.

This region was a favourite of the Mogh pirates and brigands who, with the Portuguese, used to ravage the Bay of Bengal in the 17th century. The Moghs have remained, maintaining their tribal ways through handicrafts and cottage industries, such as the manufacture of cheroots and hand-woven fabrics. To some degree the Moghs, who have a sizable population here, have assimilated more than other tribes into the ways of the dominant Muslim culture.

When the area was taken over by the British in 1760, Captain Hiram Cox founded the town as a refuge for the Arakanese fugitives who were fleeing their homeland after being conquered by the Burmese. These new refugee Mogh settlers erected quite a number of the stupas found today on the low hills around town.

The town itself, near the Myanmar border and 150 km south of Chittagong, is Bangladesh's only beach resort; although it has few amenities, except an enormous expanse of shark-free beach. You meet the occasional local who has Goan connections, and there's a very faint echo of that relaxed atmosphere here. The usual question, 'Why have you come here?' doesn't get asked because the answer is obvious – you've come to the seaside. During the winter, from November through March, it's best to avoid Cox's Bazar at weekends, when accommodation can be scarce. By 3 pm on Thursday the place is booked out. During the low season, most hotels will reduce their prices as much as 40% if asked.

Warning

Travelling east or south of Cox's Bazar, you may be checked by police due to the area's Rohingya (roh-HING-gah) camps. In late 1991, at least 250,000 Rohingyas (Muslims from Myanmar's Arakan (Rakhine) state) fled to Bangladesh and India to escape Burmese government persecution. Camps were set up by the UN and the Bangladesh government east of Cox's Bazar near the Myanmar border. While these camps functioned reasonably well, it is alleged that government security officials abused and coerced the refugees to return to Myanmar. The abuse had subsided by late 1994, when the Myanmar government agreed to accept the refugees back. Today, many of the Rohingyas have returned, though a large number remain in the camps.

Information

The Uttara Bank, next to the Hotel Sayeman (Si-mon), accepts foreign currencies and cashes travellers cheques (US dollars and UK pounds), and there's a Sonali Bank branch on Sea Beach Rd (or Jhawtola Main Rd) east of the Laldeghi Lake. The tourist office in Parjatan's Upal Hotel is more useful than most.

Though a 'tourist' town, Cox's Bazar has very little directed specifically to tourists. The Handicraft Emporium at Karpupannya Cottage Industries, Motel Rd, has a variety of excellent handicrafts. There are other handicraft and Burmese shops near the Buddhist monastery in town. Here you will find hand-woven fabrics, saris, *lungis* (Burmese sarongs), cheroots, jewellery and conchshell bangles. Bain's Rangamati Textiles, down from the Burmese shops on the opposite side of the street, sells beautiful embroidered shawls, lungis and *kurtas* from the tribal areas. Most of these goods are impossible to get anywhere else.

Police noticeboards at the beach warn you

not to stay in isolated places without informing the police; not to get too far out in the water (there are no lifeguards), and that swimming at low tide is risky. The police beach post, open during the winter season from November through March, can advise on the best times and places to swim.

The colourful Buddhist Water Festival takes place from 13 to 18 April each year.

Things to See & Do
The main reason to come to Cox's Bazar is to visit the beach. You can reach the less crowded north end of the beach from Sea Beach Rd, and the main beach from Motel Rd. In between this stretch of beach is the Shaibal Hotel's private beach which costs Tk 10 to use, though this fee is not always collected. There's a freshwater shower, but whether it's worth the large audience you'll get is debatable. You can also hire umbrellas and sun lounges for Tk 30.

Although this area affords a little more privacy than you'll get along the 'open' beach, foreign women may be hassled by young Bangladeshi men, who are paying guests at the hotel. Even the Bangladeshi upper-class are not accustomed to seeing

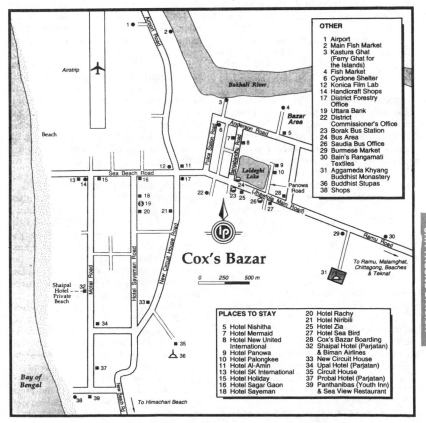

Cox's Bazar

0   250   500 m

To Himachari Beach

To Ramu, Malamghat,
Chittagong, Beaches
& Teknaf

OTHER
1 Airport
2 Main Fish Market
3 Kastura Ghat
   (Ferry Ghat for
   the Islands)
4 Fish Market
6 Cyclone Shelter
12 Konica Film Lab
14 Handicraft Shops
17 District Forestry
   Office
19 Uttara Bank
22 District
   Commissioner's Office
23 Borak Bus Station
24 Bus Area
26 Saudia Bus Office
29 Burmese Market
30 Bain's Rangamati
   Textiles
31 Aggameda Khyang
   Buddhist Monastery
36 Buddhist Stupas
38 Shops

PLACES TO STAY
5 Hotel Nishitha
7 Hotel Mermaid
8 Hotel New United
   International
9 Hotel Panowa
10 Hotel Palongkee
11 Hotel Al-Amin
13 Hotel SK International
15 Hotel Holiday
16 Hotel Sagar Gaon
18 Hotel Sayeman
20 Hotel Rachy
21 Hotel Niribili
25 Hotel Zia
27 Hotel Sea Bird
28 Cox's Bazar Boarding
32 Shaipal Hotel (Parjatan)
   & Biman Airlines
33 New Circuit House
34 Upal Hotel (Parjatan)
35 Circuit House
37 Probal Hotel (Parjatan)
39 Panthanibas (Youth Inn)
   & Sea View Restaurant

CHITTAGONG DIVISION

women in swimsuits, so while they are essentially polite, they will gawk at you. Some will even pull out a camera and want to take a few photographs. For the foreign tourist, it's a real switch being at the other end of the lens! Bangladeshi women who swim (they are a rare breed) do so in their flowing salwar kameez. Further along the beach, well out of town, there are secluded areas where swimming can be a fairly private experience.

Despite this, what was once the longest and loneliest beach in the world's most crowded country is now slowly being taken over by poor Bangladeshis and Rohingya refugees from Myanmar. For this reason the beach area is not considered entirely safe at night.

Nonresidents can use the pool at the Hotel Sayeman for Tk 20. Guests are charged Tk 40 to use the pool at the Shaibal Hotel, and for nonresidents it's Tk 50.

Aggameda Khyang

This stunning 19th century Buddhist monastery in the east end of town is representative of the Burmese style of architecture. Its distinct appearance would stand out anywhere, but nestled among trees in the middle of Cox's Bazar makes it all the more fascinating. The main sanctuary is built around massive timber columns, and the teak flooring throughout adds an air of timelessness to the place. The temple houses a number of small bronze Buddhas, mostly Burmese in origin, and a few old manuscripts. The monk-in-residence is a gracious old man who speaks English quite well.

Places to Stay – bottom end

Parjatan's *Panthanibas* (Youth Inn) has dorm beds for Tk 45 and doubles with attached bathrooms for Tk 100. It's run-down but liveable, and close to the beach at the southern end of Motel Rd.

Most other bottom-end places have a beach shack feel to them. Despite this, don't count on finding a room on a weekend during the dry season.

Hotel Rachy (☎ 3455) is often booked out

by parties, but is worth a try. Singles/doubles cost Tk 40/70. There's a restaurant next door called *Hotel Diamond* which leads to name confusion.

The pleasant *Hotel Al-Amin* (☎ 3420), on Sea Beach Rd (no English sign) and quite a way from the beach, is pricey at Tk 50/100 for singles/doubles with attached bathrooms. It's opposite the District Forestry Office.

Further east on Sea Beach Rd, *Cox's Bazar Boarding* (☎ 3565) is another shack with singles/doubles with common bathrooms for Tk 40/60.

There are several newer places in town, but it won't be long before they look like all the rest. *Hotel New United International* (☎ 4489), on Bangabandhu Rd, is decent value. Singles/doubles with attached bathrooms are Tk 80/100. Cheaper singles with common bathrooms are Tk 40.

Hotel Nishitha (☎ 4362) on Anderson Rd near the ferry ghat has singles/doubles with attached bathrooms for Tk 60/120. Its rooms on the upper floors have a good view overlooking the river and ferry ghat. *Hotel Zia* (☎ 4497), right across from the bus station, provides decent accommodation, with singles/doubles for Tk 70/130 with attached bathrooms.

Places to Stay – middle

Hotel Panowa (☎ 3282) is a cheerful place with a holiday feel and is good value. There's an excellent cheap restaurant (great fish) which is extremely popular. It's down a lane to the east of Laldeghi Lake, across the road from the bus station. Small but clean singles/doubles/deluxe rooms with attached bathrooms cost from Tk 90/120/250. Singles with common bathrooms are Tk 70.

Pleasant, but not as good, is the *Hotel Niribili* (☎ 3279; fax 3202), on New Circuit House Rd, with singles/doubles/deluxe rooms for Tk 150/200/250 with attached bathrooms. Its restaurant, in a separate building from the hotel, is said to be excellent and is good value at around Tk 125 for two.

Just west of the bus station, the *Hotel Mermaid* (☎ 3630) has singles/doubles with attached bathrooms for Tk 70/120. It's above the shops which sell electronics smuggled in from Myanmar and India.

Hotel Bilkis (☎ 3982) is in the same building as the Sonali Bank, near the entrance to the lane leading to the Hotel Panowa. Singles/doubles with attached bathrooms cost Tk 100/200. It's good value but lacks mosquito netting. Also lacking netting is the big, gloomy *Hotel Sea Bird* (☎ 3656) which has singles/doubles/triples with attached bathrooms for Tk 60/120/180.

Further down towards the beach, the *Hotel Sagar Gaon* (☎ 3445), in the tall building across and down from the Konica Film Lab (no English sign), is also fair value. Economy singles/doubles with attached (rather smelly) bathrooms cost Tk 70/150, Tk 100/200 for deluxe. Its restaurant, Biroti, serves a mean Pomfret curry dish.

Toward the beach end of Sea Beach Rd, *Hotel SK International* (☎ 3830) is not overly maintained, but nice as it's away from the hustle and bustle of the town. Singles with common bathrooms are Tk 100, and singles/doubles with attached bathrooms are Tk 150/200. Its Alpha Restaurant is popular with the locals.

Places to Stay – top end
Only just in the top-end category and good value is the town's original luxury hotel, *Hotel Sayeman* (☎ 3900; fax 4231), with doubles from Tk 250 and four-bed suites from Tk 435. The best deal here, however, are the economy doubles for Tk 150. It also has air-con doubles from Tk 850. All rooms, except economy, have satellite TV. There are two relatively basic restaurants and a bar where you can actually order a beer.

Hotel Sea Queen (☎ 3789) has a flashy foyer and a restaurant, and offers economy doubles for Tk 200 and deluxe with satellite TV for Tk 400 (Tk 600 with air-con). The *Hotel Palongkee* (☎ 3873), next door to the Panowa, is a newer place, but the rooms are nothing to write home about. Singles/doubles with attached bathrooms are Tk 200/400, and doubles with air-con cost Tk 850.

As well as the Panthanibas, Parjatan has a

number of other places to stay, all very expensive. During the low season, it has been known to reduce its prices by as much as 50%. The *Probal Hotel* (☎ 3211, 3275) on Motel Rd has a small restaurant and doubles from Tk 400; rooms with hot water cost an extra Tk 100. Down the street at the identical-looking *Upal Hotel*, rooms have balconies and cost from Tk 500. Four-person old-style cottages, somewhat on the rustic side, cost Tk 1000.

At the flagship *Shaipal Hotel* (☎ 4202, 3275) rooms run from Tk 1200 to Tk 2000. It has a decent restaurant, moderately priced, and a bar. Along with a swimming pool, other attractions include a tennis court, a large pond and a golf course with incredibly huge sand traps.

Places to Eat
There are, miraculously, no Chinese restaurants in Cox's Bazar, though many hotel restaurants, such as the *Sea Queen*, have Chinese dishes. There are many good local restaurants, mainly around the west end of Sea Beach Rd. *Hotel Diamond*, which is a restaurant connected to the Hotel Rachy, next door to Hotel Sayeman, is very popular with foreigners and locals alike.

Two of the best hotel restaurants are the inexpensive and relaxed restaurant at the *Hotel Panowa* (try the delicious, but bony Hilsa curry cooked in traditional mustard oil or the abundant biryani) and the more expensive restaurant at *Hotel Sayeman*, which has excellent seafood.

Parjatan's *Sea View Restaurant*, in the octagonal building near the Panthanibas, serves lobster and other seafood dishes along with Bengali, Chinese and American cuisine (fired chicken and burgers). Prices tend to be on the high side, but it's recommended, for both food and service. The *Shaibal* has an expensive restaurant (although cheaper than the room prices would suggest), with a mixture of Bengali and western dishes. There is an economical restaurant at the *Probal*.

If you want to try the restaurant at *Hotel Sea Queen* (which is one of the few places where you can get coffee), don't ask about it at the reception desk – it's supposedly for guests only.

Hotel Niribili, Hotel Sagar Gaon and Hotel SK International also have good restaurants.

Getting There & Away
The road from Chittagong is probably one of the worst 'highways' in Bangladesh and road repair has been going on for years. If it ever gets finished and stays that way for a period of time, the journey ought to be comfortable and speedy.

Air Biman is at the Shaipal Hotel. It operates afternoon flights to Chittagong on Monday and Saturday for Tk 312. During the winter season a Thursday flight is added. Once you're in the air, it's less than 20 minutes to Chittagong; the plane flies at only 1000m, so the views are good – try for a seat on the right-hand side. There is a direct flight to Dhaka on Thursday that departs at 2.35 pm and costs Tk 1260.

Bus Express buses to Dhaka leave throughout the day and take eight or nine hours. The last bus is at 4.15 pm and the fare is Tk 150. Chair coaches without air-con cost Tk 190. For the four hour trip to Chittagong, the last bus leaves at 4.30 and the fare is Tk 70. There are express buses to Teknaf (three hours), and they depart until 6 pm; the fare is Tk 40.

For a deluxe chair coach with air-con check the offices of Saudia, Borak or Green Line (☎ 4571), which are all close by on the main drag, Sea Beach Rd. Green Line has several departures a day to Chittagong (Tk 120); the last one at 4 pm going directly to Dhaka (Tk 315).

Myanmar Border The overland route across the Myanmar border has been closed since the early 1950s. At present, it's probably not a good idea to attempt an illegal crossing here – see the warning in the Getting There & Away chapter earlier in this book for details.

Getting Around
Most places are within walking distance, even the airport. For trips further afield, you can hire jeeps for rides along the beach. Parjatan's shiny models cost Tk 660 per hour, or Tk 100 per hour and Tk 20 per km; the beaten-up ones from the motor repair shops on Sea Beach Rd cost a stiff Tk 400 per hour.

AROUND COX'S BAZAR
Since 1994, in an effort to attract more tourists, the government began construction of a road along the beach from Cox's Bazar to Teknaf. The project is particularly controversial because of the deforestation caused along the way. As of late 1995 it had reached beyond Himachari Beach. In the process, a bridge has been constructed over the Rezu River, making it possible for the first time to drive entirely on the beach from Cox's Bazar to Teknaf. A 4WD car is required.

The evergreen and semi-evergreen tropical rainforest bordering this stretch of beach is still some of the best in the country, despite the recent heavy pressure from the Rohingya refugees and others who have settled in the area.

This forest is home to a wealth of plant and animal life. Bird-watching, especially in the patches of forest on the low hills running off the beach just south of Cox's Bazar and around Teknaf, should reveal quite a number of interesting species, including are the white-crested laughing thrush, orange-bellied flower pecker, the peacock pheasant and trogans in addition to a great number of migratory species. The staff at the District Forestry Office in Cox's Bazar are happy to give more information.

Malamghat
An hour north of Cox's Bazar on the Chittagong road is more of the same exemplary forest that is found south of Cox's Bazar. Bird-watching is also very good in this area. The village of Malamghat is well known for its excellent Baptist missionary hospital. It has a *Guest House* and charges Tk 200 per person for non-missionaries. Arrangements

should be made before arrival with the Association of Baptists for World Evangelism (ABWE) office in Chittagong (☎ (031) 210-245) or Dhaka (☎ (02) 884-699).

Himachari Beach

By reputation, Himachari is the nicest beach near Cox's Bazar, though many travellers feel that it's a bit overrated and not exceptionally beautiful. You'll find a shack where tea, soft drinks and some basic Bengali food are sold.

Just before the beach are some low cliffs and gorges; this area is very quiet. Cattle and water buffalo appear at sunset, their bells tinkling on their way to the nearby village. There is a waterfall here, though not very impressive, which sometimes dries up in late winter. If you walk a little higher you'll find forests which, sadly, are slowly being cut down.

To get here, take a public bus from Cox's Bazar to Himachari village and walk across the village to the beach. You can also take a jeep. In Cox's Bazar, jeeps leave from the shops on the southern end of the beach by the Panthanibas Youth Inn. The fare is Tk 50 but you might be able to bargain the price down to Tk 40, the fare for locals. If you have time you could walk back to Cox's Bazar.

Inani Beach

Inani Beach, one of Bangladesh's claims to fame, is considered the world's longest and broadest beach: 180m at its narrowest at high tide and 300m at low tide. Even here, some 30 km south of Cox's Bazar, it's not completely deserted, so don't be surprised if you attract a small audience.

There's a *Forestry Department Guest House* right on the beach, just south of Inani Beach, with fine views of the sea. It has three guest rooms plus common facilities; the cost is Tk 300 a room or Tk 1500 for the entire guesthouse. You have to take your own food and the facilities are limited, but it is furnished. Get permission from the District Forestry Office (☎ 3409) in Cox's Bazar, west of the bus stand area just off Sea Beach Rd.

To get here, take a Teknaf bus and get off

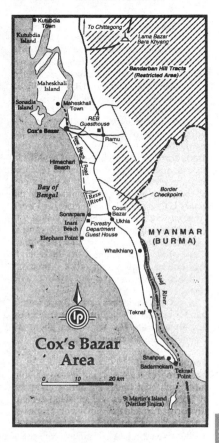

at Court Bazar (30 km), a tiny village two km before Ukhia. From there you can find rickshaws or maybe a tempo to take you west to the beach, which is 10 km away. If you're headed for the guesthouse, ask the rickshaw driver to let you off at the tiny village of Sonarpara, which is on the beach and halfway to Inani. From there you must walk south until you reach the guesthouse. Transport should not be difficult to find since locals use this route to get to nearby villages.

Alternatively, hire a jeep from Cox's Bazar to take you directly to Inani using the scenic beach route.

Ramu & Lama

Ramu and Lama (or Lama Bazar) are noted for their Buddhist khyangs and are worth visiting for that purpose. Ramu is a quiet village 14 km east of Cox's Bazar just off the Chittagong road, while Lama Bazar is roughly 50 km to the north-east in the Hill Tracts (permit required).

In addition to its khyangs, Ramu, a subsidiary capital of the Arakan kingdom for nearly three centuries, is noted for a beautiful **monastery** containing images of Buddha in bronze, silver and gold inlaid with precious and semiprecious stones. Start at the far end of the street of Buddhist buildings at the lovely U Chitsan Rakhina Temple, and work your way back towards the town centre.

The interesting Burmese **Bara Khyang** at Lama Bazar has the country's largest bronze statue of the Buddha, and in its three buildings houses a number of relics – precious Buddhist images in silver and gold, set with gems.

Buses to Ramu leave Cox's Bazar from a stand a few blocks east of the bus stand on Sea Beach Rd. The trip takes about 30 minutes and costs about Tk 5.

Sonadia Island

According to legend, centuries ago a ship laden with gold sunk here during an attack by Portuguese pirates and an island eventually formed around the ship wreck. However it formed, this tiny, 4.63 sq km island is barely seven km and 10 minutes by speedboat from Cox's Bazar. It was once a place renowned for growing pink pearls, but the economic benefits from more profitable commercial fishing has seen this tradition slowly fade away.

Sonadia, with a variety of mangroves, is noted for its bird life and, in particular, acts as a temporary sanctuary for migrating birds – petrels, geese, curlews, snipe, shanks, lapwings, ducks and other waterfowl. The western side of the island is a beach, known for its interesting seashells. There is a small bazar here with seashell crafts. Quite a few visitors come here during the winter season for beach picnics and to hunt for pink pearls.

Unfortunately, there are no public launches, so you'll have to hire a boat (Tk 700 or more for a day trip) at Kastura Ghat.

Maheskhali Island

Some six km north-west of Cox's Bazar, Maheskhali (mash-KHAL-ee) Island makes a pleasant day trip. It's large, hilly and – for a nice change – lightly populated. Arriving by ferry from Cox's Bazar, you must pass along an impressively long high jetty for about 500m until you reach the town of Maheskhali. It's a friendly Hindu community, and if there are any festivals underway you might be invited to stay and watch. Regardless, you'll find rickshaws to take you wherever you want.

Passing by the jetty into town, you'll see a small hill in the distance to the north, only about a 15 minute rickshaw ride away. This holy spot is the principal tourist attraction, with a famous stupa on top. The climb takes only five or 10 minutes. From the top you can get a good view of most of the island.

The stupa north of Maheskhali town is a popular spot with the locals.

Betel Nuts
On Maheskhali, you'll see betel trees everywhere. This island is one of the major sources of the nuts, which are sold at street stands all over the country. Taken as a digestive stimulant and mild narcotic, the betel nut is broken into tiny pieces and chewed with leaves and lime paste. There are two kinds, one with a hint of sweetness from additives. Try some – you'll see people everywhere chewing and spitting red juice. Chances are you'll find them unbearably bitter, but the locals will get a big kick out of seeing you indulge in their habit. ■

A little further north, along the cliff on the eastern side of the island, is the sole wooded area on the island. Somewhat hidden therein is **Adinath**, a Shiv Mandir (ashram) dedicated to Siva (Shiva). It's a delightfully serene place set in a beautiful garden, and the people are very friendly. It's definitely worth the effort.

If it's the dry season and you have the time you might consider some hiking. There are paths along the top of the cliff that lines the eastern side of the island. Almost no one stays overnight on the island, which is perhaps a mistake as there are lots of paths to explore besides those along the cliff. Swimming is also an option, but the sandy beaches on the island's western side are better for this.

When you return to town, ask to be pointed towards the small fishing settlement nearby, where you can watch the boat-building activity. During the dry season (which is also the fishing season) you can see fisher people, who set up temporary camps here, drying their catches.

The area is famous for its large prawns. In inlets along the coast you'll see fisher people with their nets, hauling in the catch. Fishing for other species is supposed to be good, and during the festive season of Falgoon (March to April), a visit here can be most interesting.

Places to Stay & Eat The *Sea Guard Hotel*, near the bazar, appears to be the only hotel on the island. It has singles with common bathrooms for about Tk 50 and doubles with attached bathrooms for about Tk 115. The accommodation isn't brilliant but, like the rest of the island, it's relaxed. The usual bazar food is available and there are a few reasonable restaurants.

Getting There & Away The public ferry departing from Kastura Ghat in Cox's Bazar costs Tk 20 and takes an hour. Check to see what other passengers are paying, however, as one traveller reports that the locals told him the fare is normally Tk 7 and Tk 20 only when there's foul weather. There are also faster 'speed boats' that depart from Kastura Ghat and take only 15 minutes. They depart when full (about 10 passengers) and cost Tk 50 (Tk 40 for locals). Market days are Tuesday and Saturday, when more ferries are available. The main town has an impressive jetty, but if you want to continue around the coast, which is possible, disembarking will involve balancing on ladders and wading through mud.

TEKNAF

This small town is on the southern tip of the narrow strip of land adjoining Myanmar, 92 km south of Cox's Bazar. The Naaf River forms the Bangladesh-Myanmar border here, and a creek from the Naaf divides the town, separating the flat and elevated portions. Most of the town is a crowded area of narrow alleys. From the main road where the bus stops, a narrow street runs eastward downhill and across the creek. Over the bridge, a left turn leads up to the market place, where you'll find lots of smuggled Burmese merchandise and a few food stalls.

Things to See & Do

The main reason for visiting Teknaf is to reach St Martin's Island, which lies 38 km south. Other possibilities include a walk west to Teknaf Beach and a ride south to Badarmokam at the tip of the peninsula. Particularly nice at sunset, the white sandy beach at

Badarmokam is quite deserted, except for the fisher people who bring in their catch and work on their boats and nets at various times of the day.

Back in Teknaf, just south of the market and police station you'll find jeeps that provide transport to surrounding villages. For Tk 20, a jeep will take you over a bumpy brick road to the very last village on the mainland, **Shahpuri**, a half hour ride. You'll be let off at a cafe. The left fork here leads down to the seafront and mangrove swamps. Its main attractions are the beautiful view from the embankment through the mangrove swamps across to the Myanmar coast, and the village's peaceful atmosphere, as fisher people mend their boats and nets.

In 1994, some Europeans walked from Teknaf all the way to Cox's Bazar, a trip that took three days but is better done in four. Finding a place to sleep was apparently not a major problem. On one or two nights, villagers reportedly welcomed them into their homes, offering board and lodging. A hike similar to this might be worth considering, except during the rainy season. Babu, a friendly man in Teknaf who knows everyone, is great for information and may be able to help out.

Places to Stay & Eat
The *Niribili Hotel* is a block north of the market; a sign on a lamp post points the way. Singles/doubles with fans and attached bathrooms cost Tk 50/80, but finding someone to check you in may be a problem.

Other establishments of similar quality and price are *Hotel Ajmere*, on your right just before you cross the bridge, and *Hotel Taipang*, on the main drag, south of the bus station. The Taipang also has a restaurant, but it apparently is not always functioning.

Finding cheap food is no problem, but don't expect it to be very tasty. There are some basic restaurants near the market, and some cafes on the main highway, just west of the bridge over the creek.

Getting There & Away
Between Cox's Bazar and Teknaf (70 km)

there are buses departing every hour in either direction until around 4.15 pm.

ST MARTIN'S ISLAND
Barely eight km south-west of Badarmokam and 48 km from Teknaf, St Martin's is the country's only coral island and an unspoilt paradise, with no vehicles, one single short road, genuinely friendly people' and essentially no crime. The people here are quite poor; however, begging isn't a problem, so don't create one by giving sweets etc to kids.

Amazingly, a cyclone hasn't lashed the island seriously, although in 1994 a strong storm uprooted most of the tall old trees planted by the islanders some 50 years ago. You no longer need a permit to visit, but expect some friendly attention from the border guards.

Named after a British provincial governor and called Narikel Jinjira (Coconut Island) by the locals, the dumbbell-shaped St Martin's has an area of only about eight sq km, which reduces to about five sq km – and from one to four islands – during high tide. The main island to the north, Uttar Para, gradually narrows several km southward, to a point where the width is roughly 100m. Three smaller islands – Zinjira, Galachira and Ciradia – are located just south of the main island. At low tide they're essentially one body of land, and a narrow strip of land connects them with the main island.

Hiking Around St Martin's Island
St Martin's Island is one of the best places in Bangladesh, especially in winter, to get away from it all. You can walk around the main island in a day. The island has two lagoons which support thick mangrove forests, though without the plant diversity of the Sundarbans. You'll also see numerous sand dunes, typically covered by screw pine and beach creeper. A rocky platform surrounds the island and extends into the sea, but the sand is excellent almost all the way around and is ideal for sunbathing. You may, however, encounter an oily patch here and there. If you are bothered by mosquitoes you'll love this place because there are very few in the winter and only marginally more during the monsoon. ■

Most of the island's 5500 inhabitants live on Uttar Para. The majority are Muslims and live primarily off fishing, although some plant rice and vegetables. During the peak fishing season, October to April, fisher people from neighbouring areas bring their catch to St Martin's Island, where wholesale buyers with temporary stalls stand ready to purchase their catch. It's fascinating to see so many different types of fish drying in the sun on endless bamboo racks along the beach. Much of the catch, however, decomposes because the island lacks a fish processing plant.

Information

Finding your way around Uttar Para is simple as there's only one tarred street, opposite the landing point on the beach, where the island's shops and restaurants are located. Uttar Para boasts a primary and high school, as well as a post office, police station and border patrol, a barber and tailor, a generator, and a cyclone warning centre and shelter. For information on the island, try the post office. The people there are very friendly, and will most likely invite you for a cup of tea and to hear their stories about relatives in foreign embassies. Few people on the island speak English.

Places to Stay

One of the island's two cyclone shelters serves as a rest house. From the landing, you'll find it about 300m south down the beach. It's a concrete building on stilts overlooking the sea. It has only one room with two beds, mosquito nets and a bathroom that doesn't work. The cost is Tk 100 a night. The location overlooking the water is marvellous, and every morning you'll wake up to a view of the sun rising over the mountains of Myanmar.

A better choice is the *Bay of Bengal Lodge*. It's the home and commercial inn of Kasim Master, a 76 year old retired school teacher who was the island's sole teacher when the primary school was first established. An English speaker and known by all the islanders, he is friendly, generous and

very hearty for his 76 years. He can accommodate three or four people and his family will prepare meals if you ask. The cost is Tk 100 a person. His home is on the main street on your right, a few minutes' walk from the beach.

Retired chairman Abul Quassem Chowdhury reportedly has two guest rooms at his house, and has charged guests Tk 30.

Places to Eat

There is no dearth of grocery shops and tea houses. Shops sell biscuits and bananas among other things. The tea houses serve rice with fish, lentils, roti, local vegetables and coconuts from the island. Even though limited food is available, it's probably a good idea to bring some tinned food and other goodies along as gifts for your hosts.

Getting There & Away

Between Teknaf and St Martin's Island there are apparently two ferries in operation, one leaving every morning and returning the next day. The ferry departs from Teknaf around 9 am, give or take an hour depending on the tides. To confirm the exact departure time beforehand, check at one of the hotels or the post office. Information on the boat departure is often conflicting so check a couple of sources and arrive at least half an hour early. Ignore the fishing boat owners who will probably tell you there is no ferry – they want you to use their private boats at a cost of Tk 1200 for the one way trip! The ferry, in comparison, costs only Tk 20 (3 hours). On market days (Sunday and Thursday), you might find two trawlers making the trip, and on stormy days during the monsoon season there is sometimes no service at all. The high seats on the stern are the best as they give good views and catch the breeze. There's no shade on the boat, so bring a hat and water.

When the ferry arrives, passengers must roll up their clothing and walk through knee-deep water as there is no landing. The ferry returns to Teknaf the next morning. Seats start filling up around 8.30 am but the boat may not leave before 10 am.

COMILLA

Some 90 km south-east of Dhaka on the highway to Chittagong and just a few km west of the Indian border, Comilla is a major junction. During WWII, Japanese troops penetrated the area, and graves of some 40 Japanese soldiers are amongst the hundreds on the carefully manicured grounds of the WWII Memorial Cemetery.

Comilla is easy to miss because the bypass road on the western outskirts of town has few signs suggesting that a large urban area is only several km away. A major military base is in the huge Cantonment just west of this road. Just south of the Cantonment in Kotbari is BARD (a major training institute), a cadet college and the city's major tourist attraction – the 6th to 13th century Buddhist ruins of Mainimati, some mounds of which are in the Cantonment itself. Comilla is also the home of the Academy for Rural Development and the Bangladesh Rice Research Institute.

Orientation & Information

The centre of Comilla is the Kandirpar district, the heart of which is Kandirpar Circle,

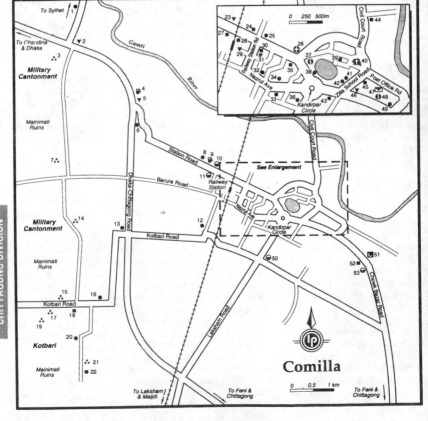

Comilla

from where four major arteries extend. Fazlul Haque Rd, heading eastward, eventually becoming Chowk Bazar Rd and the road to Chittagong, is lined with shops of all sorts and is the centre of the commercial district. Heading east along this street you'll come to Rajshinda Market, one of the city's major landmarks, and Chowk Bazar, which is another major commercial area and the location of the Chittagong bus station. Just past Chowk Bazar, on the outskirts of town, are some impressive Hindu temples.

Half a km north of Kandirpar Circle you'll find a small well maintained park, with lots of shade trees, benches and a lake nearby. This is definitely the best place for escaping the crowds. There are several hotels in the Kandirpar district, but most hotels and restaurants are well west of the Circle along Station Rd, near the railway station.

If you're an architecture buff, head for Nazrul Ave, which runs parallel with Station Rd two blocks to the south. A number of early 20th century mansions line this street. Although dilapidated, their original architectural features are largely intact.

Hindu Festivals & Temples

There are two local festivals, the Raas (Hindu) and Kathin Chibar Dan Utsab (Buddhist) festivals, which both occur 10 days into November, and are incorporated into a local trade fair.

This would be a good occasion to check the historic 17th century **Jagannath Temple**, the only one built in Bangladesh with 17 towers. On the outskirts of town, this unusual octagonal structure consists of a central brick shaft, rising in three diminishing storeys topped by a pointed roof, with murals and plaster relief inside. Unfortunately, it has lost most of its exterior artwork and its towers, so you may find it interesting only on festival days.

A more interesting and better preserved temple is the **Chandina Aat-Chala Temple**, in Chandina, 10 km north-west of town. This 19th century Siva temple, constructed in the popular hut design, is probably the best example of the 'aat-chala' variation in Bangladesh, which is a hut-style structure with a second smaller hut repeated on top to gain height. It's a small square temple but

PLACES TO STAY					
18	BARD Training Institute & Rest House	31	Jabed Restaurant Sweets Shop	21	Salban Vihara
		46	Jenny Sweets	25	Pharmacies
22	Salban Vihara Rest House & Archaeological Museum			26	Military Hospital
		OTHER		32	Colonial-Era Mansions
		1	WWII Memorial Cemetery	34	Comilla Law College
24	Hotel Abedin & Sonali Bank Branch	3	Charpatra Mura	36	Medical Centre
27	Hotel Peoples	4	Petrol Station	37	Sonali Bank
28	Melody Hotel	6	Coca Cola Plant	38	Cinema & Fuji Photo Store
30	Hotel Maynamati	7	Kotila Mura		
33	Ashique Residencial Rest House	8	Bangladesh Rice Research Institute	39	Park
35	Nirapad Guest House	9	Petrol Station	40	Our Lady of Fatima Catholic Church
43	Hotel Al-Rafique	10	Main Bus Station (for Dhaka & Sylhet)	41	Stadium
45	Lilufa Rest House	11	Baby Taxi Stand	42	Comilla Zilla School
52	Hotel Dreamland	12	Telecommunications Antenna	44	Civic Court
		13	Sign for BARD Training Institute	47	Post Office
PLACES TO EAT		14	Ananda Vihara	48	Sonali Bank
2	Kakoli Restaurant	15	Itakhola Mura	49	Rajshinda Market
5	Biroti Restaurant	16	College	50	Local Buses
23	Albarakat Restaurant	17	Rupban Mura	51	Mosque
29	Restaurant Jolin & Restaurant Alamin	19	Hitigara Mura	53	Chowk Bazar & Chowk Bazar Bus Station (For Chittagong)
		20	Cadet College		

CHITTAGONG DIVISION

very well proportioned, and the terracotta artwork on the facade and ornate entrance combine to give this building a lovely appearance.

If you happen to pass through Lalmi, a small town seven km south of Comilla towards Laksham, check the **Lalmi Temple**, one km west of town. It's small and nothing special except for its location on top of a hill – an unusual feature in most of Bangladesh.

WWII Memorial Cemetery
On the north-western outskirts of town on the road north to Sylhet, a km off the Dhaka road, this beautifully maintained cemetery is one of the city's principal tourist attractions. British, African, Indian, Irish, Australian and Japanese troops were all buried here. Coming from Dhaka, you'll arrive at the turn-off to the left for the cemetery two km before the left turn-off for Comilla.

Places to Stay – bottom end
The best area for cheap hotels is along Station Rd, just north of the railway station. Coming from Dhaka, just before the railway crossing you'll pass *Hotel Peoples* (☎ 5103), a clearly marked five storey structure. It's a bit dumpy but the cramped, single-bed rooms with overhead fans and attached bathrooms (Tk 60) are tolerable, and there's a decent restaurant across the street.

Some 70m further east is the slightly grubbier *Melody Hotel* (☎ 5506), which has similar singles/doubles with common bathrooms for Tk 40/80. The top-floor rooms, which cost Tk 100, are equally tiny but have been entirely renovated, and feature carpet and attached bathrooms.

A better deal is the poorly marked three storey *Hotel Abedin* (☎ 6014), another 70m further, on the corner. The exterior is dilapidated but inside it's OK. If you can afford Tk 100, by all means take the double on the top floor; it's spacious, bright and has reading chairs, a fan, mosquito nets, common bathrooms and great views of the city from the porch. A small single on the same floor costs Tk 60, while tolerable singles/doubles on the

lower floors cost Tk 45/80 (Tk 35 for a single with common bathrooms).

Some 50m further east is the well marked three storey *Hotel Maynamati* (☎ 6455). Popular and well maintained, it's clearly a notch above the rest. Singles/doubles cost Tk 70/135. The rooms are small but clean, with fresh sheets, overhead fans, mosquito nets and decent attached bathrooms. There's also a TV and a fridge with drinks in the lobby.

In Kandirpar, check the *Nirapad Guest House*, across from the military hospital or *Lilufa Rest House* across from the Comilla Zilla School, just south of the stadium. Nirapad is a dumpy two storey structure that has tiny singles/doubles with fans and common bathrooms for Tk40/80, while Lilufa has ventilated singles/doubles with attached bathrooms for Tk 40/70.

Hotel Meraj, just a block east of the busy Circle, has singles/doubles with attached bathrooms for Tk 50/60 and is noisy. Much better is the new *Hotel Al-Rafique* almost next door. It has fresh-looking singles/doubles with fans and attached bathrooms for Tk 55/100 and is often full. Another possibility is *Hotel Dreamland*, two km south-east of the Circle off Chowk Bazar Rd and down a lane opposite the flowery minaret. At Tk 80/125 for singles/doubles with attached bathrooms it's definitely no bargain, but it's handy for the Chittagong bus.

Places to Stay – top end
Ashique Residencial Rest House (☎ 8781), a modern four storey structure on Nazrul Ave, 50m west of Comilla Law College, has no competition in the central area. It has clean and unusually spacious rooms, with twin single beds, mosquito nets, rugs, reading chairs and large attached bathrooms. Rooms cost Tk 250 and meals are available if you order in advance.

There are at least three guesthouses in the Comilla area, but all are rather remotely located. Try for permission to stay at the modern *BARD Training Institute* (☎ 6428). Singles/doubles cost Tk 80/120 (economy), Tk 150/200 (standard), Tk 300/350 (air-con) and Tk 500 (family). Meals are available. It's near the Mainimati ruins, eight km west of town; finding a baby taxi is no problem. If you're driving, you'll find a large sign (in English) for BARD on the Dhaka-Chittagong highway.

The *Salban Vihara Archaeological Museum Rest House* (☎ 6905), two km south of BARD and much less accessible to transportation, has two rooms plus a common dining area. The charge is Tk 100/150 for one/two people. Reserve a room by calling the Director of Archaeology (Dhaka ☎ (02) 327-608).

The *Rural Electrification Board 'Guest House* (☎ 6096), 10 km north-west of Comilla in Chandina, costs Tk 50/100 for singles/doubles (Tk 120 with air-con). Get permission from' the Rural Electrification Board in Dhaka (☎ (02) 815-818, 327-828/9).

Places to Eat

For inexpensive Bangladeshi food, the area around the railway station has several very good restaurants, including *Restaurant Jolin* and *Restaurant Alamin* next door. Both places have very friendly owners and serve fresh hot naan (flat bread), curries and rice dishes for around Tk 15 to Tk 20.

Across from the Chowk Bazar bus station you'll find a place (no English sign) that serves excellent chicken with rice and tea (Tk 44) and ice-cold drinks.

Try *Albarakat Restaurant* on Station Rd just west of the railway line. The most popular dish is meat with sauce accompanied by rice and naan. It's a good sized establishment, with overhead fans.

You will also find a restaurant or two in the area around Kandirpar Circle. For sweets, tea and snacks, try *Jabed Restaurant Sweets Shop* on Railway Station Rd, a block east of the station.

The city has two upmarket restaurants, both of which are on the Dhaka-Chittagong highway on the north-western outskirts of town: the *Biroti Restaurant*, just north of the turn-off for Comilla, and *Kakoli Restaurant*, 2½ km further out of town in the Cantonment, at the turn-off for the WWI memorial cemetery in a row of shops marked with

Coca-Cola signs. Both places, which cater to individuals and families, are carpeted and have air-con. The Biroti features both Bangladesh and Chinese menus, including beef curry (Tk 20), fish curry (Tk 30), fried chicken (Tk 30) and Chinese chicken and onions (Tk 35). The Kakoli has similar prices and food.

Getting There & Away

Bus Buses for Dhaka (two hours), Sylhet (six hours) and other cities to the north leave from a bus station on Station Rd just west of the railway line. Chair coach/bus fares are Tk 125/100 to Sylhet and Tk 45/35 to Dhaka. If you're heading for Mymensingh and don't want to go via Dhaka, go north to Bhairab Bazar and pick up connections there.

Buses for Chittagong and other towns to the south leave from Chowk Bazar bus station, about two km east of Kandirpar Circle on Chowk Bazar Rd. Buses for Chittagong leave throughout the day and early evening. The trip takes three to 3½ hours and costs Tk 55/45 (chair coach/bus).

Train Comilla is on the Dhaka-Chittagong line. There are three trains daily in both directions; the morning trains are best. Trains from Dhaka arrive at 11 am (best), 6.40 pm and 2.40 am, while those from Chittagong arrive at 9.40 am (best), 5.50 pm and 2.30 am. The 1st class/sulob fare is Tk 170/55 to Chittagong and Tk 160/52 to Dhaka. Sulob on the 'best' train is about 50% more. There's one train a day to Sylhet, departing from Chittagong at 10.30 am, arriving at Comilla around 1 pm (it has a sleeper car). The six hour journey costs Tk 182/56 in 1st class/sulob. The fare to Mymensingh is Tk 233/70.

MAINIMATI RUINS

The Mainimati-Lalmai ridge is a 20 km range of low hills eight km to the west of Comilla. Famous as an important centre of Buddhist culture from the 6th to 13th centuries, the buildings excavated were wholly made of baked bricks. There are more than 50 scattered Buddhist sites, but the three most important are Salban Vihara, Kotila Mura and Charpatra Mura.

A large section of Mainimati is a military cantonment, and it was while the army was clearing the area with bulldozers that the archaeological site in the Kotbari area was discovered. This was a centre for Buddhism and was visited by Xuan Zhang in the 7th century AD. The Chinese pilgrim found 70 monasteries, about 2000 *bhikkus* (Buddhist monks) and an Ashoka stupa from the 2nd century BC.

Unfortunately, some of the major ruins are within the cantonment and cannot be visited without permission from military officers. For this reason, most visitors see only the museum and several of the ruins. If you're staying at BARD, people there can probably help you with the permission process. Independent travellers are unlikely to be successful unless they are very persistent and tactful. You can start the process by asking personnel at the cantonment entrance gate or at BARD.

Salban Vihara

This 170 sq metre monastery has 115 cells for the monks, facing a temple in the centre of the courtyard. While it lacks Paharpur's imposing stupa, the remains give a better idea of the extent of the structure, as they were rebuilt more recently.

The royal copper plates of the Deva kings and a terracotta seal bearing a royal inscription found here clearly testify that the monastery was built by Sri Bhava Deva in the first half of the 8th century. The original cruciform plan of the central temple was changed and reduced in scale during later rebuilding. The entire basement wall was heavily embellished with terracotta plaques and ornamental bricks.

Site Museum

A museum just beyond Salban Vihara houses the finds excavated there, most of which cover the 6th to 13th century AD period. The collection includes terracotta plaques, bronze statues, a bronze casket, silver and gold coins dating from the 4th century AD,

Black basalt sculptures, like this beautiful image of Buddha found in the Mainimati ruins, date from around the 10th century.

jewellery, kitchen utensils, including old grinding stones, pottery and votive stupas embossed with Buddhist inscriptions. The marvellous terracotta plaques, richly detailed with a bewildering variety of subjects, including all kinds of animals, birds, flowers, and men and women in various poses, reveal a rural Buddhist art that was alive with animation, a vivid realism of nature and a simple expression of emotionalism.

Also on display are a collection of tiny dark Buddhist bronzes which the monks kept in their cells and used for praying, an unusually large bronze bell from one of the Buddhist temples, and instructive plans of some of the major shrines and monasteries, including a model of Kotila Mura. You'll also find some Hindu art, including large black-stone carvings of the gods and goddesses Vishnu, Ganesh and Parvati etc.

The museum, which is free, is open from 10 am to 5 pm daily (10.30 am to 5.30 pm from April to September), 2.30 to 5.30 pm (3 to 6 pm April to September) on Friday and closed Thursday.

Kotila Mura

Like all the ruins in the cantonment, this one cannot be visited without permission from the military. On a hill top with a commanding view of the countryside, it's five km north of Salban Vihara and, visually, is equally impressive. It comprises three large stupas representing Buddha, Dharma and Sangha, the 'Three Jewels of Buddhism', plus some secondary stupas, all enclosed by a massive boundary wall. The ground plan of the central stupa is in the shape of a *dharma chakra*, or the 'wheel of the law'. The hub of the wheel is represented by a deep shaft in the centre, and the spokes by eight brick cells. The two stupas on either side each contain a sealed central relic-chamber which has yielded hundreds of clay miniature stupas.

Charpatra Mura

Two km north-west of Kotila Mura and not far from the Dhaka-Chittagong highway, this is another oblong Buddhist shrine perched on a hill top in the cantonment. The main prayer chamber of the shrine is to the west, and is approached from a spacious hall to the east through a covered passage. The roof was originally supported on four thick brick columns, and a covered entrance led to the prayer chamber.

Ananda Vihara

Also in the cantonment, 1½ km south of Kotila Mura, this mound is the largest of the ancient sites on the ridge, occupying an area over 100 sq metres. Similar in plan to Salban Vihara, it was badly damaged and plundered by contractors during WWII, consequently there's not much to see. Since you'll pass this monastery on the way to Kotila Mura,

however, it may be worth checking very briefly.

Getting There & Away

From Kandirpar Circle, you can get a tempo to Kotbari for Tk 7. A tempo to yourself will cost about Tk 35. You'll be dropped in Kotbari near BARD, leaving you a 1½ km walk to the museum. Most rickshaw drivers aren't interested in the long trip to Mainamati, though if you go down Laksham Rd to the intersection with Kotbari Rd (where there's a petrol station), you'll find lots of drivers willing to do the trip (about five km). If you bargain real hard, you can get a ride for as little as Tk 10; otherwise expect to pay about Tk 20.

MAIJDI

Five hours south of Dhaka by bus or car and 46 km west of Feni, Maijdi, together with Sonapur just to the south, is often labelled 'Noakhali' on maps and timetables. It's one of the principal towns in the district of Noakhali, the site of much bloodshed between Hindus and Muslims at the time of Partition. Mahatma Gandhi visited the area for several months in 1947 shortly before his death to pacify the rioting communities. Muslims here are a bit more conservative than elsewhere in the country and tend to be more reserved in dealings with foreigners. Many families have relatives working in the Middle East, so don't be surprised if you occasionally see Bangladeshi men wearing clothes of that region.

Orientation & Information

There is one long main drag running north-south through town, and virtually all the shops and offices are here. There are no handicrafts for sale but the post office is reliable should you want to mail something. You'll find plenty of baby taxis, including a stand for them on the main drag near the post office.

Places to Stay

The well marked *Mobaraka Hotel* (☎ 6266) on the main drag in the heart of town has

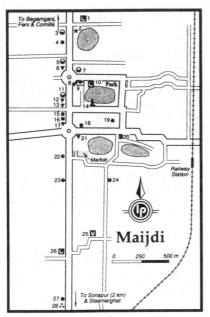

singles with common bathrooms for Tk 40 and singles/doubles with attached bathrooms for Tk 50/100. The dingy rooms have fans but no mosquito nets. The smaller *Royal Hotel* (☎ 5075) on the same block is clean and presentable, and charges Tk 120 for rooms with mosquito nets, fans, a sitting area with TV and decent attached bathrooms.

You might also try the *Circuit House* (☎ 6151) on the road to the railway station. There's a good chance the District Commissioner (who has a separate office nearby) will give the required permission. The rooms are spacious, with carpet, overhead fans and clean attached bathrooms, and meals are available for guests. There's even a tennis and squash court!

The best place is the unmarked *MCC Guesthouse* (☎ 5225), several blocks south of the Circuit House on a paved back road. To reserve a room, contact the American staff at the MCC office about two km south of the GPO on the main drag, or call their office in Dhaka (☎ (02) 815-625, 310-486). The rooms have comfortable beds, mosquito nets and attached bathrooms, and there's a sitting area. The cost is Tk 100 a person. You can also get great meals here for Tk 50 (Tk 30 for breakfast).

The *Catholic Mission* on the western side of Sonapur, several km south of Maijdi along the main drag, is reportedly quite friendly and has accepted travellers in the past. Another possibility is the *Gandhi Ashram*, 30 km to the north in Joyag. See the following Around Maijdi section in this chapter for more information.

Places to Eat

If you're not staying at a guesthouse your best bet for meals is the *Kiron Hotel* (Bangla sign), a small restaurant on the main drag on the northern side of town next to the Bilash bus station. It offers decent Bengali meals at standard prices.

You'll find the *Farid Bakery*, a block to the south, which is good for sweets and biscuits, and a shop around the corner which serves the best ice cream in town. There are also several tea houses a block further south.

At any of these places you may find some sweets, including rashmelai (RASH-mah-lie) and misti doi (or bogra doy), a sweet yoghurt served in a small bowl.

Getting There & Away
Bus The bus station is on the northern side of town, one km north of the market. The trip from Dhaka takes five to six hours and costs Tk 70. For a more comfortable chair coach try Bilash, two blocks closer to the centre of town. The fare is Tk 100 and there are three departures a day at 5.40, 6.40 am and 2.10 pm. From Dhaka buses depart from the Fakirapur area near the Green Line office at 9, 11 am and 3 pm.

Train There are daily trains between Dhaka and Maijdi, departing from Dhaka at 12.30 pm and Maijdi at 2 pm. The six hour trip costs Tk 240/82 in 1st/2nd class.

AROUND MAIJDI
Bajra Shahi Mosque
The area's most notable historical monument is the Bajra Shahi Mosque, which dates from 1741 and is in a rural setting overlooking a pond. It's a well maintained building and is completely covered in bits of broken china; the total effect is beautiful. Both men and women are allowed to enter; inside you'll find a small prayer hall pleasingly painted in bold red, blue, green and yellow.

The mosque is 15 km north of Maijdi, just off the Maijdi-Comilla road. Head north from Maijdi, pass through Begamganj (nine km) and onto Bajra (five km further). The mosque is one km further north on your left, 200m down a dirt road just south and behind a hospital.

Gandhi Ashram
The Gandhi Ashram (☎ (0321) 6017) dates from 1947 when Gandhi undertook a series of 'peace walks' through the area for several months. When a group of local Hindus presented Gandhi with a gift of about 10 hectares of land in the area, he unselfishly shrugged it off, saying it would be of no use to him, and suggested that it be used to help the poor. Gandhi promised to return but his assassination prevented him from fulfilling his word. Charu Chowdhury, who accompanied him on his trip here, began running the place, using it to help the local people as Gandhi had requested. In 1953, however, during the time of Partition, the Pakistanis confiscated the property and put Chowdhury in jail, where he remained until 1971. Chowdhury was released at independence, the property was returned and the ashram resumed its activities under his leadership until he died in 1990.

Today, the ashram, which has a staff of 32 people, is essentially a development organisation, helping both Hindus and Muslims in over 25 nearby villages to improve their lives. If you come here, you'll see some of the interesting projects: three fish ponds plus a fascinating fish-hatchery machine donated by a foreign organisation; a school covering grades one to eight; a training programme for women weaving jute; and, most fascinating, a bio-gas generator which uses dung from the ashram's six cows to produce enough fuel to run the kitchen's stove for four hours a day. They'll also be delighted to show you a prayer room dedicated to the memory of Gandhi, with old photographs dating from 1947 and one of Gandhi's spinning wheels. They'll probably offer you some tea heated by the cow-manure gas and show you some of the women's weavings, which you may purchase.

The ashram has two guest rooms; the staff are extremely friendly and staying here should not be a problem if they have beds available. Calling in advance might be wise.

To get here from Bajra Shahi Mosque, proceed 15 km further north, stay on this paved highway (rather than turning right for

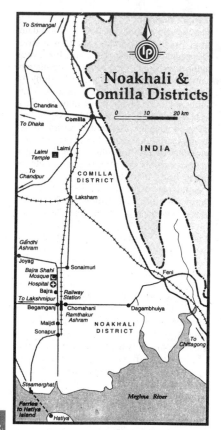

HATIYA ISLAND

For a bit of adventure, you could head south from Maijdi to Steamerghat and take a ferry to Hatiya (HAT-tee-ah) Island. Very few travellers have been here; however, there are lots of people on this large island so don't expect a tranquil paradise like St Martin's Island. Having missed the brunt of the 1991 cyclone, it's a very pretty island and one of the better places in Bangladesh for bird-watching.

Places to Stay & Eat

In the town of Hatiya, at the northern end of the island near the ferry landing, you'll find a *NGO Guest House* and a *Government Rest House*. Foreigners may stay at either. You'll also find some small tea houses serving very basic spicy meals at standard prices.

Getting There & Away

From Maijdi, take a bus headed south-west for the tiny port of Steamerghat (35 km), also known as Hatiyaghat and close to Ramgati (ram-GOH-tee), a much larger town. The route passes through Sonapur (five km south of Maijdi). Be sure to get a bus to Steamerghat, not to Ramgati. Bus connections between Maijdi and Steamerghat are frequent and good, and you'll find several restaurants at Steamerghat serving very spicy food. There is at least one ferry departing around 2 pm. The trip takes 1½ to three hours, depending on the tides. There are also daily launches from Chittagong. See the Boat entry under Getting There & Away in the Chittagong section of this chapter.

CHANDPUR

Chandpur (or Chatpur), midway on the river from Dhaka to Barisal, is a busy but dilapidated riverport town. It offers little to travellers except the opportunity to take a launch on one of the widest sections of the Meghna River.

Places to Stay & Eat

Hotel Akbari on College Rd has singles/doubles from Tk 45/70. The *Balaka Hotel* in Purana Bazar has rooms with common bath-

Laksham) and you'll come to the tiny village of Joyag (JOY-ah). Turn right through the village and after 400m or so you'll come to the ashram.

Ramthakur Ashram

The Ramthakur (ram-TAH-gore) Ashram is in Chomahani, the neighbouring city to the east of Begamganj, nine km north of Maijdi. Just south of the station, this ashram, dating from 1949, is far less interesting than the Gandhi Ashram but worth a visit if you're in Chomahani.

rooms for Tk 50. *Hotel Safina* on Bagodi Rd is similar in price and standard. You could also ask around for the *Mission*; every one seems to know it, so chances are it may take travellers.

Outside the railway station there's a long narrow eatery that serves good chicken and mixed vegetables; the cost is standard. Just around the corner, on the road leading to the bus station, you'll find a couple of places that offer more comfortable surroundings but the food isn't as good. The shacks by the ferry dock are dirt cheap but you get what you pay for.

Getting There & Away

Bus From Sayedabad bus station in Dhaka there are direct buses to Chandpur. It may be quicker to take a bus to Comilla, for which there are departures every few minutes, and connect from there to Chandpur. As with the train service between Dhaka and Chandpur, this is a long and rather roundabout route via Comilla. Taking a boat is a much better option.

Direct buses for Comilla leave from the Thompson Bridge bus stand, or you could take a more frequent Chittagong-bound bus to Feni and change there.

There is a very convenient night chair coach that leaves from the main crossroads in town (not the bus stand) for Chittagong at 1 am, arriving at Chittagong around 6 am. The fare is Tk 65. Ordinary buses charge Tk 45.

Train Travelling by train to Chittagong is quite feasible and the least nerve-racking way to go; you have to connect at Laksham and the trip is reasonably quick. Travelling from Dhaka to Chandpur by train, however, is out of the question because the route is very roundabout, with a change at Laksham.

Boat Many private launches ply between Chandpur and Sadarghat in Dhaka. You can also travel between Dhaka and Chandpur by the Rocket which leaves Dhaka on Monday, Wednesday, Thursday and Saturday at 6 pm, arriving in Chittagong around 10 pm. Coming from Khulna, it arrives in Chittagong on Tuesday, Thursday, Friday and Sunday around 3 or 4 am.

All the large nightly launches plying between Dhaka and Barisal stop in Chittagong. Those from Dhaka depart between 5.30 and 7.30 pm, arriving here four or five hours later. Coming from Barisal, they arrive here between about 1 and 5 am, continuing on to Dhaka.

See the information under Boat in the Getting There & Away section of the Dhaka chapter for more details.

Sylhet Division

Next to the Chittagong Hill Tracts, the Sylhet Division is the hilliest in the country. Sandwiched between the Khasi and Jaintia hills to the north, just across the border in India, and the Tripura hills to the south, also in India. This division is essentially one large valley. The countryside is covered mostly with terraced tea estates, small patches of tropical forests, and large pineapple plantations and orange groves.

The name 'Sylhet' could either have originated from the word *sri-hat* meaning 'central bazar', or from the Arabic term *serhed* meaning frontier town.

Part of the Assam region of India during the British era, this area has the highest annual rainfall in the country at 5000 mm. Just across the border in India is Cherrapunji, the wettest place on earth. On the whole, however, the area has the best climate in the country: it is temperate and cool with clean, crisp, fresh air in winter, and is moderately warm in summer.

This is a tea-growing region with more than 150 tea estates spread over 40,000 hectares, producing over 30 million kg of tea annually, mostly for export. Tea is Bangladesh's third-largest source of foreign exchange, after textiles and remittances from workers in the Middle East and Malaysia. Sylhet is considered the richest region of the country, with its agricultural produce, including oranges and pineapples, and mineral resources which include gas reserves and possibly oil deposits. Manufacturing industries include tea processing, cement, urea fertiliser and paper.

The valley is fed by two rivers, the Kusiyara and the Surma. The Surma passes through the city of Sylhet and eventually joins with the mighty Meghna further south. The valley is dotted with shallow natural depressions known as *haors* (HOW-ar). These low-lying marshy areas are permanent wetlands and provide verdant sanctuaries for migratory birds from places as far away as

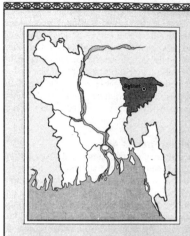

Highlights
- Tea Estates – the rolling hills are pleasant and fun to explore, especially by bike.
- Jaintiapur Megaliths – memorials of the Khasi tribe which date from the kingdom of Jaintia, and are similar to the menhirs found in Europe.
- Madhabkunda Waterfalls – this famous, remote waterfall is a popular sightseeing destination, and where you may see some of the few remaining elephants in Bangladesh
- Shahjalal Mosque – shrine to the early 14th century Sufi mystic Shah Jalal, which attracts more than 2000 pilgrims a day.
- Sunamganj Haors – a major wetlands; the premier location for bird-watching in Bangladesh.

Siberia. These haors and Sylhet's subtropical forests together make this region one of the best in the country for bird-watching. An incredible variety of ducks, other wetland birds which are scarce elsewhere in Bangladesh, Pallas' fishing eagle and other migratory birds such as geese and snipe abound. There are also reportedly a few jungle cats and wild boars roaming in the small patches of forests, but travellers are very unlikely to see any of them.

The hilly area along the northern border at the foot of the Khasi-Jaintia hills is tribal land. The Khasi, Pangou and the Manipuri, who live here, are all easily distinguishable from the native Muslim and Hindu populations by their slightly slanted eyes, a reflection of their oriental heritage, and their shorter stature. They shun regular contact with the outside world, venturing only occasionally from their settlements. The Manipuri are the exception to this; they have become artisans, jewellers and businesspeople, and have entered into the general Bangladeshi community. The Manipuri classical dance, seen only during Hindu festivals dedicated to the worship of Radha-Krishna, is the best known feature of Manipuri culture.

The Sylhet region lacks the magnificent mountainous backdrops and much cooler climate of Darjeeling, but the rolling scenery is nevertheless quite pleasant and fun to explore, especially by bike. The tea estates here are every bit as interesting to see, even though the terrain is not so steep and the tea itself is of lesser quality.

History

The history of the Sylhet Division was principally tribal until the conquest by the great Sufi mystic, the Muslim Shah Jalal-ud-din from Konya (Turkey), in the early 14th century. Upon arriving from Delhi, the warlike saint defeated the ruling Hindu raja, Gour Govinda, creating Shah Jalal's legendary stature among Muslims.

Ibn Battuta, a noted Moroccan traveller from Tangier, visited Sylhet to see the Sufi – and also picked up a slave for only Rs 7 while he was there. At about the same time as the Shah's arrival in Sylhet, Marco Polo spoke of the Sylhet region as a recruiting centre for eunuchs for the Kingdom of Kamrup.

In the 17th century, during the reign of Emperor Jahangir, the Mughal Empire overran the region. The Mughals, who apparently considered the area of little importance, gave way in the 18th century to

the British East India Company, which developed it as part of its Assam tea-growing region. Though Sylhet was a centre for Muslim pilgrimage during the era of the Tuglukh Dynasty, the town itself was most influenced by the British occupation. They have given this town a unique style of architecture: tall windows shaded by large, curved awnings, and roofs topped by several enclosed glass cubicles to provide light and ventilation.

SYLHET

The town of Sylhet has a faint British atmosphere and, while hardly charming overall, does have a few picturesque sights. Apart from the usual administrative buildings, the former residences and social structures seem to have weathered the transition from independence better than many other pieces of British Raj flotsam. For example, the old clocktower, made entirely of corrugated iron sheeting, and the British Council House, on the northern bank of the Surma, remain picturesque. Colonnaded residences are still fronted by neatly trimmed lawns, and verandahs still have leather armchairs and sofas arranged for delicate tastes. Most wealthy Bangladeshis and expatriates, however, now live in the more modern eastern quarter of town, Upashahar.

Sylhet has various religious festivals – Muslim, Hindu and Buddhist. The Hindu melas (fairs), the Laspurnima, Jolung Jatra, Rota Jatra, are the most colourful, all dedicated to Radha-Krishna. Only during these Hindu melas are the Manipuri dances held.

Warning

You cannot enter India from Sylhet without a permit from the Indian High Commission in Dhaka (now routinely issued) as the eastern region of India is a restricted and protected area (see To/From India in the Getting There & Away entry later in this section).

Orientation

Across the Surma River to the south is where you'll find the railway and bus stations. This section of town, which is newer but hardly modern, has little of interest other than the market and river life. The river is traversed by two bridges. The older more central one, Kean Bridge, is a narrow steel structure and continually congested with rickshaws, usually pushed by 'assistants' who get paid 50 paisas for the crossing. If you walk across, (often faster than taking a rickshaw), watch out for rickshaws hurtling down the steep slope whenever the way is clear. Just east of that bridge on the northern side is a dock with some speed boats. If you'd like to rent one for a trip on the river, ask here or at the nearby Circuit House, which has friendly helpful staff.

Information

Money The Sonali Bank in the heart of town on Shah Jalal Rd exchanges foreign currency.

Pharmacy The Central Pharmacy on Airport Rd at Chowhatta intersection is highly recommended. The owners speak excellent English and are very friendly and helpful.

Forestry Office If you're heading to Srimangal and want to stay at the guesthouse in Lowacherra (lau-ah-CHAIR-ah) Forest, get permission here at the District Forestry Office (☎ 6358), located near the post office;

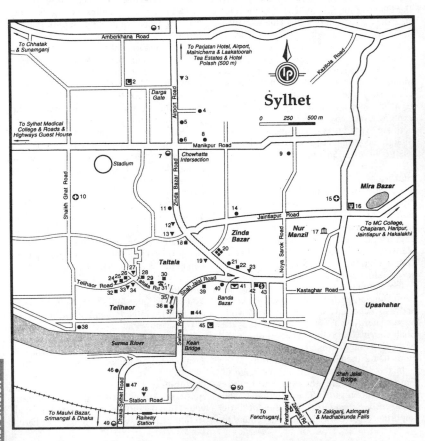

it has sole authority over this guesthouse. If the District Forestry Officer (DFO) is not in, call his residence (☎ 5104).

Mosques & MC College

There are a number of mosques of the pre-Mughal and Mughal periods in and around the town. On the northern bank of the Surma and east of Kean Bridge is a Mughal-period **mosque** enclosed by high walls and topped by a low dome. In the city, off Airport Rd, the old round-domed **Shah Jalal Mosque** is the shrine of the aforementioned 14th-century Sufi mystic Shah Jalal, and a major pilgrimage place for Muslims of Bangladesh. His sword and robes are preserved within the mosque but are not on display. The pond next to it is filled with huge sacred catfish who are fed by the pilgrims and are, according to legend, the transmogrified followers of the Hindu Raja Gour Govinda, who was defeated by Shah Jalal in 1303. There is also a tiny tank around the back with ordinary goldfish which attract attention; they too are apparently considered sacred.

Nearby, on a hillock named **Rama Raja's Tilla**, are the ruins of Gour Govinda's palace. They are no longer visible, but you can get some partially blocked views of the city here.

Some 11 km east of town, just off the highway to Jaintiapur, is a second old **Shah Jalal Mosque** in Chaparan, a tiny village. It's a similar looking single-domed mosque which attracts some 2000 pilgrims a day; you'll see charter buses from Dhaka all around the place. Like the former mosque of the same name, it cannot be visited inside. En route, on the city's eastern outskirts, you'll pass **Murali Chand (MC) College**, which dates from 1921. The main building, just off the highway, has a grand appearance and is worth a short stop.

Osmani Museum & Rama Krishna Temple

The Osmani Museum is a small, plain colonial-era house in Nur Manzil, near the centre of town, east of Noya Sarok Rd and on the same block as the jail. It's open Saturday to Wednesday from 10.30 am to 4.30 pm and Friday from 3.30 to 7.30 pm. A block to the north-east is Rama Krishna Temple, which is worth checking out.

Manipuri Village

East of the Shah Jalal Bridge is a pleasant village inhabited mainly by people of the Manipuri tribe. Their houses are decorated

PLACES TO STAY				
18	London Rest House & London Plaza	12	Chow King Chinese Restaurant	
22	Modern Rest House	13	Diner King Chinese Restaurant	
25	Hotel Bilash & Cinema	19	Ponchokhana Restaurant	
26	Hotel Sufia	23	Oriental Restaurant	
28	Hotel Gulshan	24	Jamania Restaurant	
29	Romania Boarding	27	Hotel Bye-Bye	
30	Hotel Shahban	33	Banani Restaurant	
32	Hotel Hiltown	34	New Green Restaurant	
36	Hotel Monoram	35	Suruli Restaurant	
39	Surma Valley Rest House & Kushiara Department Store	48	Food Stalls	
42	Mojlish Rest House & Restaurant	**OTHER**		
44	Circuit House	1	Local Bus Depot	
47	Hotel Cassana	2	Shahjalal Mosque	
		4	Rama Raja's Tilla	
PLACES TO EAT		5	Gulf Air & British Airways Agent	
3	Aajrani Restaurant	6	Central Pharmacy	

7	Rental Minibus Stand
8	Roads & Highways Office
9	Catholic Mission
10	Hospital
11	Biman Airlines
14	Aarong Handicraft Shop
15	Hospital
16	Rama Krishna Temple
17	Osmani Museum
20	Sylhet Plaza
21	Fujiphoto
31	Business Centre
37	Surma Market
38	Kagil Market
40	Town Hall
41	Post Office
43	Sonali Bank
45	Mosque
46	Vegetable Market
49	Comilla Bus Terminal
50	Dhaka Bus Terminal

with carved awnings, and there are several small Hindu shrines nearby. Many of the friendly locals wear traditional costume, and you can purchase handicrafts from them, though there is no pressure put upon you to do so.

Organised Tours
Sylhet Tourism Agency (☎ 2995) at Hotel Polash offers two standard one-day tours. One covers the scenic area of Tamabil, Jaflang and Sripur, with a visit to the stone megaliths in Jaintiapur and several tea estates en route (Tk 300 a person). Another heads south-east to Madhabkunda waterfalls (another scenic area), also with a visit to a tea estate en route (Tk 400 per person).

Places to Stay – bottom end
There is a good range of hotels in Sylhet. A number of the lower-end choices are in the centre of town in Taltala, along Taltala Rd and the adjoining Telihaor area, west of Kean Bridge. Unless otherwise stated, rooms at all of these places have overhead fans and attached bathrooms.

The cheapest in this area is *Romania Boarding* (☎ 4939). It's a friendly place with tolerably clean singles/doubles for Tk 40 to Tk 50/Tk 70 to Tk 80. Another is *Hotel Monoram* (☎ 7307), a five storey establishment down a side alley near Surma market. The singles/doubles, which cost Tk 45/80, look like cells, but this place is clean enough, staff are friendly and there is a lobby with TV.

A block further west is *Hotel Sufia* (☎ 4697). Singles/doubles here cost Tk 40 to Tk 50/Tk 90 to Tk 120. The Tk 120 rooms are a bit grubby, but they're fairly spacious, with one large bed and a large bathroom. The cheaper rooms are smaller. It's on the 2nd floor, with a TV viewing area that's large if not attractive.

A little further on Telihaor Rd is the four storey *Hotel Bilash* (☎ 4659), which has a Bangla sign and offers better value. It has standard singles/doubles for Tk 50/90 and more deluxe rooms for Tk 135/250. The economical units are reasonably clean and

are not too cramped, while the deluxe rooms have carpets, comfortable armchairs and large bathrooms with western facilities.

Even better, but more expensive, is the four storey *Hotel Gulshan* (☎ 6437), across from the Hotel Sufia. It's unusually clean and well managed, with singles/doubles for Tk 69/115 (Tk 840 for air-con rooms with TV, carpeting and western-style bathrooms). The spotless standard rooms are spacious, with mirrors, desks and mosquito nets.

There are also inexpensive hotels around Banda Bazar, which is lively until midnight. The cheapest is *Mojlish Rest House & Restaurant* (☎ 6701) on Shah Jalal Rd. Its singles/doubles cost only Tk 35/60, but they're tiny and you get what you pay for. Staff are friendly, it's central and has a restaurant on the 2nd floor, overlooking all the action. A better choice, however, would be *Hotel Al-Kwachwa* next door. It has a very pleasant owner, and a better and quieter restaurant (on the 2nd floor). Its rooms are similarly priced with common bathrooms.

The *Modern Rest House* (☎ 7713), a modern five storey building also in Banda Bazar, is much more presentable and features a small reception area with TV. The rooms cost Tk 75 to Tk 100/150 for singles/doubles, and are very clean, with wide and relatively soft beds. Three blocks north-west along Zinda Bazar Rd is the *London Rest House* (☎ 6081), which charges just Tk 50/80 for its singles/doubles. It's in a modern but noisy five storey commercial building. The rooms are OK but have windows opening onto the hallway and thus offer little privacy if you want sunlight.

Another possibility is *Hotel Cassana* near the railway station. Singles/doubles cost only Tk 30/60, but getting a room is difficult unless you come early. If you're down to your last taka, pass by the *Catholic Mission*. The legendary Irish priest here is exceptionally friendly and might be able to help out.

Places to Stay – middle
Sylhet has only two mid-range hotels. Both are in Telihaor and have decent inexpensive restaurants. The best is *Hotel Hiltown* (☎ 6077,

8263), which has singles/doubles for Tk 135 to Tk 165/Tk 245 to Tk 315 (Tk 475/565 with air-con). Well run, this place has spotless rooms, with tiled floors, comfortable beds, desks, bureaus and neat bathrooms with soap and towels.

The other is the six storey *Hotel Shahban* (☎ 8040) off Taltala Rd. It has four categories of rooms, two with fans (Tk 70/120 and Tk 150/250) and two with air-con (Tk 500 and Tk 700). The rooms are reasonably clean, though beds in the cheaper units are harder than those of the Hiltown.

Hotel Polash, listed under top-end places to stay, also has economical units.

Places to Stay – top end

The small new *Surma Valley Rest House* (☎ 2670) in the town centre on Shah Jalal Rd, above a modern department store, has 12 units with singles/doubles for Tk 800/900 with air-con (Tk 500/600 with fans). Rooms, which are modern, large and truly 1st rate, have colour satellite TVs, telephones, minibars, comfortable chairs, big beds and tile bathrooms.

The modern *Hotel Polash* (☎ 8811, 8309), on Airport Rd has a travel agency and one of the city's best restaurants. It has air-con singles/doubles with TVs for Tk 650 to Tk 750/Tk 850 to Tk 950, including breakfast, plus 15% Value Added Tax (VAT). It also has singles/doubles with fans for Tk 400/550, and more economical units for Tk 200/300 and Tk 300/400.

The *Parjatan Hotel* (☎ 2426) is spacious and modern but it's well out of town on a hill just south of the airport and is thus quite isolated. It has ventilated rooms for Tk 400, air-con rooms for Tk 800 (Tk 900 with TV) and a decent but unatmospheric restaurant. It can also arrange car rentals.

Those with pull should try staying at the *Circuit House*, but it seems very busy. A better choice is the *Roads & Highways Guest House* (see its office near the centre of town on Manikpur Rd) or, best of all, the lovely *Laakatoorah Tea Gardens Guest House* (☎ 2600). Located just north of town in the Laakatoorah tea estate, it has two large nicely furnished guest rooms with air-con (Tk 450 a room). You can reserve by calling the manager's office (☎ 6016). It features a front porch with wicker furnishings, a comfortable living room with sofas, TV and library, and a dining room where you can eat fairly cheaply.

Places to Eat – bottom end

If you're staying in the Telihaor area, you'll have lots of choices, including the friendly *New Green Restaurant*, *Banani Restaurant* (no English sign) and the well marked *Jamania Restaurant*, all on Telihaor Rd. For example, you can get delicious hot puris (Tk 3) at the Banani and good vegetable kebabs (Tk 3) at the New Green, plus full meals for Tk 15 to Tk 20 at both. The similarly priced Jamania has received even better reviews from travellers. *Hotel Bye-Bye* (no English sign) nearby is not as friendly or as good. There are lots of similar places closer to Kean Bridge at Surma Market, including the popular *Suruli Restaurant* (no English sign) on Taltala Rd.

Similar places in Banda Bazar include *Mojlish Rest House & Restaurant* (on the 2nd floor) and the *Oriental Restaurant* across the street. The *Ponchokhana Restaurant* up on Zinda Bazar Rd is a bit more upmarket, with areas curtained off for women (local women are never seen at the preceding restaurants). The 2nd floor restaurant at the nearby *London Rest House* is also very popular, with tasty but limited choices, such as Tk 29 for chicken (or fish), rice and sauce. A few doors down on the same block is the *Jala Abad Hotel* (no English sign outside), which offers a choice of vegetable dishes (rare in Bangladesh); a tasty meal can come to less than Tk 10!

If you're further north on the same road, which becomes Airport Rd, you could try the similar, well marked *Aajrani Restaurant* or the more ordinary unmarked establishments just south of Hotel Polash.

Places to Eat – top end

Two of the city's very best restaurants, both near the town centre, are the *Chow King*

Chinese Restaurant (☎ 3651) on Zinda Bazar Rd and Diner King Chinese Restaurant (☎ 8647) around the corner to the south. Both are nicely decorated and the food is excellent – good places to splurge if you've been eating meals for Tk 15 for too long. Dishes served at the Chow King include beef and onions (Tk 80), Thai prawns (Tk 125) and Thai chicken (Tk 80). It also has non-oriental selections. The Diner King is similar but cheaper, serving dishes such as sweet and sour chicken (Tk 80), Mandarin steamed fish (Tk 70) and fish with mushrooms (Tk 45).

The Shapnil Restaurant at Hotel Polash features mostly Bangladeshi cuisine (eg chicken tikka for Tk 95 and fish curry for Tk 55) but also serves a number of Chinese selections. The Parjatan Hotel is another possibility as is the Moghal Restaurant at Hotel Hiltown. The latter is much more modest and cheaper, with only Bangladeshi selections, such as beef bhoona (Tk 50), chicken dopiaza (Tk 38) and dhal butter fry (Tk 24). Hotel Shahban has a TV and a wide selection of similar Bangladeshi dishes at comparable prices.

Things to Buy

The city's liveliest area is Banda Bazar, which is in the heart of town and is bustling until midnight. You'll find just about anything and everything here. Smuggling goods from India is widespread, and around this bazar products from India such as cosmetics, confectionery and saris are widely available. The city also has some modern shopping establishments, in particular the ultramodern three storey Sylhet Plaza on Zinda Bazar Rd and Kushiara department store on Shah Jalal Rd.

Sylhet is well known for its wide variety of exquisite handicrafts, including chairs, baskets, handbags, trays and lampshades made from locally grown cane. Floor mats called 'sital patis' are a speciality, and the exquisite home-spun fabrics of the Manipuri make colourful souvenirs. The best selection of such handicrafts and textiles are available at the Aarong outlet on Jaintiapur Rd, 1⅓ blocks east of Zinda Bazar Rd.

Getting There & Away

It's worth taking a day trip by bus or train between Dhaka and Sylhet, as it's an interesting journey through varied countryside, with bits of seemingly wild jungle in the hills. At the Meghna River, buses must cross by ferry, although there is a rail bridge. The crossing takes a few minutes but often involves a wait of half an hour, sometimes more. Day buses sometimes make a brief stop in Brahmanbaria, although many do not stop at all. Near Brahmanbaria, in the village of Sorail, north-east of Ashuganj on the Sylhet-Dhaka road, the Sorail Mosque of 1670 has three domes and short towers.

Air Biman has three flights a day between Dhaka and Sylhet. The fare is Tk 792 (plus Tk 50 airport tax) and flights are reasonably on schedule most of the time. The Biman office (☎ 7076) is on Zinda Bazar Rd, south of Chowhatta intersection.

Bus Buses for Dhaka, Zakiganj and Fenchuganj leave from the large bus station south of the river, most often referred to as Dhaka terminal, even though there are actually several separate terminals. Non-stop chair coaches to Dhaka cost Tk 140 (Tk 110 for an ordinary bus), the last bus departing around 11.30 pm. The trip takes about 6½ hours (7½ hours by ordinary bus). Buses to Fenchuganj cost Tk 9 and take about one hour, with the last bus departing from Sylhet around 8 pm. Those to Zakiganj (Tk 32) take two hours, departing between 6 am and 7 pm.

In Dhaka, buses leave from Sayedabad bus station. There are lots of bus companies; one of the better ones is Romar.

There are no direct buses to Chittagong. Those to Comilla leave from Comilla terminal on Dhaka Rd, south of the railway station. Fares are Tk 100 for ordinary buses and Tk 125 for a chair coach.

Buses north-east to Tamabil, Jaintiapur and the Indian border leave from the small Jaintiapur bus station on Jaintiapur Rd, several km east of the centre of town, just beyond a UCB bank branch. They depart between 6.45 am and 5.35 pm. The trip to

Jaintiapur (Tk 21) takes just under three hours; the Indian border is just eight km further.

If you're headed west for Chhatak or Sunamganj, you'll find the bus station for these towns on Amberkhana Rd. It's possible to travel from Sunamganj to Mymensingh via Mohanganj, which involves a seven hour boat ride from Sunamganj to Jaysiri and hiking or taking rickshaws from there to Mohanganj (see under Bicycle later in this section). The main route to Mymensingh from Sylhet, however, is via the Sylhet-Dhaka highway all the way back (south-west) to the Meghna River ferry crossing. On the opposite side is Bhairab Bazar, which is a road and rail junction where there are connecting buses and trains north-west to Mymensingh.

Train The railway station (π 7036 for reservations) is on the south side of town. There are three express trains a day for Dhaka, departing at 5.55 am, 1.30 and 9.30 pm (summer hours). The trip normally takes about seven hours. There's also one daily express to Chittagong, departing from Sylhet at 12.20 am and taking about nine hours. Only the night train to Dhaka has a sleeper car (Tk 445/600 fan/air-con). First class/sulob fares are Tk 274/135 to Dhaka, Tk 182/56 to Comilla and Tk 298/92 to Chittagong. Departures are reasonably punctual, so don't arrive late.

Car If you rent a vehicle at the Parjatan, it'll cost you between Tk 1500 and Tk 2000, with petrol and driver. You can save money by negotiating with one of the taxi or minibus drivers at the airport, or in town on Airport Rd at the Chowhatta intersection where they all hang out. A fair price would be Tk 1000 a day plus petrol. The easiest way to calculate petrol usage (vehicle petrol indicators rarely work) is to agree to pay for one litre for every eight to 10 km travelled in the van (slightly more km in a car).

Bicycle If you want to cycle in Sylhet, consider coming here by train from Dhaka with your bike, cycling around the Sylhet region and then cycling back to Dhaka via Mymensingh. The best route in this respect is the alternate less-travelled route to Mymensingh via Chhatak, Sunamganj and Mohanganj. The trip takes three or four days to Mymensingh, depending on whether you stop the first day in Chhatak. There are hotels in all of these towns.

The really fun section is between Sunamganj and Mohanganj where the route virtually disappears from the maps. At Sunamganj, you can take back roads and dirt tracks south-west to Mohanganj (you'll have to ask directions every few km) or, much easier, you can catch a launch on the Surma River all the way to Jaysiri (an interesting and fun seven-hour trip), which is 15 km or so from Mohanganj. Along the short route between Jaysiri and Mohanganj, you'll pass through Chandrabara and some very pleasant countryside.

From Mohanganj, which is a major town and the halfway point between Sunamganj and Mymensingh, you can continue cycling south-west to Mymensingh (about 60 km) or catch a train if you'd prefer.

To/From India In the early 70s, the route to Shillong in India via Tamabil was closed on the Indian side to both regional and international traffic because of problems in Assam caused by the influx of illegal immigrants from Bangladesh. In 1995 the permit requirement was dropped; it may take awhile before crossing here becomes problem free. Moreover, if you are driving, you still need a permit, actually two (see Road Permits under India in the Land section of the Getting There & Away chapter for details). If you're travelling by bus and border officials demand such a permit, you may have to educate them a bit on the rules.

It takes 2½ hours to get to Tamabil from Sylhet by bus, and a 15 minute hike to the border. It is then a further 1½ km walk to Dawki in India, from where buses run to Shillong, a 3½ hour trip. From Shillong (elevation 1496m), if it's not cloudy, the views over Bangladesh are superb.

Getting Around

The Airport Located 10 km north of town, the airport has a post office, snack bar, and numerous taxis and baby taxis waiting outside. If you wish to rent a car or van by the day, do it here and save yourself the extra cost of a taxi into town (see under Car earlier in this section). For a vehicle into town, expect to pay about Tk 200 for a taxi, Tk 100 for a baby taxi and Tk 10 for a seat in a 10 seat tempo.

Baby Taxi To catch a baby taxi to the airport or around town, go to the baby taxi stand on Airport Rd, just south of Hotel Polash.

AROUND SYLHET
Tea Estates & Jaflang Area

To see the process of tea manufacturing, try the Laakatoorah Tea Estate, where the manager may lecture you on the history and production of this beverage in exchange for a tour of the factory. Malnicherra Tea Estate, which was the first tea estate in Bangladesh, dating back to 1857, offers tours as well. The Laakatoorah and Malnicherra tea estates are just beyond the city's northern outskirts on Airport Rd.

Just east of Sylhet are the Khadim Tea Gardens. From Khadim Bazar, which is 10 km east of town, you can take a tempo there as they transport estate workers to and from

---

The Tea Estates

Tea production in Bangladesh dates from 1857 when Malnicherra Tea Estate, just north of Sylhet, was set up by the British. The tea grew well here and by the end of the century, there were some 150 tea estates, almost all under British ownership. Approximately the same number exists today, but since independence, only 48% are British owned. The rest mainly belong to wealthy Bangladeshis, and to a lesser extent, the government's Tea Board. In some cases, British companies, most notably Finlays and Duncan, manage the estates but are not themselves the owners.

When the British began growing tea in Sylhet, they didn't bother training the indigenous people. Rather, they brought over experienced Indian labourers, mainly from tea estates in Bihar, Orissa and West Bengal. Today, virtually all of the labourers, or 'coolies', are descendants of these original Hindus, living in colonies established by those first brought here. Small Hindu shrines are a common feature of tea estates with worker colonies.

Each estate provides an elementary school (and a doctor). Since many of the estates are in remote locations, few of the workers' children are able to go beyond the primary grades. However, the tea workers have the only trade union in Bangladesh that effectively bargains with management, so their contracts often include special privileges, such as a festival allowance. New Year's Eve is one of the most festive times, in part because the tea season is over. The Hindu religion does not ban alcohol and many workers get a bit tipsy at festival time. Several private 'clubs' outside Srimangal cater to the owners and managers year round. Faced with these long-standing traditions, the Muslim government looks the other way.

Generally even the smallest estates are at least a thousand hectares. Because each requires its own processing plant, a sizable production is necessary to be profitable. Most estates have excess land from which timber can be sold in bad years to generate a profit.

The trees can last for 80 years, but they are usually replaced after 50. Since the mid-1980s, production has increased significantly with a new dwarf variety of tea plant that allows the trees to be planted much closer together. Experts from the British ODA Tea Estate, who go around advising individual owners, have been pushing this changeover. However, tea production in Bangladesh is continuing to decline (by 16.8% between 1980 and 1994) and now represents only about one percent of the country's total export earnings.

Bangladeshi tea is a black variety of ordinary quality and is mainly combined with teas which must be blended, such as Kenyan tea. Virtually all of it is sold by auction companies in Chittagong and shipped to Europe to be mixed. It ends up mostly in lower-end markets, typically Eastern Europe, Russia and parts of the Middle East.

If you come to Srimangal or Sylhet, visiting a tea estate is a must. The colourfully dressed female pickers are a picturesque sight, and a tour of the factory can be fascinating. The equipment in some of these factories is very old, some original. However, don't make the mistake of touring on a Friday, the day of rest, or visiting between mid-December and the 1st of March, as everything will be at a standstill. The picking season is during the rainier months from early March to early December and the factories are in full operation. ■

their villages. Some 23 km further east, seven km before Jaintiapur, you'll pass Lalakal Tea Estates on the right side of the road; it's accustomed to receiving visitors and will gladly show you around.

The largest number of tea estates in the northern half of Sylhet Division are further on, around **Jaflang** and **Sripur**, just beyond Tamabil and near the Indian border. This is one of the most scenic areas in the division, so definitely try to get here. It is also a major tribal area, where many Khasi are found. The bus from Sylhet takes 2½ hours to Tamabil and another half hour to Jaflang. You must constantly ask to be let off in Jaflang as there are no signs and you can easily pass by it, causing much lost time.

There's a Bangladesh Tea Board guesthouse in nearby Sripur where you may be able to stay (there's also more basic accommodation in Tamabil). If you take a tour of Laakatoorah Tea Estate, the manager there (☎ 6016) may be able to help you make a reservation.

Jaintiapur

Two hours by bus (40 km) north-east of Sylhet, on the road to Tamabil, the town of Jaintiapur (JOINT-tah-poor) was, until the annexation of Sylhet by the British in 1835, the capital of the Jaintia kingdom of Jaintiapur, which included the Khasi and Jaintia Hills and the Plains of Jaintia.

Today, nothing remains of the old splendour of the Jaintia kingdom except a **rajbari** (palace built by zamindar) in town and the **Temple of Kali** on its grounds. Now in an extremely ruinous state and hardly worth seeing, the rajbari, which had outer wall reliefs representing, among other things, horses and lions prancing in a tree, formerly consisted of two grandiose palaces, one of which contained the Kali temple. This temple was widely feared in the district due to the frequent human sacrifices that took place upon its altars, and which ultimately led to the downfall of the Jaintia family.

Even more unusual and unexpected – and definitely worth seeing – are a small group of striking **stone megaliths** nearby, which are a prominent landmark in the countryside. They're about 2½ metres high and grouped in odd numbers of three, five, seven or nine. There are around 20 such monuments in the vicinity of the rajbari, scattered over an area of about one km.

Also found in the hills of Assam in neighbouring India, and very similar in shape to the menhirs found in England, Brittany, Ireland, Denmark and Scandinavia, these megaliths, blackened with age, bear important historical and social significance, and are believed to be associated with the religious practices of the Khasi tribe. It's most likely that they were memorials to deceased ancestors, or they commemorated some important event of the Khasi tribe.

The Jaintiapur megaliths, which bear a striking resemblance to the menhirs found in Europe, are monuments of the Khasi tribe, who are held to be of Mongolian origin.

Madhabkunda Waterfalls

A three hour drive south-east of Sylhet (and equally accessible from Srimangal by road and rail), three km from Dakhinbagh railway station, there is the famous remote waterfall of Madhabkunda, which is pictured in many tourist brochures and attracts a good number of sightseers. This general area is also where you may be able to find some of the few elephants in Bangladesh, which are still being used as work animals, hauling huge logs.

Hakalakhi, Fenchuganj & Chhatak

Twenty km north-east of town in the direction of Jaintiapur, Hakalakhi is a flat area reportedly good for bird-watching and angling.

Fenchuganj, a 45 minute bus ride south of Sylhet, is a fairly scenic town despite the huge fertiliser factory which operates on natural gas and produces half of the country's total requirement of urea. There is reportedly a wildlife reserve nearby.

Thirty-eight km north-west of Sylhet, Chhatak has orange groves and cement and pulp factories, plus a sky ropeline used to transport lime from the hills. The cement factory, which is the largest of its kind in the country, has a *guesthouse* with four air-con rooms.

SUNAMGANJ

Approximately 70 km west of Sylhet, this small town offers little for the tourist except as an interesting rural backwater. However, The haors (wetlands) in the area are rife with bird life, however, especially during mid-winter through to the end of March, and sometimes until the end of April. At this time, migrants, winterers and residents all get together for one big bird party. Varieties of rails, raptors, ducks, sandpipers, lapwings, crakes and more congregate here. There are three haors which seem to be the best for bird-watching several hours upriver from the Sunamganj River. It's too far for a day trip, but overnight excursions and longer can be arranged in town.

Organised Tours

The best trip, which includes visiting all three haors, is a four day affair. Except for true bird enthusiasts, this is probably more than most travellers want. Nevertheless, an overnight trip would get you out into some of the most fascinating rural areas in Bangladesh.

Bird-Watching in the Sunamganj Haors

For a worthwhile tour of the Sunamganj haors, you'll need at least four days to find some exciting bird species. Baer's pochard is probably the rarest bird, and not difficult to spot if you're there at the right time; other pochards include the white-eyed and red-crested varieties. The baikal teal and the falcated teal are both impressive winterers, along with an assortment of crakes, including the ruddy crake and the little crake. You'll also see the spotted redshank and the blue-breasted rail, and the assortment continues with various sandpipers and lapwings. A number of raptors are here as well, including several fishing eagles, such as the Pallas', grey-headed and spotted eagles. So little has been done to record species here, that it's not unreasonable to expect to see new, previously unrecorded birds during each trip.

The trip begins at Aila Haor, four hours upriver. A knowledgeable boatman will know exactly where to go. It's another two hours on foot into the haor area, but it's worth it for the rich birdlife awaiting. It may be dark by the time you return to the boat, so carry a torch. You'll sleep on the boat and continue to Pasua early next morning.

Pasua Haor, four hours upriver, lies just over an embankment from the river. You can sit and watch the wildlife or walk for a couple of kms on the fringes of the marshy basin. After another four hours' travel the next morning, you'll arrive at Tangua Haor, bordering India and the furthest point of the trip. In this area, scrub and grassland are a bonus, and you'll see some interesting grassland species of birds.

On the return to Sunamganj, river travel is spartan yet peaceful, and it is an exceptional way to experience rural life in Bangladesh, where so much of it takes place on or near a river's edge.

Dave Johnson

To arrange a trip into the haor area, the best person to see is Mr Shokat, master of two boats, the *Rubaia* and *Al-Amin*. He has considerable experience with bird-watchers and the haors, and has worked for ornithology survey teams. Ask for Mr Shokat, or mention either of his two boats by name, at the boat dock area, Sachna Ghat (the entrance into Sunamganj). Smack in the middle of a line of food/tea/dry goods stalls is an 'office' with a desk and a few chairs, and, more than likely, several men sitting around. This is the Sunamganj Boat Owner's Association. If he's not there, someone will fetch him.

You can contact him during the day or evening before you want to go to set up a departure time (6 to 7 am is recommended) and length of trip. His rate is Tk 1200 per day, but if there is a group (four sleeps comfortably on the boat; more than six – someone may have to curl up on the outside deck) it's not a bad deal. The boatmen cook the meals, you provide the food, or the money for food, and Mr Shokat will buy all supplies that evening. He'll need a cash advance to buy fuel and a few other necessities.

For the trip, you'll need water, a mat, a sleeping bag of some sort and a torch. A mosquito net would also be a good idea. Bird-watchers will want a scope; binoculars will suffice for the less serious.

Places to Stay

In the Sachna Ghat area there are two basic hotels which are spartan but not bad. In town, the best accommodation is at the *Circuit House*.

Getting There & Away

From Sylhet, there are regular buses to Sunamganj. The trip takes about two hours.

SRIMANGAL

Some 75 km south of Sylhet, Srimangal, not the regional capital, is the actual tea centre of the Sylhet Division. This hilly area, with tea estates and shade trees everywhere, is unquestionably one of the most picturesque sections of Bangladesh. For miles around, you can see tea estates forming a perennially green carpet on the sloping hills. It's the one area besides the Sundarbans where in certain parts you can look around and not see a single human being. This is particularly true of the dense Lowacherra Forest Reserve, which is eight km east of town. In short, if you're feeling overwhelmed by people everywhere, spend a few days in Srimangal. Visits to the rainforest and several of the tea estates, plus the slightly cooler climate, are the main attractions, although getting here by train from Dhaka is often half the fun.

The town itself is quite small. A single road, the Dhaka-Sylhet highway, passes from one end to the other, with a four-way intersection in the middle. While Srimangal is of no particular interest, it has the bare essentials, including several banks, a restaurant or two, a tourist agency and several reasonably decent lower-end hotels. Also, the people are quite friendly and more of them seem to speak English.

If you're lucky, you might get to stay in a guesthouse. A number of companies and organisations have them; however, you'll have no chance unless you book in advance, usually by contacting the company's head office in Dhaka or Chittagong. The luckiest ones are those who get invited to stay for free at one of the private tea estates, virtually all of which have tiny guesthouses.

Places to Stay

There are at least three lower-end hotels, all well marked three storey establishments on the main drag. Coming from Dhaka, the first you'll pass is *Hotel Mukta* (☎ 310), which is 1½ blocks before the town's main intersection. It's very inviting and relatively new, with private parking and singles/doubles for Tk 55/80. The rooms are well maintained, with fans, mosquito nets and clean attached bathrooms. *Hotel Lalrahaman*, which is just beyond, is equally nice with similar prices .

If you're running short of money, check *Hotel Ara International*, which is 500m north of the main intersection. It has 30 singles/doubles with overhead fans, mosquito nets

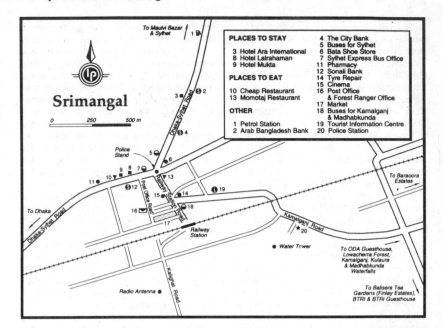

Srimangal

0   250   500 m

PLACES TO STAY

3 Hotel Ara International
8 Hotel Lalrahaman
9 Hotel Mukta

PLACES TO EAT

10 Cheap Restaurant
13 Momotaj Restaurant

OTHER

1 Petrol Station
2 Arab Bangladesh Bank

4   The City Bank
5   Buses for Sylhet
6   Bata Shoe Store
7   Sylhet Express Bus Office
11 Pharmacy
12 Sonali Bank
14 Tyre Repair
15 Cinema
16 Post Office
    & Forest Ranger Office
17 Market
18 Buses for Kamalganj
    & Madhabkunda
19 Tourist Information Centre
20 Police Station

To Maulvi Bazar & Sylhet

To Baraoora Estates

To Dhaka

To ODA Guesthouse, Lowacherra Forest, Kamalganj, Kulaura & Madhabkunda Waterfalls

To Balisera Tea Gardens (Finlay Estates), BTRI & BTRI Guesthouse

Police Stand

Police Stand

Post Office Road

Railway Station Road

Kalighat Road

Kamalganj Road

Railway Station

Water Tower

Radio Antenna

and attached bathrooms for Tk 30/60 and doubles with common bathrooms for Tk 50, but the rooms are tiny, grubbier and definitely inferior.

The wonderful *ODA Tea Estate Guesthouse* (☎ (08626) 207) and the *Bangladesh Tea Research Institute Guesthouse* (☎ (08626) 225) both have excellent facilities, but it's difficult to get a room without connections. Bookings for the ODA Guesthouse must be made in advance at the British High Commission in Dhaka (☎ 882705), and only the Bangladesh Tea Board in Chittagong (☎ 210239, 212448), not the Dhaka office, can give permission to stay at the BTRI Guesthouse. Other organisations which have guesthouses in or just outside Srimangal are the Jalalabad Gas Co and the Rural Electrification Board.

For real solitude, you can't beat the lovely *Forestry Guest House* inside Lowacherra Forest Reserve (see the Around Srimangal section later in this chapter for information).

Places to Eat

The *Momotaj Restaurant* in the heart of town, a few steps south of the town's main intersection, has good Bangladeshi food and you can get a filling meal for around Tk 20. There's a restaurant on the main drag close to Hotel Mukta, and you may find tea stalls around the market near the railway station.

Only overnight guests are allowed to eat at the *ODA Guesthouse*, which cost Tk 120 for breakfast, Tk 150 for lunch and Tk 200 for dinner. However, if you're not staying there but are desperate for a meal, see the administrator.

Getting There & Away

Bus Buses for Sylhet, including Sylhet Express, all have their offices on the main drag near the town's main intersection. Those headed east towards Kamalganj and Madhabkunda leave from around the two petrol stations on Railway Station Rd. If you're headed to Dhaka or Comilla, you can catch one from Sylhet on the main drag in the centre of town. They stop along this route and hail passengers. Expect to pay about Tk 90 (Tk 120 for a chair coach to Dhaka), Tk 80 (Tk 110 for a chair coach) to Comilla and Tk 30 to Sylhet.

Train Most travellers from Dhaka take the train. There are three trains a day in either direction. At the time of writing, departure times from Dhaka station (☎ 413-137, 409-686) were at 7.45 am (7.20 am during the winter months), 2.00 pm and 10 pm. According to the schedule, the trip takes five hours (eg, arrivals in Srimangal at 12.45 pm, 7 pm and 3 am), but the trip normally takes 5½ hours. These trains continue on to Sylhet. The summer and winter train schedules vary slightly but it's best to check.

Fares vary per train, for example, Tk 240/120 for 1st class/sulob (Tk 355 for an air-con compartment) on the morning train; Tk 200/100 for 1st class/sulob on the afternoon train; and Tk 355/120 for 1st class (sleeper)/sulob (Tk 510 for an air-con sleeper) on the evening train. Only the evening train has sleepers. Air-con compartments and sleepers must normally be booked at least several days in advance, and in practice you must book them to Sylhet, which costs about 20% more.

Heading back to Dhaka, you can take trains at 8 am, 3.50 pm and 11.50 pm. Only the afternoon and evening trains have air-con compartments and only the evening train has sleepers. If you book one, you should purchase a ticket which reads Sylhet-Dhaka (Tk 600 for an air-con sleeper), otherwise your cabin reservation cannot be guaranteed.

You can also travel from Chittagong to Sylhet via Comilla and Srimangal once a day by express train; the trip takes about eight hours to Srimangal and 9½ hours to Sylhet. The train departs from Chittagong around 10.30 am, arriving in Srimangal in the late afternoon, and departs from Sylhet at 12.20 am, arriving in Srimangal a little over an hour later. The fare is Tk 240/74 1st class/sulob.

AROUND SRIMANGAL
Cycling
The area around Srimangal is one of the best in Bangladesh for cycling. No one has caught on to this yet, so if you should bring a bike here or rent one in town, you'll definitely be the only foreign traveller cycling around. Despite the hilly terrain, the roads are reasonably level, so even the ubiquitous one-speed Chinese bike can be used. Certainly the Bangladeshis find the hills no trouble for cycling.

There's an intricate network of roads connecting all the tea estates to the main highways. Only the major routes are tarred or bricked, but even the numerous dirt roads are, by necessity, in good condition so that the tea can be easily transported to market.

Most tea estates have guest lodges for housing friends, relatives and visitors from Dhaka. If you show up at a tea estate in the afternoon, you'll be such a novelty as a cyclist (foreigners visiting the tea estates by car are not a novelty) that if you ask for a room for the night, chances are they may be only too happy to oblige. If not, you can try the next tea estate down the road. There are so many tea estates all over the area that your chances of getting a room for the night are good. Cycling around here could well be your most enjoyable time spent in Bangladesh.

Tea Estates
There are so many tea estates that it's not easy to determine which are the best for visiting. Some are more receptive to showing visitors around than others. One of the most frequently visited gardens is Madabpore Tea Gardens, which has a lake on its premises. The turn-off for the gardens is about 1¾ km beyond the ODA compound.

Two of the largest estates are Deanston and Rajghat, which are close to one another and well south of Srimangal, many km past the BTRI complex and the Balisera Tea Gardens managed by Finlays. Other tea estates which are good for viewing are scattered far and wide in the greater Srimangal area, and are shown on the regional map, Tea Estates & Cycling Trails Around Srimangal.

Tea Estates & Cycling Trails Around Srimangal

Lowacherra Forest Reserve

Some eight km east of Srimangal on the road to Kamalganj, Lowacherra Forest is not to be missed, especially if you're a bird-watcher. It extends only a few km, but the terrain is hilly and the vegetation is fairly thick, thus slowing your walk. Fortunately, this forest is in an area that's not so heavily populated, consequently it's less threatened than Madhupur Forest.

Some logging goes on nearby, so you may hear some chopping sounds. Otherwise, it's perfectly tranquil. There are unmarked trails to follow, but you can wander off without fear of getting lost. Look for wild orchids growing in the upper branches of trees, and keep an eye out for gibbon apes that make lots of noise as their troupe swings through the branches in the upper canopy. The blue-bearded bee-eater and the red-breasted trogon are a couple of interesting birds to watch for in addition to the variety of forest birds, some rare oddities, that show up. Take care during the wet season, as leeches are not unheard of here.

Inside the forest is a lovely *Forestry Guest House* with a caretaker. It's possible to sleep here and get meals, or camp. Get permission from the District Forestry Office in Sylhet (near the post office), not the forestry office in Dhaka or in Srimangal. There is no charge, and you couldn't hope to find a more tranquil place to stay in all of Bangladesh.

Getting There & Away From Srimangal, take the paved road east towards Kamalganj. The poorly marked turn-off to your left (north), which is easy to miss, is about 4¾ km past the ODA compound and another 2¾ km beyond the well-marked turn-off for the Nurjahan and Madabpore tea estates. The dirt road into the forests, which crosses the railroad tracks, is less than a km long and thus an easy walk. The guesthouse is just up the hill from the end.

Telepara/Satcheri Forest Reserve

About 60 km south-west from Srimangal on the Dhaka-Sylhet highway is this small preserve. Similar in vegetation and species to the Lowacherra Forest Reserve, the mixture of evergreen and teak provides a good habitat for quite a number of forest birds and small animals. There is a track heading into the forest from the main road which eventually leads to a sandy ravine and an old, grown-over logging road/path. By following this path, you'll come to a tea plantation at the edge of the forest and will be able to loop back (going left) across the ravine and follow the continuation of the path through the forest. Though this 'logging' path is the best one, there are other ill-defined tracks throughout the forest. The area is also littered with bits of petrified wood.

Getting There & Away The forest is on the south side of the main road about one km east of the Satcheri bus stop/Telepara Tea Estate, just where the highway takes a sharp left (hairpin) bend. You could get the driver of the Dhaka-Sylhet bus to drop you here but you'd miss the early hours when bird-watching is best. Alternatively, you could get a bus from Srimangal to Telepara, which is well marked, and walk to the trailhead a km away. To return to Srimangal, you could try flagging one of the Dhaka-Sylhet buses, which tend to be full, or walk back to Telepara and catch one there.

Glossary

baby taxis – mini three wheeled auto-rickshaws

baksheesh – donation, tip or bribe, depending on the context

Bangla – *see* Bengali

bangla – architectural style associated with the Pre-Mauryan and Mauryan period; bamboo-thatched hut with a distinctively curved roof

baras – old houseboats

bas-relief – sculpture in low relief

bawalis – timber workers in the Sundarbans

bazar – market

Bengali – the national language of Bangladesh, where it is known as Bangla, and the official language of the state of West Bengal in India

bhikkus – Buddhist monks

bigha – 1600 sq yd

BIWTC – Bangladesh Inland Waterway Transport Corporation

BNP – Bangladesh National Party

BRAC – Bangladesh Rural Advancement Committee

BRTC – Bangladesh Road Transport Corporation

buraq – a winged creature who carried Mohammed from Jerusalem to heaven and back

cantonment – administrative and military area of a Raj-era town

carnapuli – a zoo of painted cement animals

cha – milky sweet tea

chair coach buses – modern buses with adjustable seats and lots of leg room

chan-chala – type of hut design

chaturmukhar – a structure with all four walls decorated with stone bas-reliefs of gods

chilla – place of meditation

coasters – minivans

crore – 10 million

cupola – domed roof or ceiling

dacoity – armed robbery

encaustic – ceramics decorated by burning in colours, especially by inlaying coloured clays

fakir – a Muslim who has taken a vow of poverty, but also applied to Hindu ascetics

ganja – the dried flowering tips of the marijuana plant

gema – type of wood felled in the Sundarbans

ghat – steps or landing on a river

guarni jaur – winds which whirl up from the Bay of Bengal, then U-turn at the Himalaya and carry their icy cargo back to Bangladesh

haors – wetlands

hartaals – strikes

jamdani – ornamental loom-embroidered muslin or silk

Jamuna River – the name for the Brahmaputra River when it flows into Bangladesh

jatra – folk theatre

jhum – slash-and-burn agriculture

jor bangla – twin hut architectural style

Kabigan – debate conducted in verse

kantha – embroidered, quilted patchwork cloth, often with folk motifs

katha – 30 sq yd

kuthi – factories

lakh – one hundred thousand (100,000)

lingam – phallic symbol of Siva the Creator

madan-tak – adjutant bird

mahavihara – large monastery

maidan – open grassed area in a town or city, used as a parade ground during the Raj

mandir – temple

mau (madhu) – honey

maualis – honey gatherers in Sundarbans

maund – 37 kg

mazars – graves

mela – fair

mihrab – niche facing Mecca
mishuk – smaller, less colourful version of a baby taxi
mohajons – rickshaw, taxi fleet owners
Mughal – alternative spelling for Moghul – the Muslim dynasty of Indian emperors from Babur to Aurangzeb (16th-18th century)
Mukti Bahini – the Bangladesh Freedom Fighters, led by Ziaur Rahman during the War of Independence
mullah – Muslim scholar, teacher or religious leader
mustan – mafia-style bosses who demand, and receive, payment from baby taxi drivers, roadside vendors, people living on public land...

naan – Indian flat bread
nava-ratna – nine towered

oshot – banyan tree

Padma River – the name for the Ganges River when it flows into Bangladesh
pagoda – *see* stupa
paisa – unit of currency; there are 100 of these in a taka
pancha-ratna – five-spice powder
Parjatan – the Bangladesh government tourist organisation
pashi – a blistering wind which blows through the day in April
pelligiti – village songs
pukka – genuine

Raj – British Raj
raj – rule or sovereignty

raja – ruler, landlord or king
rajbari – Raj-era palace built by a zamindar
REB – Rural Electrification Board
rekha – buildings with a square sanctum on a raised platform
rest house – government owned guesthouse
rickshaw – small, two wheeled bicycle-driven passenger vehicle
rickshaw wallah – rickshaw driver

sadhus – spiritual men
sal – hardwood tree
salwar kameez – a long dress-like tunic worn over baggy trousers
Shankhari – Hindu artisans
shishu – children's park
Siva (Shiva) – Hindu god; the destroyer, the creator
slash-and-burn – a form of agriculture
sona – gilded dome
stupa – Buddhist religious monument
Sufi – ascetic Muslim mystic
sulob – upper 2nd class (with reserved seating)

tea estate (tea garden) – terraced hillside where tea is grown
tempo – auto-rickshaw
tik-tiki – gecko
tolars – motorised passenger boats

uchamgo – classical music

veena – Indian stringed instrument

zamindar – landlord

Index

MAPS

TEXT

LONELY PLANET PHRASEBOOKS

**Building bridges,
Breaking barriers,
Beyond babble-on**

Nepali phrasebook

Listen for the gems

Ethiopian Amharic phrasebook

Speak your own words

Latin American Spanish phrasebook

Ask your own questions

Ukrainian phrasebook

Master of your own image

Greek phrasebook

Vietnamese phrasebook

- handy pocket-sized books
- easy to understand Pronunciation chapter
- clear and comprehensive Grammar chapter
- romanisation alongside script to allow ease of pronunciation
- script throughout so users can point to phrases
- extensive vocabulary sections, words and phrases for every situation
- full of cultural information and tips for the traveller

'...vital for a real DIY spirit and attitude in language learning' – **Backpacker**

'the phrasebooks have good cultural backgrounders and offer solid advice for challenging situations in remote locations' – **San Francisco Examiner**

'...they are unbeatable for their coverage of the world's more obscure languages' – *The Geographical Magazine*

Arabic (Egyptian)
Arabic (Moroccan)
Australia
  Australian English, Aboriginal and Torres Strait languages
Baltic States
  Estonian, Latvian, Lithuanian
Bengali
Brazilian
Burmese
Cantonese
Central Asia
Central Europe
  Czech, French, German, Hungarian, Italian and Slovak
Eastern Europe
  Bulgarian, Czech, Hungarian, Polish, Romanian and Slovak
Ethiopian (Amharic)
Fijian
French
German
Greek

Hindi/Urdu
Indonesian
Italian
Japanese
Korean
Lao
Latin American Spanish
Malay
Mandarin
Mediterranean Europe
  Albanian, Croatian, Greek, Italian, Macedonian, Maltese, Serbian and Slovene
Mongolian
Moroccan Arabic
Nepali
Papua New Guinea
Pilipino (Tagalog)
Quechua
Russian
Scandinavian Europe
  Danish, Finnish, Icelandic, Norwegian and Swedish

South-East Asia
  Burmese, Indonesian, Khmer, Lao, Malay, Tagalog (Pilipino), Thai and Vietnamese
Spanish (Castilian)
  Basque, Catalan and Galician
Sri Lanka
Swahili
Thai
Thai Hill Tribes
Tibetan
Turkish
Ukrainian
USA
  US English, Vernacular, Native American languages and Hawaiian
Vietnamese
Western Europe
  Basque, Catalan, Dutch, French, German, Irish, Italian, Portuguese, Scottish Gaelic, Spanish (Castilian) and Welsh

---

LONELY PLANET JOURNEYS

JOURNEYS is a unique collection of travel writing – published by the company that understands travel better than anyone else. It is a series for anyone who has ever experienced – or dreamed of – the magical moment when they encountered a strange culture or saw a place for the first time. They are tales to read while you're planning a trip, while you're on the road or while you're in an armchair, in front of a fire.

JOURNEYS books catch the spirit of a place, illuminate a culture, recount a crazy adventure, or introduce a fascinating way of life. They always entertain, and always enrich the experience of travel.

IN RAJASTHAN
Royina Grewal

Indian writer Royina Grewal's travels in Rajasthan take her from tribal villages to flamboyant palaces. Along the way she encounters a multitude of characters: snake charmers, holy men, nomads, astrologers, dispossessed princes, reformed bandits . . . And as she draws out the rarely told stories of farmers' wives, militant maharanis and ambitious schoolgirls, the author skilfully charts the changing place of women in contemporary India. The result is a splendidly evocative mosaic of life in India's most colourful state.

Royina Grewal lives on a farm in Rajasthan, where she and her husband are working to evolve minimal-impact methods of farming. Royina has published two monographs about the need for cultural conservation and development planning. She is also the author of *Sacred Virgin*, a travel narrative about her journey along the Narmada River, which was published to wide acclaim.

SHOPPING FOR BUDDHAS
Jeff Greenwald

Here in this distant, exotic land, we were compelled to raise the art of shopping to an experience that was, on the one hand, almost Zen – and, on the other hand, tinged with desperation like shopping at Macy's or Bloomingdale's during a one-day-only White Sale.

Shopping for Buddhas is Jeff Greenwald's story of his obsessive search for the perfect Buddha statue. In the backstreets of Kathmandu, he discovers more than he bargained for . . . and his souvenir-hunting turns into an ironic metaphor for the clash between spiritual riches and material greed. Politics, religion and serious shopping collide in this witty account of an enlightening visit to Nepal.

Jeff Greenwald is also the author of *Mister Raja's Neighborhood* and *The Size of the World*. His reflections on travel, science and the global community have appeared in the *Los Angeles Times*, the *Washington Post*, *Wired* and a range of other publications. Jeff lives in Oakland, California.

LONELY PLANET TRAVEL ATLASES

Lonely Planet has long been famous for the number and quality of its guidebook maps. Now we've gone one step further and in conjunction with Steinhart Katzir Publishers produced a handy companion series: Lonely Planet travel atlases – maps of a country produced in book form.

Unlike other maps, which look good but lead travellers astray, our travel atlases have been researched on the road by Lonely Planet's experienced team of writers. All details are carefully checked to ensure the atlas corresponds with the equivalent Lonely Planet guidebook.

The handy atlas format means no holes, wrinkles, torn sections or constant folding and unfolding. These atlases can survive long periods on the road, unlike cumbersome fold-out maps. The comprehensive index ensures easy reference.

- full-colour throughout
- maps researched and checked by Lonely Planet authors
- place names correspond with Lonely Planet guidebooks
  – no confusing spelling differences
- legend and travelling information in English, French, German, Japanese and Spanish
- size: 230 x 160 mm

Available now:
Chile & Easter Island • Egypt • India & Bangladesh • Israel & the Palestinian Territories •Jordan, Syria & Lebanon • Kenya • Laos • Portugal • South Africa, Lesotho & Swaziland • Thailand • Turkey • Vietnam • Zimbabwe, Botswana & Namibia

---

LONELY PLANET TV SERIES & VIDEOS

Lonely Planet travel guides have been brought to life on television screens around the world. Like our guides, the programmes are based on the joy of independent travel, and look honestly at some of the most exciting, picturesque and frustrating places in the world. Each show is presented by one of three travellers from Australia, England or the USA and combines an innovative mixture of video, Super-8 film, atmospheric soundscapes and original music.

Videos of each episode – containing additional footage not shown on television – are available from good book and video shops, but the availability of individual videos varies with regional screening schedules.

Video destinations include: Alaska • American Rockies • Australia – The South-East • Baja California & the Copper Canyon • Brazil • Central Asia • Chile & Easter Island • Corsica, Sicily & Sardinia – The Mediterranean Islands • East Africa (Tanzania & Zanzibar) • Ecuador & the Galapagos Islands • Greenland & Iceland • Indonesia • Israel & the Sinai Desert • Jamaica • Japan • La Ruta Maya • Morocco • New York • North India • Pacific Islands (Fiji, Solomon Islands & Vanuatu) • South India • South West China • Turkey • Vietnam • West Africa • Zimbabwe, Botswana & Namibia

The Lonely Planet TV series is produced by:
Pilot Productions
The Old Studio
18 Middle Row
London W10 5AT UK

For video availability and ordering information contact your nearest Lonely Planet office.

Music from the TV series is available on CD & cassette.

PLANET TALK

Lonely Planet's FREE quarterly newsletter

We love hearing from you and think you'd like to hear from us.

When...is the right time to see reindeer in Finland?
Where...can you hear the best palm-wine music in Ghana?
How...do you get from Asunción to Areguá by steam train?
What...is the best way to see India?

For the answer to these and many other questions read PLANET TALK.

Every issue is packed with up-to-date travel news and advice including:

- a letter from Lonely Planet co-founders Tony and Maureen Wheeler
- go behind the scenes on the road with a Lonely Planet author
- feature article on an important and topical travel issue
- a selection of recent letters from travellers
- details on forthcoming Lonely Planet promotions
- complete list of Lonely Planet products

To join our mailing list contact any Lonely Planet office.

Also available: Lonely Planet T-shirts. 100% heavyweight cotton.

LONELY PLANET ONLINE

Get the latest travel information before you leave or while you're on the road

Whether you've just begun planning your next trip, or you're chasing down specific info on currency regulations or visa requirements, check out Lonely Planet Online for up-to-the minute travel information.

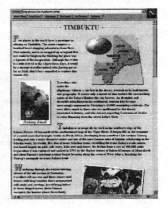

As well as travel profiles of your favourite destinations (including maps and photos), you'll find current reports from our researchers and other travellers, updates on health and visas, travel advisories, and discussion of the ecological and political issues you need to be aware of as you travel.

There's also an online travellers' forum where you can share your experience of life on the road, meet travel companions and ask other travellers for their recommendations and advice. We also have plenty of links to other online sites useful to independent travellers.

And of course we have a complete and up-to-date list of all Lonely Planet travel products including guides, phrasebooks, atlases, Journeys and videos and a simple online ordering facility if you can't find the book you want elsewhere.

www.lonelyplanet.com
or
AOL keyword: lp

LONELY PLANET PRODUCTS

Lonely Planet is known worldwide for publishing practical, reliable and no-nonsense travel information in our guides and on our web site. The Lonely Planet list covers just about every accessible part of the world. Currently there are eight series: *travel guides, shoestring guides, walking guides, city guides, phrasebooks, audio packs, travel atlases* and *Journeys* – a unique collection of travel writing.

EUROPE

Amsterdam • Austria • Baltic States phrasebook • Britain • Central Europe on a shoestring • Central Europe phrasebook • Czech & Slovak Republics • Denmark • Dublin • Eastern Europe on a shoestring • Eastern Europe phrasebook • Estonia, Latvia & Lithuania • Finland • France • French phrasebook • Germany • German phrasebook • Greece • Greek phrasebook • Hungary • Iceland, Greenland & the Faroe Islands • Ireland • Italian phrasebook • Italy • Lisbon • Mediterranean Europe on a shoestring • Mediterranean Europe phrasebook • Paris • Poland • Portugal • Portugal travel atlas • Prague • Russia, Ukraine & Belarus • Russian phrasebook • Scandinavian & Baltic Europe on a shoestring • Scandinavian Europe phrasebook •Slovenia •Spain • Spanish phrasebook • St Petersburg • Switzerland •Trekking in Spain • Ukrainian phrasebook •Vienna •Walking in Britain • Walking in Switzerland • Western Europe on a shoestring • Western Europe phrasebook

Travel Literature: The Olive Grove: Travels in Greece

NORTH AMERICA

Alaska • Backpacking in Alaska • Baja California • California & Nevada • Canada • Florida • Hawaii • Honolulu • Los Angeles • Mexico • Miami • New England • New Orleans • New York City • New York, New Jersey & Pennsylvania • Pacific Northwest USA • Rocky Mountain States • San Francisco • Southwest USA • USA phrasebook • Washington, DC & the Capital Region

CENTRAL AMERICA & THE CARIBBEAN

Bermuda • Central America on a shoestring • Costa Rica • Cuba •Eastern Caribbean •Guatemala, Belize & Yucatán: La Ruta Maya • Jamaica

SOUTH AMERICA

Argentina, Uruguay & Paraguay • Bolivia • Brazil • Brazilian phrasebook • Buenos Aires • Chile & Easter Island • Chile & Easter Island travel atlas • Colombia • Deep South • Ecuador & the Galápagos Islands • Latin American Spanish phrasebook • Peru • Quechua phrasebook • Rio de Janeiro • South America on a shoestring • Trekking in the Patagonian Andes • Venezuela

Travel Literature: Full Circle: A South American Journey

ANTARCTICA

Antarctica

ISLANDS OF THE INDIAN OCEAN

Madagascar & Comoros • Maldives• Mauritius, Réunion & Seychelles

AFRICA

Africa - the South • Africa on a shoestring • Arabic (Moroccan) phrasebook • Cape Town • Central Africa • East Africa • Egypt • Egypt travel atlas• Ethiopian (Amharic) phrasebook • Kenya • Kenya travel atlas • Malawi, Mozambique & Zambia • Morocco • North Africa • South Africa, Lesotho & Swaziland • South Africa, Lesotho & Swaziland travel atlas • Swahili phrasebook • Trekking in East Africa • West Africa • Zimbabwe, Botswana & Namibia • Zimbabwe, Botswana & Namibia travel atlas

Travel Literature: The Rainbird: A Central African Journey • Songs to an African Sunset: A Zimbabwean Story

MAIL ORDER

Lonely Planet products are distributed worldwide. They are also available by mail order from Lonely Planet, so if you have difficulty finding a title please write to us. North American and South American residents should write to Embarcadero West, 155 Filbert St, Suite 251, Oakland CA 94607, USA; European and African residents should write to 10a Spring Place, London NW5 3BH; and residents of other countries to PO Box 617, Hawthorn, Victoria 3122, Australia.

NORTH-EAST ASIA

Beijing • Cantonese phrasebook • China • Hong Kong • Hong Kong, Macau & Guangzhou • Japan • Japanese phrasebook • Japanese audio pack • Korea • Korean phrasebook • Mandarin phrasebook • Mongolia • Mongolian phrasebook • North-East Asia on a shoestring • Seoul • Taiwan • Tibet • Tibet phrasebook • Tokyo

Travel Literature: Lost Japan

MIDDLE EAST & CENTRAL ASIA

Arab Gulf States • Arabic (Egyptian) phrasebook • Central Asia • Central Asia phrasebook • Iran • Israel & the Palestinian Territories • Israel & the Palestinian Territories travel atlas • Istanbul • Jerusalem • Jordan & Syria • Jordan, Syria & Lebanon travel atlas • Lebanon • Middle East • Turkey • Turkish phrasebook • Turkey travel atlas • Yemen

Travel Literature: The Gates of Damascus • Kingdom of the Film Stars: Journey into Jordan

ALSO AVAILABLE:

Travel with Children • Traveller's Tales

INDIAN SUBCONTINENT

Bangladesh • Bengali phrasebook • Delhi • Hindi/Urdu phrasebook • India • India & Bangladesh travel atlas • Indian Himalaya • Karakoram Highway • Nepal • Nepali phrasebook • Pakistan • Rajasthan • Sri Lanka • Sri Lanka phrasebook • Trekking in the Indian Himalaya • Trekking in the Karakoram & Hindukush • Trekking in the Nepal Himalaya

Travel Literature: In Rajasthan • Shopping for Buddhas

SOUTH-EAST ASIA

Bali & Lombok • Bangkok • Burmese phrasebook • Cambodia • Ho Chi Minh City • Indonesia • Indonesian phrasebook • Indonesian audio pack • Jakarta • Java • Laos • Lao phrasebook • Laos travel atlas • Malay phrasebook • Malaysia, Singapore & Brunei • Myanmar (Burma) • Philippines • Pilipino phrasebook • Singapore • South-East Asia on a shoestring • South-East Asia phrasebook • Thailand • Thailand's Islands & Beaches • Thailand travel atlas • Thai phrasebook • Thai audio pack • Thai Hill Tribes phrasebook • Vietnam • Vietnamese phrasebook • Vietnam travel atlas

AUSTRALIA & THE PACIFIC

Australia • Australian phrasebook • Bushwalking in Australia • Bushwalking in Papua New Guinea • Fiji • Fijian phrasebook • Islands of Australia's Great Barrier Reef • Melbourne • Micronesia • New Caledonia • New South Wales • New Zealand • Northern Territory • Outback Australia • Papua New Guinea • Papua New Guinea phrasebook • Queensland • Rarotonga & the Cook Islands • Samoa • Solomon Islands • South Australia • Sydney • Tahiti & French Polynesia • Tasmania • Tonga • Tramping in New Zealand • Vanuatu • Victoria • Western Australia

Travel Literature: Islands in the Clouds • Sean & David's Long Drive

THE LONELY PLANET STORY

Lonely Planet published its first book in 1973 in response to the numerous 'How did you do it?' questions Maureen and Tony Wheeler were asked after driving, bussing, hitching, sailing and railing their way from England to Australia.

Written at a kitchen table and hand collated, trimmed and stapled, *Across Asia on the Cheap* became an instant local bestseller, inspiring thoughts of another book.

Eighteen months in South-East Asia resulted in their second guide, *South-East Asia on a shoestring*, which they put together in a backstreet Chinese hotel in Singapore in 1975. The 'yellow bible', as it quickly became known to backpackers around the world, soon became *the* guide to the region. It has sold well over half a million copies and is now in its 8th edition, still retaining its familiar yellow cover.

Today there are over 180 titles, including travel guides, walking guides, language kits & phrasebooks, travel atlases and travel literature. The company is one of the largest travel publishers in the world. Although Lonely Planet initially specialised in guides to Asia, we now cover most regions of the world, including the Pacific, North America, South America, Africa, the Middle East and Europe.

The emphasis continues to be on travel for independent travellers. Tony and Maureen still travel for several months of each year and play an active part in the writing, updating and quality control of Lonely Planet's guides.

They have been joined by over 70 authors and 170 staff at our offices in Melbourne (Australia), Oakland (USA), London (UK) and Paris (France). Travellers themselves also make a valuable contribution to the guides through the feedback we receive in thousands of letters each year.

The people at Lonely Planet strongly believe that travellers can make a positive contribution to the countries they visit, both through their appreciation of the countries' culture, wildlife and natural features, and through the money they spend. In addition, the company makes a direct contribution to the countries and regions it covers. Since 1986 a percentage of the income from each book has been donated to ventures such as famine relief in Africa; aid projects in India; agricultural projects in Central America; Greenpeace's efforts to halt French nuclear testing in the Pacific; and Amnesty International.

'I hope we send the people out with the right attitude about travel. You realise when you travel that there are so many different perspectives about the world, so we hope these books will make people more interested in what they see. These are guidebooks, but you can't really guide people. All you can do is point them in the right direction.'
– Tony Wheeler

LONELY PLANET PUBLICATIONS

Australia
PO Box 617, Hawthorn 3122, Victoria
tel: (03) 9819 1877 fax: (03) 9819 6459
e-mail: talk2us@lonelyplanet.com.au

USA
Embarcadero West, 155 Filbert St, Suite 251,
Oakland, CA 94607
tel: (510) 893 8555 TOLL FREE: 800 275-8555
fax: (510) 893 8563
e-mail: info@lonelyplanet.com

UK
10 Barley Mow Passage, Chiswick,
London W4 4PH
tel: (0181) 742 3161 fax: (0181) 742 2772
e-mail: 100413.3551@compuserve.com

France:
71 bis rue du Cardinal Lemoine, 75005 Paris
tel: 1 44 32 06 20 fax: 1 46 34 72 55
e-mail: 100560.415@compuserve.com

World Wide Web: http://www.lonelyplanet.com